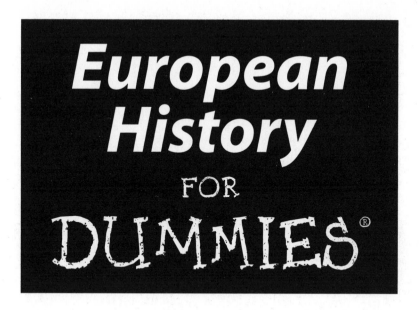

European History FOR DUMMIES®

by Sean Lang

JOHN WILEY & SONS, LTD

European History For Dummies®

Published by
John Wiley & Sons, Ltd
The Atrium
Southern Gate
Chichester
West Sussex
PO19 8SQ
England

E-mail (for orders and customer service enquires): cs-books@wiley.co.uk

Visit our Home Page on www.wileyeurope.com

Copyright © 2006 John Wiley & Sons, Ltd, Chichester, West Sussex, England

Published by John Wiley & Sons, Ltd, Chichester, West Sussex

Wiley also publishes its books in a variety of electronic formats. Some content that appears in print may not be available in electronic books.

British Library Cataloguing in Publication Data: A catalogue record for this book is available from the British Library.

ISBN-10: 0-7645-7060-9 (PB)

ISBN-13: 978-0-7645-7060-5 (PB)

Manufactured in the United States of America

10 9 8 7 6 5 4 3 2 1

WILEY

About the Author

Sean Lang studied history at Oxford and has been teaching it to school, college, and university students for the past 20 years. He is the author of *British History For Dummies* and has written textbooks on nineteenth and twentieth century history. He is Honorary Secretary of the Historical Association and co-editor of *Twentieth Century History Review*. He writes regularly for the *Times Educational Supplement* and for *BBC History Magazine* and has written on history teaching for the Council of Europe. Sean is currently based in Cambridge where he is Research Fellow in History at Anglia Ruskin University.

Author's Acknowledgements

I must thank my editors at John Wiley, Samantha Clapp and Rachael Chilvers, who have shown a lot more patience with my hectic schedule than I am sure I deserve. Alan Palmer was invaluable on the history of the Baltic region and Nicolas Kinloch and Marc Polonsky both gave me good ideas for the Part of Tens. To my in-laws, Phyllis and Monica Graham of Cockermouth, and my friends Laure and Alain Renouf of Aix-en-Provence, all of whom put me up (and put up with me) over the summer while I was writing this, I owe special thanks. Finally, my thanks go to John Hooper – writer, journalist, European, and very forbearing Kraftwerk fan.

Publisher's Acknowledgements

We're proud of this book; please send us your comments through our Dummies online registration form located at www.dummies.com/register/.

Some of the people who helped bring this book to market include the following:

Acquisitions, Editorial, and Media Development

Project Editor: Rachael Chilvers

Content Editor: Simon Bell

Commissioning Editor: Samantha Clapp

Development Editor: Kelly Ewing

Copy Editor: Kate O'Leary

Proofreader: Juliet Booker

Technical Editor: Matthew Bennett, Liverpool Hope University

Executive Editor: Jason Dunne

Executive Project Editor: Martin Tribe

Special Help: Jan Withers and Jennifer Bingham

Cover Photo: © CORBIS: Sandro Vannini, Bettmann, David Lees, Archivo Iconografico, S.A., Austrian Archives; Getty Images: Dante Gabriel Rossetti, French School, BAVARIA

Cartoons: Rich Tennant, www.the5thwave.com

Production

Project Coordinator: Maridee Ennis, Jennifer Theriot

Layout and Graphics: Carl Byers, Andrea Dahl, Stephanie D. Jumper

Proofreaders: Brian H. Walls

Indexer: Techbooks

Publishing and Editorial for Consumer Dummies

Diane Graves Steele, Vice President and Publisher, Consumer Dummies

Joyce Pepple, Acquisitions Director, Consumer Dummies

Kristin A. Cocks, Product Development Director, Consumer Dummies

Michael Spring, Vice President and Publisher, Travel

Kelly Regan, Editorial Director, Travel

Publishing for Technology Dummies

Andy Cummings, Vice President and Publisher, Dummies Technology/General User

Composition Services

Gerry Fahey, Vice President of Production Services

Debbie Stailey, Director of Composition Services

Contents at a Glance

Table of Contents

Part II: Europe of the Ancients 33

Chapter 3: You're Ancient History! 35

Chapter 4: The Ups and Downs of the Roman Empire 51

Part III: Middle Ages 65

Introduction

· ·

*O*ne afternoon in 1983, when I was living and working in Paris, I was heading into the Place de la Concorde when I noticed some people running across it, something you don't usually do unless you've got an advanced death wish. Some sort of student demonstration was going on. The students chanted '*Etudiants en colère!*' ('Students are anger-y!' though in my experience 'Students are still-in-bed!' is usually more accurate.) Older people stood in doorways and shook their heads. And then things turned nasty. The riot police made their first charge. Yes, they had batons, and yes, they used them. Hard.

'Place de la Concorde' means 'Square of Peace and Harmony', which was always rather a pious hope, because before that it had been called the Place de la Révolution (you can probably work out the translation) and this place was where the guillotine stood that executed King Louis XVI. The Tuileries palace used to be there too, but in 1871 the Paris mob stormed it and burnt the palace to the ground. If you're going to take on the French riot police – and I wouldn't entirely recommend it – the Place de la Concorde is certainly the most appropriate place to do it.

Teaching European history, as I do, you are forever explaining scenes like that one I witnessed. Always remember that what happened in the past wasn't always history, and it wasn't always told in history-book language: it was *now*, it was *real*, and – very often – it hurt. Of course, my students might think that about my lessons, but I hope you won't think it about this book.

About This Book

We'd better get one thing straight. This is my history. I don't mean it's my life story, but this book is my version of Europe's history. Historians certainly try to get their facts right, but what we say *about* the past, whether what happened was a good thing or a bad thing or an act of God or whatever, is down to us. Or, in this case, me.

Europe is the world's smallest continent, yet it has an incredible history: Greek gods; mad Roman emperors; Roman emperors who weren't Roman; and Holy Roman Emperors who weren't holy (or Roman). You meet Visigoths in Africa and Normans in Sicily; an Italian who talked to his books and another who conquered a kingdom and gave it away. You meet the two Catholic kings of Spain, one of whom was a woman, and the Spanish king who never smiled. You discover a German monk who split Europe in two because he was so afraid of going to hell. And what about the great European war that started when two nobles were thrown out of a window onto a dungheap? Well, at least they had a soft landing.

Scared of Europe and its history? Think you'll never get your head round all those foreign names? Relax. You're going to enjoy this.

Conventions Used in This Book

I follow the usual conventions for history books. Most of these are fairly straightforward, such as arranging history in centuries or decades. I also keep to the sort of terms you've probably heard before, such as 'ancient' and 'medieval', even though they were not how the people at the time referred to themselves.

Most of the world numbers its years from the notional date of the birth of Jesus Christ. (I say notional, because they miscalculated and got it wrong by some four years or so.) In Latin – these things were all worked out by the Catholic Church in the Middle Ages, so it's all done in Latin – that comes out as A.D., which stands for *Anno Domini*, or 'Year of Our Lord'. Dates from before the birth of Christ are labelled B.C., 'Before Christ'. Some people nowadays prefer to use C.E. and B.C.E. for 'Common Era' and 'Before Common Era', but I use B.C. and A.D. because it's what I'm most comfortable with.

Foolish Assumptions

I assume, perhaps wrongly, that you:

- Never learned anything about European history at school except a bit about Hitler and maybe Stalin, and anyway, you've forgotten it
- Didn't like those school textbooks with lots of documentary extracts in them with endless questions you had to answer
- Think European history sounds a bit hard
- Are prepared to give it a go, but this had better be good

How This Book Is Organised

The great thing about *For Dummies* books is that you don't have to read them all the way through. You can simply turn to the bit you want – a chapter, a section, even just a paragraph. The Table of Contents and the Index help you out. Of course, history has all sorts of links and connections from one period to another, but I show you how to follow these links if you want to. The great thing is, you don't have to. This section gives you an idea of what lies ahead:

Part I: Origins of a Continent

This part is about how Europe was actually formed. Chapter 2 covers the Stone Age: that's all those incredible cave paintings and stone monuments. You probably know of Stonehenge, which is actually rather later than the Stone Age proper, but you can find some pretty impressive monuments on the continent as well. And talking of 'the Continent', Part I explains how Europe took its present shape, and how Europe fits into the story of the formation of the world.

Part II: Europe of the Ancients

Part II is all about the history behind those sword and sandal movies, such as *Troy*, *Alexander*, and *Gladiator*. The writers, mathematicians, and statesmen of Ancient Greece and Rome laid the foundations for western society. This part looks at how a rich civilisation grew up in the raggedy coastline of Greece and Turkey (though it wasn't Turkey then), and a mighty empire took shape on the banks of the River Tiber: Rome.

Part III: Middle Ages

Nowadays people say something is 'medieval' when they mean it's primitive and barbaric, but this judgement is a gross slur on one of the brightest and most dazzling periods in European history, a time of art, chivalry and cathedrals.

The kings of Europe fought each other over land and titles, and set off for the Holy Land to redeem the holy city of Jerusalem, and in 1282, the people of Sicily seized the opportunity of evening vespers to murder every Frenchman they could find. Europe came face to face with the terrible Black Death, and a German printer called Johannes Gutenberg created an information technology revolution that changed the world.

Part IV: New Ideas, New Worlds

Part IV begins with the Renaissance, when the people of Italy rediscovered the heritage of the ancients, when Europeans took on new ideas that made them look at the world *in a different way*. This part also explains the dramatic changes that took place in the Church, starting with Martin Luther's doubts about whether or not he would ever get to heaven, and ending in terrible religious wars that tore the continent apart.

Meanwhile, Europeans were taking to the sea in small ships and setting foot on what they thought of as new worlds: America, yes, but also China, India, and the islands of Asia.

Part V: Europe Rules the World

In the 18th and 19th centuries Europeans took over the world. Quite literally. There is not a single continent on the face of the globe that was not conquered or settled or mapped or evangelised by Europeans.

At home, new ideas about man's natural rights helped lead to the French Revolution, which sent a shiver down the spine of the crowned heads of Europe (and a blade through the spine of one of them!). The revolution spawned a host of important ideas about nationalism and about democracy that would dominate the centuries ahead, as another revolution, industrialisation, created a whole new type of European – the industrial worker.

Part VI: Europe Tears Itself in Two

Part VI deals with the calamitous 20th century, which saw Europe torn apart by two World Wars – which some people, understandably, prefer to call 'European civil wars' – and a Cold War, which brought the continent, and the world, to the brink of destruction. This part looks at how the mighty European empires crumbled and fell after the Second World War, and how in 1989, amid incredible scenes of rejoicing, the barriers of the Cold War and the Berlin Wall itself came down and Europe could reunite. Well, sort of.

Part VII: The Part of Tens

Here you find a handy list of ten Europeans who had a pretty good go at dominating the continent and some good ideas for places to visit in Europe that you might not have considered. But what about things – and people – Europe could well have done without? You'll have your own ideas; have a look at mine.

Icons Used in This Book

This book won't throw lots of questions at you, but it should certainly set you thinking. These icons highlight some of the points you may be thinking about.

The wooden horse of Troy. Luther nails his ideas to the church door. Queen Marie Antoinette says the people can eat cake. Quick reality check: did it really happen? Find out when you see this icon.

What happened long ago affects our lives today in all sorts of ways. When you see this icon you see yet another way in which you too were created from the past.

You can always find *at least* two ways of looking at anything in history, which is why historians are always arguing and rewriting it. Okay, I give you my version, but this icon highlights when opinions differ.

This icon draws your attention to an important point to bear in mind.

For the nerd in you. Small details, little points that add a touch of interest to your life and mean that people steer clear of you at parties. Read or skip them as you like.

Where to Go from Here

Where to go? Wherever you like. You can home in on the Middle Ages, run-in with the Renaissance, or gather round the foot of the guillotine. But if you're really not sure where to start, why not have a look at Chapter 1, which gives you a bit of a general survey and may give you a few ideas. The history of Europe is at your fingertips. All you have to do is turn the page.

Part I
Origins of a Continent

The 5th Wave   By Rich Tennant

"And believe it or not children, some of your ancestors could be related to this fellow right here."

In this part . . .

Europe offers much more than a summer backpacking around the Eiffel Tower and the Leaning Tower of Pisa. Europe is the smallest of the world's continents but it's one of the most varied. This part introduces you to Europe and its history and gives you some idea of why Europe's had such an impact on the world. You'll see something of Europe's long, fascinating Stone Age, with its mysterious cave paintings and stone circles, and you can consider the strange case of Neanderthal Man – the advanced form of life that just didn't seem to go anywhere.

You'll also consider the *idea* of Europe. General De Gaulle used to talk about 'a certain idea of France', but you can say the same of the whole continent. Europeans have a strong idea of their separate national identities, but they are also aware that they are part of a much wider unit, with its own distinctive culture.

Chapter 1

Not So Much a Continent
As a View of Life

*O*ne thing that hits you very quickly about Europe is how varied it is. In some areas, you can take a two-hour drive and go through three or four different language zones, sometimes with different alphabets to write them with. General De Gaulle once said that you could not unite a nation like France that had 265 different types of cheese; it's even harder for Europe, a small continent that can't decide which language to speak, which religion to follow, which money to use, or even where exactly it begins and ends.

Where Is Europe?

Most continents have a pretty obvious land mass, but Europe's a bit different. Because Europe's part of the same land mass as Asia, you could make a case for saying that, geographically, it's not really a separate continent at all. The border between Europe and Asia is usually taken as the Ural mountains in Russia, but that line is a bit arbitrary.

The border becomes even more arbitrary in the Mediterranean region. The city of Istanbul sits officially at the meeting point between Europe and Asia, with just a narrow waterway, the Bosphorus, between them. But if you're expecting to find yourself in a different world as soon as you step off the ferry, you may be disappointed. Much of Turkey looks pretty similar to much of Greece, which is not surprising because they were both part of the same culture. Cyprus is part of 'Europe', but it has a lot more in common with 'Asian' Turkey than it has with other European islands, such as Iceland, Ireland, or the islands of the Baltic. In fact, for much of Europe's history, the Mediterranean world has operated as a single unit, with trading ships going back and forth from one coast to another and mighty empires seeking to rule the whole area, without anyone making too much of the fact that, strictly speaking, three separate continents exist there.

How Many Europes?

Once you start looking for similarities that hold Europeans together, you end up with some unexpected results. For one thing, you soon find that more 'Europes' have existed than you may have thought.

A Christian Europe?

The idea of Europe as a Christian continent works, up to a point. However, Europe has a substantial Muslim population, and not just post-war immigrants but communities first created when the Ottoman Turks overran eastern Europe back in the 15th century. Much of Spain used to be ruled by Muslims from North Africa, who established what they called the Caliphate of Cordoba; you can still get a sense of their rich cultural legacy in the beautiful Alhambra Palace in Granada.

Christianity did spread across Europe, so much so that talk focused on *Christendom*, a sort of united Christian Europe. However, Christendom split into two geographic and theological camps: the Catholic Church based at Rome and the Orthodox Church based at Constantinople.

Medieval Catholics regarded Orthodox Christians as little better than *infidels* (that is, non-believers), and in 1204, an army of western Crusaders on its way to Jerusalem decided to teach them a lesson by trashing the great Christian city of Constantinople. (You can find out more about this deplorable episode in Chapter 7.)

Fast forward three centuries, and you find Europe tearing itself in two over the religious ideas of Martin Luther and John Calvin. This period is called the *Reformation* (Chapter 10 has the details), and it divided Europe into Protestant (England, Scotland, northern Germany, Scandinavia, the Netherlands, parts of

Switzerland) and Catholic (Italy, France, Spain, Poland, Hungary, southern Germany, Ireland), not to mention eastern Orthodox (Russia, Greece, the Balkans). Christian Europe? Take your pick: there were three!

A royal Europe?

When religious leaders weren't claiming divine fiat over parts of Europe, European royals claimed – or tried to claim – their own divine right to rule.

Royal flush . . .

Does it make sense to think of Europe as a continent that, historically at any rate, relates easily to monarchy? Europe has thrown up a lot of kings who were born to rule and knew it. Among these men were:

- Medieval kings, such as St Louis IX of France or Henry II of England, who held all the lands of their kingdoms, so that everyone else, even the most mighty nobles, were their tenants.

- Holy Roman Emperors who ruled Germany and saw themselves as the leaders of Christian Europe, like Frederick II, known as 'Stupor Mundi', the 'Wonder of the World'.

- The Tsars of Russia, such as Ivan IV 'the Terrible'; autocrats of a vast empire who could expect their every word to be obeyed.

- King Philip II of Spain, who ruled a worldwide empire from a simple bedsit inside the vast bureaucratic palace he built for himself outside Madrid, *El Escorial*.

- Louis XIV of France, the 'Sun King', so called because his court at Versailles was meant to be as magnificent as the sun itself. He believed in the divine right of kings to rule – absolutely.

You could say – and some historians have said it – that all those dictators in 20th-century Europe were simply following a pattern set by their royal predecessors. Stalin sometimes gets called a Red Tsar, and Mussolini certainly saw himself as a latter-day Roman Emperor (he ended up like some of them, too).

. . . and royals flushed

But another Europe exists that has never believed in the divine right of kings and is rather proud of having kept its rulers under tight control. The English forced King John to accept Magna Carta in 1215, and by the end of the 17th century, they had cut off one king's head, kept another in exile for years, and forced a third to flee for his life. The Swiss banded together to kick out the Austrians back in the 13th century and have been fiercely proud of their republican tradition ever since. The Italians set up a series of city republics in the middle ages and were forever on their guard – not always successfully, it has to be said – against would-be rulers who might try to take them over. The Dutch and the Germans have very strong traditions of city republics, banding together to defend their independence. All these countries looked for inspiration to the city states of ancient Greece, and to the big daddy of them all, the ancient Roman Republic.

The danger, as the Romans and later the Italians were to find out to their cost, didn't come from foreign enemies but from their own successful generals. The Roman word for an army commander was *imperator*; it's no coincidence that it gave us the word *emperor*, because that's what Roman imperators turned into. (Head to Chapters 4 and 6 to find out what went wrong with the Romans' noble experiment in republican government.)

A democratic Europe?

The Council of Europe, which was set up after the Second World War, likes to promote the idea that to be properly European, you have to stand up for the ideals of democracy – and you can see why. Ancient Greece was the birthplace of democracy – even the word is Greek – Britain's 'Mother of Parliaments' is generally regarded as the model for representative government, and the French can claim, with their 1789 *Declaration of the Rights of Man*, to have given the world the first authentic statement of human rights (but see Chapter 16 before you take their word for it).

The trouble with this notion is that European democracy is a fairly recent idea, and it hasn't put down very deep roots. Greek democracy was very different from modern democracy, not least because Greek freedom rested on a class of slaves known as *helots*, and women – you just *know* what's coming, don't you? – had none of the rights that men enjoyed. Even in modern western Europe, it took years of battling to get equal democratic rights for women.

Democracy has only really flourished in European history in the period since the end of the Second World War in 1945 and then – and never forget this – only in half of the continent. Eastern and central Europe did not taste democracy until the Berlin Wall came down in 1989, bringing the communist dictatorships with it. Since that time, many of these countries in *democratic transition*, as the phrase has it, have found democracy very difficult to adjust to. Plenty of Russians today look back nostalgically to the good old days of Stalin and the labour camps; at least you knew where you were then, they say. It would be nice to say that democracy somehow comes naturally to Europeans, but the evidence is against it.

Is There Such a Thing as European Civilisation?

Europeans have been very quick to promote 'their' civilisation, and to do so by scoffing at everyone else's. The Greeks used to talk of other peoples as *barbarians*, by which they meant that anyone who didn't speak Greek came out with a sort of animal bah-bah noise. Greeks used the alarm 'The barbarians are at the gates!' to mean that civilisation was in danger.

Exactly who the barbarians were changed over time: Gauls, Goths, Huns, Turks, Mongols, and, of course, Jews have all been seen as foreign threats to European civilisation, but so have European liberals, nationalists, socialists, communists, anarchists, and fascists. The 19th-century pope, Pius IX, thought that the greatest threat to Christian civilisation was posed by railways and promptly banned them from the papal states (no doubt he railroaded that law through). More recently, people have said similar things about migrants, immigrants, and asylum seekers. But what exactly is the civilisation that all these people and ideas are supposed to be threatening?

Strictly speaking, *civilisation* simply means people living in towns and cities, but if you think about it, this notion in itself has big implications for the way people organise themselves. Living at close quarters inevitably means a bit of give and take, with rules and regulations and residents' associations. In the 18th century, being civilised meant keeping your animal instincts in check both in everyday society (that is, be polite) and in society as a whole (that is, obey the law). Nothing scared the bewigged ladies and gentlemen of 18th-century polite society more than the thought of the *Mob*, the underclass of the destitute and unemployed whom you could see on the streets of every city – not just because they could be violent, but because they were a constant reminder that European civilisation was not as deeply rooted as they liked to think.

Why Does Europe Have So Many Languages?

If you like foreign languages, then Europe is the place for you – it can sometimes seem difficult to find two adjoining countries that actually speak the same language. The main reason for all these languages lies in the way people have moved through history, often in great tribal migrations. Most of Europe's languages are descended from an original one called Indo-European, which started off in northern India and travelled westwards with all those nomadic

Unsolved language mysteries

We haven't completely resolved on the origins of all of Europe's languages. Scandinavian languages are all pretty similar until you hit Finnish, which is unlike any other language in Europe except Estonian. Quite why this corner of northern Europe should have such a different language from everyone else we just don't know.

Even odder is that Finnish seems to be connected with Magyar, the language of Hungary. It may suggest that some sort of common ancestral people exists for three nations in very different parts of Europe, but not for anyone else, though who it may have been we just don't know.

tribes central Asia is so good at producing; the Celtic languages, for example, are Indo-European. The Romans did their bit for linguistic harmony by conquering so much of Europe and making everyone speak Latin. The extent of the Roman Empire is why Italian, Spanish, and French are all so closely related; Celtic only really survives in the areas the Romans found hardest to control. A lot of Latin influence exists in English, but German overtook it when the Angles and Saxons invaded Britain, and later French, when the Normans came over. You can trace Europe's conquests through its languages.

Is There a European Culture?

If you love Mozart and go ape over the Impressionists (and quite a lot of people do both, I find), then clearly you can find culture in Europe. To some extent, these 'high' artists all fed off each other, so that they collectively created a sort of unity to much of European culture. The painters of the Renaissance consciously sought inspiration from the ancient world, and they, in turn, influenced the painters who came after them. Printing and Europe's network of patrons and universities allowed ideas and techniques to spread across huge distances.

Nevertheless, acknowledging high art is a very limited way of looking at European culture. You can find just as much richness in the folk tales and tunes with which Europe's peasants kept each other amused over the centuries. Luckily, in the 19th century, there was quite a vogue for collecting examples of folk culture (it was all part of the great romantic movement, which Chapter 17 can tell you more about), so many of them have survived. The German brothers Jakob and Wilhelm Grimm amassed a huge collection of German folk tales, which, quite wrongly, have been categorised in English as *Grimms' Fairy Tales* for children – more like *Grimms' Fairy Tales* for twisted psychopaths, if you actually read them.

Cinema with style – and subtitles

One aspect of modern culture in which Europeans have carved out a very distinctive niche is cinema. Cinema began in Europe, and Europeans have never been entirely happy to leave the medium entirely to Hollywood. The French and Italians have developed a reputation for producing stylish studies of human relationships, while Sweden's Ingmar Bergman is known for his darker portraits of tormented souls. Both Hitler and Stalin placed great emphasis on the importance of cinema: The German film-maker Leni Riefenstahl and the Russian Sergei Eisenstein were both commissioned to make grand-scale propaganda films, which are still admired by film buffs today. Eisenstein employed more people in his 1927 reconstruction of the Bolshevik Revolution, *Oktober*, than had taken part in the real thing! If you want an insight into the development of 20th-century Europe, looking at the films it produced is a good way to go about it.

What of Europe Lies beyond Europe?

'What should they know of England,' wrote Rudyard Kipling, 'who only England know?' You can't really claim to know all about Europe and its history if you restrict your gaze to Europe itself – even if you have worked out exactly where Europe begins and ends.

From the Holy Land

Although geographically part of western Asia, the Middle East – and especially the seaboard lands of modern-day Israel, Syria, Lebanon, and Egypt – has always been built into Europe's pattern of development. European civilisation can trace its origins to the development of cities in Mesopotamia (Iraq) and Jordan, and the corn lands of Egypt kept the Roman Empire supplied with bread.

Christianity bound Europe even more closely to what Europeans called 'the holy land'. Every year thousands of Europeans went on pilgrimage on foot all the way to Jerusalem. When the region fell to the Turks, it was a huge blow, and young men from all over Christendom volunteered to go off on crusade. The crusaders even set up European kingdoms in the Holy Land, and although they eventually fell to the Turks, the Europeans never quite forgot them. (If you don't want to forget these kingdoms either, have a look at Chapter 7.)

In 1798, Napoleon led a French army into Egypt, in 1917, the British General Allenby entered Jerusalem, and it was the Jews from Europe who set up the state of Israel in 1948. People sometimes wonder why Israel competes in the Eurovision Song Contest, but it's a sign that, in this part of the world at least, 'Europe' extends far beyond its geographical boundaries.

Back to Africa

Humankind began in Africa, and in the 19th century, Europeans went back to their roots in a big way – though that's not how they saw it, of course. In the space of 20 years, the Europeans virtually wiped the vast tribal continent of Africa off the map and replaced it with a continent of colonies with borders and capital cities and railways and roads; in short, they turned Africa into an extension of Europe.

In some of the most tragic cases, the borders drawn for these African countries by European administrators – with straight rulers – caused terrible trouble. The Nigerian province of Biafra and the Congolese province of Katanga were both scenes of ghastly civil wars in the 1960s, prompted by artificial boundaries drawn by Europeans. The bloodbath that erupted in Rwanda in the 1990s was also caused originally by European meddling with the local balance of power.

Europe's presence in Africa has not been a happy story (look ahead to Chapter 24 to find out just how unhappy), but it has left its legacy, and modern Africa is very much a part of the story of modern Europe.

To a new world

When Europeans spoke of a New World across the Atlantic, they really meant it. America wasn't just another land mass that Europeans had stumbled upon; it was an *empty* land – give or take the thousands and thousands of native peoples – where they could start all over again. This dream of a new life is why the settlers named so many places after places back home, and they often put the word 'new' in front of them: New Orleans, New Amsterdam (later New York, though named after the Duke of York rather than the city), New Hampshire, New Jersey, Nova Scotia (that is, New Scotland), and, of course, New England. All these place names meant 'new *and* improved'.

In South and Central America, the Spanish and Portuguese did a pretty good job of re-creating the society and structures of their homelands. The first permanent stone building that Spanish settlers erected in the New World was a church. New Spain looked an awful lot like the old one, with nobles overseeing large *haciendas* (estates) just as they did at home. Even the climate and terrain felt familiar, though when the native peoples fled attempts to enslave them for work in the gold and silver mines, the Spanish and Portuguese began the process of importing large numbers of Africans as slave labourers instead, thus changing the demography of America forever.

Europeans transported

America's most famous symbol, the Statue of Liberty, is such an icon of America that it's easy to forget that it was actually French, a gift from the French Republic to the American one in 1886. Thousands of immigrants who came into America from all over Europe gazed at the statue hopefully as they arrived in New York seeking a new life. This scene has been captured on film many times, including Charlie Chaplin's *The Immigrant* and Francis Ford Coppola's *The Godfather Part II*.

The American West was full of European immigrants, and you would have heard plenty of British and German accents out on the range (you just had to listen out for the occasional cry of 'Tally ho!' while everyone else was hollering 'Yee haw!'). But Europeans didn't just head for the States. They took boats for South America, Australia, New Zealand, and South Africa. Missionaries headed for China and India. By the 20th century, Europeans had established outposts of Europe all over the world, not just colonies ruled under European flags but places where Europeans tried to re-create the feel and the look of the lands they had left behind. European history is obviously not world history, but Europeans are part of the history of just about everywhere in the world.

Divided Europe or United Europe?

When you hit the 20th century, understanding European history becomes urgent. This period is when Europe tore itself apart in two disastrous wars that spread around the world. However, the 20th century is also when Europeans made their greatest efforts to pull the continent together and unite it as it had never been united since the days of the Romans. So, is Europe naturally divided or united?

Long division

Historians may tell you, rightly enough, that the First World War had many causes, and I deal with them properly in Chapter 20. But for now, the important cause to get hold of is *nationalism*.

Nationalism was always rather more than just patriotism. Nationalism came out of the French Revolution, which had conceived the idea of the nation as a sort of mystical union of the people all clothed in liberty and equality rather than being downtrodden subjects of a king. Nationalism caught on, and by the end of the 19th century, proud nationalists were fighting for their nations' rights all over Europe, especially where their nation was ruled by another one.

No surprise then, that the First World War actually began as a nationalist conflict between the Serbs and the Austrians, and that it spread as a nationalist conflict between all the Great Powers of Europe – France wanted her land back off the Germans; the Russians stood by their fellow Slavs, the Serbs; the Germans wanted their nation's right to an empire; and so on. Result: Division and disaster.

If you think about the causes of the Second World War, you can understand that it started for almost exactly the same reasons as the First World War: the Germans were claiming lands – Austria, the Sudetenland, the Polish Corridor – that they said had been German and should be again. But just like other nationalists before him, Hitler didn't stop there and started taking over rather large chunks of all his other neighbours' lands, too. Result: More disaster and division.

After the Second World War, Europe was divided in a rather different way. In 1945, two superpowers, the Soviet Union and the United States, effectively divided Europe from the outside along ideological lines: the Capitalist West versus the Communist East. (Chapter 24 gives you the low-down.) The division was particularly keenly felt in Germany, which was divided down the middle (though it's not the only European country to have been divided in the 20th century: Ireland, France, Poland, Czechoslovakia, and Cyprus have all experienced it). The Iron Curtain made it difficult for westerners to visit the East, and virtually impossible for east Europeans to visit the West. Right across Europe the post-war generations grew up with the idea that a divided Europe, even a divided Germany, was the natural order of things and never expected to see it change.

Europe united?

Of course Europe did change, and very quickly, in 1989 when the Berlin Wall came down. Immediately, talk turned to reuniting Germany.Next, the European Union really began pushing ahead with its plans for a closer political union.

The idea of a united Europe isn't quite as new-fangled as it may seem. The Romans had united the continent, or as much of it as they could conquer, under Roman law. Napoleon had attempted to unite the continent under the principles of liberty established by the French Revolution – or at least that was what he said he was doing. Even the great European nationalist leaders had dreamed of a united Europe of nation states all living in perfect harmony (dream on, my friends), and Hitler actively promoted the idea of a united Europe standing firm against Communism – not (as German leaders were often at pains to point out) so *very* different from the post-war American idea.

So, is Europe really a united continent that only gets divided by accident? History doesn't really support that idea. All the attempts at union I mention involved using a degree of force. The exception is the European Union, but the evidence by the start of the 21st century was that the ordinary people of Europe were much less happy about uniting than their leaders. And in the end, if you haven't united the people, you haven't united anything.

This Must Never Happen Again!

European history is full of moments, normally after wars, when people have drawn breath and said something along the lines of 'This must never happen again!'. People said it in 1648 after the Thirty Years' War (*thirty years* of war – just think about it! Better still, turn to Chapter 13 and read about it). And people said it again in 1815 after Napoleon was finally defeated and the nations of Europe decided to set up regular summit meetings, known as Congresses, to solve problems without going to war. People said it after the First World War ('the war to end all wars'), when they set up the League of Nations, and again after the Second World War, when they set up the United Nations. The line was repeated after the Holocaust, and then again after the genocide in Bosnia and Rwanda: 'This must never happen again!' War and atrocity always do happen again, though. This books shows you why.

Chapter 2

The Stone Age Rocks

*T*he Stone Age gets a bit of a raw deal. Many people think that it's the dull bit before the real history begins. There's no dialogue, the costumes are *awful*, and you have to pretend to be interested in all those bits of old stone in museums while people in safari jackets enthuse about the Palaeolithic or the Neolithic.

Well, hang on – there's a lot more to those stones than you might think.

Three Stone Ages for the Price of One

The Stone Age is so-called because the people who lived through it used stone for their tools, and because their tools have survived. Later ages are named after bronze and iron for the same reason. But the Stone Age was a lot *lot* longer than these later ages. If this book were arranged in proportion to the time each chapter covers, the Stone Age chapter would take up all but the last few pages.

Archaeologists and anthropologists divide the Stone Age up into three main periods:

> ✔ **Palaeolithic (Old Stone Age):** The oldest part (and since it began about 1 million years ago, they divide *that* up into three periods, too)

> ✔ **Mesolithic (Middle Stone Age):** The middle period (10,000 to 9,000 B.C. – a millennium)

> ✔ **Neolithic (New Stone Age):** The most recent period (9,000 to 4,000 B.C. – 5 millennia)

Strange ruts in Malta

Some of the earliest evidence for human activity in Europe is in Malta: great standing stones, known as *megaliths,* strange tombs and a temple carved into the rock. This evidence suggests that humans had a sophisticated set of beliefs in Neolithic times, not to mention an efficient labour service. Fossilised ruts in the rock may indicate some sort of prehistoric drag carts – two poles dragged along by a horse or ox for carrying loads. If so, these ruts could have major implications; these people had domesticated animals, they had something to load on their drag carts (and what might that have been?), and they had somewhere to take it to – not to mention a reason for making the journey in the first place. Also significant is that this evidence for early Europeans lies so close to Africa – almost certainly the cradle of humankind.

This chapter focuses on the Neolithic stage in a bit more detail, because that's when people began emerging in what we recognise as human form and setting up small human societies that were built on the tremendous advances made by their predecessors. If you think our ancestors were stupid (and who knows, they may just be thinking that about their descendants), try taking yourself somewhere far from human habitation with only stones to work with, and then fashion yourself a workable tool to cut things with. Then, go back to that museum and look at the ones in the glass cases. I bet you'll be even more impressed!

Rummaging Through the Dustbins of History

Remember all those *things* you had when you were a child? Not just the toys – the ordinary things. The plates and furniture and gadgets and tools and those knick knacks on the mantelpiece, not to mention your clothes and school books. What happened to them all? Some no doubt got thrown away, some got sold, and some are probably still knocking around somewhere, but ultimately they all end up where we all end up: in the ground, my friends. Most of them never see the light of day again, but those that do – oh, what stories they can tell. Welcome to the world of archaeology.

Archaeologists explore the past through the things that get left behind. Not just the ancient past; there's archaeology of 19th-century industry and even of recent history such as the Cold War. But archaeology is particularly useful for finding out about societies that have left no written record.

Archaeologists get excited by things most of us wouldn't give a second glance to and would probably throw away. In fact, things that have been thrown away are often the very best evidence for how people live, as any police officer or downmarket journalist can tell you. However, finding the material is only the start of the process. Archaeologists carefully note which layer of earth the find was in and then compare it with other finds from the same layer (in case the soil has been displaced over time). Any archaeologist can tell you that the moments that you see on television, when someone uncovers a grave or a mosaic pavement, are only a tiny part of the work. Archaeologists do a lot of distinctly unglamorous digging and hauling and sifting and brushing as well, because even the tiniest find can add to the overall picture of the past.

Is there a palaeobotanist in the house?

Archaeologists are very good at bringing in other experts. Some experts can tell an amazing amount from pollen and seeds preserved from ancient times (yes, folks, they're the _palaeobotanists_), whereas others can 'read' fabric or recover writing from waterlogged papyrus or wood. The police use a method for reconstructing crime and accident victims' mutilated faces that was originally developed for 'rebuilding' the faces of Egyptian mummies.

A lot of technology has gone into dating archaeological finds. _Radiocarbon dating_ measures the rate of decay of radioactive elements such as carbon or potassium that are found in many objects, and researchers can use DNA to trace genetic links in human remains. But a lot of dating work is done through older techniques, such as measuring tree rings in a piece of wood.

Archaeological digging is very expensive and always carries the risk of destroying as much as is discovered, so archaeologists are always open to alternatives to digging, such as these:

- ✔ Aerial photography and satellite images can pick up the shape of solid structures or field patterns.
- ✔ Hand-held equipment can send radar waves and electric currents into the ground to detect buried objects.
- ✔ Computer imaging can reconstruct whole buildings and scenes from the bits and pieces that come to light in the earth itself.

Learning from the neighbours

If digging or using modern technology seem a bit tame, you can always try learning from experience. Archaeologists sometimes re-create artefacts or dwellings and get people to try them out, to find out what practical problems the original people may have encountered and how they may have overcome them. The Norwegian Thor Heyerdahl reconstructed sailing vessels of people of ancient Polynesia to find out just how far they could have sailed – and then discovered that they could have gone a lot farther than they had been given credit for. Archaeologists also call in the help of anthropologists who study different communities, especially when they're looking at people who still live much as they did in ancient times. Such study doesn't *prove* how things were in the past, but it can give a pretty good idea.

Out of Africa . . . We Think

The oldest human, or *hominid* (not-quite-ape and not-quite-human), remains have been found in southern and eastern Africa, and no one has offered any serious scientific challenge to the idea that humankind first emerged there. The earliest hominids were called *Australopithecus*, which means 'southern ape man', by Professor Raymond Dart, who found the skull of an Australopithecus child at Taung in southern Africa in 1924. Many different types of skulls and bones have come to light since then, and scientists still enjoy blazing rows about exactly how all these australopithecines relate to each other.

After the era of Australopithecus, archaeologists start finding bones and skulls of various types of *homo* – that is, humans:

- ✔ *Homo habilis:* Very early human, only found in Africa so far. Not the sort of character you'd want to take your daughter out for the evening (though you might think that's just who is).
- ✔ *Homo erectus:* Recognisably human, and found in Africa, Asia and Europe.
- ✔ *Homo sapiens neanderthalis:* Otherwise known as the much-maligned Neanderthal man, who was actually just as clever as you are (though not quite as good-looking, of course).
- ✔ *Homo sapiens sapiens:* Our very good selves.

OK, now come the bits archaeologists don't yet know.

Archaeologists don't know how these different species relate to each other, nor how one evolved into another (if, of course, they did). Archaeologists don't know what, if anything, was the famous 'missing link' between the unmistakably animal and the unmistakably hominid. Nor have these explorers of the past pieced together how hominids became human, or how we developed speech or beliefs or a sense of morals or ethics. And, although archaeologists are pretty sure that hominids came out of Africa, we don't really know how they came to spread to other parts of the world, including Europe.

The First Europeans

The story of how humans first appeared in Europe has bigger implications than might at first appear. For example, if humans *don't* have a common ancestor of some sort, if they appeared spontaneously in different parts of the world, what are the implications for relations between different branches of the human family? That we're not just different races, but different *species*? Then again, how, when, and why did the skin colour of humans in Europe become so much paler? Why did Europeans develop different eye and hair colours from those you find in Africa? At the moment, no one knows the answers to these questions, but for anyone who saw Europeans as different from, or better than, other peoples (and there has been no shortage of Europeans who believe just that), these questions are very interesting indeed.

The Beagle has landed

The somewhat romanticised version of Charles Darwin's place in history goes like this: In 1832, the young Charles Darwin, fresh out of Cambridge, set sail on HMS *Beagle* on a long voyage of scientific discovery. He amassed an enormous collection of scientific specimens and made careful observations of the species he found, especially in the South Atlantic and the Galapagos Islands in the Pacific. Darwin's observations led him to conclude that nature operates according to *natural selection*, and that creatures adapt to their environment in such a way that over time the same species, if placed in different environments, will evolve differently. Darwin published his ideas in *The Origin of Species* in 1859, and the novelty of his theory of evolution created a storm of controversy. Although he hardly mentioned the idea in *The Origin of Species*, Darwin went on to dwell particularly on the idea that human beings have also evolved over time, and that the story of the creation as told in the Book of Genesis cannot be literally true.

Neanderthal man: International Man of Mystery

Ever since his big bones were first dug up in 1856, Neanderthal man has posed a lot of difficult questions. The first one was probably 'What the –?!', but the questions have become rather more sophisticated since then. In 1908, a whole Neanderthal skeleton turned up in France, and it was so deformed that it had scientists seriously worried about our ancestors, until it turned out that particular specimen had suffered from rickets, poor chap. Nevertheless, Neanderthal remains gave the impression of early man as a rough creature living in caves, muttering 'Ugh, ugh' and dragging his knuckles along the floor.

Now we know that Neanderthals were highly intelligent, built shelters for themselves, made their own clothes, and very probably had some form of spoken language. This species buried their dead with full ritual, which almost certainly points to a system of religious belief. Neanderthals certainly looked different from us, but they were recognisably human. But what's even more intriguing is how these people fit into the grand pattern. Neanderthals have been found in Europe and Asia but nowhere else. Why? *Neanderthalis* started earlier than *Homo sapiens sapiens*, but the two species overlapped and coexisted for a time, which means that – barring individual cases of interbreeding (unlikely but not impossible) – Neanderthal man is not our ancestor. The Neanderthals died out, while our forebears survived, and we still don't really know why.

The idea of some sort of evolution had been around for a long time before Darwin, and selective breeding to develop new species was familiar to anyone who had visited an 18th-century English farm. By no means did everyone uphold the strict biblical account of the creation even before Darwin published his book. The controversy soon died down, and Darwin's ideas became widely accepted, even by many churchmen. You can think of Darwin as a pioneer figure if you like, but he was very far from alone, – more like a scout with a full regiment of cavalry only just behind him.

Darwin followed up *The Origin of Species* with a number of books on evolution in plants and animals, and then in 1871, he published *The Descent of Man*, which argued that humankind was related to the great apes and that we all probably have a common ancestor. So far the prize for the oldest human fossil in Europe goes to a female *Homo erectus* skull dug up at Swanscombe in Kent, in southeast England. But don't expect that to be the end of the story!

The painting's on the wall

It's not always the great scientists who make the big discoveries. It was four young French boys who in 1940 – a busy year in France – went to their schoolteacher to ask whether he'd like to see what they had found. What they had found were the magnificent cave paintings of Lascaux.

The paintings at Lascaux show animals, such as bison and antelope, in vivid colours, some of them apparently being hunted by stick men. (If the artists could paint animals so well, why the stick men? One of many questions about Lascaux.) There are also outlines of hands, which seem to have been made by blowing paint through a tube. There have been all sorts of theories about what all these cave paintings mean. Some say that they formed part of a ritual for hunting, others say that they tell us about the roles of men and women, and others say that they're evidence of belief about the afterlife. We just don't know.

What we do know is that they were made by humans, *Homo sapiens sapiens*, often called *Cro-Magnon* after the cave in the Dordogne region of France where their bones were first found. These humans needed the caves because they were living through the Ice Age.

Go easy on the ice

To get an *Ice Age* in Europe, you only need a temperature drop of 4 degrees Celsius, and for most of the last million and a half years up to today, Europe had just that. For much of the Ice Age, the arctic ice cap spread to the south coast of England, northern Germany, and Poland. Southern Europe was a sort of tundra – the south of France or Tuscany would have looked like modern-day Greenland. Summers were still warm, but the long winters were severe, and it was almost certainly this climate change that did in poor old *Homo erectus*. Neanderthals adapted well to the cold, and so did Cro-Magnon. At Predmost in the Czech Republic, the remains of some 900 woolly mammoths have been found, and the evidence suggests that early people made good use of them for food and clothing, while the bones and tusks made a great frame for a tent. Nevertheless, by the time the ice melted and left Europe in more or less its modern shape (though with forests to replace the tundra and ice caps), the Neanderthals had disappeared. The future lay with *Homo sapiens sapiens*. That's us.

Down on the (Stone Age) Farm

The period after the Ice Age is called the *Neolithic period*, or the New Stone Age (not to be confused with the New Age, many of whose proponents are indeed stoned). That's because the Neolithics took to a way of life that seems to have spread from the Middle East – it was called farming.

A very Fertile Crescent

It may seem odd to say that European history has its roots in the Middle East, but evidence supports the idea. The area between the rivers Tigris and Euphrates in modern Iraq (known to historians as Mesopotamia, 'the land between two rivers') was always being flooded, with the result that it became extremely fertile. In fact, the whole region, through to modern-day Israel, is known as the *Fertile Crescent*. And while Europeans were remarking on how warm it was now that the Ice Age was over and wondering where all the woolly mammoths had gone, people in the Fertile Crescent were experimenting with crops and animals and working out how to plough.

The first cities

There's nothing like farming for tying you down to the land, and it wasn't long before the people of the Fertile Crescent (see the nearby sidebar) began building more permanent residences, and even towns and cities. Some of these places have become very well known, such as Ur on the Euphrates, where Abraham is supposed to have come from, or the famous city of Jericho in the Jordan Valley. We know a lot about Jericho because it was excavated in the 1950s, unearthing houses, trade goods, a large circular stone tower, and, yes, city walls – still standing.

Another important Neolithic city is Çatal Hüyük in Anatolia, in modern-day Turkey. This city started as a farming village, but it grew into a town of about 6,000 people – huge by Stone Age standards – with a full irrigation system. The people had fine clothes and jewellery, and they traded with the whole of Anatolia. Their houses were plastered and painted, but they hadn't worked out about doors – you entered by a hole in the roof ('Hi, honey, I'm . . .' *Crash!*).

The farmers of Greece

The first Europeans to take up farming were the Greeks; they were the nearest to the Fertile Crescent. We don't know exactly how the knowledge spread. It's nice to think of a Neolithic Greek version of Will Parker in *Oklahoma!* coming back all excited from a visit ('I got to Çatal Hüyük on a Friday, by Saturday I'd larned a thing or two!'), and that sort of thing may very well have happened, though it's just as likely to have been visitors from the east making helpful suggestions. It seems pretty clear that we're talking about seafarers by now, because there's evidence of farming in Sicily and southern Italy as well.

However, knowledge of farming didn't change the way of life in southern Europe overnight: much of Greece was ill-suited to farming, and we reckon it was some time before they gave up their hunting and fishing for this new-fangled idea of sitting around watching plants grow.

You say you want a (Neolithic) revolution

Somehow, the knowledge of farming spread up from southern Europe into the colder northern parts. It was probably done through trade along the Danube and then along the other rivers of northern Europe (northern Europe being particularly well-off for navigable rivers). For many years, historians talked of this as the *Neolithic revolution*, a complete change in people's way of life, from a hunter-gatherer society (where you hunt for food or gather it from the trees) to a settled farming way of life, with villages and enclosed fields and the very first utterance of the immortal line 'Get off my land!' For those who like their history neat and simple, this idea is attractive.

Guess what? The process probably wasn't quite like that. Neolithic people certainly built substantial settlements, such as the village of Lepinski Vir on the Danube, or the settlement of Starr Carr in Yorkshire, or the village built on stilts at Lake Neuchatel in Switzerland. At Karanovo in Bulgaria, archaeologists have even found the earliest evidence yet of a town street. Some of these places may have been temporary bases for people who were still essentially nomads. If there was a Neolithic revolution, it took a very long time for everyone to notice.

Meet the Flint Stones

The trouble with talking about the Stone Age, or even the New Stone Age, is that it doesn't tell you which 'stone'. For the Neolithics, the stone was flint, and it's still impressive to see what they were able to achieve with it. These people could refine flint to a sharp edge that could cut like a razor, and those flint arrowheads you can see in museums are so perfect that some archaeologists think that they must have been for display rather than use. Without flint, the Neolithics could never have taken up farming, because they used flints for the cutting edge of their sickles at harvest time. In fact, we've even found a sort of flint tool factory at Grimes Graves in Norfolk, in England. The Neolithic revolution was a sort of agricultural and industrial revolution rolled into one.

The Neolithics are best known not for sickles or arrowheads but for the enormous stones, known as megaliths, erected as burial chambers or arranged in mysterious stone circles. There aren't many man-made structures that make you scratch your head and ask 'Why?' – well, okay, London's Millennium Dome – but that's precisely what archaeologists have long been asking about Neolithic monuments. Why?

Tombs and what they tell us

At least we know what tombs are for, even if we don't know quite why the Neolithics went to so much trouble to set them up. There are two big burial grounds in Brittany in northern France; elaborate burial chambers in Denmark, where the people who built them are known as the Mound People; and a huge grave complex at New Grange in Ireland. In Portugal, Neolithics even had burial chambers underneath mounds created from hundreds of years' worth of shells from the local seafood – not the best advertisement, I'd have thought. All of these mounds must have taken a lot of highly organised labour to build (we're talking about 1,000 years before the pyramids went up), and unless it was all forced labour, these people must have had some strong sense of the meaning of what they were doing.

Some of these tombs, such as the simple *dolmens* of France, are essentially one stone balanced on top of two others and were probably built for one person. Others, such as the huge burial mounds at West Kennet in Wiltshire in England, were for groups, though whether these mounds were for a chief's family or whether it was communal is harder to say. Some of the burial mounds are aligned to the winter solstice or some other movement of the sun, which raises all sorts of tantalising suggestions about what these people actually believed in, not to mention their powers of observation. Either way, it suggests organised religion of a very sophisticated sort – and some very weak unions.

Standing stones (and some that have fallen over)

The famous Neolithic standing stones (megaliths or *menhirs*) are quite another matter. Archaeologists just don't know what they're for. There are thousands of them, some on their own, some in circles, and some in long lines, spread across Britain, France, and Ireland. The most famous example has to be the great stone circles of Stonehenge in Wiltshire, which is so carefully aligned with the movements of the sun that it has even been suggested that it was some sort of early computer or astronomical observatory. In fact, Stonehenge was probably even bigger than we thought, because archaeologists have shown that a number of stand-alone stones on the very edges of the site were almost certainly part of the original setup, and that there was another huge henge (circle) nearby, only made of wood.

When they're not trying to work out what these stone monuments were for, historians and archaeologists have puzzled over how on earth they were constructed. Simply raising the stones must have been difficult enough, not to mention lifting one stone on top of others, but some of them had to be transported long distances first. There have been all sorts of theories, some involving rolling the stones on logs, some involving carrying them by sea (though some stone circles are a long way inland) or even sliding them on ice. One thing we do know is that the Neolithics were getting help from some new kids on the block. We call them the Beaker People because we've found lots of their drinking beakers in their graves. The beakers were made of metal.

Mining Metal

You won't be surprised to hear that metalworking probably began in the Middle East – in this period, just about every technological advance did. Archaeologists have found beads from Çatal Hüyük made of lead, and other Turkish sites have thrown up small copper objects that were mined in Neolithic times along the Tigris, where it is still mined today. Clearly, these people knew how to smelt and how to fashion some quite intricate objects out of copper, and it wasn't long before Europeans learned the knack as well. The Balkan region of south east Europe is rich in metals, and we have found copper earrings and tools in a big excavation at Karanovo in Bulgaria, which show a Neolithic metal industry in full swing. And just for once, all this technical achievement was happening some 2,000 years *before* the Chinese caught up!

At the same time as they were crafting metal in the Balkans, elsewhere in Europe people were still shaping (knapping) finely crafted flints. There was no neat division between the Stone Age and the age of metals.

Some of this metal knowledge spread peacefully. The Beaker People (see preceding section) who helped build Stonehenge, for example, seem to have integrated quite happily with the Neolithic natives. But life didn't stay peaceful for long. The excavations at Karanovo show that it changed from being a sort of extended village into a full-fledged fortress, and we have found evidence of other fortified towns elsewhere in the Balkans. These people were scared, and with good reason. A new metal had arrived, and it was very tough. So were the people who brought it. And they were *not* friendly.

These people came from the steppe lands of central Asia, they were called Kurgans, and about 6,000 years ago, they decided to leave their homelands (possibly because the grazing was dying out so it was migrate or die). The Kurgans headed for the Balkans, where the natives hurriedly threw up defensive walls because the newcomers had two distinct advantages:

- ✔ Horses
- ✔ Bronze

Bronze is an alloy of copper and tin, and it's much harder than either of them. The Kurgans had learned how to use it to make very effective battle axes, and judging from the number and quality of the ones we have found, they had a very efficient mass production line. Bronze meant power (they were quite brazen about it!), especially when you could wield it from on top of a galloping horse. This source of power enabled the Kurgans to sweep through southern and central Europe, killing as they went. Europe would see many other peoples over the centuries who did the same thing.

Part II
Europe of the Ancients

The 5th Wave　　　By Rich Tennant

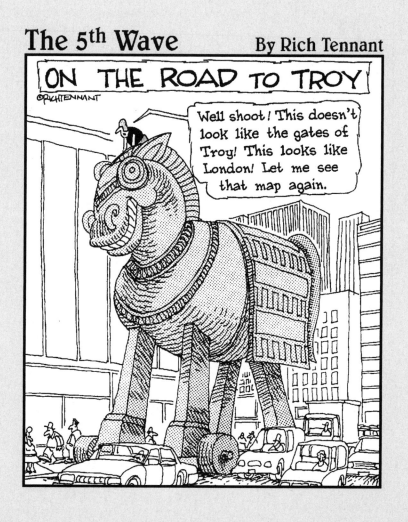

In this part . . .

People still talk about Europe's Graeco-Roman heritage, and you get a very strong sense that modern Europe grew out of its ancient forebears. The Ancient Greeks virtually invented European civilisation single-handed: everything from architecture and mathematics to literature and government. If your knowledge of the Greeks is a bit patchy, and you never know how the Spartans fit in, or what actually happened to Alexander the Great, this part will help put you right.

Thanks to Hollywood everyone has an image of the Romans, with their scarlet cloaks and plumed helmets hailing Caesar like there was no tomorrow (which, for some of them, there wasn't). This part shows how the Romans fitted into the wider picture of the ancient world, what they owed to the Greeks, and what they lost to the barbarian tribes, who were never *very* far away.

Chapter 3

You're Ancient History!

In This Chapter

▶ Following the adventures of the ancient Greeks

▶ Overcoming Greek hegemony

▶ Meeting Alexander the Great

▶ Building a Republic, Roman-style

*I*f you want to know why historians pay so much attention to ancient Greece, look at a map. Greece was the nearest European land to all those new ideas and techniques coming in from the Middle East and the Fertile Crescent. (Look back to Chapter 2 for more about these topics.) In this chapter, I follow suit, looking at ancient Greece and its impact on Europe's history.

Greece Is the Word

Greece is made up of an archipelago of hundreds of islands and narrow peninsulas, with lots of nice, safe natural harbours for keeping boats in. The interior is very rocky – good for goats, not so good for town planning – so Greek communities tended to be on the small and manageable side. To the Greeks, mountains were the ultimate barrier: they even believed that the gods lived at the top of one. The Greeks had picked up on how to use sails, so it's no surprise that Greek civilisation began on Crete and the Cyclades islands of the eastern Mediterranean, handy for hopping over to the towns of Anatolia (modern Turkey) and the Middle East.

An Englishman on Crete

We know about the people of Crete thanks to an English archaeologist named Sir Arthur Evans, who went there in 1894 to look for evidence of the story of Theseus and the Minotaur. (See the sidebar 'That's a lot of bull', later in this chapter, for the details.) Evans dug up the ruins of a huge palace complex called Knossos, which was clearly the centre of a highly sophisticated civilisation. Evans named it 'Minoan', after King Minos, the king in the Minotaur story; we don't know what the Minoans called themselves. Thanks to Knossos's wall paintings and pots and objects of daily living, we know a lot about the people who lived there in 2000 B.C. We'd know even more about the Minoans if we could read their writing. Evans found lots of clay tablets with writing on them, some in a sort of hieroglyphic picture writing, some in a written script known as Linear A. Sadly, we can't read either of these scripts. Even more sad is what happened to the Minoans. In about 1450 B.C., the island of Thera, just north of Crete, blew up. Scientists reckon it may have been the biggest volcanic eruption for 10,000 years. You can still see the results in the ruins of a Minoan village on Akrotiri, the small Greek island which is about all that's left of Thera. The eruption utterly destroyed Knossos – Crete's glory days were over.

The destruction of Thera and Knossos may be behind the legend of Atlantis. When the philosopher Plato wrote of a thriving civilisation called Atlantis that sank beneath the sea, he may have had the Minoans in mind.

New kids on the block: the Mycenaeans

The Mycenaeans get their name from the city of Mycenae, though they lived in other places as well. They were a very tough lot, who dominated the whole Greek mainland for about 500 years, from 1600 to 1100 B.C. We know a lot about the Mycenaeans from their *shaft graves*, so called because you reached them via a very deep shaft; bad news for grave robbers but very good news for archaeologists. We also have the magnificent Mycenae *acropolis* ('high city') with its famous Lion Gate, with two lions carved above it. We have found lots of weapons, as well as evidence of trade, and some magnificent golden jewellery, including some gold face masks, probably of Mycenaean kings. The Myceneans also had a form of writing known as Linear B – a sort of transition phase between the Minoans' Linear A and Ancient Greek. Archaeologists have worked out how to read Linear B; unfortunately, all the examples of it we have seem to be rather dull lists and inventories.

You steal my wife; I trash your Troy

The story of Troy that we have today comes from an epic poem called the *Iliad* (from 'Ilium', the Greek name for Troy) by the poet Homer. According to the story, it all started with Helen, a Greek princess so fabulously beautiful that Greek kings (she seems to have attracted only VIPs) fell in love with her. In the end, Helen chose Menelaus, king of Sparta, but they had hardly finished choosing curtains when young Paris, son of King Priam of Troy, caught Helen's eye, and they slipped away together over the sea to Troy. Well! Talk about scandal!

That's a lot of bull

According to legend, Zeus, the king of the gods, spotted a beautiful princess called Europa, fell in love with her, changed himself into a bull (as you do), and promptly swam over to Crete with the girl on his back. Europa and Zeus's son, Minos, became king of Crete and built his palace at Knossos – where Arthur Evans found it, a year or 4,000 later. Unfortunately Minos's wife, Queen Pasiphaë, promptly fell in love with a bull sent up as a present by the sea god, Poseidon, who arranged for the bull to, er, mate with the queen (inside a specially constructed hollow cow, would you believe?) Result: The famous half-bull half-human monster, the Minotaur. Minos, understandably, did not want the Minotaur hanging around the palace – quite apart from the awkward paternity question, it ate people – so he imprisoned it in an impenetrable maze, known as the *labyrinth,* specially designed by a canny architect called Daedalus, where it lived on a special diet of seven Greek boys and girls every nine years, until a dashing young Athenian called Theseus turned up. With the help of Minos's daughter, Ariadne, who gave him a long ball of wool to help him find his way back out of the labyrinth, Theseus killed the Minotaur and sailed off into the sunset with Ariadne at his side – though he then unceremoniously dumped her on an island and married her sister instead. Okay, how much of this story is true? The labyrinth may actually have existed, and the kings of Crete may well have worn a bull's head mask for special ceremonies, which may be the origin of the Minotaur idea. There are certainly paintings from Knossos showing young Cretans – men and women – leaping over charging bulls as a form of sport. And for all you astrology fans, Europa's bull is said to have ended up in the heavens as the constellation Taurus – the bull.

Agamemnon, king of Mycenae, organised a vast army of all the kings of Greece to sail over to Troy and get Helen back, and the result was ten years of bloody war, in which the Greeks couldn't get into Troy and the Trojans couldn't get out. Eventually, wily old King Odysseus of Ithaca thought of a cunning plan. The Greeks would pretend to sail away, leaving a large wooden horse on the beach. The Trojans would think it was an offering to the gods and take it into the city, whereupon the Greek soldiers hidden inside ('Surprise!') would creep out, open the gate to let the rest of the Greeks in, and burn the city to the ground. Desperate though that strategy sounds, according to Homer, it worked: They destroyed the city, Menelaus got Helen back (she no doubt protesting, 'Oh, Menelaus darling, I can explain everything . . .'), and the Greeks set off home, braving all sorts of dangers and adventures on the way.

It's hard to imagine the Trojans allowing Helen to stay, especially if it was going to mean a major war. Rather more prosaically (but more likely), by about 1200 B.C., the real Mycenaeans were desperately short of food, and their trade was collapsing. They started launching raids overseas, and one of these raids may have been the origin of the story of the Trojan War. There is evidence that horses were regarded as sacred in that part of the Mediterranean, and that models of animals, sometimes even very large ones, were sometimes left as offerings to the gods. So that part of the story *might* be true.

Gods and goddesses

The Mycaeneans originally drew up the set of Greek gods and heroes. The Greeks liked to think that the gods looked after different aspects of everyday life, but they also conceived of them bickering and generally carrying on like a soap opera at the top of Mount Olympus. Later, the Romans adapted the Greek gods for their own purposes – as they did with just about everything else the Greeks left behind. Here's a handy checklist of some of the most important Greek gods:

- **Zeus (Roman: Jupiter):** King of the Gods, usually shown with a thunderbolt. Zeus married his sister, Hera, but that didn't stop him from pursuing other women, usually disguised as an animal. Gross!

- **Hera (Roman: Juno):** Sister and wife to Zeus, patron of put-upon wives. No wonder.

- **Poseidon (Roman: Neptune):** Zeus's brother and King of the Sea, usually shown with a trident. Causes earthquakes.

- **Hades (also known as Pluto or Dis):** Lord of the Underworld and of the Dead. 'Hades' was also used as the name for his underworld kingdom. Hades kidnapped his niece, Persephone (Roman: Proserpina), and married her, so she had to spend half the year underground – which is how the Greek explained the germination of plants each spring.

Homing in on Homer

For one of the greatest poets in European history, we know precious little about Homer, who wrote the *Iliad* about the Trojan War and the *Odyssey* about the adventures of Odysseus. Homer is supposed to have been blind, probably a travelling bard, though some historians think that he may not have been one person at all. Homer's tale fired the imagination of the young Heinrich Schliemann, who was born in Germany in 1822 and spent a pretty adventurous life himself: he was shipwrecked, escaped a hotel fire in Sacramento by the skin of his teeth, and came within an inch of dying of fever. Schliemann set off for Turkey with only Homer's description to guide him and pinpointed the exact site of Troy. Schliemann's methods seem very crude today – they sometimes included using dynamite! – but he was in many ways the first modern archaeologist. Unfortunately, what Schliemann thought was the golden mask of Agamemnon is too old to have been, the treasure he found at Troy is not old enough to have come from Homer's Troy, and the Troy he identified as *the* Troy almost certainly wasn't. As another Homer would say, *D'oh!*

Going under

The Greek idea of the Underworld was of a dull, grey, lifeless place where hope died and souls existed in an unending state of misery and despair – rather like Kettering. However, for a fortunate few singled out by the gods for special favour, a more pleasant prospect beckoned: they were sent to walk in the pleasant fields of the island of Elysium, there to live the life of the blessed. The Champs Elysées in Paris are named after the Elysian Fields, though if you walk across the Champs Elysées without taking due care, you could quickly end up in the Underworld yourself.

- **Ares (Roman: Mars):** God of War and lover of Aphrodite (Roman: Venus), Goddess of Love, behind the back of her lame husband, the blacksmith Hephaestus (Roman: Vulcan). There's nothing new about the attraction of a man in uniform!

- **Apollo (also known as Phoebus):** Twin brother of Artemis (Roman: Diana), Goddess of Hunting. Apollo was God of the Sun, Music, Medicine, and Poetry, and also managed to fit in time to kill the great serpent, Python, who guarded the entrance to the Oracle of Delphi, where Greeks went to find out what the future held in store for them.

- **Athene (Roman: Minerva):** Goddess of Wisdom and War, and patron of the city of Athens. Athene is supposed to have sprung fully armed from Zeus's head when he asked Hephaestus to cure his headache by splitting his head open. (How did she get in there? Zeus had fathered her and then eaten her mother!)

You can have a lot of fun learning about all these gods, but for historians, the big question is: Did the Greeks actually *believe* all this stuff? The answer, which may surprise you, is yes. However sophisticated their philosophy later became, the Greeks never got rid of their need for these gods and their stories to explain the world they lived in.

Decline and fall . . . and rise

Sometime around 1200 B.C., the Mycenaean world collapsed, probably through famine. Some of the Mycenaeans settled overseas, and some operated as pirates – until an Egyptian fleet put a stop to *that*. Greece entered its Dark Ages, not because it was chaotic, but because the people who moved in, the Dorians, didn't read or write, and didn't go in for elaborate burials. But around 800 B.C., there was a big rise in population, and the new people not only knew how to read and write, but they also knew how to build and think and fight. The glory days of *Classical* Greece were about to start.

Living in a Polis State

These new Greeks set up self-governing cities, such as Athens, Corinth, and Sparta – and their word for such a city was *polis*, from which we get 'politics'. A polis was drawn up on very simple lines: There were free men, and there were slaves, known as *helots*. Free men had rights; slaves had none.

Later, the Athenians decided that for full rights, you had to have been born in Athens; if you were born anywhere else, you were a *metic* and had fewer rights (you could say this was an early version of the metic system . . .). Oh, and women had no rights at all, wherever they were born.

Each polis was an *oligarchy*, run by a small group of the richest free (male) citizens. In time of war or emergency, all power was handed over to one man, called a *tyrant*, which in those days just meant 'ruler' – though one of them, Draco, drew up a set of laws for Athens, which were so harsh that we still talk of 'draconian' laws today.

Luckily for Athens, a new ruler, called Solon, repealed Draco's laws and generally introduced a much fairer system of government. But Solon made enemies, and these adversaries forced him to leave Athens. Cue for a power struggle and civil war, until an Athenian aristocrat called Cleisthenes set up a new system: It got its name from *demos* (people) and *kratos* (power), and it was called *democracy*.

Hmm . . . it's not that democratic, is it?

Don't get too excited by the Greek idea of democracy. Europeans like to point to it as the origin for modern democracy, but there were big differences. Here's how the system worked:

- Citizens – and only citizens – had the vote. No helots, no foreigners, no metics, and no women.
- The citizens were grouped into tribes and each tribe elected 50 representatives to sit on the City Council. Citizens also elected ten military commanders, called *strategoi,* and nine civil officials called *archons*.
- Every citizen also had the right to sit and vote in the Assembly, which met every ten days on the Pnyx hill outside the city. Slacking was not an option: If you didn't turn up, the police were sent to fetch you.

Could we have our marbles back?

Pericles rebuilt the Acropolis above Athens, including the famous Temple of Athene, the Parthenon. By the 19th century, Greece was under Turkish rule and the Acropolis was crumbling away. An English nobleman, the Earl of Elgin, bought the marble statues from the Parthenon's frontage off the Turkish government and shipped them back to England. Buying archaeological antiquities was quite common practice at the time, but in recent years, the Greek government has lobbied ceaselessly for the 'Elgin marbles' to be returned from the British Museum to Athens.

The most successful Athenian statesman was Pericles, a very popular *strategoi* who was regularly re-elected and helped Athens recover from its disastrous war with Persia. (See the section 'Squaring Up to the Persians', later in this chapter, to find out what the war was about.) Unpopular officials were thrown out of Athens for ten years on a vote of 600 of the citizens (on the basis that 600 Athenians can't be wrong!). The evicted official's name was written on a piece of broken pot called an *ostrakon*, which is where the word ostracise came from.

Greek geeks

The Greeks produced a set of writers and thinkers who for their contribution to our understanding of the world have never really been equalled. Greek writers can seem a bit off-putting – it's easy to get the idea that you have to be terribly clever to read them – so here's a handy Who's Who.

We only have a *fraction* of what the Greeks originally produced. The poet Pindar wrote 17 volumes of writings; all that's survived are four small books of songs, but they're enough to make some experts think Pindar may have been the best Greek poet of them all.

Polis Academy

Socrates was the big daddy of Greek philosophy. Socrates didn't write anything down (unless that, too, has been lost), but he taught the importance of careful, sceptical questioning (the *Socratic method*) in order to tease out the truth. Socrates was condemned to death (by drinking hemlock – nasty) for 'corrupting' the city's youth with his subversive ideas. Socrates's most famous pupil was *Plato*, who founded a famous school in a grove called the Academy to carry on spreading his old teacher's ideas. Plato wasn't too impressed by democracy – it gave power to the sort of ignorant oafs who had condemned Socrates to death – so in his book, *The Republic*, he argues that states should be run by a small number of properly educated 'Guardians', with property held in common, and marriage and reproduction all carefully geared to the requirements of the State. Plato's most famous pupil was *Aristotle*, who lectured on everything from politics to mathematics, biology, and even music. Aristotle had more faith in the people than Plato had: He thought that extremes would cancel each other out, and you'd end up with a sensible middle course.

Plato's ideas appealed to the 19th-century British, who used their public schools and universities to turn out an educated elite along platonic lines to run the British Empire. Plato has also been blamed for inspiring 20th-century dictatorships, such as Nazi Germany and Soviet Russia.

Greek philosophy included science and mathematics. *Archimedes* worked out in the bath that a body displaces its own weight of water and ran down the street shouting 'Eureka!' ('I have found it!'). *Euclid* worked out the principles of geometry, which is hard to forgive, and *Pythagoras* worked out the intervals of the musical scale. Pythagoras is also the one with the famous theorem about the square on the hypotenuse, though it seems that it was originally set out by Euclid. We'll leave it to them to fight it out.

Tragedies, comedies, and history

The Greeks enjoyed a night out at the open-air theatre. The audience sat in a semicircular auditorium, with pefect acoustics. Seeing was more of a problem, so the actors – all men, surprise, surprise! – wore masks with exaggerated expressions to make it clear who they were and what sort of a mood they were in. You could catch the latest tragedy from *Aeschylus*, who wrote the Oresteia trilogy about King Agamemnon coming back from Troy and finding his marriage in a bit of a mess – and ending up in a bit of a mess himself, on the floor; or you could try *Sophocles*, who wrote about King Oedipus, who accidentally killed his father and married his mother (oh, well, these things happen); or possibly *Euripides*, who wrote about the mad witch Medea (who murdered her own children to get back at her husband, Jason) and Agamemnon's daughter Electra, who joined with her brother to avenge their father by killing their mother. No one does a dysfunctional family like the Greeks!

These tales too grim for you? Try a comedy. *Aristophanes's* 'The Frogs' is a wickedly funny parody of Greek tragedy, 'The Wasps' is about a man who puts the family dog on trial (they gave the dog the lead!); and 'Lysistrata' is about women forcing men to stop a war by staging a sex strike.

The Greeks also created the modern art of writing history. *Herodotus* wrote about Greece's wars with Persia, which he saw as a clash between the civilised west (Greece) and the decadent east (Persia). Herodotus checked his sources carefully and is often referred to as the 'Father of History'. *Thucydides* wrote about the later civil war between the Greeks, known as the Peloponnesian War, looking both at its long-term causes and at the moral lessons it threw up.

Squaring Up to the Persians

Don't forget that while the Greeks were developing their civilisation, in the Middle East, where civilisation had actually begun, there were still some very powerful kingdoms. In the sixth century B.C., the Greek colonies in Asia Minor (modern-day Turkey) staged a rebellion against the mighty Persian empire. Bad idea! The Persians crushed the rebellion, and Persian King Darius decided the time had come to teach these insolent Greeks a lesson they wouldn't forget. In 490 B.C., Darius invaded the Greek mainlands and the Persian Wars had begun.

Here they come!

The Persians invaded but got unexpectedly beaten by the Athenians at the Battle of Marathon, thanks to the professionalism of the Athenian *hoplites* (citizen soldiers) and their highly disciplined formation known as the *phalanx*. Pheidippides ran all the way to Athens with the news (yes, folks, that's the origin of the marathon race) and then dropped dead from exhaustion.

Here they come again!

In 480 B.C., Persian King Xerxes led a massive invasion to avenge Marathon. A small group of Spartans held the Persians up at the narrow pass of Thermopylae. The Persians got past them, however (thanks to a Greek traitor), took Athens, and burned the Acropolis. But the Athenian leader Themistocles lured the Persians into a great sea battle off the island of Salamis. King Xerxes confidently set up his chair to watch the fun and finds himself watching the Athenians destroy all his ships.

My Big Fat Greek Civil War

The Greek states had all stood together in the *Delian League* against the Persians, but 50 years later, this unity was shattered by a war between the two leading Greek states, Athens and Sparta. Spartans left weakling babies out on the hillside to die, and Spartan women expected their men to die in battle if they didn't win. The Spartans deeply distrusted the Athenians with their strange democratic ways, and when the Athenians started building long defensive walls to protect the road to their port at Piraeus, the Spartans decided that the Athenians must be preparing for war. In 431 B.C., Sparta and its allies in southern Greece (known as the Peloponnese – hence the Peloponnesian War) went to war with Athens and its allies in the Delian League. Neither side ever recovered.

The Olympic Games

The Olympics may have started as funeral games for one Pelops, who, poor chap, was killed and served up to the gods as a tasty snack by his own father! The games were held every four years in honour of Zeus and staged in a specially constructed complex, at Olympia. Athletes were invited from all over the Mediterranean world, and all warfare had to stop to allow people to get there. The events included running, wrestling, boxing chariot races, horse races, and the pentathlon of running, jumping, wrestling, javelin,

and discus. Synchronised swimming wasn't featured (and no women's events either, though there were separate women's games dedicated to the goddess Hera), but there may have been competitions in poetry and music. The modern Olympics were created in 1896 by the Frenchman Baron Pierre de Coubertin, who wanted to recreate the amateur ideals of the original games, although in fact, the Greeks had no qualms about paying their athletes very handsomely.

The Peloponnesian War lasted from 431 to 404 B.C. Like so many wars in history, it's rather complex, so I've divided it up into phases to make it a bit clearer as to who was annihilating whom:

- **Phase 1: Stalemate.** The Spartans were stronger on land, and the Athenians were stronger at sea. After ten years, including a disastrous outbreak of plague in Athens that killed their great leader, Pericles, the two sides signed a truce.

- **Phase 2: Things go badly wrong for Athens.** Athenian general Alcibiades suggested an attack on Sparta's ally, Syracuse in Sicily. Unfortunately, Alcibiades was wanted for questioning back in Athens about a nasty case of sacrilege (mutilating sacred statues of genitals, would you believe?), and when the arrest warrant arrived, he took himself off and joined the Spartans instead. Result: The Athenian attack on Syracuse was a disaster. The Athenians' position was so bad that they even invited Alcibiades back – it didn't help.

- **Phase 3: Just when Athens thought things couldn't get any worse, they did.** In the final phase, the Athenians' allies deserted them, and the Persians (remember them?) agreed to help the Spartans build a fleet in return for land in Asia Minor. The Athenians didn't know what'd hit them. The Spartans destroyed the Athenian fleet, executed some 1,400 prisoners, besieged Athens, and starved it into surrender. Athens had to dismantle its democratic system and agree to be ruled by a small group known as the Thirty Tyrants. Game, set, and match to Sparta.

Or so it looked. The Spartans soon found that they couldn't control all of Greece, the Athenians got rid of the Thirty Tyrants and slipped back into their old democratic ways, and the Greeks were all so preoccupied that no one noticed that one of their northern neighbours was becoming very powerful: The Macedonians.

Macedonia and Alexander the Great

The Greeks were always rather snooty about their neighbours, but the kingdom of Macedonia, to the north of Athens, was about to teach them, and the rest of the world, a lesson in humility. King Philip II of Macedonia, gave his soldiers longer spears and new tactics, and conquered Greece. To keep the Greeks happy, Philip proposed launching a big campaign against the Persians – *everyone* hated the Persians, remember! – but in 336 B.C., before he set off, he was murdered. The killing may have been the work of Persian agents, or it may have been his ex-wife – either way, the task of fighting the Persians now fell to Philip's 20-year-old son, *Alexander*.

Alexander had been taught by Aristotle and had impressed his father by taming and riding a wild stallion, Bucephalus. Now Alexander showed that he could tame Persians, too. Alexander conquered Asia Minor, Egypt – where he founded a new city named Alexandria – and utterly destroyed the Persian army at the Battle of Gaugamela in modern-day Iraq before moving into Persia itself. Poor King Darius of Persia had to run to keep out of Alexander's clutches until eventually he was murdered by his own men, whereupon Alexander became King of Persia. Alexander didn't stop there: he pressed on into Afghanistan and even into northern India, winning every battle he fought. Alexander's men wanted to go home and forced him to turn back, and in 323 B.C. Alexander caught a fever and died at Babylon on the River Euphrates. Age: 32. No wonder he's gone down in history as *Alexander the Great*.

Alexander founded cities, usually called Alexandria, and spread Greek ideas and language across a huge territory; historians call this the *Hellenistic Age* (from *Hellas*, meaning Greek). But Alexander was always open to the ideas and cultures of the peoples he conquered. Like most Greek men of the time, Alexander probably indulged in both homosexual and heterosexual love – his close male friend was called Hephaestos, but Alexander also married a Persian princess called Roxanne. Although Roxanne was pregnant with his child when he died, Alexander's heir never got to inherit his empire: It was split up between his generals. The Greeks tried to shake off Macedonian power, but they never managed it, and by the time the Athenians bribed the Macedonians to withdraw their garrison, the Greeks had some different neighbours to worry about – the *Romans*.

What a Way to Run a (Roman) Republic!

The Romans began as *Latins,* one of many people living in Italy, including Greeks in the south and a rather mysterious people called the Etruscans in the north. Historians still don't know where the Etruscans came from, but they had a big influence on the Romans. Aqueducts, togas, even gladiators, and chariot races – these all came originally from the Etruscans.

A revolution and a (not very democratic) republic

The early history of Rome is such a mixture of fact and fiction that it's very difficult to know where the truth lies. An old story exists that the early Romans felt the lack of female company, so they invited their neighbours, the Sabines, to a sports festival and then took the opportunity to run off with all their daughters. Not a very likely tale, though it does rather reflect the Roman view of women. In the early days, Rome was ruled by kings – according to tradition, there were ten of them, but we don't know for sure – and the last ones seem to have been Etruscans and deeply unpopular. The worst king was Tarquin the Proud, who is supposed to have set up a murderous regime of terror. When Tarquin's son, Sextus, attacked and raped a married Roman lady named Lucretia, the Romans decided that they'd had enough. Led by a noble-man called Lucius Junius Brutus, the Romans threw Tarquin and his son out and vowed that they'd never again have a king ruling over them. From now on Rome was to be a *republic.* That last bit at least is true.

Later on, other European republicans took inspiration from the example of the Romans overturning King Tarquin. The Roman action was a very popular theme in the French Revolution at the end of the 18th century, and it was much in the minds of the Americans as they set up their own republic after sending the British King George III packing.

Just like the Greeks, the Romans weren't great believers in equality, even within a republic. To be a citizen, you and your parents all had to be born in Rome, and even then, it was only the top people, known as *patricians,* who could vote or stand in elections to the Roman *Senate.* Once elected, the senators were in for life. Instead of a king, the Romans elected two *consuls* to lead the Senate – two, so that one could keep an eye on the other.

Rome wasn't built in a day (and it wasn't built this way either)

The Romans believed that they were descended from a Trojan prince called Aeneas, who escaped from Troy with his small son and aged father, whom he carried on his back. After many adventures, Aeneas is supposed to have landed in Italy, married a Latin princess, and founded a new people. Two of Aeneas's descendants were the twins, Romulus and Remus. The twins' wicked uncle, Amulius, had them set afloat in their cradle on the River Tiber, but they were rescued and suckled by a passing she-wolf. When the boys grew up, they killed their uncle and decided to build a new city on the seven hills on the banks of the Tiber. Remus laughed at how low Romulus's wall was, so Romulus, who was obviously very touchy about his bricklaying, killed him. Romulus then became the first king of the new city, which, of course, was named after him. Clearly, none of this story is actually true, but it's important as a *foundation myth*. The Romans always felt inferior compared to the Greeks, so it was important to them to claim a link with the Trojans, the Greeks' great rivals. The Roman poet Vergil wrote the *Aeneid* telling Aeneas's story as a deliberate attempt to provide the Romans with an equivalent of Homer's *Iliad* and *Odyssey*. The story of Romulus and Remus shows the Romans as chosen by fate or by the gods, but not prepared to stand for any nonsense. The twins' story also shows that sibling rivalry can be taken too far.

Conquering the neighbours

These early Romans didn't have it all their own way. Not only did they often get defeated by the Etruscans and the Samnites, another big tribe in central Italy, but in 390 B.C., Rome was attacked by fierce red-haired warriors from the far north – the *Gauls*. The Gauls sacked the city and would have taken the Capitol, the hill with all government buildings on it, if the sacred geese of Juno hadn't raised the alarm – or so legend has it, at any rate. But gradually, by a mixture of good generalship and shrewd politics – if you surrendered quickly, the Romans were surprisingly generous to you, but they could be merciless if you resisted – the Romans defeated their enemies and took over the whole of Italy.

Trouble on the bridge over water

According to a story very dear to Roman hearts, King Tarquin didn't take his fall lying down: he went straight off to the Etruscan king, Lars Porsena, and got him to help get his throne back. Lars Porsena had a huge army, but it needed to cross a narrow bridge over the Tiber to reach Rome. An enterprising chap called Horatius volunteered to hold up the army while the Romans demolished the bridge behind him, and so he did, fighting furiously and even managing to swim to safety afterward. This event is highly unlikely to have happened (after all, the Etruscans only needed to shoot him with an arrow), but it shows how the Romans liked to think of themselves: brave, public-spirited, and effective fighters, even in the face of impossible odds.

The Phoenicians – Coming to a Coastline Near You

The Phoenicians came from the eastern Mediterranean, more or less modern-day Israel and Palestine, and they set up a trading empire that spread right as far north as Cornwall. One of their trading outposts along the southern shore of the Mediterranean grew into a prosperous and powerful trading city in its own right, with an army and empire – *Carthage*.

Ain't room for both of us: Rome versus Carthage

At first, the Romans and Carthaginians left each other alone, but trouble flared up when they both decided that they wanted the island of Sicily. The Romans were happier fighting on land, and the Carthaginians were good at fighting at sea, so it came as a surprise when the Romans managed to copy a Carthaginian ship, make a few improvements, and defeat the Carthaginian navy. (The Romans weren't always very original thinkers, but they were very good indeed at developing other people's ideas.) Round One to the Romans.

Here comes Hannibal

To cheer themselves up after losing to the Romans, the Carthaginians decided to conquer Spain instead. But the Romans were allied to some of the Spanish cities, so in 219 B.C., Rome and Carthage went to war again. This time the Carthaginians' brilliant young commander, Hannibal, took an army from Spain and attacked the Romans from behind – over the Alps, just where the Romans *weren't* expecting any trouble. Hannibal even took his war elephants with him, and even though all but one of them died on the way, the mere idea that anyone could do it scared the Romans witless. More to the point, Hannibal took on a much larger Roman army at Cannae, in southern Italy – and slaughtered it.

US Second World War general, George C. Patton, was a great admirer of Hannibal, and General 'Stormin' Norman' Schwarzkopf, who led the coalition forces in the Gulf War with Iraq in 1991, said he based his successful campaign in Kuwait on Hannibal's tactics against the Romans. Neither commander, it has to be said, made any use of elephants.

The Romans could only force Hannibal to go home by attacking Spain and Carthage itself. Hannibal rushed back, but this time he met his match: The Roman general, Scipio, defeated him and forced Carthage to surrender. Hannibal was hunted down and eventually killed himself to evade capture. But the Romans weren't satisfied with mere surrender: In the words of a famous Roman statesman called Cato, *'Carthago delenda est!'* – 'Carthage must be destroyed!' In the last of the Punic Wars (from the Latin word *Poenica* for Carthage), the Romans did utterly destroy Carthage – so no stone stood on another, according to the official Roman version of events. The people were driven out and sold as slaves, and the Romans even sowed salt into the fields so that the crops wouldn't grow back.

The Senate and (rather grumpy) people of Rome

No sooner had the Romans defeated Carthage than they started fighting each other. Ordinary Romans, known as *plebeians*, wanted more of a say in running the Republic, and the top people who sat in the Senate, known as *patricians*, wouldn't let them. The Gracchus brothers both suggested that the rich give back the lands they'd taken from the poor – and got murdered for their pains. Then General Marius allowed plebeians to become soldiers, which scared the patricians because now the poor were armed. Marius was challenged by Consul Cornelius Sulla, and a fine old – and very deadly – power struggle followed between the two men, with Marius posing as the people's champion and Sulla standing up for order, class, and discipline. When Marius died, Sulla was able to take power and rule as a dictator. Sulla had all Marius's followers put to death, but he wasn't able to catch Marius's nephew-by-marriage, an ambitious and able young officer called *Julius Caesar*.

Spartacus

Just when Sulla thought he had control of Rome, there was a huge slave uprising led by a gladiator from Thrace called *Spartacus*. It took the Romans two years to crush the uprising, though by the end, many of Spartacus's men were drifting off – something the Stanley Kubrick film doesn't really mention. The stakes were very high: Crassus and Pompey, the generals who finally defeated the rebellion, became consuls; Spartacus and his followers were crucified along the Appian Way, the original road that led to Rome, but they passed into legend. Years later, Spartacus remained a popular symbol of freedom against oppression, and the German communists after the First World War called themselves Spartakists in his honour.

Chapter 4

The Ups and Downs of the Roman Empire

*T*he Romans established a mighty empire which changed European history for ever. Rome was ruled by a succession of emperors, some good, some bad, and some certifiably insane. The army started deposing emperors and fighting over whose commander should be emperor. In the end, the Romans divided their empire in two, with one emperor based in Rome and a second emperor based at the Empire's smart new eastern capital, Constantinople.

War, Seduction, Murder, and War Again: The New Roman Empire

Ever since the Romans got rid of their kings, they'd been very wary of giving absolute power to one man – Cornelius Sulla got it, however, after winning the power struggle with Marius. (Chapter 3 has the thrilling details of all this early Roman history.) Sulla set himself up as a ruthless dictator until he retired (he then died peacefully in his bed – there's no justice).

Sulla's loyal follower, Gnaius Pompey, made himself very popular by clearing the seas of pirates and defeating the Romans' sworn enemy, King Mithridates of Pontus. But even Pompey couldn't ignore young Julius Caesar, whose hired thugs were building him a power base among the ordinary people in the streets. Pompey agreed to share power with Caesar and another of Sulla's old henchmen, called Crassus, in a *triumvirate*, or three-man rule. Pompey, Caesar, and Crassus were about to prove that three-man rule doesn't work.

Forget Crassus – he went on a campaign and got himself killed – Caesar and Pompey are who mattered. The Senate didn't trust Caesar, so they sent him off to govern southern Gaul, but he took the opportunity to conquer the whole of Gaul, launch an invasion of Britain, and make himself a national hero. Oops. The Senate summoned Caesar to come and explain himself but he didn't come alone – he took his troops over the border at the River Rubicon (crying out as he did so, 'The die is cast!' like a gambler risking everything – or so he said) and marched on Rome. Pompey had to get out fast, and the great Roman Civil War began.

Unfortunately, the best account we have of this war was written by Caesar himself, which is ever-so-slightly one-sided ('Then Caesar, stunned by his own brilliance, came up with yet another extremely clever scheme . . .' – that sort of thing), but it's clear that although Pompey was a very good general, he lost. In 48 B.C., Pompey went to Egypt hoping to get help, just when the King of Egypt was trying to think of a good present to send to Caesar. So, the king cut off Pompey's head and sent him that.

The Senate appointed Caesar dictator for a year and consul for the next five. (Strictly speaking, you were meant to be consul for only one year, but the Senate seems to have thought, 'What the heck.') Then Caesar won some more battles so the Senate declared him Father of the Country, dictator for life, consul for the next ten years, put his portrait on the coins – oh, and they decided that his person was sacred and probably divine. But at least Caesar wasn't actually a king wearing a crown. Yet. Enter Cleopatra, Queen of Egypt – wrapped up in a carpet according to Caesar's version of events.

Cleopatra was in the middle of a power struggle with her little brother when Julius Caesar first arrived looking for Pompey, and she immediately set her cap – well, her carpet – at him. Making glad eyes worked. Caesar put Cleopatra on the throne, and she took him on a slow boat trip down the Nile, which somehow resulted in a little boy called Caesarion.

The Romans were always rather suspicious of eastern ways – nothing but autocratic rule and strange sexual practices, they thought – and Cleopatra confirmed all their worse fears. Sure enough, Caesar started toying with the idea of wearing a proper crown, not that set of laurel leaves he wore to hide his receding hairline. A group of senators, led by Marcus Brutus and his brother-in-law, Gaius Cassius (both of them old Pompey supporters), decided to act. With a group of co-conspirators, Brutus and Cassius stabbed Caesar to death in the Senate House. With a nice touch of irony, Caesar fell dead in front of a statue of his old rival, Pompey.

Wow! What a nose!

The only lifelike portrait we have of Cleopatra is on a coin and shows her looking, frankly, rather dumpy, but she must have had *something* going for her (apart from money, power, Egypt, more money . . .). According to tradition, she had a nose so beautiful, so bewitching, it was to die for – as Julius Caesar and Mark Antony both found, to their cost. The 17th-century French philosopher Blaise Pascal wrote that had Cleopatra's nose been a bit shorter, the whole history of the world would have been different, and this has given rise to the 'Cleopatra's nose theory of history', which holds that big events are caused by little accidents of nature or behaviour that can't be predicted. Some historians are convinced, but others are a bit more sniffy about it.

No sooner was Caesar dead than civil war broke out: Brutus, Cassius, and company against Caesar's old generals, Mark Antony and Lepidus, and Caesar's adopted son, Octavian. In a big showdown battle at Philippi in Greece (the great thing about ruling most of the Mediterranean world was that the Romans always choose nice sunny places for their battles), Caesar's side won. Brutus and Cassius did what the Romans considered the decent thing, and killed themselves. Mark Antony, Octavian, and Lepidus set themselves up as another triumvirate. What happened next was all Cleopatra's fault.

Octavian didn't approve of Cleopatra who was talking about her son, Caesarion, being Caesar's true heir. He sent Mark Antony to deal with her. Unfortunately, Cleopatra dealt with him: Antony was besotted with her, and they were soon openly living together and planning a coup. But Octavian moved first – he put a fleet together and defeated Cleopatra and Antony's ships at the *Battle of Actium*. Antony and Cleopatra both killed themselves (she used a poisonous asp hidden in a bowl of fruit). From now on, Octavian ruled on his own.

The Emperor's New (Purple) Clothes

After the Battle of Actium, Octavian was given the Latin name 'Augustus', which means 'great, powerful, revered' and so on. From now on, I refer to Octavian as Augustus. More important were Augustus's titles, which in Latin were *imperator* and *princeps*:

- ✔ 'Imperator' simply means a military commander, but under Augustus it began to mean something much closer to 'emperor'.

- ✔ 'Princeps' originally meant 'first citizen', in the sense of first among equals, but now it came to mean something very close to the English word that derives from it – prince.

Great balls of fire!

Ironically, Nero almost certainly *didn't* carry out the most famous crime he's usually remembered for: the Great Fire of Rome of 64 A.D. In fact, evidence suggests that Nero took a hand in fighting the flames. However, the spectacle of Rome burning like Troy would have appealed to the artist in him, and it's entirely plausible that he might have improvised an epic song about it, though he wasn't 'fiddling while Rome burned' – there were no violins in those days. What we do know, is that Nero took full advantage of the Great Fire. Nero blamed the Christians for it and had hundreds of them put to death; he also built a huge palace for himself, the Golden House, on the ruins. No, he didn't call it Dunromin.

To make his status absolutely clear, Augustus started to wear a toga made of the most expensive colour there was – purple. Augustus always said he'd look after things for a while and then step down to let the Republic get going again, but somehow it was never quite the right time for it. Funny, that.

Augustus was utterly ruthless. When he decided he wanted to marry the lady Livia, he didn't worry about the fact that they were both already married. Augustus divorced his wife (according to some accounts he did it the day she gave birth to their daughter, Julia) and told Livia to divorce her husband and marry him. The marriage was actually very successful, but it didn't have the most auspicious of starts.

Augustus did rule wisely. It was said – well, okay, he may have said it himself – that he inherited a city of brick and left it in shining marble. Augustus certainly built temples and saw to the city's water and grain supply and generally kept things ticking over. Unfortunately, Augustus and his wife Livia also produced an imperial family that was nothing but trouble. Meet the *Julio-Claudian emperors*:

- ✔ **Tiberius (14–37 A.D.):** Livia's son by her first husband. Became violently paranoid as he got older. Tiberius left governing to his henchman, Sejanus, and went off to Capri, living for (mainly sexual) pleasure and throwing unwanted visitors off a cliff. Tiberius was probably murdered, and no one cried.

- ✔ **Gaius ('Caligula') (37–41 A.D.):** Great-grandson to Livia. Young, handsome (well, going bald), and very popular to start with: Caligula's father, Germanicus, had been a national hero. Unfortunately Caligula was also barking mad. He convinced himself that he was the god Jupiter, had an affair with his sister (and killed her), declared that he rather wished all Romans had one neck so he could cut it off (tactless), and appointed his favourite horse a priest and a consul. Well, it was a stable job. Caligula was assassinated by his own guards.

✔ **Claudius (41–54 A.D.):** Grandson to Livia. Claudius only became emperor because the praetorian guards found him cowering behind a curtain after they'd killed Caligula and thought having Claudius as emperor would be a bit of a laugh. Some historians think Claudius was just as bloodthirsty as the rest of his family. Claudius conquered Britain; he also put down an attempted coup by his wife, killing as many people as he could lay his hands on. To cheer himself up, Claudius married his niece, Agrippina. She poisoned him.

✔ **Nero (54–68 A.D.):** Son of Claudius's niece (and wife) Agrippina, by her first husband. To start with, Nero ruled jointly with his mother Agrippina, but you know how it is: they had a row, he sabotaged her boat, and when she swam to the shore his men bashed her head in with the oars. Then, Nero killed Claudius's son, Britannicus (a rival heir – very wise), murdered his wife Octavia, and kicked his (pregnant – ouch) second wife, Poppaea, to death. Nero promptly proposed to Claudius's daughter and was amazed when she turned him down. So, Nero killed her. Nero fancied himself as a poet, actor, dancer, charioteer. Romans found his exhibitionism very *undignified*. Finally, the army staged a coup to get rid of him – he killed himself. Last words: 'What an artist dies in me.' Which, in the Romans' eyes, said it all.

After Nero's death, there was a confused power struggle, with three emperors in one year. The man who came out on top was a successful general who had made his name fighting in Judaea: Vespasian. Vespasian restored law and order; he also built a vast amphitheatre on the site of Nero's Golden House – the Colosseum. Vespasian died in his bed – his last words were a nice little ironic comment on the Romans' habit of declaring their emperors divine: 'Oh dear,' he said, 'I think I'm becoming a god.'

You Probably Wouldn't Want to Be an Emperor

Being in sole charge of most of the known world might sound attractive, but it had its drawbacks, as the emperors who followed Vespasian found out.

✔ **Titus (79–81 A.D.):** Vespasian's son. Titus's reign was certainly eventful: Mount Vesuvius erupted in A.D. 79 and destroyed Pompeii and Herculaneum, and the next year Rome caught fire again and the people suffered an outbreak of plague.

✔ **Domitian (81–96 A.D.):** Titus's younger brother. Domitian took pleasure in having his opponents put to death, preferably slowly. Domitian was paranoid about enemies and had more and more people put to death until a group of senators decided he had to be stopped and assassinated him.

✔ **Nerva (96–8 A.D.):** A respectable old senator, who was brought in so everyone could have a bit of a breather after all the killing of Domitian's reign.

✔ **Trajan (98–117 A.D.):** Trajan was Spanish. He set up poor relief schemes and public work projects and won lots of military victories. Trajan died on campaign, which, the Romans thought, was just how an emperor *ought* to die.

✔ **Hadrian (117–138 A.D.):** Another Spanish emperor. Hadrian built fortifications to mark the empire's boundaries, including *Hadrian's Wall* across northern Britain. He also built himself a beautiful, luxury palace complex outside Rome at Tivoli where he could get away from his in-tray and relax.

✔ **Antoninus Pius (138–161 A.D.):** A good governor and administrator, who kept the empire at peace and dispensed balanced justice and fair taxes. Sounds too good to be true, doesn't he?

✔ **Marcus Aurelius (161–180 A.D.):** A stoic philosopher, which was just as well because he had a lot to put up with: a German attack along the Rhine and the Danube, and war and rebellion in the east. Marcus Aurelius wrote a series of meditations that still inspire people today. Marcus Aurelius died on campaign against the Germans and handed over to his son, Commodus. Commodus was *not* a philosopher.

✔ **Commodus (180–192 A.D.):** Commodus is the emperor in the film *Gladiator*, though unlike in the film he did not kill his father; he was miles away at the time. Commodus drew up long lists of people to be murdered. His mistress Marcia found them lying around and saw her own name. She got in touch with an athlete friend of hers and had Commodus strangled.

The emperors had always relied very heavily on their bodyguards, the elite *Praetorian Guard*. After Commodus was assassinated, the Praetorians held an auction to decide the next emperor. Soon lots of emperors were going, going, gone. In the 60 years after Commodus's death in A.D. 192, there were *19* emperors, and only three of them *weren't* assassinated – usually by their own bodyguards!

Two (crowned) heads are better than one – we hope

In A.D. 284 yet another general was declared emperor by his troops. This man's name was Diocletian. Diocletian decided that the empire had become too big to be controlled by one man in Rome, especially with the Praetorian Guards forever on the look-out for someone with a better offer. So, Diocletian decided to divide the empire in two: One half in the west, based in Rome (or in Italy at any rate), and the other half in the east. The two emperors would each have an assistant and a successor, called a Caesar (note to the Praetorian Guards: Sorry lads, the party's over). Diocletian chose a well-positioned city in Greece, with a good harbour that could be easily defended – *Byzantium*.

Emperor or god?

Diocletian gave up the old laurel wreath that previous emperors had worn and started wearing a rather natty *diadem* – a headband with a great precious jewel on it, worn by the kings of Persia and Parthia. Visitors had to kneel down and kiss Diocletian's robe. If these actions sounds a bit like worshipping a god, you're right – Diocletian declared that he was divine and that people were to burn incense in front of his statue in their local temples. For most Romans this was just another admin chore they had to do, but it posed a big problem for one increasingly important group within Diocletian's empire: The Christians. When the Christians refused to worship him, Diocletian saw it as undermining his authority so he ordered the first really big wave of persecution of Christians since Nero. (For more information about Christianity and how it changed the empire, see Chapter 5.)

Diocletian hoped that his two-ruler system would put an end to all the in-fighting in the empire, but that was a bit optimistic. In A.D. 312, only seven years after Diocletian retired, Constantine managed to fight his way to the top and reunite the empire, but he had to overcome five rival emperors to do it.

Getting an Empire

After the Romans destroyed Carthage, they took over the Carthaginian Empire, which included Spain and much of North Africa. (Chapter 3 has the low-down on the wars with Carthage.) The Romans then got dragged into a dispute in Greece and ended up conquering all the Greek lands, including Sicily and a province in southern Gaul (which is why the South of France is still called Provence to this day). All this expansion brought the Romans into contact with some deeply scary red-headed people – the Celts.

Getting a precise picture of the Celts is difficult because the only written descriptions we have come from the Greeks and Romans, who generally didn't like them one bit, though the Greeks did give them the name, *Keltoi* or Celts. Luckily, archaeologists have dug up beautifully crafted pottery and weapons, early material known as Hallstatt, after the place in Austria where much of it was found, and a later, much more sophisticated style of design known as La Tène, after the Swiss town where a rich hoard of Celtic crafts was found. From these discoveries, we can see that the Celts were highly skilled craftsmen, and that they had a complex social hierarchy of chiefs, nobles, warriors, and slaves – much like the Romans and Greeks, in fact.

Meet the Celts – er, literally

In the 1950s grisly corpses began appearing in peat bogs in Denmark. At first, people thought they were local murders, and so in a way they were: These were the bodies of bronze age Celts who had been sacrificed to the gods and dumped in lakes where their bodies had been preserved as the lakes turned to peat. In 1991, a rather different body came to light, frozen solid, in the Alps, between Austria and Italy. This body was fully clothed, with a bow and a sort of framed rucksack on his back, and he had raised his arm across his face as if to ward off some terrible danger. Many theories exist about how this man might have died; the latest is that he died during fighting between rival tribes. All these bodies have yielded a lot of detail about how people lived in northern Europe during the bronze age, from their clothes and weapons right down to the food they had in their stomachs.

The Greeks and Romans first encountered the Celts in the fifth century B.C., when overcrowding and possibly a change in the climate brought them south. The Celts sacked Rome and trashed the shrine of Apollo at Delphi. Some Celts pushed on to Anatolia, in modern Turkey, where they became known as Galatians, and Saint Paul (a Roman citizen, note) wasn't particularly impressed with them: 'You foolish Galatians!' he wrote in his famous biblical letter to them.

Eventually the Romans beat the Celts, or *Gauls*, back to Gaul, where the different Celtic tribes were just as ready to fight each other as they were to fight Romans. One tribe, called the Aedui, made an alliance with Rome against their neighbours and enemies (and among the Celts these were usually the same thing), the Arverni. When the Romans wiped out a huge Arvernian army, Rome got a big slice of southern Gaul – and the Celts got something to think about.

When is a Celt not a Celt?

The best-known examples of modern Celts are the Bretons of Brittany and the Scots, Welsh, Cornish, and Irish. Some historians dispute that the peoples of Britain were ever Celtic at all – the Romans never called them so, for one thing. Other historians say this is just silly quibbling. You may like to debate the matter. But be warned: Don't go into a Glasgow pub and tell the people they're not Celts, at least not if you want to come out alive.

The fall of Gaul

The year 59 B.C. may not be a date that rings many bells for you but it was momentous for the Celts. Three major events all happened that year:

- The Helvetii of Switzerland decided that the mountain life was no longer for them – perhaps they couldn't stand the yodelling – and decided to go looking for new territory in Gaul.

- A Gallic tribe called the Sequani invited a fearsome Germanic chieftain, Ariovistus, to help them fight their old enemies, the Aedui. (Bad idea; the Aedui had powerful friends, remember?)

- The Roman Senate decided to post the uncomfortably ambitious Julius Caesar to southern Gaul to keep him out of harm's way. (The section 'War, Seduction, Murder, and War Again: The New Roman Empire' above explains the politics that lay behind Caesar's posting to Gaul.)

The Aedui sent a message to Caesar complaining that the Helvetii were trampling all over their land, so Caesar got his troops together, marched north in double quick time, crushed the Helvetii, and then had lunch. Only about a third of the Helvetii made it back to Switzerland. 'While you're at it,' said the Aedui, who knew a useful ally when they saw one, 'could you do something about Ariovistus?' Caesar charged north, negotiated with Ariovistus, the talks broke down, Caesar fought a battle, crushed Ariovistus, and sent him and his men back to Germany – all within six days.

The powerful Belgae tribe of northern Gaul decided to stop Caesar right there and started gathering their allies for a showdown. But Caesar was quicker on the draw; he came storming up north and crushed the Belgae before they knew what day it was. That defeat only left the Nervii, a rather tough, snooty Belgian tribe who gave Caesar a long and very difficult battle – but at the end it was the Nervii, not the Romans, who were annihilated. Caesar had conquered Gaul and it was safe to go over the Channel and take on the tribes of Britain. Or, so he thought.

Rebel rebel

The Gauls were a sophisticated, proud people, and they did not take kindly to being made to look fools by Julius Caesar. While Caesar was away campaigning in Britain, the Gauls rose up in rebellion.

The Gauls had found just the leader they needed: Vercingetorix of the Arverni – tall, strong, fearless, and he *hated* Romans. Vercingetorix gathered people of many different tribes into his army, tribes which had only recently been at each others' throats. He even got the Romans' old allies the Aedui to join the rebellion. Caesar moved quickly – he always did – and seized Vercingetorix's capital, but when he besieged Vercingetorix himself in the fortified town of Gergovia, the unthinkable happened: *Julius Caesar lost.* The Gauls were so excited that it was touch and go whether the Romans were to be driven out of Gaul altogether. But then, Caesar trapped Vercingetorix in another fortified town, at Alesia – we still don't know exactly where that was – and brought up all his siege engines. The Gauls couldn't break through the Roman lines, and Vercingetorix surrendered. The Romans recognised Vercingetorix as a noble and worthy opponent, and gave him pride of place in Caesar's victory parade through the streets of Rome – then they strangled him.

Rocking all over the (Roman) world

After Gaul fell, the main areas for the Romans to expand their empire were

- **Germany:** In A.D. 6, in the greatest disaster in Roman military history, a Roman general called Varus led three whole legions straight into an ambush in the German forests. Apparently, Augustus used to cry out in anger 'Publius Quintilius Varus, *where are my legions?*' (No doubt Livia would call back, 'They're in the wash!') The Romans never tried to conquer Germany again.

- **Britain:** To everyone's surprise it was limping, stammering Claudius who organised a successful invasion, in A.D. 43. Mind you, the Romans nearly lost Britain again when Queen Boudica staged a huge revolt against Nero in A.D. 60, but they regained their nerve and restored (Roman) order.

- **Judaea:** The whole Middle East region was very important to the Romans for food and for security. When the Jews rose in revolt in A.D. 66 General Vespasian destroyed Jerusalem and surrounded the Jewish resistance in the hilltop fortress of Masada. The Jews killed themselves rather than surrender.

- **Romania, Armenia, Iraq:** Or Dacia, Armenia, Mesopotamia, and Assyria, as the Romans called them. The emperor Trajan conquered them all.

  Trajan's successor, Hadrian, decided the empire should stay within its boundaries: thus far and no further, or *ne plus ultra*, as the Romans used to say.

The Roman Peace

The Romans liked to think they were bringing peace, law, and order to people who otherwise lived in barbarism. Romans spoke of the *Pax Romana*, the

'Roman Peace', though the Roman historian Tacitus, writing about Rome's conquest of Carthage, put it rather differently: 'They make a wilderness and call it peace.'

The secret of the Romans' success was their army, which was divided into regiments known as *legions*. All well-bred young Romans served a spell in the army, and the soldiers were well equipped and often highly motivated. The pay was good, and when the soldiers retired there was the chance of a big lump sum plus a bit of land to farm. However, a legion that failed in its duty could be decimated – one man in every ten was taken out and killed, which certainly concentrated the soldiers' minds.

A Civilised People – Give or Take the Odd Gladiatorial Combat

A lot of evidence exists about how the Romans lived. Some of our knowledge comes from their writings, especially satirical poets like Juvenal and Martial, who always had a sharp eye for detail. We can discover a lot from archaeological sites like the Roman forum or Pompeii, though you have to be careful with Pompeii: it was a rather up-market seaside resort, so relying on it too heavily is a bit like basing our knowledge on modern France entirely on the remains of Monte Carlo.

Roman social climbing

Like the Greeks, the Romans had a strict class system, though it was a bit more flexible: you could buy your way up from one class to the next. Going from top to bottom, the Roman classes were:

- **Patricians:** Top class of Roman citizen. Only patricians became senators.

- **Equites:** Originally descended from the cavalrymen of the early days of Rome, these people were the Roman middle class, and often ran the business side of the empire. Think of the equites as people who wanted to keep up with the Januses.

- **Plebeians:** The Roman working classes. Without rich families to house and feed them, the Roman poor were often worse off than slaves and there was a flourishing network of robbers, muggers, and highway thieves.

- **Slaves:** Slaves belonged to their owners, but they were often very well treated and could win or buy their freedom. Freed slaves, known as *freedmen*, sometimes became surprisingly rich and powerful.

Daddy knows best

The Romans placed great importance upon the family. The *paterfamilias* – father of the household – had enormous power over his family. Father's word was law, and he could beat or imprison his children and divorce his wife if she grew ugly or talked too much. If his wife was unfaithful, the paterfamilias could put her to death. When Augustus discovered that his daughter, Julia, had been sleeping with half the Roman aristocracy, he had her exiled to a tiny island for the rest of her life. Parents also arranged their children's marriages, and a hot-blooded young Roman man counted himself very lucky if he got a wife anything like his own age: Girls could marry at 12, and they often did.

Cool, clear water

The Romans were the first and probably the last people before the 19th century to grasp the importance of a proper water supply, not just for drinking, but for bathing and public health as well. The Romans built miles of precision-designed aqueducts to carry water to their cities, where it supplied the famous Roman baths as well as the toilets and the sewers – and they had separate pipe systems to keep the two uses apart, you'll be glad to hear. Romans went to the toilet *en masse*: There's nothing like a public latrine for catching up on the gossip. If you couldn't afford the latrine, you had to use a bucket, but you could always sell your urine to a laundry, where it was used to whiten togas! Don't you just hope not many Romans knew that?

Follow the military road

Roman roads began as a way of giving their armies the power of speed. Legions or, just as important, information, travelled fast the whole length of the empire, so that the imperial government in Rome kept in close touch with what was happening even in the farthest provinces. The roads were properly paved and drained, and they went in such sensible straight lines that many European roads today still follow the routes the Romans laid down.

Bread and circuses

The Roman satirist Juvenal used to say that the way to keep the people in order was to offer them bread and circuses, which is more or less what the Romans did. The Romans didn't actually chuck loaves into the crowd, as they do in the film *Gladiator* – the bread would've gone off within a day or two. Instead, grain was handed out at official distribution points – less photogenic but rather more practical.

Thrown to the lions

The Romans were particularly fond of wild beast fights: Big-game hunters penetrated deep into Africa to keep the Flavian amphitheatre supplied. Animals were also used for executing criminals. Someone found guilty of patricide (killing your father) was sewn up in a sack with a cock, a monkey, and a viper, and thrown into the sea, which usually did the trick. Murderers or anyone convicted of other serious offences were tied to posts in the arena and then set upon by lions, specially starved to make sure that they were peckish. The same thing was done to Christians when they began to fall foul of the emperors. To the Romans, this practice was a good way of combining punishment with public entertainment – just as public hangings would do in the 19th century.

The biggest towns had circuses for chariot races, where you'd bet on your favourite teams and watch them crash into each other, and even the smallest Roman town had an arena for gladiatorial contests. The audiences liked a bit of variety: Gladiators, wild-beast fights, gladiators versus wild beasts, or re-enactments of events from history or mythology – with the right characters getting killed (for real), of course. The emperor Commodus was such a fan of gladiator contests that he even fought in the arena. (Letting your boss win at golf is bad enough; imagine if he wanted to fight you to the death.) For light relief there were special fights, between dwarfs or people who had lost a limb – whatever the organisers' imagination ran to. Which didn't usually include taste.

The Beginning of the End of Empire

The Roman Empire looked strong, but by the fourth century A.D. it had serious problems:

- ✔ The population of the empire had fallen, possibly by about one-third so the Romans depended more than ever on non-Romans, especially in the army.

- ✔ The empire was fast running out of money. To save money the emperors debased the coinage, so there was hardly any silver in it. Prices went through the roof.

- ✔ To save on army pay, the Romans started taking prisoners to use as slaves, and even as troops. Most of these foreigners were Germans, known as *foederati*. The Romans appropriated so many of these foederati that the empire was becoming more and more German even before the *real* trouble began.

In the fourth century A.D., a fierce, warlike, and utterly ruthless people had come charging across the plains of Russia all the way from China: *The Huns*. The Huns cut one German tribe, the Ostrogoths, to pieces and made them a subject people (and if that doesn't impress you, you obviously haven't met many Ostrogoths lately), and now they were pressing hard against the Ostrogoths' neighbours, the Visigoths. The Visigoths lived along the Danube, modern-day Romania, which meant that they were close to the Roman frontier. The Visigoths decided to ask the emperor Valens, emperor of the eastern Roman Empire, for asylum.

Valens decided to do a deal. The Visigoths were allowed to settle if they agreed in return to defend the Danube frontier against the Huns. This arrangement should have worked, but unfortunately food got scarce and a bunch of unscrupulous Roman officials decided to start trying to extort money out of these new arrivals. Not such a good idea. The Visigoths turned on the Romans and, with a little help from the Huns (who were only too pleased to stir things up), they defeated a large Roman army at Hadrianople in Greece. Thousands of Romans were killed – including the emperor.

That outcome made the Romans sit up – they couldn't ignore the Visigoths, but they couldn't welcome them either. The Romans started paying the Visigoths protection money, which worked for a while, until the Visigoth king, Alaric, asked if he could be a general in the Roman army. The emperor said no. 'All right,' said Alaric, 'you'll be sorry.' So, Alaric got his Visigoths together, invaded Italy, and in 410 A.D. they all entered Rome. And sacked it.

Part III
Middle Ages

Oh for gosh sake, Richard! It's a couple of mice in the basement stealing grain. Quit making a crusade out of everything!

In this part . . .

This part shows you that the Romans weren't the only civilised people around: German and Frankish tribes set up highly sophisticated Christian kingdoms in places as far apart as France, Italy, and North Africa. Out of these western peoples grew two institutions that were to fight it out for supremacy in the medieval world: the Holy Roman Empire and the Papacy.

While Popes and Emperors were battling it out in the west, in the east the Roman empire carried on, known now as Byzantium. Byzantium developed a distinctive style and culture of its own that spread from Greece and the Balkans to embrace the vast lands of Russia. But it was the Byzantine emperor's desperate call for help against the threat of the Turks that unleashed the great clash of east and west that we know as the Crusades.

In this part, you'll encounter plenty of battles and leaders slugging it out, but you'll also get a sense of what it was like to live in the Middle Ages, and of the incredible feats of building and learning that medieval people achieved.

Chapter 5

Dancing in the Dark Ages

*W*hen people today talk of the legacy of the Roman Empire they usually think in terms of roads or drains, but one of the most important things the Romans left to their successors was Christianity. Christianity spread out from its base in Judaea in the first century A.D., and spread right across the Roman world. Meanwhile, warlike tribes, such as the Visigoths, the Ostrogoths, and the Vandals, fell on the Roman frontier with frightening speed and terrifying strength. Christian scholars were deeply divided on some of the fundamentals of Christian doctrine. And a young man named Muhammed was winning converts throughout Arabia and the Middle East, and across North Africa. Christian Europe confronted the spread of Islam head-on – in battle.

Meet Constantine

The Roman Empire didn't close down just because the Visigoths had trashed Rome. (Refer to Chapter 4 if you missed all the excitement.) To understand why the Empire survived – in the east it grew *stronger* – you need to meet one of the most famous Roman emperors of all, *Constantine*.

At first, Constantine was just another Roman general who got himself declared emperor by his troops . Constantine beat off his rivals, took power in the West, went to war with Licinius, the eastern emperor, and put him to death. Constantine was now emperor of the whole of the Roman Empire, and poor old Diocletian must have wondered why he bothered dividing the Empire in the first place (if you're not sure what I'm on about, have a look at Chapter 4).

If he'd called it 'New Rome', at least you could spell it

Constantine decided to build a state-of-the-art capital city in the East, at Byzantium, where the eastern Roman emperors had been based, and he called it *Constantinople* ('the City of Constantine', now Istanbul). The city was a port (always useful) on a cape called the Golden Horn, right where Greece met Asia – which is what military buffs call a prime strategic position.

Constantine gave orders for huge walls to be built to keep the city safe from attack. These walls must have been good, because they even deterred Attila the Hun. The city was to be Christian, with churches rather than temples, and it remained the greatest Christian city in Europe, every bit as important as Rome, for over a thousand years.

Constantine's mother Helena was a Christian, and before one important battle in the power struggle (at the Milvian Bridge against the Emperor Maxentius, if you're keeping score) Constantine saw – or said he saw – a great cross in the sky with the message 'By this you will conquer'. 'All right,' thought Constantine, 'I'll buy it' – and conquer he did. Poor unfortunate Maxentius ended up drowned in the River Tiber. These events set Constantine thinking that maybe this Christianity business might be worth looking into.

Changing My Religion

Christianity began with the teachings of Jesus, which his disciples then started spreading around the Middle East and the eastern end of the Roman Empire. The exact details of all the comings and goings of these early Christians are a bit hazy, but there seems good evidence to suggest that St Peter, the man Jesus put in charge of the Church, travelled to Rome and spent the last years of his life there; according to tradition, his bones lie buried on the Vatican hill, where St Peter's Basilica now stands.

To the early Christians, it made perfect sense that Peter should have gone to Rome, the centre of the Roman Empire. Later on, Christians started calling Peter and the bishops of Rome who followed him 'popes', from *papa*, the Italian word for 'father'. The Church even began to see itself as a sort of spiritual successor to the Roman Empire with 'Catholic' ('universal') authority, just like the Roman emperors. From now on, when I speak of the 'Catholic' Church, I mean the Church based in Rome, under its bishop, known as the Pope.

When the Romans first heard about Christianity, they thought it was just a branch of the Jewish religion – all very interesting but not necessarily important. However, it soon became clear that Christianity wasn't Jewish. For one thing, the Jews started persecuting it, and for another, Christians, unlike Jews, wanted to convert people to Christianity.

The Romans were usually very tolerant of different religions. But Christians believed that their God was the *only* god – if you became a Christian you had to drop Jupiter and Mithras and all the other Roman gods. Aspects of Christianity sounded very suspect – eating flesh and drinking blood and everyone loving each other. 'Hmm,' thought Mr and Mrs Average Roman, pursing their lips, 'we all know what *that* means . . .'

Christians also believed that everyone was equal in the sight of God, which could give slaves and poor people all sort of ideas (and it did). So when Nero blamed the Christians for the Great Fire of Rome and started sending them in to the lions (Chapter 4 has the low-down on this) no one actually believed they'd done it, but many Roman citizens were quite happy to see the Christians being taken down a peg or two.

You can see why the Christians were so relieved when Constantine decided to make their religion one of the official religions of the State. By then, *everyone* was talking about Christianity, because it was just doing for the first time what it would do many, many times in the future – splitting opinion right down the middle on a question of doctrine.

That's a Very Interesting Question, Arius

You know the Christmas carol 'O Come, All Ye Faithful'? A line in the second verse goes 'Very God, begotten, not created', which is always a bit awkward to fit into the rhythm, and most people who belt it out each year don't know what it means anyway. The people of Constantinople in Constantine's time knew what that line meant, though – it was *the* topic of conversation. If you had a haircut, the barber asked you how much you wanted off the sides and did you reckon Jesus was begotten or created? The fuss was all because of a Syrian priest called Arius, who had spotted what appeared to be a flaw in Christian doctrine.

Arius's thinking went like this:

    a) Jesus is the Son of God. Right? *Yes.*

    b) Therefore, at some point God must have become Jesus's father. *Er, yes.*

c) Therefore, there must have been a time when Jesus hadn't yet been born or created or whatever you want to call it. *Hmm. I'm not sure I like where this is heading . . .*

d) Therefore, if there's a time *before* Jesus was created, he can't be eternal, and if he isn't eternal, he can't actually be God. Therefore, the whole idea of the Trinity is wrong. *Arius, you are a dangerous heretic and ought to be driven out of the Church.*

The Church didn't know what to make of Arius's logic. In A.D. 321, a big Council of Bishops was held at Alexandria which decided that Arius was wrong and threw him out of the Church. However, two years later there was another big Council which decided he had a point and let him back in again.

Constantine couldn't afford to have his empire torn in two in this way, so, in A.D. 325 he summoned a big Council of the Church to the town of Nicaea to thrash the whole thing out. Constantine decided to chair the Council himself, which was a bit cheeky since he wasn't actually even baptised. Constantine probably didn't worry too much about the rights and wrongs in the begotten–created debate, but he did worry about splits in the Church, so he found against Arius: God the Father had *begotten* (i.e. fathered) Jesus but hadn't actually *created* him – hence the line in the carol. Arius and a couple of bishops who supported him were excommunicated – thrown out of the Church – and that, Constantine thought, was that. Wrong.

Arius's supporters ('Arians') went on preaching, and they managed to convert some of the later emperors, like poor old Valens, the one killed in battle by the Visigoths (and you can find out what all *that* was about in Chapter 4). The Arians even sent missionaries into Germany, where they won over many of the barbarian tribes. These Arian converts were about to carry their new religion – as well as a lot of military hardware – westwards into the very heart of the Roman Empire.

And Lo, There Came Invaders from the East

Everyone talks about the 'barbarian invasions', but 'barbarian' is rather unfair. These 'barbarians' had a well-developed culture, with their own laws and forms of art and codes of ethics and everything else you need to keep a people going. What the barbarians didn't have was written language, and this was fatal for their reputation, because it meant that the only written descriptions we have come from their Roman enemies.

Sorry, old boy, once a Vandal always a Vandal

Flavius Stilicho was a Vandal (one of the German tribes that the Romans called barbarians) and a Christian who served the Roman Empire loyally as an ambassador and a general, and ended up marrying the niece of the Emperor Theodosius. Theodosius made Stilicho guardian of his half-wit son, Honorius, who in turn married Stilicho's daughter (which must have made for a tricky father-of-the-bride speech: 'I'm delighted that my daughter has married into the imperial family. What a pity she couldn't find one with a brain cell.').

Stilicho kept Alaric and the Visigoths under control, saved Italy from the Ostrogoths, and put down a rebellion in North Africa.

Unfortunately, many jealous Romans hated the idea that they were being saved from disaster by a barbarian, and an Arian barbarian at that,

no matter how Roman he'd become. This sentiment is called racial and religious prejudice – you shall meet its like again in later chapters.

By now, the barbarian attacks were so frequent that Stilicho had to start stripping outlying provinces, like Britain, of troops to enable him to concentrate on defending Italy. Stilicho even tried to talk Alaric round to fighting on the Roman side. 'We knew it!' said the Senate, 'Stilicho's executing a cunning barbarian plot to weaken the Empire and take power himself.'

So the Senate had Stilicho declared a public enemy, and when he fled to Ravenna they had him murdered. Whereupon thousands of loyal barbarians decided that if that was how the Romans treated their friends, they'd be better off joining Alaric, and frankly, who can blame them?

Because the written sources are so scarce, historians have often referred to the period after the end of the Roman Empire (in the West) as the 'Dark Ages', which is a rather misleading term, because it gives the impression that it's a time of nothing but fighting, destruction, and general gloom – like an English town centre on a Friday night. Nowadays, historians prefer to give the period a more neutral name like 'the early Middle Ages' – boring but fair.

The following sections take these invading tribes one by one (which the Romans would have loved to do, if they'd ever had the chance).

Can we come and stay? The Visigoths

The Visigoths settled in Dacia, modern Romania, until the Huns drove them out, so they asked the Roman Emperor Valens for permission to come and live in the Empire. (Refer to Chapter 4 for the whole story.) The relationship ended in tears at the Battle of Hadrianople where the Visigoths killed the Emperor Valens. The new emperor, an astute chap called Theodosius, did the

Visigoths a deal. The Visigoths could stay within the Empire as long as they helped Theodosius defend it against other tribes, like the Visigoths' old rivals, the Ostrogoths.

This arrangement worked well until Theodosius died, when everything went pear-shaped. Theodosius's two young sons, Arcadius in the East and Honorius in the West, didn't have a clue about governing (they weren't actually all that bright), so it was open house for anyone wanting to scheme their way into power. The one man who was able to keep order was General Stilicho, but he had enemies in the Senate who had him murdered. (See the sidebar 'Sorry, old boy, once a Vandal always a Vandal' for more about this unedifying business.) 'Here's our chance!' said the Visigoth king, Alaric, who'd already started ravaging the eastern Empire, and now decided to go and do the same in the West. In A.D. 410, the Visigoths reached Rome and sacked it.

After sacking Rome the Visigoths wandered around aimlessly in Italy for a while looking for somewhere to live until they gave up and headed for Gaul. The Romans let the Visigoths settle in the South West, near Toulouse, but the Romans didn't trust them one bit, and took care to stay on good terms with the Visigoths' old bogeymen, the Huns. Just in case.

Uh-oh: Here come the Huns

The Huns were incredibly fierce, and very smelly – they washed their babies in cold water every day for the first six months to put them off the idea of ever being clean again. Huns also bound their babies' heads so tightly that their skulls ended up elongated in a most peculiar manner; people even wondered if Huns were quite human. The Huns had perfected a way of firing arrows while riding at full gallop (*not* easy), and they dealt utterly ruthlessly with anyone who opposed them.

The Huns set up a base of sorts in Hungary, and in A.D. 444 or 445, a young prince named Attila killed his brother Bleda and seized the throne for himself. *Attila the Hun.* You may have heard of him.

Attila took over a huge kingdom stretching from the Baltic to the Black Sea (which comprises the whole of eastern Europe north to south). Attila had a go at attacking Constantinople but the walls were too strong, so he decided to chase the Visigoths out of their land in southern Gaul, instead. All Attila needed was an excuse to invade, and in A.D. 450 he got one. The Emperor Valentinian's sister, a nasty piece of work called Honoria, asked him to come and rescue her from a boring marriage, so Attila, knowing an opportunity when he saw one, acted all outraged on her behalf and demanded that

Valentinian hand over power to Honoria – and himself, of course. When Valentinian told him to get lost, Attila unleashed his Huns. The Huns swept over the border and headed for Gaul.

An epic battle took place in A.D. 451 on the Catalaunian Plains near Troyes, south east of Paris (though for many years historians wrongly called it the Battle of Châlons) where the Roman General Aelius pulled off the seemingly impossible – he defeated Attila the Hun. Attila pottered around northern Italy for a while, married a German princess called Ildico, and headed back to Hungary where, in A.D. 453, he died. In bed. Some say that Attila ruptured an artery in the middle of a night of passion with Ildico, some say he was murdered, but however it was, Attila died with his boots off.

Hungary isn't actually named after the Huns who made it their homeland, it was probably named after a later people, called the Onunguns. But, the Hungarians have never forgotten the Huns and won't hear a word said against them. Attila is a very popular name in modern Hungary, and the Hun art of horseback archery has been revived recently. Hungarians draw the line at washing their babies in cold water and binding their heads though.

The Vandals go clubbing (in the Mediterranean)

The Vandals, who came from the Baltic area of northern Germany, do have a bit of an image problem, caused by their name (the Philistines suffer the same and they were actually quite a cultured people). The Vandals reputation may stem from that time in A.D. 406 when they caught the Romans on a bender at New Year, crossed the Rhine and trashed the city of Mainz, but hey, it was the Decline and Fall of the Roman Empire – my dear, _everyone_ was trashing Roman cities.

The Scourge of God

Attila the Hun was certainly scary – Christians called him the 'Scourge of God'. It's said that Attila was going to sack Rome but that he was persuaded to spare the city by the saintly figure of Pope Leo I coming out to plead with him in person. According to the 1950s film _The Sign of the Pagan,_ heavenly choirs were singing at this point and the Pope came riding through the mist. Nice image; bad history. Attila never had any time for religion. His men were up against famine and disease and it made perfect sense to turn back and give Rome (which was surrounded by marshes and notoriously unhealthy, as Leo almost certainly pointed out) a very wide berth.

Eventually the Vandals settled in Spain, where they learned how to build ships (the Romans put the – Roman – people who had taught them to death) and invaded North Africa. North Africa supplied Rome with almost all its corn, so whoever controlled it had Rome by the short and curlies. The Vandals set up camp in the city of Carthage and in A.D. 455, just to rub it in, they sailed over to Rome and sacked it – revenge for what the Romans had done to Carthage years before (see Chapter 3.).

Not until A.D. 533, over a hundred years after they first crossed into Africa, did the Emperor Justinian finally defeat the Vandals, and he did to their kingdom what his ancestors had done to Carthage – destroyed it utterly. Vandal prisoners were sold off as slaves throughout the Roman world and the Vandal race was wiped out – you could call it Roman vandalism.

How the West Was Won

If you read the section 'And Lo, There Came Invaders from the East', earlier in this chapter, you've probably got the picture: Although the Roman Empire was still very strong in the East, it had more or less collapsed in the West. From A.D. 472–476 the western emperors were overthrowing each other at the rate of one a year.

The last western emperor, who took over in A.D. 475, was a young lad called Romulus Augustus, after the founder of Rome and the first emperor, but he was such a feeble character that he was given a sort of comic name, Romulus Augustulus, like calling a US president Washington Boshington.

In A.D. 476, the Roman commander in chief, a barbarian chief called Odoacer (or possibly Odovacer – there's some confusion about the correct form of his name) decided enough was enough. Odoacer overthrew Romulus and took the throne for himself. In theory, Odoacer was ruling Italy in the name of the *eastern*, and now, of course, the only, Roman emperor, a shrewd character by the name of Zeno, but in reality Odoacer ruled Italy on behalf of himself. This situation didn't suit Zeno one bit. And Zeno had a *very* useful friend . . .

Your mission, Theodoric the Ostrogoth, should you choose to accept it . . .

The man Zeno turned to was Theodoric, king of the Ostrogoths. The Ostrogoths (or 'eastern Goths') had declared their independence from the Huns back when Attila died and asked the Roman emperor if they could settle within the empire if they promised to defend it. The emperor, thinking 'Hmm. Now where have I heard that before?' agreed, but said that the Ostrogoth king had to send his 8-year-old son to Constantinople as a hostage – which is how little Prince Theodoric the Ostrogoth came to be brought up at the imperial court.

Everyone liked Theodoric. Prince Theodoric was polite and well-mannered, and he became a senator and an officer in the imperial bodyguard, and all in all seemed more Roman than Ostrogoth. When he was 18, Theodoric asked the emperor, very politely, if he might go home. The emperor, thinking Theodoric was harmless and might even be a good influence on the Ostrogoths, agreed. Boy, was the emperor wrong.

Theodoric immediately sprang into life as a fully fledged Ostrogoth warrior. He got an army together and took the city of Singidunum (Belgrade) and then refused point blank to hand it over to the emperor. But in fact, Theodoric didn't want to destroy the Empire; twice he even saved the emperor Zeno from attempted coups. What Theodoric wanted was a homeland for his people. So when Zeno started looking for someone to go and deal with Odoacer, Theodoric was the obvious man to approach. Zeno's offer was simple: Get rid of Odoacer, and you can have Italy. But you'll have to deal with Odoacer yourselves, with no help from Constantinople. Theodoric agreed.

St Augustine of Hippo

In the 21st century, we're so used to thinking of North Africa as a Muslim region that imagining it as the heartland of Christianity in the early days is difficult. The leading Christian scholar in the fifth century A.D. was St Augustine (*not* the missionary who travelled to England: he's a quite different, later character, called St Augustine of Canterbury). Augustine had led rather a wild youth (the salacious details are all in his *Confessions* on the top shelf in all good theology departments) and only became a Christian in his thirties. In A.D. 395, Augustine became bishop of the North African town of Hippo, where his speciality was in refuting the arguments of *heretics,* Christians whose beliefs and preaching had gone a bit wonky.

Like just about everyone else in the Roman world, Augustine was horrified when the Visigoths sacked Rome in A.D. 410, and he wrote his famous book *City of God* to try to work out why God had let it happen. (The City of God wasn't Rome but a more general idea of all Christians, in heaven and on earth, joined in one cosmic 'city'.) Augustine decided that God wasn't punishing the world or anything like that, but that – and here was the surprise – if you thought it through properly, the fall of Rome *didn't really matter.* Empires come and go, and people can't do much about it; everything that happens is part of God's plan. What matters is to keep a sense of justice alive – which, incidentally, was the main thing Augustine thought the Romans had lost sight of.

Second-class (Roman) citizens

Using Theodoric to get rid of Odoacer worked – just. Odoacer put up a massive fight and held out for three years in the fortified city of Ravenna, which was the real capital of Italy by then. Theodoric had to starve Odoacer out. When Odoacer finally surrendered, Theodoric invited him to dinner – Odoacer was feeling very peckish – but his spies told him that Odoacer was plotting to kill him. So, during the meal Theodoric drew his sword and cut Odoacer in two (you try doing that next time you're carving a joint) and then calmly had all his family, generals, friends, and anyone else who might possibly be dangerous rounded up and killed, too.

Theodoric gave the Italian Romans a taste of the colonial rule they had dished out to the rest of Europe for so long. Theordoric ruled them very fairly, but the law was administered and enforced by the Ostrogoths. The Romans were second-class citizens in their own land.

In theory, Theodoric was ruling Italy on behalf of the emperor in Constantinople, but in reality he ruled pretty much as he liked. Theodoric married his family into all the other kingdoms in Europe, conquered the Vandals of North Africa and took over the Visigoth lands in southern Gaul and Spain. The eastern emperors were very nervous of Theodoric's success, especially as the Ostrogoths, like all the other Goths, were Arians. Emperor Justin I started persecuting Arians in the East, so Theodoric retaliated by closing down Catholic churches and arresting anyone who seemed to be in close touch with the emperor. He even arrested the Pope.

Yet More Barbarian Raiders

The Visigoths, Ostrogoths, Huns, and Vandals weren't the only peoples rising up and attacking the Roman Empire. You could also count among Rome's enemies:

- **Angles, Saxons, Jutes:** These were all sea-faring peoples (unlike most of the others, who preferred to stay on dry land) from north Germany and the Baltic who sailed over the North Sea and settled in Britain.

- **Franks:** Unlike other tribes, they didn't abandon their homeland (north Germany and the Netherlands), which may be why they were so successful. The Franks threw the Visigoths out of Gaul and moved in (Gaul changed its named to Francia, after the Franks. The German name for France is still *Frankreich*, which means Kingdom of the Franks). Meet the Franks again in Chapter 6.

- **Burgundians:** A fierce lot, with a penchant for throwing axes, these people settled for a time in northern Italy, but were conquered by the Franks. The Burgundians settled eventually in the area of France still named after them today.

Oh, and a grim lot called the *Sassanids* had taken over in Persia and were attacking from the East.

The (Eastern) Empire Strikes Back

If the Roman Empire was well on its way out, no one seems to have told the Emperor Justinian I. Justinian came from a very humble background (which means that his family were peasants and he'd rather you didn't know) from Illyria, which is modern-day Croatia and Slovenia. But Justinian was a Latin speaker and proud of it; he'd have been even more proud had he known that he was the last Roman emperor who would speak Latin. From the moment Justinian was crowned in Constantinople in A.D. 527, he was determined to restore the Empire to its former glory. And most historians agree that Justinian more or less succeeded – though at a cost.

From now on, the Empire is generally called the Byzantine Empire, or just Byzantium, the name of the original town on the site of Constantinople. Using this name is not wrong exactly, but the Byzantines did not use it of themselves. The Byzantines spoke Greek and wrote Greek but they called themselves Romans. (Mind you, everyone else just called the Byzantines Greeks!)

Justinian was in partnership with his formidable wife, the Empress Theodora. Theodora started life as a dancer and, er, general entertainer in the circus – and in various rooms off the circus. Justinian was one of Theodora's clients and he had to get special senatorial permission to marry her. We know a lot about Theodora because of the most amazing 'secret history' written by the

---

Chariots and fire

Everyone in sixth-century Byzantium was mad on chariot racing at the hippodrome (Greek for horse arena). Two main teams competed, the Greens and the Blues, causing so much rivalry between them that it was like having two political factions in the city. The Empress Theodora was a Blues supporter – her dad had worked for the Blues – which meant that the Greens disliked her and Justinian. Usually Justinian just had to do a bit of divide and rule to stay in control, but in A.D. 532 both groups went on the rampage in the hippodrome demonstrating against high taxes and chanting 'Nika! Nika!',

which was the Byzantine equivalent of shouting out 'Go on, my son!' to your team in a race. The riots got completely out of hand and the crowds burned down whole sections of the city, and even elected a new emperor.

Justinian was just getting ready to run for it when Theodora saved the day, telling him 'There's the sea and there are the ships. I'm staying here. I'd rather be buried in purple.' So Justinian, feeling rather foolish now, ordered his guards to restore order, and they went out and killed some 30,000 people in one day – and that did the trick.

court historian, Procopius, which turned up in the Vatican library in the 17th century. Procopius, who may possibly (but only possibly) have had a rather overactive imagination, thoroughly disapproved of Theodora and her influence on Justinian, and he disapproved of her in graphic detail. And if you get hold of a copy of Procopius's *Secret History* you can disapprove of Theodora, too.

Justinian was Roman Emperor, and Italy, Spain, Gaul, and North Africa had all been part of the Roman Empire – now he wanted those places back. In A.D. 533, Justinian sent his general, Belisarius, to North Africa to start the ball rolling. Belisarius was a very able soldier and beat the Vandals of North Africa fairly easily. Next stop: Italy.

Italy was under the Ostrogoths, who were deeply divided among themselves. Theodoric's daughter, Amalasuntha, wanted to stay friendly with the Romans, but her husband, Theodahad, wasn't interested. In fact, Theodahad was so uninterested that he had Amalasuntha locked up, and just when the Romans started asking what he thought he was doing, she had an accident in the bath – someone strangled her. Right!

Belisarius was soon on his way to Italy with an army of – well, mostly of other barbarians, actually. There just weren't that many genuine Romans left, which is why historians talk about 'Imperialists' or Byzantines instead of Romans. Belisarius and the imperial eunuch General Narses did reconquer Italy, but it took them five long years, and the Italians, who had become quite used to being ruled by the Ostrogoths, weren't all that happy to be liberated. How's that for ingratitude?

All this fighting cost so much that Justinian had to keep raising taxes, and the Imperial Tax Collector, John of Cappodocia, took great pleasure in making the process as painful as possible. The one bit of good news was that Belisarius was able to add southern Spain to Justinian's collection of reconquered provinces, thanks to a handy split among the Visigoths.

And then the whole empire was struck with a devastating outbreak of bubonic plague. Historians don't know exactly how many people died but it was many thousands – on a similar scale to the later Black Death (Chapter 8 has the grisly details of the Black Death). All in all, Justinian may have recovered much of the Empire, but it took a long time for the Empire to recover from him.

Roman law

Justinian collected all the existing laws and all the important judges' rulings in a single 'code', with handy FAQs, that you could point to and say '*That* is the law'. Justinian's code remained in force in the Byzantine Empire, and eventually became the basis for Church law. Justinian's Roman law still underpins European law and the European courts to this day.

Let's Be Frank

If you get a bit confused with all these different peoples attacking the Roman Empire, remember this: *the Franks came out on top*. The Franks started in the Netherlands and moved into northern Gaul, and very early on they hit on a winning formula – work out which side the Romans are on and stick to it. The king of the Franks, Clovis I of the *Merovingian* dynasty, added a masterstroke – he made his people drop Arianism and become Catholics. Immediately, the Franks became the Romans' favourite barbarians, and there was nothing Rome or Constantinople wouldn't do to help them.

Clovis quickly united all the different Frankish kings under his leadership (okay, he had them all assassinated). Next, Clovis forced the Visigoths to flee to Spain and settled in as king of what the Franks now called Francia. Then Clovis destroyed the Kingdom of Burgundy, took Provence off the Ostrogoths, and generally made Francia the most powerful kingdom in the West.

The Merovingians had an odd custom of giving so much power to their royal officials, known as mayors, that mayors like Charles 'the Hammer' Martel and his son, Pepin the Short, were kings in all but name. In fact, Pepin overturned the last Merovingian king in A.D. 751 and set up his own dynasty – you can meet them in Chapter 6.

The Incredible Rise of Islam

The Prophet Muhammed was originally just a poor boy from Mecca who had a vision of the Archangel Gabriel, who told him to recite the message that there is one God and to spread the word. Westerners nowadays often think of Islam as a separate religion from Christianity, but doing so is not quite right. Much of Muhammed's message made sense to Christian ears: One God, a duty to pray and fast regularly, give alms to the poor, go on pilgrimage – nothing very new there. Even Muhammed's idea that Jesus was a prophet rather than the Son of God was not that different from what the Arians had been saying for years. In fact, some Christians saw Islam in the early days as simply another Christian heresy. What these Christians weren't expecting was the speed with which Islam spread.

Muslims date the calendar from A.D. 622, when Muhammed left Mecca, where no one had wanted to listen to him, and set off for the much more sympathetic city of Medina. This event is known as the *Hejira,* which means 'the cutting of the ties', but Muhammed didn't cut them for long. Eight years later, Muhhammed was back at the head of an army, and Mecca decided that maybe Muhammed had a point after all. Scholars note that the verses of the *Koran* which date from after the *hejira* are a lot more hardline than the earlier ones, and they include the idea of *jihad* – holy war to spread the faith.

By the time of his death in A.D. 632, Muhammed and his men had conquered Arabia, but his successors went on to conquer a lot more, incredibly fast. In the East, the Muslims defeated the mighty Persian Empire; in the West, they headed for Egypt, Syria and Palestine, known as the Holy Land, and to the horror of the Emperor Heraclius in Constantinople, they overran the lot. Actually, Heraclius had no one to blame but himself. Heraclius had tried to force the Syrians and Egyptians to accept the idea of the Trinity, whereas they preferred their own 'Coptic' (Egyptian) Church, which said that Jesus was God only and not part-God-part-man. So the Syrians and Egyptians could appreciate the logic of the Arabs' idea that Jesus was human, not divine. The Syrians and Egyptians appreciated the logic even more when the Arabs kicked Heraclius out and let everyone worship as they liked.

The Arabs even won over the Berber people of North Africa when they realised that the Arabs were just as anti-Roman as they were. Newly converted to Islam, the Berbers launched the first Muslim invasion of Europe and landed in Spain. Spain was ruled by the Visigoths (they'd been pushed out of Gaul by the Franks – do try to keep up); the Arabs and Berbers went through Visigothic Spain like a warm knife through butter. The Muslims reached the Pyrenees and crossed into France, but it was there that they had their first big defeat. Charles Martel ('Charles the Hammer'), ruler of the Franks, stopped the Muslims at the great Battle of Poitiers in A.D. 732 and drove them back into Spain. This event was one of the decisive moments in European history.

Sound your horn in good time, Mr Roland

After the Battle of Poitiers, many clashes took place between Christian and Muslim warriors in the Pyrenees. One battle or skirmish at the pass of Roncevaux became immortalised in the legend of *The Song of Roland,* which is all about how a heroic Christian knight called Roland is guarding the pass with his friend, Oliver, when a great Muslim army appears. The Frankish king, Charles (Charlemagne), had given Roland a horn to sound if he got into trouble, and Oliver reckons that this may be a good time to see if it works, but Roland isn't having any of it. 'We can head 'em off at the pass!' he cries, while Oliver is no doubt thinking that of all the knights to get paired up with he has to end up with a heroic half-wit. Sure enough, Oliver gets blinded in the fighting and Roland finally blows the horn ('which was heard throughout Francia') too late. According to the legend, Roland was killed by poor old Oliver who couldn't see what he was doing, and they fell dead on each other's breasts, but *I* reckon Oliver did it deliberately.

Chapter 6

Gold, Murder, and Frankish Sense

. . . .

In This Chapter

▶ Splitting the Church into east and west

▶ Discovering how Charlemagne became an emperor

▶ Encountering the Vikings raiding and settling right across Europe

. . . .

*Y*ou can't really understand medieval Europe without a grasp of the importance of Christianity – in fact, Europe was often called 'Christendom'. But during the medieval period the Christian Church split into two, east and west. The Franks set up an empire under Charlemagne to counter-balance the Byzantine Empire in Constantinople, and then a forceful band of import–export dealers from Scandinavia sailed into the picture – the Vikings.

Let's Get This Church on the Road

Jesus's apostles spread out through the Roman world setting up little communities known as *ecclesiae* or 'churches', but that didn't mean a big building with a spire and a hall for hire; a church just meant a group of people who all believed in the same God.

Each church was run by an *episcopus* or 'bishop', though in the biggest churches the bishops had priests called *presbyters* and admin officers called *deacons* to help them. In theory, all bishops were equal, but in practice the most important bishops (also known as *metropolitans,* because they were based in big cities) were from Antioch, Alexandria, Constantinople, and Rome.

Now don't leap to conclusions. No one was assuming that the Bishop of Rome should be in charge. In fact, Rome was the Johnny-come-lately in this story; Christianity began in the East, so people generally assumed that it should be led from the East – just as the Roman empire was.

Crisis in the East

Ever since the Emperor Constantine made Christianity one of the Roman Empire's official religions (refer to Chapter 5 for more about why Constantine made this choice) the Church's fate had been closely tied to the fate of the Roman Empire, and especially its eastern, Byzantine half. And Byzantium was in trouble. Sclavs (or 'Slavs') and Avars came sweeping down from northern Russia, Arabs attacked in the East, Lombards attacked in Italy and Bulgars attacked in the South: Byzantium's days seemed numbered. The Bulgars defeated the Emperor Nicephorus I, killed him and used his skull as a drinking goblet. Ouch.

The emperors strike back

The Byzantine emperors came up with a very ingenious two-pronged response to these threats:

- **Reorganise the army.** The whole empire was reorganised into military zones called *themes* and put onto a war footing. A new dynasty of Macedonian emperors, starting with Basil I, regained control of Greece and southern Italy and pushed the Arabs out of Anatolia (modern-day Turkey). Maybe things weren't so bad after all.

- **Send missionaries.** Converting some of these people to Christianity relieved the pressure on the Empire enormously. But would they find someone brave enough to go and preach to the Bulgars?

Incredibly, the Byzantines did find someone. Two brothers, St Cyril and St Methodius, set out to spread the gospel among the Slavs and Bulgars and very successful they were, too. Cyril even worked out a special alphabet – the Cyrillic alphabet – based on Greek letters but specially adapted to suit the way the Slavs and Bulgars spoke (which is why Bulgaria and Russia still use the Cyrillic alphabet to this day).

In theory, the Bulgars were less of a threat once they'd become Christian, but Emperor Basil 'Bulgar slayer' II wasn't taking any chances. In 1014, Basil took terrible revenge on the Bulgars, defeating them in battle, taking some 15,000 prisoners, and *blinding* them (blinding prisoners was something of a Byzantine speciality). The exception was the prisoner who only had one eye taken out, so he could lead all the blind Bulgars home. The Bulgar king is said to have died of shock, and then the Bulgars became a Byzantine province. Rather a sulky province, but one not prepared to take on the Empire again – which, of course, was the general idea.

Icons and politics

St Cyril and St Methodius weren't just introducing the Slavs and Bulgars to Christianity; they were helping to create a distinctive eastern culture based around the Church. Unfortunately, one aspect of that culture was about to spark off an almighty row – *icons*.

You've probably seen icons, those rather flat, oddly unreal pictures of Jesus or the saints, all looking the same, which you get in eastern churches. Icons aren't meant to be portraits; they illustrate eternal truths, which go beyond temporary details like an individual's features. An icon is a message, and every detail has a meaning, which is why people spend so much time contemplating them and meditating on what they might mean.

The trouble was, that praying and lighting candles in front of icons looked suspiciously like idol worship. An eighth-century group called the *iconoclasts* (icon smashers) reckoned God was punishing idol worship by allowing the Muslims to conquer so much Christian land, and that the only thing to do was to rip icons out of churches and smash them – which they did, with great enthusiasm.

The bishops were very worried about iconoclasm, but in 730 Emperor Leo III decided that the iconoclasts were right and banned icons from churches throughout the Empire. Anyone caught using icons was arrested. The bishops protested, and the *Iconoclastic Controversy* dragged on for years, until finally, in 843, Emperor Michael III relented and allowed icons back.

These people were fighting a cosmic war of Good and Evil, and if icons *were* evil, getting them out of churches fast became imperative (and if icons were good, stopping the iconoclasts destroying them became equally imperative).

Don't Live Like an Egyptian: Christianity in the West

While the eastern churches and Byzantine emperor were having their issues (see preceding section), the Church was developing in the West in a very different way.

Monks, monasteries, and more

The first big difference between Christianity in the East and West concerned monks. Now, when you think of monks, you think of men with long brown habits, cord tied round the waist, and deeply bad haircuts, all living together in a monastery, but that wasn't what monks were like in the early days. Early monks were people who had read about John the Baptist living in the wilderness and eating locusts and wild honey and thought, 'If he can do it, so can we.' So the monks went and dug themselves holes in the Egyptian desert and lived off scraps.

An Egyptian *monastery* looked rather like a shanty town, except that these people had chosen to live like that. When the eastern Church talked of a monastery, this shanty town arrangement is what they meant.

To add to the air of unreality, these early monks competed with each other to do ever crazier things to show how holy they were. St Simon Stylites, for example, decided to get closer to heaven by spending his life living on top of a pillar, never sitting or lying down, not even to sleep. I mean, frankly, what was the point?

A young Italian called Benedict of Nursia also pondered on the point of such behaviour. Benedict agreed that Christians should withdraw from the world and devote themselves to prayer, but he thought all this Egyptian-style masochism was rather unhealthy. So, when Benedict set up a new monastery at Monte Cassino, near Naples, he drew up a set of rules known as the *Rule of St Benedict* for how to run a monastery without putting people off. Benedict suggested that there should be discipline, but 'nothing harsh or burdensome'. In the years that followed, thousands of young men and women found that the Rule of St Benedict offered just the right sort of structured life of prayer. People still live by the Rule of St Benedict today. (See the sidebar 'St Benedict's Rule' to find out more about this lifestyle.)

The Rule of St Benedict was one thing that set the western Church apart from the eastern Church; the other was the growing power of the Bishop of Rome – the Pope.

St Benedict's Rule

The basic idea behind the Rule of St Benedict is a combination of humility and obedience. You obey your abbot or mother superior (there are Benedictine nuns as well as monks) without question – very like the Army. The idea of the habits and haircuts (called *tonsures*) is to demonstrate humility and to show that you have cast-off worldly concerns for fashion or appearance. The Benedictine day is tightly structured, with regular prayers and services, even in the night, and the lifestyle is certainly not for people who enjoy a lie-in.

Gregory the Great

The man who almost single-handedly made the papacy into the leading power in western Europe was Pope Gregory I, also known as Pope Gregory the Great, yet he never wanted to be pope at all and always craved a quiet life tucked away in a monastery.

Gregory certainly had the right background for a pope – he came from a leading Roman family and his great grandfather had been Pope Felix III (no vows of celibacy in those days) – but he really wasn't interested in the role. Instead, Gregory became a Benedictine monk and used his family wealth to found seven new monasteries. Aiming for a quiet life was no good, however; the Lombards were invading Italy and Pope Pelagius I needed a good ambassador to go to Constantinople to get help. Pelagius sent Gregory (who spent six years there and got no help from the Byzantines at all).

When Pelagius died the people of Rome enthusiastically elected Gregory to succeed him. Gregory was so horrified that he fled the city, until he reflected that if God wanted him to be pope, he was wrong to refuse. So, Gregory turned round and went back to Rome.

Gregory insisted on a special title for himself: *Servus servorum Dei*, which means The Servant of the Servants of God. The title was meant to signify how Gregory would serve the people just as Jesus had served his apostles, and it remains the official title of the popes to this day. Not all the popes have taken the title quite as seriously as Gregory, though.

Gregory proved just as good a leader of Rome as any of his imperial predecessors. Gregory overhauled the city's system of poor relief. and when the Lombards got too close for comfort he took over the defences of the city and negotiated a peace settlement. But Gregory's really important work was in extending his authority a long way outside the city of Rome.

The English patent

Gregory had always taken a special interest in the way that slaves were treated, and in the slave market in Rome a couple of fair skinned young slaves caught his eye. These slaves were Angles, from the island of Britain – or England as it was beginning to be called.

Gregory became very interested in England because it seemed to be a land that had completely lost touch with Christianity after the Romans left. If Gregory were to arrange for England to be converted back to Christianity, then he'd have a large overseas Christian province under his control. So Gregory selected a Benedictine monk called Augustine – Gregory was a monk himself and one thing Benedictines had drummed into them was the need to obey orders – and sent him with a group of other monks off to England.

Today Germany, tomorrow . . .

England proved a very wise investment, because a few years later two English monks called Willibrord and Wynfrith volunteered to take the gospel message into the heart of Germany. The monks asked the Pope for permission first. The Pope agreed to the mission, as long as the monks changed their names, and being obedient English monks they did so, which is why history knows them as St Clement and St Boniface. The monks were very successful – St Boniface had a particularly good party trick involving chopping down the Germans' sacred idol and surviving to tell the tale as a way of convincing them that their gods didn't exist – and now the papacy controlled the Church in Italy, England, and Germany.

Next up: The eastern churches?

Gregory had one last trick up his sleeve. Gregory said that each new bishop had to be given a ceremonial scarf known as a *pallium*, and that he had to travel to Rome to get the scarf, from the Pope himself. In effect, Gregory was claiming the right to appoint all new bishops. Gregory wasn't claiming the right to rule the whole Church (not yet at any rate) but the eastern churches certainly didn't like the way things seemed to be shaping up in the West. The papacy wasn't yet strong enough to face up to the eastern churches, but was getting nearer to this goal. Remember this pallium business – you'll meet it again.

Who You Gonna Call? The Franks!

By the eighth century the popes had more pressing concerns to worry about than missions to England or Germany or even who to appoint as bishops (see preceding sections). The Lombards were advancing through northern Italy and closing in on Rome. In theory, the popes should have turned for help to the emperor in Constantinople – Italy was still supposedly in the Roman Empire – but they didn't bother doing that; the popes turned straight to their very good friends, the Franks. And yes, the emperor did notice.

With love from me (via St Peter) to you

The Franks had set up the strongest barbarian monarchy in Europe, and since they were also Catholics, the popes and the Frankish kings enjoyed a mutual admiration society. The popes anointed the Frankish kings at their coronation and gave them impressive Roman-style titles like 'Patrician', and the Franks came riding to the rescue whenever the popes were in trouble.

Something fishy in the shoes of the fisherman

The Donation of Constantine was a forgery, but it didn't come to light until the 15th century when a Renaissance scholar called Lorenzo Valla showed from its style that it could not possibly date from Roman times. The Donation of Constantine shows how the eighth-century popes were allowing their bid for power to lead them away from the strict path of truth. Not a very good example for others to follow.

And very effective the Franks proved too; by the end of the century the Frankish king, Charlemagne, had completely conquered the Lombards and taken them into his empire; but the important date comes a little before that. In 756, the Frankish king, Pepin the Short, took the city of Ravenna from the Lombards. Nothing so odd about that action, you may think, but what matters is what Pepin did with Ravenna afterwards. Pepin didn't keep the city; he gave it to St Peter. Doing so was a roundabout way of giving the city to the Pope, who was, of course, St Peter's representative. (Pepin wasn't able to give Ravenna directly to the Pope because bishops weren't supposed to be rulers.) The bishops of Rome, unlike any other bishops in Christendom, now had land under their control – and important land at that.

Just then, by an astonishing coincidence, the Pope found an old document signed by Emperor Constantine himself called the *Donation of Constantine*, which stated that the Pope was God's special representative on earth, that he was in charge of all other bishops, and that he was to rule Rome, Italy, and the West. Now wasn't that handy?

You scratch my back, Your Holiness, and I'll scratch yours

The Franks were ruled by a dynasty called Merovingians (see Chapter 5). The Merovingians had a refreshingly novel approach to the business of government – they left it all to their household officials called *mayors*.

In 751, the Mayor of the Palace, Pepin the Short, decided that since he was doing all the ruling that he might as well take over the crown as well – so he did. But Pepin didn't actually have any *right* to be king, and among the Franks this lack of legitimacy mattered. Pepin, therefore, wrote to the Pope and asked him to confirm his title as king. The Pope was only too pleased to help; the Franks were the only Catholic people in western Europe outside Italy itself, and Pepin's *Carolingian* dynasty looked a safe bet for a very useful alliance.

Feudal Franks

The Franks had a very successful secret weapon – they were Europe's first fully-fledged knights in armour, with chain mail and shields and lances and all the rest of it. Each knight had a small army of armed maintenance people, who owed loyalty to their knight in return for his protection. The Frankish knights thus ended up in charge of their own private armies, which the king could call on when he needed help. This system was rather like the tribal armies that the Romans had allowed to live within the Empire in the old days. The Romans had called these armies *feodali,* which is why this system of knights and private armies was known as the *feudal system.*

Pepin wouldn't have called his dynasty 'Carolingian' because the term comes from his son Charles; the Latin for Charles is *Carolus*. In fact, even Charlemagne probably didn't use the term 'Carolingian' – like so many terms used in history, it was invented by historians writing much later.

Pepin was the first western king to hold his title 'by the grace of God' and to be made king by the Pope. In fact, the whole Carolingian state was closely tied to the Church. Nobles, called counts, came and went, but once a bishop had been confirmed by the king he had a job for life, so bishops often became the real rulers of the provinces within the kingdom. Bishops were even expected to lead troops into battle. So it was natural for Pope Stephen II to turn to his very good friend, Pepin, for help against the Lombards; he even left Rome to go and see him in person. The young lad who took the Pope in to meet the king was Pepin's son Charles, later to be known as Carolus Magnus, 'Charles the Great', or as we know him, Charlemagne.

Thanks to Charlemagne, kings ain't wot they used to be

Charlemagne believed in the idea of a Christian king, who had a duty to lead and protect his people and to see them safely into heaven. The king's favourite reading (Charlemagne was literate, which was pretty remarkable to start with) was St Augustine's *City of God* (see Chapter 5), but where Augustine had been talking of a virtual city made up of all Christians past and present, Charlemagne saw it as a union of Church and State here on earth. So Charlemagne took it on himself to fight God's enemies (who luckily were also the neighbours of the Franks), but he also gathered a remarkable collection of scholars at his court at Aachen to promote truth, justice, and the Carolingian way.

The leading scholar at Charlemagne's court was an English monk called Alcuin of York. These scholars gave each other Greek and Latin names, because they were so conscious of the debt they owed to the classical authors. Charlemagne himself was a keen linguist; he spoke Latin and was learning Greek, though as his biographer, the scholar Einhard, tactfully put it, 'he had started rather late'.

Capital city, desirable location, hot and cold running water

Charlemagne maintained a splendid court at a purpose-built imperial capital. The king chose Aix-la-Chapelle (German name: Aachen) because it had nice warm springs and Charlemagne loved bathing – another thing that set him somewhat apart from his contemporaries. Charlemagne wanted Aachen to be a fittingly dazzling place, so he imported artwork and handy home hints from the old imperial capital at Ravenna, which in turn had got its ideas from Byzantium. The Byzantines were a bit snooty about it ('My dear, I thought if I saw one more decorated arch I should scream...') but Aachen was the first city since Rome which was purpose built to be a capital of Europe, and for that reason alone is well worth a visit. And you may like the decorated arches.

The main work of all these scholars was to improve standards in the Frankish Church. There were to be neat new copies of the Bible, with all the mistakes corrected (the trouble with copying by hand is that people make mistakes and before you know it everyone thinks the Israelites were rescued by Noses). The court scholars even produced a clear, uniform style of handwriting called Carolingian minuscule, and so good were the results that years later, in the Renaissance, scholars thought it was the original handwriting of the ancients.

If it's Tuesday, this battle must be against the Lombards

Charlemagne didn't spend too long in Aachen; he was spending a lot of time fighting. The main war zones were

- **Spain:** Most of Spain was now the Islamic Caliphate of Cordoba. It was riven by faction-fighting, and one of these factions invited Charlemagne to come and invade. Charlemagne saw this invasion as a holy war against the enemies of Christ, and he took over a considerable strip of northern Spain while he was at it. Charlemagne had started the long process of Christian reconquest.

- **Italy:** Pope Stephen III asked Charlemagne to come and sort out the Lombards, who were still around and making a thorough nuisance of themselves (though Lombard historians no doubt say the same about Pope Stephen III). Charlemagne conquered the Lombards and made himself king of Lombardy. Was the Pope grateful? Not a bit. The Pope had wanted northern Italy himself. Charlemagne also defeated the Count of Benevento in southern Italy, so that his empire actually hemmed the Pope in on two sides, north and south. You can see why the popes were very wary of their big protector.

✔ **Germany:** The pagan Saxons of north Germany still worshipped the old gods, including a large tree which they reckoned held the sky up, so Charlemagne saw this as a holy war. After Charlemagne had chopped down their tree and massacred a few thousand of them, he insisted that the Saxons become Christians – by force if need be. Alcuin protested that this was not in the spirit of Jesus, and that forced converts were no good to anybody. Charlemagne, however, reckoned that he wouldn't have any security until the Saxons became at least nominal Christians – they could always be properly converted later. And in the meantime, Charlemagne now added Germany to his collection of European conquests.

Charlemagne was the first ruler since the Greeks to talk of 'Europe' as a single entity. And now, many years later, the French–German alliance is the basis for the European Union, and they naturally look back to Charlemagne as a sort of patron saint. The Charlemagne Prize remains the EU's highest award for people who have done most to promote the spirit of European friendship and unity.

Emperor? Moi?

The defining moment in Charlemagne's reign happened on Christmas Day 800, when Pope Leo III rather unexpectedly crowned him Roman emperor. Pope Leo had lots of enemies, especially among the family of the previous pope, and in 799 they ambushed him during a papal procession (quite literally – they tried to cut out his eyes and tongue and he only just managed to escape to a monastery). Pope Leo's enemies declared him overthrown, but he ran to Charlemagne for help. Charlemagne duly came to Rome and put Leo very firmly back on his throne. So Leo may have crowned Charlemagne emperor as a one-good-turn-deserves-another gesture, or it may have been a way of making sure of his continued support.

Charlemagne always protested that he hadn't known what Leo was going to do. Some historians believe him, though others think Leo could never have done it if Charlemagne hadn't known about the plan in advance, and maybe even rehearsed it. The truth about the coronation of Charlemagne as Roman emperor may never be known.

The eastern churches were furious about the coronation, and it was eight years before the Byzantine Empire grudgingly accepted Charlemagne's right to call himself an emperor. Charlemagne was pleased with his new title, but not with having received it from the Pope. As soon as his son Louis was old enough, Charlemagne had him crowned co-emperor at Aachen, not Rome (crowning your heir while you were still alive was much safer than risking a succession dispute once you were dead). Charlemagne didn't invite the Pope.

Charlemagne died in 814. His sole surviving son, Louis the Pious, inherited the empire, but Louis's three sons followed standard Frankish practice and divided the empire up between them by the 843 Treaty of Verdun. The French and Spanish bits went to Charles the Bald, the German bits went to Louis the German, and a great slice down the middle, from the Netherlands, through the borderlands of Germany and France, into Provence and Italy, went to the third brother, Lothair.

Charles's lands eventually became the kingdoms of France and Spain, and Louis's lands in time became the German Empire. Lothair's kingdom was known as Lotharingia – and it didn't last long. Lothair's sons divided the kingdom up between them and all except the Italian bits ended up being subsumed into France and Germany. The French border region called Lorraine is all that remains of Lotharingia today.

Holy Doctrinal Difference, Batman!

While Charlemagne was building an empire, a very unholy row was developing between the eastern and western branches of the Church. These branches were meant to be parts of the *same* church (see earlier in this chapter), but you would never have known it from the way in which they behaved.

Some of the differences between the eastern and western churches may seem fairly minor now, but they mattered a lot at the time:

- ✔ Their priests dressed differently.
- ✔ The eastern Church didn't like the way that the western Church used unleavened bread at Mass.
- ✔ The western Church didn't like the eastern Church's icon cult.
- ✔ Above all, the eastern Church resented the way that the Pope was presenting himself as a sort of universal ruler. They thought that if anyone was in charge of the Church it should be their boy, the Patriarch of Constantinople, because Constantinople was where *real* Roman emperors lived, not Frankish imitation emperors.

The final split came in 1054, over a bit of highly technical religious doctrine. The western Church added a single Latin word, *filioque*, to the creed, which is the bit in the Mass when everyone says exactly what they believe in. 'Filioque' means 'and from the Son'; the western Church was saying that the Holy Spirit came from God the Father *and* from the Son.

'So?' I hear you ask. So the eastern Church said that the western Church was changing the whole basis of Christianity. 'Oh no we're not,' said the West. So the Pope excommunicated the Patriarch of Constantinople and the Patriarch of Constantinople excommunicated him back, and they both cut each other out of the list of people they prayed for and each Church said that the other one had started it, and they still haven't made up the quarrel to this day.

Axes of Evil: Enter the Vikings

The year 793 was the 9/11 of the early medieval world. A gang of armed men landed on the island of Lindisfarne, way up in northern England, burned down the famous monastery, and slaughtered the monks or carried them off as slaves. The Vikings had arrived.

No one really knows what made the people of Scandinavia set off in their longships and start terrorising the rest of Europe. Overcrowding may have been a problem at home, but for the most part, the Vikings were probably just after a quick buck. Well, if someone told you that there were holy places overseas full of gold and silver (nothing but the best for worshipping God, you see) guarded by unarmed men who believed fighting was wrong, wouldn't you be tempted to go and have a look?

The Vikings raided monasteries all over England, Scotland, Ireland, and along the coast of France. Charlemagne built coastal defences to keep them at bay, but his grandson, Lothair, invited the Vikings to help him fight his brothers and they moved in wholesale. The Vikings found that they were able to sail or row their longships up the rivers deep into the heart of France; they also found that the French were prepared to pay protection money. So were the English. The Irish weren't quite so rich, but they made very good slaves.

Eventually, Alfred the Great in England and Eudes and Charles the Simple in France (when it came to nicknames the French weren't called Frank for nothing) managed to give the Vikings a taste of their own medicine and kicked them out. The situation didn't last – the Danes came back and conquered England in 1016 and their King Cnut became king of England. In France, a Viking leader called Rollo defeated King Charles the Simple, and Charles agreed to give Rollo and his men a large area of land at the mouth of the Seine – they called it Normandy.

Purveyors of luxury goods, wholesale pillagers by appointment

That the Vikings have such a reputation for raiding and pillaging is unfortunate because that isn't the whole story at all. For one thing, the Vikings did *not* wear horned helmets – that was a complete invention by 19th-century illustrators. 'Viking' meant pillaging, and 'a Viking' was a pirate, which was not at all how the Vikings saw themselves; they were traders, and they carried out their raiding along strict business principles. The town of Hedeby in Denmark was one of the most important trading centres in Europe.

Ethical pillaging policy

The Vikings had a finely tuned sense of right and wrong. One story tells of a Viking who was running off with a bag of booty during a raid when he had a sudden crisis of conscience about stealing. So, the Viking ran back and killed the owner. Then, the Viking ran off with *all* the owner's worldly goods.

The Vikings built their longships (or *knörrs* if your Old Norse is up to pronouncing it) fairly shallow in the water – good for long voyages, not so good for carrying goods in bulk. So these traders concentrated on high-quality luxury goods that offered better value per shipload: furs, amber, and slaves. If you wanted to sell slaves – and slaves fetched very high prices all over the Mediterranean (including the Christian parts) – you had to go and get them, so the Vikings did. The Vikings' trading methods were not so *very* different from those employed by Europeans in later more 'civilised' times.

Hey, guys! We can trash places in the East as well!

The Vikings settled in England, Ireland, France, Iceland, Greenland, and even for a while in North America. But, the Vikings also went east, through Russia and the Byzantine Empire, into the Mediterranean, the Caspian Sea, and even into Persia.

The Swedes led the drive eastwards. The Slavic people they met called them *Rus*, which probably comes from their word for rowing (Rus-land became 'Russia'). These Vikings founded a sort of city state far inland called Novgorod ('New City') the Great, and another at Kiev. Two enterprising Vikings called Askold and Dir led a fleet of 200 ships all the way down the River Dnieper to the Black Sea and into the Byzantine Empire. It just so happened that the Byzantine army and navy were away fighting the Arabs at the time, so the Vikings moved in and helped themselves. The Vikings had a fine old time raiding and pillaging in the sun, then they sailed away back up the Dnieper to tell their friends.

Er, I'm not sure that you've quite got the hang of this, old boy

The Vikings had some suitably bloodthirsty gods of their own, who sometimes required human sacrifice. The Vikings soon found, however, that these gods could be bad for business, because Christians were only supposed to trade with other Christians. So some Vikings started going along to churches instead of just torching them and soon became rather over-enthusiastic converts. Olaf Tryggvason, King of Norway, was so keen for his fellow Vikings to embrace Christian love and peace that he had their eyes and tongues cut out if they refused, and when one Viking chief refused to give up the old gods, Olaf forced a poisonous snake down his gullet to devour him from inside. Sorry, were you eating?

In 907, the Viking Prince, Oleg, decided to try a raid on Constantinople itself (or Miklagard, the 'Great City', as the Vikings called it). The Byzantines cunningly strung a heavy chain across the Golden Horn to stop Oleg's longships, but Oleg even more cunningly gathered all his men at the back end of their ships and then just as they got to the chain they all rushed to the front so their ships tipped over the chain. Luckily for the Byzantines, Oleg hadn't thought to pack any ladders to scale the city walls, so he did a deal: the emperor paid him *tribute* (a posh word for protection money) and the Vikings settled in the city for six months – free food, wine, and baths (the Byzantines probably thought they needed them). After six months, the emperor paid for their packed lunches for the journey home and let them trade tax-free. Oleg sailed home with a smile on his face and with sails made of fine Byzantine silk.

Norman conquests

The Vikings who settled in northern France became known as Normans (from 'norsemen'). The Normans did even better than their distant cousins in Russia:

- ✔ **1066:** Rollo's grandson, William, conquers England at the Battle of Hastings. The Normans now control a first-rank European power.

- ✔ **1071:** Norman brothers Robert and Roger Guiscard go to war with the Byzantines and take the south of Italy from them. Robert gets the mainland and Roger gets Sicily.

Ironically, those Vikings who settled in Byzantium made up the emperor's most-trusted group of bodyguards, a sort of Byzantine Foreign Legion known as the Varangian Guard ('Varangians' was the Greek name for Vikings). So now there were Vikings fighting both for the emperor and against him. Just to add to the fun, one Varangian Guardsman was Harald Hardrada, who became king of Norway and died in 1066 trying to become king of England. Only a few months later, after the Battle of Hastings, lots of Saxons fled to Byzantium and joined the Varangian Guard – alongside distant cousins of the very men who had forced them to flee England in the first place!

Chapter 7

Knock, Knock, Knocking Heads at Heaven's Door

. . . .

In This Chapter

▶ Discovering how the Holy Roman Emperors quarrelled with the Pope

▶ Exploring the Crusades

▶ Introducing new kingdoms in Europe, and saying goodbye to Byzantium

. . . .

The Middle Ages specialised in religious wars. A splendid set-to occurred between the Holy Roman Emperors and the popes, and wars broke out between the French and the English, where Joan of Arc claimed she was getting messages directly from God. The most famous wars, however, were the Crusades, in which Christians and Muslims squared up to each other from Spain to Syria; we're still living with their legacy today.

I'm the King of the Germans

King Henry I was elected king of the Germans in 918 but had to spend the first few years of his reign persuading the other German princes of that fact. Henry also had to fight the Magyars (pronounced *Modyars*), who had come charging in from the East and were busily ravaging Hungary, Germany, and northern Italy. Henry died in 936 and passed his throne to his son, Otto.

Three guys called Otto

Otto proved a very good king, defeating the Magyars decisively at the Battle of the Lechfeld in 955. Otto also more or less united the Germans into a single empire, and had himself crowned emperor at Charlemagne's old capital at Aachen.

But Otto wanted a proper coronation, in Rome. When the coronation finally happened, Otto I took a slightly different title: Holy Roman Emperor (which rather suggested that the 'real' Roman emperor, the one in Byzantium, somehow *wasn't* very holy, which didn't go down well in the East, I can tell you).

Otto's son became Otto II and his grandson, Otto III. In fact, this Holy Roman Empire (which, as people never tire of pointing out, wasn't very holy, wasn't Roman, and wasn't really an empire) lasted until Napoleon's day. But before Otto I even started to think about posterity, he had to get one thing clear: Who was in charge, himself or the Pope?

Heavyweight championship of the world: Pope versus Emperor

The Pope who agreed to crown Otto I as Holy Roman Emperor was a rather unimpressive character called John XII. John became pope at the age of 18 as part of a hard-nosed political deal between his natural father and the leading Roman citizens.

John XII was into what most 18-year-old young men are into: sex and drink, which wouldn't have mattered quite so much if he hadn't just been elected pope. Drunken partying and sexual carousing are not quite the behaviour one expects at the Vatican.

John XII was also at war with Berengar, king of Italy, and losing. So John wrote to Otto I asking for help. In return, John said he would crown Otto I Holy Roman Emperor in a proper ceremony, in Rome. Otto was only too delighted to help – at a price.

Otto operated what historians call the *Ottonian system*: Otto was in charge of all appointments – including church appointments. John XII was happy enough to go along with this plan while he needed Otto's help ('Yeah, yeah,' he said, 'Whatever.'), but once Otto started telling John to grow up and mend his ways, John decided to double-cross Otto. This decision was a very, *very* bad idea. Otto came storming back to Rome, accused John of a whole string of violations (ordaining a deacon in a stable, running a brothel without a licence, gambling at dice and invoking the old Roman gods for help while he was at it, treason – oh, and castrating a cardinal), deposed him, and installed a new pope to replace him, called Leo VIII. (Leo wasn't even a clergyman, so they had to ordain him one day and elect him pope the next.) For good measure, Otto got Leo to agree that no pope in the future was to be consecrated until he had sworn loyalty to the emperor.

I am an antipope

Now *two* popes claimed to lead the Church: John XII and Leo VIII. John excommunicated Leo, and said that he was an *antipope* – a sort of antichrist figure – but Otto stood by his man. When John died (in bed with a married woman, or so they say), the Romans tried to elect their own man, a genuinely saintly character called Benedict V, but Otto held a court and condemned Benedict, who showed great dignity during the hearing, especially when Pope Leo broke his papal staff over his head. Round One to the emperor.

Quite often two popes existed at the same time, one real pope and one antipope. Historians list popes and antipopes separately, but it wasn't so clear cut at the time, and both the Romans and the emperors supported popes that historians have listed as antipopes.

Some of these popes were genuinely pious; some weren't, like the antipope Boniface VII, who had the emperor's representative strangled (and got a priest to do it for him!) or Gregory V, who had the antipope John XVI blinded and driven through the streets sitting back to front on a donkey, with his nose, tongue, and hands cut off. Emperor Otto III took up residence in Rome so he could dethrone the Pope if necessary; emperor Henry III overturned two. Round Two to the emperor? Not so fast.

The Pope's new friends

In 1016, the Normans landed in Sicily and southern Italy, found that they liked being there, and decided to stay. They also agreed to help Pope Nicholas II to keep the emperor's grubby hands out of future papal elections. In 1073 the cardinals elected a new pope called Hildebrand, who became Pope Gregory VII and they didn't bother checking it with the emperor Henry IV. Round Two to the pope.

Gregory versus Henry: The Investiture Contest

Pope Gregory VII wanted to make a few changes in the Church. Specifically:

- ✔ No more married priests (Gregory thought that priests were to concentrate on their spiritual role and not have to worry about whose turn it was to put the bins out)

- ✔ No more bishops buying their way into office (this was called *simony*)

✔ No bishops were to be appointed by laymen (kings or emperors)

✔ All new bishops were to travel to Rome to receive the *pallium* (a bishop's ceremonial scarf) from the pope himself, and not from the emperor.

'Oh yes,' said Gregory VII, 'about the emperor. That reminds me:

✔ Popes are superior to kings (and emperors) and can depose them.'

The history books call the rivalry between Gregory and Henry the *Investiture Contest*, because the quarrel was about who had the right to invest – appoint – bishops, but it was also a face-off between two very stubborn men. Henry said that Gregory wasn't pope any more, so Gregory excommunicated Henry and said that he wasn't emperor any more.

Unfortunately for Henry, plenty of German princes felt distinctly uncomfortable having an excommunicated emperor. 'You say sorry to Gregory,' they told Henry, threateningly So in January 1077, Henry IV gritted his teeth and set off to see Gregory. 'And say it like you mean it!' the princes shouted after him. Henry found Gregory staying at a little place in the mountains called Canossa. Henry took off all his warm clothes and knelt barefoot in the snow, pleading with Gregory to come out and forgive him, though he looked like he was chewing a wasp at the time. *Three days* Gregory kept Henry waiting in the cold ('Let him freeze', he thought, toasting himself another crumpet by the fire) before he let him in, forgave him, and let him put his socks back on.

For years afterwards, the Germans never forgot or forgave what happened to their emperor at Canossa. 'Never again to Canossa!' was one of the Nazi slogans, explaining partly why they refused to accept the Treaty of Versailles at the end of the First World War (which they saw as another 'Canossa') but also why they didn't listen to religious criticism of their regime.

You may think that Canossa was game set and match to the Pope, but you'd be wrong. In the eyes of most of Europe, the Pope's humiliation of the emperor had gone too far, especially as Gregory immediately seemed to go back on his forgiveness. Gregory started supporting Henry's enemies and declared him excommunicated and deposed all over again. This time even the cardinals were on Henry's side. Henry stormed down to Rome, deposed Gregory, and set his own pope up in his place. Gregory had to flee for the south, where he died.

Russia Gets Religion

The Rus (see Chapter 6 for more on the Rus) still worshipped the old Viking gods like Odin and Thor, who were looking a tad dated now. Had the time come to trade them in for a new religion? The new prince of Rus, Vladimir, decided that the moment had arrived, but which faith was the best one to adopt? Three religions were on offer:

- ✔ Islam
- ✔ Christianity according to Rome
- ✔ Christianity according to Constantinople

Islam was no good as a new religion: you weren't allowed to drink. That left Rome (the universal or 'Catholic' Church) or Constantinople (the proper or 'Orthodox' Church). The Catholic churches didn't sound like anything special, but Constantinople sounded amazing.

'We didn't know if we were in heaven or on earth. We only know that God dwells there among men,' said the reports. 'Okay, Constantinople it is,' said Vladimir. So, Vladimir sent a letter to the Byzantine emperor asking him to send a few missionaries and colouring books for the children, and Russia joined the Greek Orthodox Church. If Vladimir had chosen differently, a lot of European history would have been very different.

Turkish Delight

When the Turks came charging out from central Asia in the 11th century the Arabs didn't know what had hit them. The Turks took Baghdad and in 1071 they took Jerusalem. The Turkish sultan, Alp Arslan, looked for a Christian city to take. He chose Constantinople.

Red Alert in Byzantium. The Emperor Romanus IV Diogenes led his men out in person to fight the Turks, and in 1071, at the Battle of Manzikert, they lost. The Turks took Romanus prisoner and headed for Constantinople. But, the Turks weren't able to get into the city (those walls again), so they simply settled all over Anatolia, which is why the area is called Turkey, to this day.

This situation was serious: Anatolia was where the Byzantines recruited most of their soldiers. Emperor Alexius I Comnenus decided to get help. In 1095, the emperor sent out an SOS to the pope.

The Crusades

The Pope was a Frenchman called Urban II. Urban saw Alexius's request for help as his big chance to make the Papacy the undisputed leader of Christendom. In 1095 Urban crossed the Alps and at Clermont in France in 1095 he preached the second most famous sermon in history. 'All of Christendom must rise up as one to fight the infidel!', said Urban. 'Amen! God wills it!', said the congregation. 'And they must march to – Anatolia?', thought the Byzantine ambassadors. 'Jerusalem!', said the Pope. (Crack of thunder, climax from heavenly choir, pope throws his arms heavenwards, congregation fall to knees, Byzantine ambassadors ask if they can possibly have a brief word . . .)

Urban sympathised with the Byzantines about Anatolia, but Urban was much more interested in who ruled Jerusalem. Recapturing Anatolia would help the Byzantine emperor; recapturing Jerusalem would bring blessings on all Christendom – and it would be an enormous coup for the papacy.

The Crusades (=holy wars, from the French *croix* for cross) spanned a long stretch of history and were led by different groups for different reasons each time, so the following sections offer a handy guide.

1095: The People's Crusade

A visionary (and probably raving mad) character called Peter the Hermit got a huge army of ordinary people together, mainly from France and Germany, who thought that with God's help they could liberate Jerusalem on their own. Just as a starter they massacred of all the Jews they could find. Emperor Alexius sent this rag-taggle army on to Turkish territory before they could do any more damage and the Turks promptly massacred the lot of them.

Live and let live

Jerusalem is a holy city to three religions: Jews, Christians, and Muslims. The Arabs were very tolerant of these other 'religions of the book' and let Christian pilgrims come and go pretty freely. Unfortunately, the Seljuk Turks weren't so tolerant of other faiths (often the way with converts) and they certainly didn't want Christian pilgrims walking all over their property. So Pope Urban did have a point about fighting the infidel at Jerusalem. Whether this point justified what followed is quite a different matter.

Monks with attitude

The Crusaders founded three military orders of monks: the Order of the Hospital of St John, known as the *Knights Hospitaller*; the Order of the Temple of Jerusalem, known as the *Knights Templar*; and a German order, known as the *Teutonic Knights*. These monks carried out the usual duties of prayer and charity, but they were also armed to the teeth.

The Turks hated the military orders with a vengeance and usually executed any of them they captured. After the Crusades, the French King Philip IV got Pope Clement V to close the Templars down. Philip was after their treasure, and he had the leading French Templars, including the Grand Master of the Order, Jacques de Molay, burnt at the stake for everything from treason to heresy and even sodomy. Jacques de Molay, smouldering in more ways than one, uttered a loud curse on Philip and Clement, and guess what? They both died six years later. Spooky.

1095–1099: First Crusade

The 'official' First Crusade was led by a mixture of French knights and the Pope's Norman pals from Sicily. Rather against the odds, the Crusade succeeded. The Crusaders took a string of cities including Edessa and Antioch (where they very conveniently found a piece of the Holy Lance that had pierced Jesus's side on the cross. Now don't spoil everything by saying that it looked just like an old piece of wood) and finally captured Jerusalem.

The Crusaders slaughtered the Muslim population of Antioch (and quite a few Christians as well) and in Jerusalem they massacred all the Jews as well.

Emperor Alexius was horrified at the news of the killings going on ostensibly in his name. To make the situation worse, the Crusaders had no intention of keeping their oath to give him back all the land that they took. Instead, the Crusaders set up four new states in what they called the land of *Outremer* (Over-the-Sea). These states were Antioch, Edessa, Tripoli, and a brand-new Kingdom of Jerusalem.

1146: Second Crusade

The Turks took back Edessa, so Abbot Bernard of Clairvaux preached a rather unnecessary Second Crusade. The Crusade was a fiasco. The Crusaders didn't go to Edessa; they went to Jerusalem, which wasn't actually in any danger, and attacked Damascus, which just happened to be about the only friendly Muslim city in the region. The Crusaders lost.

Very heavy cavalry

A charge of armoured knights was deadly and could decide a battle, *if* (big if) they all kept together. The Turks preferred to use their mounted archers to wear the Crusaders down, though their arrows didn't always penetrate the Crusaders' armour, so knights sometimes ended up walking around with lots of arrows stuck in them.

The Byzantines were more subtle and tried to entice some of the enemy to defect, or else left letters lying around suggesting that some of them already had. Then, when the Byzantines heard the enemy all shouting at each other – 'I knew it; you're a traitor!' 'No, I'm not, you are!' – they sent in their cavalry. The Byzantines also had a terrifying weapon called *Greek Fire*, a highly inflammable mixture of naphtha, nitre, and sulphur, which was fired from a gun or packed into hand grenades. Greek Fire worked a treat against the Arabs. The Arabs pinched the idea and used it against the Crusaders.

The Turks reckoned that if that attack on Damascus was the best the Crusaders could offer, they were easy meat. Turkish leader Nur ed-Din conquered Damascus and Syria and sent the head of Raymond, Count of Antioch, to the Caliph of Baghdad as a present. Then Sultan Saladin utterly destroyed the army of the Crusader states at the Battle of Hattin, in 1187 and captured Jerusalem. Time for a Third Crusade.

1190–1192: Third Crusade

The Third Crusade is the famous one led by King Richard I, 'the Lionheart', of England and King Philip Augustus of France (not forgetting the German emperor Frederick Barbarossa, who fell off his horse and drowned). Richard and Philip Augustus were deeply suspicious of each other; after they took the port of Acre, Philip went home and left Richard on his own. Richard beat Saladin soundly at the Battle of Arsuf – revenge for Hattin – but he didn't have the resources to take Jerusalem and both he and Saladin knew it (and so, of course, did Philip Augustus). Also, Richard was urgently needed at home. So Richard and Saladin signed a truce. Honours more or less even.

1199–1204: Fourth Crusade

The Fourth Crusade was a shambles. A couple of French knights put this Crusade together, but they didn't have enough cash. Prince Alexius of Byzantium offered to pay them handsomely if they helped him overthrow his father, the emperor, but when the Crusaders sent in their bill, Alexius said there must be some mistake, he'd never met these people, and could someone show them the door? Alexius got himself murdered (Byzantine politics was very dangerous) and his successor refused point blank to pay up. By 1204, the Crusaders had had enough of being mucked about so they got their weapons out and destroyed Constantinople – slaughtering the people and burning the city.

Think about that event. Constantinople was the greatest Christian city in Europe. Constantinople had seen off the Huns, the Vikings, and the Turks; now it had been destroyed by Christian knights from the West.

Fifth, Sixth, Seventh, and Eighth Crusades

The Fifth Crusade (1216–1221) was led, rather unusually, by a priest, Cardinal Pelagius. The Crusaders invaded Egypt and took the important port of Damietta for a while. Most of the Crusaders fell in the Nile and drowned.

The Sixth Crusade (1228): The Holy Roman Emperor Frederick II retook Jerusalem by negotiating a deal with the Turks, sensible man, and the Pope, who hated Frederick, said the deal didn't count. Fifteen years later, the Turks took Jerusalem back again.

Finally, in 1248, King Louis IX of France (St Louis), who got himself into the right mood for crusading by buying, ahem, Jesus's crown of thorns from the Byzantine emperor, led the Seventh Crusade (1248–1252) into Egypt, where he took Damietta, lost half his men to plague, and got himself captured.

Louis had another go at crusading in 1270, this time in Tunisia (the Eighth Crusade) and died.

Child catchers

One of the most tragic episodes of the Crusades happened in 1212 in France and Germany, and historians are still not sure quite what to make of it. A boy called Stephen went round France and a lad called Nicholas went round Germany, calling on all children to join them in a great crusade, which would succeed, with God's help, where the grown-ups had failed. Stephen and Nicholas said that God would part the sea for them and they would simply walk over to Jerusalem, which would be liberated by their innocent prayers.

What actually happened was that when the children reached the south coast of France they were sold as slaves by unscrupulous French and Arab dealers and hardly any of them ever got home again. Historians now think that these Crusaders may have been young men rather than children, but they were young enough for their parents to go crazy about what happened to them. Nicholas's neighbours back in Germany turned on his father and lynched him.

By now, the new head honchos in the Muslim world were the Mameluks of Egypt. In 1291, the Mameluks took Acre, the last Christian possession in the Holy Land, and threw all Christians out. The Crusades were over.

The end of the Crusades wasn't the end of the battle for control of Jerusalem. The British retook it from the Turks in 1917 during the First World War, and the future of Jerusalem, the city sacred to three religions, has been a running sore throughout the recent history of Israel and Palestine.

Playing Crusades at Home

If you weren't able to travel east to fight the infidel, there were plenty of people closer to home to go and whack in the name of God, for example:

- **The Cathars:** An engagingly loopy sect in southern France, also known as *Albigensians*, who believed that the world was evil. A fair point. The Cathars murdered a papal legate, so the Pope ordered a Crusade to crush them. The Cathars were burnt at the stake, and then the Inquisition arrived to sniff out any more.

- **The Prussians and Lithuanians:** The Teutonic Knights, back from the Holy Land and at a loose end, decided to launch a Crusade against the Prussians and Lithuanians, Europe's last genuine pagans. In the process, the knights established a considerable empire for themselves along the Baltic coast.

The Nazis saw the Teutonic Knights as bringing (German-style) civilisation to the pagan Slavs; the Russians, on the other hand, saw the Teutonic Knights as western imperialist invaders. Eisenstein's famous film *Alexander Nevsky* is about a hero who saves Russia from the evil clutches of the Teutonic Knights.

Who were the Moors?

The Romans called the sallow-skinned people of north Africa *Mauri* and named their homeland 'Mauretania'. The Mauri were conquered by the Arabs in the seventh century, became Muslim, and then invaded Spain and turned it into an Islamic caliphate (refer to Chapter 5 for more on the Muslim conquest of Spain). The Europeans called all these people 'Moors', just as the Arabs called all Crusaders 'Franks' whatever their nationality. Some of these 'Moors' had black skin, and soon the Europeans began to connect all 'Moors' with black skin. Shakespeare's Othello, the Moor of Venice, is constantly described as a black man, even though that meant he probably wasn't actually of Mauri 'Moorish' stock at all.

✔ **The Moors:** Moorish Spain was a highly developed culture which let Christians practise their religion largely unmolested, but the Christian kings still launched what was known as the *Reconquistá* (Reconquest). Toledo, the old capital of Spain, fell in 1085, and in 1212 King Alfonso VIII of Castile finally broke the Moors at the Battle of Las Navas de Tolosa. By the 13th century the Moors were left with just the Emirate of Granada in the south and those Spanish eyes were firmly fixed on it.

Too Much Power to the Pope

Pope Innocent III (1198–1216) launched two crusades, excommunicated the Holy Roman Emperor Otto IV and King John of England, decided who was going to be king of Bulgaria, tried to decide who ought to be Holy Roman Emperor (not, he thought, Otto IV), declared England's Magna Carta null and void, and took special charge over the Spanish kingdom of Aragon, Portugal, and Poland.

A lot of kings thought that the papacy needed its wings trimmed. In 1303, King Philip IV of France even sent men to arrest Pope Boniface VIII, which infuriated the Italians, who regarded the Pope as *their* leader. The relationship between the French and the Italians had become so bad that in 1309 the French pope, Clement V, decided to leave Rome altogether to go to live in France. Clement settled in Avignon. Over the next 68 years there were seven popes, all French, and they all lived in Avignon.

Living at Avignon was very nice (and it still is) but even French popes knew that they really ought to be in Rome. However, when the popes went back to Rome in 1377, the fun really started. The following year, the cardinals elected an Italian pope, Urban VI, who appeared to be mad. The French cardinals decided to elect their own pope, resulting in two popes, one Italian and one French, each saying that he was the real pope and the other one was the antipope. This situation was known as the *Great Schism*.

The Great Schism was great fun for all the kings and emperors, because they played these popes off against each other, but everyone agreed it was getting a bit silly. So in 1414, the Holy Roman Emperor took charge; he held a big council of the whole Church – with him in the chair – declared all three (yes, three!) popes overturned and got the cardinals to agree on one single pope, called Martin V. Martin wasn't one of history's great popes, but hey, who was counting?

The German Emperors Fancy Ruling Somewhere Warm

A tough character was needed to control the 400-odd German states, and Frederick 'Barbarossa' ('Red beard') (1123–1190) of the house of Hohenstaufen was as tough as they come. Frederick crushed all opposition in Germany, but he also wanted to control Italy. The popes hated Frederick and his family – 'that viper-breed', as they called the Hohenstaufens – and some very broad grins appeared in the Vatican when they heard that he'd fallen in a river and drowned during the Third Crusade.

Frederick II (1194–1250) was a fighter with a great interest in learning, known as *stupor mundi*, the Wonder of the World. He gathered Jewish and Muslim scholars at his court in Sicily (the Pope took a very dim view of that action) and founded the University of Naples. Frederick II negotiated a deal with the Turks, which got Jerusalem opened to the Christians and made him king of Jerusalem, but the Pope just thought he was keeping in with his Muslim friends and refused to recognise his title.

Eventually, the strain of fighting the Pope for control of Italy while also trying to keep the princes of Germany under control proved too much even for the Hohenstaufens. The family began to lose power to an up-and-coming family from Austria – the Habsburgs.

- ✔ **1266:** Manfred, the last of the Hohenstaufens, loses the Battle of Benevento to the Pope's French champion, Charles of Anjou. That event signifies the end of the German Empire in Italy.

- ✔ **1356:** Emperor Charles IV issues his 'Golden Bull' setting out the rules for governing the Holy Roman Empire. Seven leading princes are to be the 'electors' who choose the emperor. The electors then just choose Charles IV's family.

- ✔ **1438:** The electors choose Albrecht II of the Austrian Habsburg family. The title stays in the Habsburg family until the empire ends in 1806.

- ✔ **1477:** The Habsburgs marry into the very wealthy Ducal family of Burgundy and their fortune is made.

Vespers in Sicily

While all the fighting was going on between the Hohenstaufens and the popes (see preceding section), the Italians split into two groups: *Guelphs*, who supported the popes, and *Ghibbelines*, who supported the emperor. Despite this division, most Italians were only too pleased to see the back of the Hohenstaufens – they just weren't so sure about what they got instead.

What the Italians got was Charles of Anjou, the highly ambitious brother of the king of France. Charles took over southern Italy, and then he took over northern Italy, and it looked as if he might take over Rome itself – when he was suddenly stopped. At Easter 1282, at vespers, the people of Palermo rose up and murdered every Frenchman they could find.

The *Sicilian Vespers* is still remembered as an awful warning of what happens when rulers forget the people. (Sicilian Vespas, on the other hand, are rather different.)

Just Who's in Charge in France?

The kings of France were called *Capetians*, after Hugues Capet who became king back in 987, but they never really controlled the whole country. Whole regions of France, including Brittany, Burgundy, Provence, and Languedoc, were effectively independent of the Crown. Henry Plantagenet, Count of Anjou, even became King Henry II of England in 1154, which meant that a huge area of western France came under the English Crown. So the Capetians spent much of their time fighting against their own nobles or trying to take land off the Plantagenet kings of England. The master at this game was Philip Augustus, who outfoxed the English King John (and that took some doing) and took back nearly all the Plantagenet lands after the Battle of Bouvines in 1214.

A few more highlights from France:

- **1285–1314:** Philip IV 'the Fair' expels France's Jews and suppresses the Knights Templar; arrests pope; gets papacy moved to Avignon; and executes two knights for having affairs with his daughters-in-law (call it two nights of passion!).

- **1337:** Edward III of England claims the throne of France, and starts the 'Hundred Years' War' between England and France.

- **1364–1380:** Bertrand du Guesclin, Constable of France, fights a heroic guerrilla war against the English and takes most of France back.

- **1380:** Charles VI 'the Mad' comes to the throne, convinced that he is made of glass (he must've been cracked). In 1415, Henry V of England defeats the French at Agincourt and becomes heir to the French throne. The Duke of Burgundy backs the English; the Dauphin, Charles VI's son and the real heir to the throne, sulks.

- **1422:** Both Henry V and Charles VI die. Officially, the new king is Henry's son, Henry VI, but he is only a baby. The Dauphin plucks up courage and claims the throne for himself, and immediately wishes he hadn't because the English trounce him and besiege his men in Orléans. Dauphin prays for a miracle.

Joan of Arc

Joan was a teenager in the village of Domrémy when she first claimed she heard voices and had a vision of St Michael the Archangel, St Catherine, and St Margaret who all told her to drop what she was doing and go to save France. When she went to meet the Dauphin, he tried to trick her by disguising himself as a courtier but she identified him, which helped convince everyone that she had God on her side. Joan stood next to the Dauphin when he was crowned King Charles VII in Reims Cathedral; however, the voices in her head had told her she wouldn't live long after the coronation. Sure enough, almost immediately things started to go wrong – Joan's big attack to liberate Paris failed and she began to make enemies at court. When the Burgundians caught her, many people at the French court were pleased to see the back of her.

Her trial was run by a French bishop, the Bishop of Beauvais. The court was particularly shocked that Joan insisted on cutting her hair short and dressing like a man. At one point she recanted – said her visions were false – and agreed to go back to skirts, but then she changed her mind, recanted her recantation, and put her trousers on again. That meant that she had rejected the Church's mercy and could be burnt at the stake.

In 1920, Joan of Arc was declared a saint. The French adopted Joan as their national patron, and the Vichy government, who collaborated with the Nazis, used Joan's image to harden people's opinions against the English (see Chapter 23 for more on Vichy).

✔ **1429:** Miracle arrives in the form of a peasant girl called Jeanne d'Arc ('Joan of Arc' in English) who tells the Dauphin she has a mission from God to drive the English out of France and put him on the throne. Joan beats the English at Orléans and just about everywhere else. Dauphin is finally convinced when Joan has him crowned King Charles VII, in Reims Cathedral.

✔ **1431:** Joan is captured by the Burgundians (who are on the English side, remember) and burnt as a witch. Charles VII does nothing to help her. By the time Charles VII dies in 1461 the English only hold Calais.

A Sunset in the East: The Ottoman Turks

The French and the Germans and the English and the Italians might have kept slugging it out, but one power seemed unstoppable – the Ottoman Turks. The Ottoman Turks took their name from their founder, Osman I, and they were committed to Islamic *jihad* (holy war). The Ottomans looked down at the once-mighty Byzantine Empire and decided it was well past its sell-by date. The Ottoman Turks didn't go straight for Constantinople – for one thing the walls were a problem, and for another the Turks were briefly defeated by the even more terrible Mongols of Tamurlaine the Great. But the Turks crossed into Europe and crushed the Serbs, who had only just declared independence from the Byzantine Empire, at the Battle of Kosovo in 1389.

By 1453 Sultan Mehmet II 'the Conqueror' was ready to turn on Constantinople. The Byzantines appealed desperately to Christian western Europe for help. The westerners, however, weren't interested; they didn't think the Orthodox Church was really Christian, anyway. The Ottoman Turks sailed across the Golden Horn, broke into the city, and finally destroyed all that was left of the Roman Empire.

Chapter 8

Don't Call Us Medieval!

The Middle Ages have always had an image problem – even the name was originally an insult by later historians. People use the term to mean barbaric, as if you could hardly walk down a medieval street without seeing a witch being burnt or someone being tortured by the Inquisition. But it was in the Middle Ages that Europeans achieved some of their most breathtaking advances in art and architecture and set in place much of the thinking and many of the ideas we still rely on today. This period was the age of the great cathedrals and theologians, after all. The Middle Ages were also when medieval people had to face up to probably the single most devastating natural disaster since the ice age: the Black Death.

Why the Term 'Middle Ages'?

No one at the time talked of living in the Middle Ages! This term only came into use much later, during the Renaissance (another term no one used at the time). Renaissance scholars were great admirers of the writers and artists of the ancient world, and they used to refer rather scornfully to the time in-between as 'medieval', rather as scholars used to talk about the 'Dark Ages', or everyone used to sneer at 'Victorian' things when they went out of fashion. The Middle Ages meant the time between the times that mattered.

We're All Doomed! Religion

Medieval people had a very strong sense of God and of their own mortality. Every time these people went to church they saw paintings or stained glass windows reminding them of the Day of Judgement, and this image was a powerful incentive to them to sort out their own relationship with their Maker. So what exactly did medieval people believe in?

In a nutshell, thanks to Adam and Eve disobeying God in the Garden of Eden (well, thanks to Eve really), we are all of us damned:

- ✔ We're all going to die.
- ✔ We've all sinned (even newborn babies – blame Eve) so we're going to burn in hell unless we accept salvation from the Church.

And, just in case you thought that you hadn't sinned *that* much, at least not so's you'd notice, the Devil and his imps and demons are lurking around every corner to tempt you into more sin and even more sin until your soul looks like an old boot, which will condemn you to the fiery furnace for eternity. Can nothing be done to save us from hell? Yes, it can. The Church is here to do the saving.

Amazing grace

The medieval approach to religion was like balancing a budget. In the debit column you amassed lots of sin that put you ever deeper in debt in the heavenly bank. What you needed was 'grace' to put in the credit column so you could be in the black by the time you had to present your account on Judgement Day. You got grace from the Church.

You could do all sorts of different things to get grace. Some tasks were small, like helping your mum make the beds, and others were much bigger (and, therefore, worth more grace), like going on a pilgrimage or, better still, a crusade. Going to Mass, receiving communion, or doing a bit of charity work all earned grace. That way, when the great day came and the recording angel looked over your books, he'd see you were in credit and send you straight up to heaven in time for tea; whereas if you were still in the red, you'd expect the fires of hell and no supper.

Pilgrims progress

The idea of a pilgrimage was to travel to a place with a special shrine – a saint's tomb, say, or the site of a vision – and the whole journey would be a spiritual experience, like a particularly deep and meaningful road movie. Going on a pilgrimage would earn you grace and get you time off from the fires of purgatory after you died, which is not available from a Club 18–30 holiday.

Each shrine had its own badge emblem for you to collect and wear in your hat, like scout badges, though getting caught by two medieval anoraks discussing the merits of alternative pilgrim routes wasn't a good idea. The ultimate pilgrimage, the one you built up to in easy stages, was the one to the Holy Land, but with the Turks running the place many pilgrims opted for the next best thing, the great shrine of St James the Apostle at Compostela, in northern Spain.

No convincing evidence exists to suggest that St James ever went anywhere near Spain, not even on holiday, but the story went the rounds very early on and soon became accepted. The Spanish adopted St James – Santiago in Spanish – as a patron saint of the reconquest of Spain from the Moors. Later, they adopted Santiago as the patron saint of another 'crusade' – the conquest of America.

Any self-respecting cathedral had a set of splendid gold and silver cases housing a collection of holy relics. Top banana were relics of Jesus himself. So many bits of the True Cross were knocking around that people said that you could reconstruct it twice over. People believed that holy relics could work miracles, and would swear their most solemn oaths over them. (Don't smile too much – people who believe in *feng shui* are in no position to feel superior.)

The crucial point in the medieval view of religion was that most of these grace-bearing acts could only be done through the church, so if you were ever to get to heaven, having a church handy became essential.

A monastic life for me!

A number of reformed monastic orders cropped up in France, including these three influential movements:

- ✔ **Cluniacs:** The Abbey of Cluny in Burgundy led a big reform movement with strict rules for the monks, and set up a huge network of Cluniac abbeys all over Europe. Cluniac monks often proved very able administrators, which kings tended to approve of, and they were independent of bishops, which kings liked even more.

Take a chant on me

Monks and nuns may have led rather enclosed lives, but they started Europe's music industry. Every day they would sing their *plainsong* chants, using a notation system first worked out by Pope Gregory the Great; and known, therefore, as a Gregorian Chant. The idea was to let the chant emphasise the rhythm of the words rather than to come up with anything you could hum as you came out of church. The original idea came from the Byzantines, and you can still hear a similarity between western plainsong and the liturgical chants of the Orthodox churches to this day.

The monks also borrowed a Jewish practice of having two separate choirs tossing the lines between them like a singing dialogue, which is why church choirs are still often divided in two and sit facing each other. Then, someone had the idea of having two tunes going at once, if you were able to work out how to make them sound right (medieval music sounds a bit empty to our ears because they hadn't mastered the major third – the note in the middle that makes a chord sound nice), and before long they were writing music on four-line staves and paving the way for harmony.

✔ **Carthusians:** Founded at Chartreuse in 1084 by St Bruno of Cologne, Carthusians lived in separate one-up-one-down cells within their monasteries in silence and contemplation. Carthusians also produced books rather well (and probably passed each other little notes).

✔ **Cistercians:** Founded at Cîteaux in 1098 by St Bernard of Clairvaux, who also preached the Second Crusade, the Cistercians went for tighter control and more uniformity, which gave them the strength to stand up to rulers when need be. The Cistercians refused point blank to recognise any of emperor Frederick Barbarossa's three antipopes (refer to Chapter 7), and only a brave man would tell *him* where to go.

The only trouble with all these monastic orders was that they tended to cut themselves off from the world. The abbeys were all built in remote valleys or on inaccessible hillsides, and once monks went in, they didn't usually come out. If you fancied a more hands-on approach, you could always try:

✔ **Franciscans:** Named after St Francis of Assisi, the soldier son of a rich Italian merchant who just wasn't able to understand why his son decided to renounce the world and live as a tramp. Francis started the first *friars* – monks who came out of the monastery and worked directly with the poor. People told all sorts of tales about Francis: The famous one about him making friends with the animals was probably designed to stress his sense of simple, unsophisticated spirituality. Francis is also said to have received the *stigmata* – a special sign of holiness where your hands, feet, and side bleed in exactly the places where the nails and spear went into Jesus.

What about nuns?

Although we use 'monastery' to mean a community of men and 'convent' for a community of women, in the early days both terms were used for communities of either sex. St Benedict, founder of the Benedictines, had a sister called St Scholastica who was in charge of a nunnery near Benedict's famous monastery at Monte Cassino, and brother and sister used to meet up once a year to discuss spiritual matters and settle whose turn it was to write to mother.

Some holy women became famous mystics. The 12th-century St Hildegard of Bingen set up a Benedictine nunnery at Rupertsburg on the Rhine and became celebrated for her denunciations of vice and her visions of doom. Hildegard wrote theology and a life of St Benedict, as well as poetry, drama, and books on natural history and medicine. Hildegard was also an accomplished artist and musician.

Another German mystic was St Gertrude the Great, who lived in the 13th century. She became famous for going into ecstasy and having visions in the middle of Mass, which must have done wonders for attendance figures.

✔ **Dominicans (Order of Preachers):** St Dominic Guzmán was a Spaniard, who enjoyed a good debate, and he had a powerful sense of the need to spread the word of God. Dominic decided to set up a special order of preaching friars to travel around and face down heretics or infidels in open debate, showing the world the truth of the gospel. These Dominicans or Black Friars (because they wore black), tended to be well educated and impressive intellectuals; they were also tailor-made for running the Inquisition.

✔ **Augustinians:** Very popular monks who lived according to a rule derived from the writings of St Augustine of Hippo (you can find out more about this charismatic doctor of the early Church in Chapter 5). The Augustinians ran schools and hospitals and made important advances in learning. St Norbert, Archbishop of Magdeburg, founded a rather austere group of Augustinians named Premonstratensians, after their first base in the French town of Prémontré, and helped to spread the order into eastern Europe. Augustinians tended to be more open to debating new ideas than some of the other orders. Martin Luther, the monk who set the Reformation going, was an Augustinian (see Chapter 10 to find out more about his impact on Europe).

University Challenge

Historians get very excited about the 12th century (1100s) and even talk about a 12th-century renaissance. Europe's oldest universities – Bologna, Paris, and Oxford – were all founded in the 12th century (later Bologna and Paris both closed and had to be refounded, which makes Oxford the oldest continually-running university in the world). Student unions or graduation days did not exist, though. A university was a community of scholars, usually gathered around a handful of masters who lectured on the classical texts. These universities were monastic foundations, where the lecturers were usually friars and students were made aware that learning was all aimed at gaining an understanding of at least a tiny part of the mind of God.

Nowadays, university graduates still wear gowns, hoods, and academic caps derived from the monastic dress of the medieval lecturers. The monks took vows of poverty, chastity, and obedience. Modern students are still poor, and there's no reason why they can't be chaste and obedient as well.

The idea of a university was to study the nature of God's creation, which might encompass the heavens, the principles of mathematics, or the structure of the body. This sort of natural science was also known as natural philosophy – scholars didn't make the same rigid distinctions between subjects that we do today. Students were expected to study the Bible and the fathers of the early Church, and to debate them in public (and in Latin), but they also studied the works of the great classical writers from Greece and Rome, especially Aristotle, whose works had been translated into Latin and were proving very popular. This way of learning from the ancients was known as *scholasticism*.

Medieval universities drew up of the basic principles of law. The Church was also developing its own codes of law, known as *canon law,* thanks to a Benedictine monk called Gratian, so plenty of work was available for able law graduates (there always is).

Scholarly inquiry

Medieval scholars were surprisingly open to ideas from other cultures. These scholars introduced Arabic numbers from the Muslim world, which were much easier than Roman ones because they used 0. (Try doing even basic arithmetic in Roman numerals, and you'll soon see why scholars adopted Arabic ones instead.)

The things we do for love

When he was lecturing in Paris, Peter Abelard tutored the beautiful young Héloïse, niece of canon Fulbert of Notre Dame. Well, Peter and Héloïse fell in love and eloped and one thing led to another, and when the baby was born – it was a boy – they married. Now, Peter could either be a top-flight theologian at the University of Paris or he could be a doting dad – not both. So to save Peter's career, Héloïse stoutly denied that they were married. Doing so meant that both Peter and Héloïse had to go into separate monasteries (which was alright for Peter, because he continued his work, but wasn't much fun for Héloïse). Don't think Peter got off lightly, however – Canon Fulbert had him castrated.

However, when the great French scholar Peter Abelard pointed out contradictions in the Bible and argued that a sin might sometimes not be a sin if the sinner meant well, he got himself accused of heresy, by St Bernard of Clairvaux, no less.

When they weren't scratching their heads over Roman sums or castrating eminent theologians (see the nearby sidebar, 'The things we do for love'), medieval scholars were arguing the toss between the two leading religious thinkers of the age, the Italian Dominican Thomas Aquinas and the Scottish Franciscan Duns Scotus. The gist of their differences was:

- ✔ **Thomas Aquinas, the 'Angelic Doctor'** used the ideas of Aristotle to support the mysteries of Christianity against Muslim and Jewish objections; he argued that you could deduce the existence of God by observing the natural world. To the delight of his followers, known as *Thomists*, Aquinas's great work, the *Summa Theologica*, became a standard church textbook, telling you all you'll ever need to know about Christian doctrine.

- ✔ **John Duns Scotus, the 'Subtle Doctor'** believed that having faith was not just an intellectual exercise but a positive act of will – something you went out and acted on. Duns Scotus thought that Aquinas was too taken up with theory and ought to get out more.

The Dominicans and Franciscans argued for years, each supporting their boy against the other. Aquinas won in the short term, and his ideas were adopted by the Church and are still the basis of Catholicism today. But Duns Scotus's ideas echo some of the criticism of the Catholic Church that later reformers would make, and which would lead to the Reformation (head to Chapter 10 for the low-down on that period).

Corpus Christi Carnival

In 1263 a priest reported that as he was saying Mass he had seen blood coming out of the bread and the wine. Some people thought he'd overdone the communion wine, but the Pope decided that this was a splendid opportunity to institute a new public holiday in the summer dedicated to the Body of Christ (Latin: *Corpus Christi*), and he asked Thomas Aquinas to come up with a suitable liturgy for it. The whole plan proved a big hit: All over Europe people staged colourful processions and fairs, as they carried the host (the bread representing Christ's body) through the streets.

Corpus Christi is a good reminder of why the Church meant so much to people in the Middle Ages. This festival wasn't just about serious-minded monks debating the Bible. This festival was about giving ordinary people a chance to have a bit of fun with just a touch of mystery added in.

The Great Cathedrals

Easily the most impressive buildings the Middle Ages produced are those great cathedrals with their spires soaring away into the heavens. These cathedrals still have the power to overawe; think what they must have been like for the medieval people who first saw them.

Cathedrals took hundreds of years to build. Sometimes, a church that already existed was extended to form a cathedral, which is why when you visit them today you often see ground plans with different periods in different colours. The cathedral in Aix en Provence has got the parts from different periods all in a line next to each other, so you start with the Merovingian section on the right, and move to your left, going through the Romanesque, the Gothic, the baroque, and the gift shop.

Cathedrals took hundreds of years to build because they were meant to reflect the eternal nature of God, and you couldn't convey that in a building which would be up and ready in a matter of months. The money for these Cathedrals came from rich patrons, who gave generously in the hope that it would count in their favour on the Day of Judgement. Patrons often insisted on having their emblems or coat of arms worked into the decoration of the building, and sometimes they were painted into pictures of biblical scenes, showing the patrons present at the Nativity or the Sermon on the Mount. Accuracy wasn't important, as all that mattered was that everyone should know who had put up the money.

The building itself was in the form of a cross, facing east, toward Jerusalem. Bible stories were carved onto the doors or painted in glass in the windows. Don't forget that glass was extremely expensive, and even quite rich people couldn't afford it, so to see a beautiful rose window high in a cathedral gave people a sense that they were looking into heaven itself. The patterns were carefully designed to show the pattern of life: circular, showing that we come from God and go back to God, or with twists to illustrate the pitfalls and traps along the way to heaven.

Modern visitors can work out the symbolism from a guidebook, but remember that the people who originally saw these pictures and patterns had to work out their meanings for themselves. Churches and cathedrals weren't just buildings – they were prayers and meditations in stone.

Originally, the builders more or less copied the Romans' style of building using rounded arches, which are good and sturdy but need a lot of space. On the continent, this style of architecture is known as *Romanesque*, though in England, the term 'Norman' is usually used because it came over with the Normans.

But then, engineers discovered that with a pointed arch you could span different widths much more easily, and that with flying buttresses you can prop walls up, like bookends. Now builders built walls which were virtually all glass and filled the cathedral with light. This style of building became known as *Gothic*.

Abbot Suger of St Denis, north of Paris, is normally credited with creating the first Gothic cathedral in Europe. He wanted it to have a great soaring central nave with a high altar for the really big occasions, and lots of side chapels, with masses being said continually throughout the week, so you could always pop in and catch one. Cathedrals were full of visitors or pilgrims (and cathedral guides to show them round), beggars, people selling candles or pilgrim badges, people conducting church business, the cathedral choir practising, not to mention builders installing the latest style of arch. People often get annoyed with the streams of tourists traipsing through Europe's great cathedrals, but in the Middle Ages they were even noisier.

Castles, Chivalry, and Knights

All those dark, ruined castles you can see now were colourful places in the Middle Ages – with rich tapestries and carpets hanging on the walls to keep the heat in and next door's noise out – and they were teeming with people. A castle took a lot of managing; lords (and ladies) of castles had to recruit and train guards, collect rents, keep accounts, write letters, order food and clothes, ensure beds were made, and so on. A well-run castle needed a lot of people and a lot of rooms: store rooms, guard rooms, offices, strong rooms, bedrooms and dormitories, usually a chapel, and certainly stables. Above all, the lord of a castle needed a great hall, where everybody ate (and, therefore, a big kitchen not too far away), where the lord received guests, and which his servants could clear quickly and turn into a courtroom for the lord to hear cases. Think of a cross between a barracks and a small but animated town, and you've got the measure of a medieval castle.

The central tower of a castle was known in English as the *keep* and in French as the *donjon*. We get the word 'dungeon' from *donjon*, but if you're thinking in terms of dripping walls with prisoners hanging on them, think again. Most prisoners were fined; the cellars of the *donjon* were only used as a short-term lock-up until the lord of the castle got round to hearing the case.

Knights in shining armour

Knights were the heavy cavalry of the Middle Ages, but being a knight implied a lot more than that. The role meant that you kept to certain codes of behaviour, both on and off the battlefield, that you treated people with courtesy and politeness, that you ate nicely and didn't pick your teeth at table, that you upheld the right and defended the weak – in short, that you were the soul of *chivalry*.

Arthur's song

The tales of King Arthur – the Arthurian legend – were *the* big stories of the Middle Ages. We tend to think of these stories as English because Arthur was king of Britain, but in fact troubadours sang them all over Europe (no paperbacks in those days, and most people couldn't read anyway). The Knights of the Round Table represented an ideal of courageous knighthood that everyone aspired to, and many of the best-known aspects of medieval chivalry have their origins in the Arthurian legend.

The most perfect knight was Sir Galahad, who was so impossibly good that he was allowed to see the holy grail; most people probably identified more with Sir Lancelot, who was equally brave and noble but also managed to have an affair with the queen.

The idea of a quest to find the holy grail was a metaphor for devoting your life to seeking God. Nowadays, the grail is just an excuse for conspiracy theorists to sell books.

Becoming a knight was a serious business. You started as a child, working in a knight's household as a page (helmet-carrier and general dogs-body). When you got older, you became a squire (knight's assistant and trainee) until you were ready to be dubbed a knight. Any knight was able to dub someone else a knight, but it wise to be picky – you always got more respect if you'd been dubbed by someone with a bit of prestige.

The ceremony was like joining a religious order. First you had to show that you were brave in arms and leading a virtuous life (or at least that no one could prove that you weren't). Then, you kept vigil all night in church, praying for God's help. Next, you took a ritual bath to make you pure, until you were deemed ready to put on the ceremonial robes – white for purity, red for blood – and receive your knightly sword. (Later on, when knights had their own swords the king or whoever was dubbing them just touched them with it.) Arise, Sir Knight!

If you were really lucky, you might get to join one of the Orders of Chivalry, like the English Order of the Garter or the Burgundian Order of the Golden Fleece. The Burgundian Order was the most prestigious; unfortunately, joining it meant that you had to wear a gold chain with a dead sheep on it round your neck.

Is this a war? No, it's the regional semi-final

Tournaments were a rehearsal for war, but you are forgiven for not realising the difference.

Every knight for miles around turned up, armed to the teeth. The knights just met in the middle in a giant mêlée and knocked the stuffing out of each other (except people thought it rather unsporting to shoot the other team with a crossbow). In 1241, more than 80 knights died in a tournament in Neuss in Germany, mostly by getting knocked over and suffocating in their armour.

Pope after pope tried to ban tournaments and the papacy even decreed that if you got yourself killed in a tournament then you couldn't have a Christian burial, and serve you right. Eventually, even the knights decided that taking a few precautions might be sensible, so they began using blunted weapons and introducing a few rules. Tournaments began to lay more and more emphasis on something else that knights enjoyed – single combat.

Coming up next – jousting from Hicksted

The knights enjoyed jousting, because it gave them a chance to be like the Knights of the Round Table, who went through the forest jousting at anything that moved. Single combat was good practice and required a lot of skill. If you think riding a horse at full gallop in heavy armour, balancing a long lance in one hand and a shield in the other while another knight tries to knock you into the middle of next week is easy, then you clearly haven't tried it. If you knocked your opponent off, you often got to keep his horse (and if you killed him you could have his room). Jousting made a much better spectator sport than a tournament. Strict rules applied and the action occurred in special fields called *tiltyards*. More importantly, jousting was a splendid chance to show off in front of the ladies.

Don't ring us, Sir Knight, we'll ring you

Troubadours were romantic young men, often of very good family, who went round from castle to castle singing of their love for some unattainable lady and generally driving the neighbours mad. Sighing with passion for a married lady and singing about it was quite acceptable, as long as that was as far as it went. Being a troubadour was more a phase you went through than a career choice, rather like busking.

Duke William IX of Aquitaine was one of the most famous troubadours. William sighed and sang about his mistress; he painted her face on his shield, saying he would bear her in battle as she had borne him in bed – there are some things you feel you just don't need to know, aren't there?

On the castle catwalk

If you've ever been caught wearing a bad colour combination, spare a thought for the fashion-policed Middle Ages. Strict rules existed about which colours and materials you were *allowed* to wear. Bright colours were strictly nobles only. Peasants had to make do with rough homespun in a riot of brown. Rich cloths like velvet were reserved for the ruling classes, too, though the price probably did the job on its own. But even nobles got in trouble for wearing purple, which had been the colour of the Roman emperors and was reserved for royalty or bishops.

In the later Middle Ages, men went in for power dressing: padded tops and skin-tight leggings to give that triangular shape the ladies go for. A slash effect was even cultivated to make men look as though they'd just that moment come in from single combat – the last time slashed clothes were to be fashionable until the advent of ripped jeans. Men also liked to show off their nether regions. By the 15th century so many tight leggings and prominent cod pieces were on display that the poor ladies can't have known where to look. Or, maybe, where to begin.

And looking demurely at the ground was no good either. Long, tapered shoes were supposed to be an indication of the size of their wearer's manhood. If you really wanted to show off, you stuffed the ends of your long shoes with sawdust and made them stand up. Hence the medieval chat-up line: Is that a bunion on your foot or are you just pleased to see me?

Heraldry

As knights got a taste for regular weekends bludgeoning each other, armourers very sensibly started designing bigger helmets, until a knight's face was completely obscured, which was good from the safety angle but made it impossible to recognise who was on which side. The only way to tell knights apart was by the decoration on their shields, which meant rules governing that aspect of jousting had to be introduced.

Soon, everyone wanted a coat of arms – knights, towns, churches, merchants, trade guilds – so heraldry developed into a highly complex system, with strict rules (having the same design as someone else was an absolute no-no). Noblewomen had coats of arms, too, so some families developed mind-bogglingly complex coats of arms, showing their own arms and granddad's and the in-laws'. But beware: Changing your coat of arms in the wrong way could mean trouble – you could even be charged with treason.

Some historians think that, being a literate lot, we in the 21st century tend to overstate the importance of books and underestimate just how important all this visual culture of heraldry was in the Middle Ages, when very few people could read or write or saw any reason why they should.

Managing Money – The Medieval Way

The Middle Ages soon put those Arabic numerals to very good use. Some bright spark invented – wait for it – double-entry bookkeeping. Now, okay, maybe this skill won't win you many admiring looks at parties, but double-entry bookkeeping is one of the great inventions of history. For the first time, you were able to keep tabs on your money. Double-entry bookkeeping also facilitated the very first proper banking system, so that you didn't have to travel round with great chests of silver and gold crying out to be stolen. These bankers became very rich (what a surprise) and the Italian banking families went on to become the great patrons of the Italian Renaissance.

The Germans had gone a step further and set up a self-governing trading federation of towns in the Baltic, which they called the *Hanse*, with important outstations known as *Kontors* in Bruges, Bergen, London, and Novgorod. The Hanse did very well trading in candlewax (think how much it takes to light a single cathedral for a week) and in dried cod known as stockfish – the church said you had to eat fish every Friday and all through Lent, so demand was high. The Hanse became so powerful that it started standing up to the rulers of the countries that it traded with, and at one point it even engineered a coup against the king of Denmark. The Germans are still very proud of their Hanseatic heritage, and in cities like Hamburg and Lübeck they still put H for *Hansestadt* (Hanseatic town) in front of their letter on German car number plates.

Perhaps ironically, by sending ships across all the known oceans and linking Europe with the far-off lands of the East, all this trading activity was also responsible for ushering in the single greatest disaster in European history – the Black Death.

The Black Death

Historians still argue over exactly how many people died in the Black Death (1347–1350). Some people put the death toll at around *50 million*, something between a third and a half of the population of Europe. No wonder 14th century art is so full of images of death and the grim reaper.

The Black Death (the name wasn't used till much later, but people would've known what you meant) was an epidemic of bubonic plague carried in the stomachs of the fleas that infested the black rats that were always hanging round people's barns and larders. The plague probably started in China, and came to Europe thanks to some Italian merchants who got caught up in a city in the Crimea which was being besieged by the Mongols.

Outwitted by the Black Death

Medieval medicine was ill-prepared to cope with the Black Death. Some doctors suggested that there must be something foul in the air that the victims were breathing. So, the doctors started recommending that people hold bunches of herbs to their noses to protect themselves from the poisonous miasma in the air. But still people died. The doctors were baffled.

The bubonic plague started with a fever and blotches all over the body, with huge swellings under the armpits known as *buboes* (hence 'bubonic' plague). If the buboes burst you were okay, but if they didn't you were dead in a matter of hours (and bursting them with a knife didn't save you).

Medieval Europe simply couldn't understand what had hit it, especially because they had already had disastrous food shortages thanks to some of the hottest summers and coldest winters of the millennium. Medieval people assumed that God must be punishing them for something, though they weren't sure what. One response was the cult of *flagellants*, who travelled round in groups praying for forgiveness and whipping themselves as a sign of their repentance. Other Christians did the usual thing and blamed the plague on the Jews, resulting in appalling attacks on Jewish communities across Europe during the Black Death.

One effect of the mortality rate was to make living, working peasants suddenly a rarity, and they soon cottoned on. Peasants started demanding more money and better conditions from the lords, and if they didn't get them they'd get nasty. A major peasants' revolt broke out in England in 1348, and ten years later, an even more serious one took place in France. The revolt degenerated into an orgy of killing that the French called a *jacquerie* (from Jacques Bonhomme, the name given to any peasant, like Fred Bloggs or John Doe today). The word *jacquerie* is still used today to indicate a violent uprising of an underclass.

Part IV
New Ideas,
New Worlds

The 5th Wave   By Rich Tennant

"I've arranged for you to have lunch with Leonardo, Your Highness, a scholar and man of extraordinary abilities."

In this part . . .

Europeans really discovered the world in the 16th and 17th centuries – and the world discovered Europeans. Mariners such as Columbus and Vasco da Gama, sailed the world's oceans and sent back excited tales of the lands they encountered. Other Europeans, excited at the idea of adventure, Christian mission, or (usually) the chance of making a fortune, set off in their wake and spread European ideas and influence, not to mention military power, political domination, and disease, all over the globe.

But this was also the age when Europeans grew to understand the world in a deeper sense, exploring the natural world and learning through careful observation the rules that governed it. This deep exploration meant that, like it or not (and many Europeans didn't like it one bit), they were also delving in the mind and intentions of God. And exactly how best to understand God was something that divided Europeans dangerously. This part explores a period of growing knowledge and understanding, but the 16th and 17th centuries also brought devastating religious civil war, the persecution of witches, and organised state intolerance.

Chapter 9

Back to the Future: The Renaissance

. . . .

In This Chapter

▶ Introducing the Italian city states

▶ Reading about Renaissance scholars and artists

▶ Witnessing wars in Italy, and the end of Muslim Spain

. . . .

*A*19th-century Swiss historian called Jacob Burckhardt coined the term 'Renaissance' (rebirth) for the big changes in thinking and the arts which took place in Europe in the 15th and 16th centuries. The rebirth in question was of the world of the ancients, the Romans, and especially the Greeks. The writings and ideas of these civilizations seemed to offer meanings which were applied to every aspect of life – education, music, politics, painting, religion, even falling in love. Renaissance scholars called this new learning *humanism* – everything you'll ever need to know about being human. You'd never know it from the clothes, but this period was when the modern age began. We are looking at an early photograph of us.

Small City States – Beautiful but Very Vulnerable

The Renaissance story starts in Italy. The Italians had set up lots of separate states based around individual cities, such as Florence, Venice, Milan, and Pisa. City states were small enough to be run along proper republican lines, where everyone – well okay, some of the richer men – was able to have a say in making decisions, just like in ancient Greece. These city states didn't have huge resources of manpower to draw on, but they did have the next best thing: money.

Fifteenth-century Italy was *the* place to be if you were a mercenary, or *condottiere* as the Italians called them. Some enterprising condottiere simply took over states like Milan, Mantua, and Ferrara. Condottiere were not to be messed with. Duke Galeazza of Milan was a James Bond-type villain, very well spoken and obsessed with how beautiful his hands were, but cruel and sadistic; he enjoyed humiliating prisoners by making them eat excrement. (Galeazza was stabbed to death as he was coming out of church, you'll be pleased to hear.)

Some city states, such as Parma or Genoa, were fairly small; others were a bit bigger and weightier. The main city states were:

- **Florence:** Florence was ruled by a small elite group of feuding families called the *signoria*. The signoria expelled the up-and-coming banker Cosimo de Medici in 1433, but he came back the next year and took the city over himself. The Medici were popular, but they had powerful enemies.

- **Milan:** Milan had been a republic, but it had been taken over by a dynasty of condottiere, the Visconti family. When they died out, another condottiere dynasty, the Sforza family, replaced them.

- **Pisa:** Pisa was an important port, always wary of being taken over by Florence. The Pisans also very much wanted a word with the surveyor regarding their bell tower, but according to his secretary he was always in a meeting.

- **Rome:** Ruled by the papacy. Pope Sixtus IV appointed his own relatives cardinals and bishops so blatantly that it gave nepotism a bad name; Innocent VIII made his 13-year-old grandson a cardinal; Alexander VI fathered a string of illegitimate children and tried for years to get hold of the Romagna region for his son Cesare; Julius II went to war with Venice and led his troops in person, in a special papal suit of armour. These successors to St Peter had moved a long way away from the message of the gospels.

- **Naples:** Naples was ruled by King Ferrante, an appalling character, who ruled by terror and had his enemies embalmed after execution as a keepsake. The Neapolitan nobles were always plotting against Ferrante, and no wonder.

- **Genoa:** An important seaport, increasingly eclipsed by Venice.

- **Venice:** Venice was known as *la Serenissima*, the Serene Republic – serene, but wet. Venice was a major trading centre for the Adriatic and eastern Mediterranean, and very jealous of its independence. The city fathers elected a prince called a Doge, who had to wear a very silly hat and go through an annual marriage ceremony with the sea. More importantly, the Venetians made sure the Doge had virtually no power. The other Italians tended not to like Venice very much as they felt the city was far too full of itself. And too full of water.

At home with the Borgias

The Borgias were a Spanish family who had already produced one pope, Callistus III. Callistus's nephew, Rodrigo, became Pope Alexander VI in 1492, by the simple means of wholesale bribery. Pope Alexander had his priorities sorted: most of his time and energy went on pocketing as much money as possible and making a serious attempt at the all-time record for the greatest number of illegitimate children fathered by a pope.

Alexander's daughter, Lucrezia, worked her way through a string of political marriages, had at least one of her husbands murdered, and ran Rome while her father was away. Lucrezia's brother, Juan, always his dad's favourite, married a Spanish princess and became a duke twice over. Sadly, Juan's brother Cesare had

him murdered – obviously a bad case of sibling rivalry.

Alexander was so shocked by the murder of one son by another that he nearly decided to give up being pope and become a humble priest, but he got over his distress, and decided to remain as pope. To show that he bore no hard feelings, Alexander made Cesare (age: 17) a cardinal and set about conquering the whole of central Italy for him. 'Conquering' meant having leading Romans murdered and then confiscating their lands.

In 1503, Alexander and Cesare went to a farewell supper for the Cardinal of Corneto, intending to poison him. Unfortunately, a mix-up occurred at the table, and Alexander and Cesare got the cardinal's food by mistake. Cesare survived, just; Alexander didn't.

Forty Years of 'Peace': The Italian League

In 1454, Florence, Naples, and Milan decided to patch up their differences and sign the *Peace of Lodi*. These major city states got the other Italian states to join in and set up a special Italian League, to keep the peace and keep foreigners out. Italy got a breathing space of approximately 40 years to concentrate on other things, like encouraging artists and writers. You may not have heard of the Peace of Lodi or the Italian League, but without them we probably wouldn't have heard of Michelangelo or Leonardo or any of the other great figures of the Renaissance either.

The Medici had a very effective way of maintaining peace. Whenever another state threatened Florence, they wrote saying that in the circumstances the Medici bank would regretfully have to foreclose on them and call in their loans. Because these states were all deeply in debt to the banks, this method worked very well.

However, not everyone took kindly to the Medicis's way of doing business. When the Medici bank refused a loan to Pope Sixtus IV, he turned instead to the Medicis's great rivals, the Pazzi family, who gave him his money, and they all hatched a plot to get rid of the Medici. At the high point of Mass under the great dome of Florence's magnificent cathedral, Pazzi hitmen stabbed Giuliano de Medici and tried to stab his brother Lorenzo. Lorenzo got away, turned the tables on the Pazzi, talked the king of Naples (who'd also been in on the plot) out of attacking, and sent the Pope's men packing. Lorenzo wasn't called 'the Magnificent' for nothing.

The Roots of the Renaissance: Italy

Fifteenth-century Italy had all the ingredients for an artist's paradise. Rulers and rich merchants abounded, all with cash to spend and looking for some way of showing off their wealth to everyone else. What better than to get the latest Renaissance painter to come and decorate your reception area?

A city didn't even need to have a university to take advantage of the 'new learning', as it was called. Venice's Aldine Press produced editions of all the great Greek authors for libraries right across Europe. Pope Nicholas V founded the great collection of books that became the magnificent Vatican Library. Later, the new learning would penetrate the universities and take them over.

Francesco Petrarch: The man who loved books

You can't usually date movements and trends like the Renaissance from one event or person, but Francesco Petrarch has a good claim to having started off the Italian Renaissance. Francesco was a poet with a reputation for pure and spotless love, which was just as well because the lady who was the object of his passion was a respectably married mother of 11 children.

Petrarch developed the sonnet, but his real importance was as an avid book collector. Petrarch didn't just collect them – he used to sit stroking their pages and talking to them. And Petrarch couldn't read Greek so he used to kiss his Greek copy of Homer instead. Er, quite.

Digging around in attics and cellars in Florence, Petrarch found lots of old Latin manuscripts, and when he read them he was astounded by the purity of their language. The only Latin Petrarch or anyone else knew was the rather clumsy Latin of the Church and universities. Imagine for a moment that the only English you ever heard, the only English that *existed*, was the language of a firm of chartered accountants, and then you opened an old cupboard and found the complete works of Shakespeare. Soon, not an attic in Italy was safe from scholars prising open old chests and cupboards to see if any old documents were inside. This period was the only time in history when the season's must-have was a book of Latin grammar.

Yes, but can you do anything with humanist scholarship?

In Petrarch's eyes, poetry and literature were for scholars only; his book collection formed the basis for the library of Florence's new university. However, one of Petrarch's followers, a scholar and civil servant called Coluccio Salutati, came up with a more far-reaching idea.

Salutati had come across the speeches of the great Roman lawyer Cicero. These documents were all top quality stuff – lots of rhetorical flourishes and learned allusions – but what interested Salutati was that these were not composed for private reading or scholarly study, but for use in court, to get Cicero's client off with a caution. Salutati liked that notion and he called it *negotium* – applying your learning to practical life. Salutati became Chancellor of Florence, and started writing his diplomatic correspondence in the style of Cicero (though obviously he had to remember to write 'Dear Sir' and not 'I put it to you, members of the jury'). Soon, other states started to get interested in the new 'humanist' scholarship being pioneered in Florence.

Nowadays, a humanist is someone who does not believe you need religion in order to lead a good life and treat other people properly. In the Renaissance, a humanist was someone who studied the ancients in order to understand the human condition and the mind of God. Same word, two very different meanings.

Florence soon became a major centre of humanist scholarship, thanks to another scholar-Chancellor, Leonardo Bruni. When Constantinople fell to the Turks in 1453, many Greek scholars ended up in Florence and introduced the Florentines to some of the ancient Greek masters, like Aristotle in the original (previously they only had a very bad Latin translation) and the big new discovery, Plato. Forty years later, the whole Jewish population of Spain was kicked out, so now Hebrew scholars headed for Florence too. The new learning was about to become very practical indeed.

Lost in translation

The humanist scholar Lorenzo Valla looked closely at the *Donation of Constantine* (see Chapter 6), the charter that the Emperor Constantine supposedly gave to the popes to say that they were in charge of the Church, and showed that it was a medieval forgery. Oops. Humanists started looking at the official Latin translation of the Bible, known as the Vulgate, and found mistakes there, too. Hmm.

All this comparison of translations and questioning of texts didn't go down well with the universities. The universities were run along *scholastic* lines – you studied certain texts by the great masters of the past and while you might debate their implications and even how best to interpret them, you didn't dispute the texts themselves. The scholastics found this new trend for questioning accepted doctrines very difficult to take.

Purely platonic: Neoplatonism

The humanists' big find was Plato (and you can find him in Chapter 3). The humanists wanted to create a philosophy called *neoplatonism*, that married Plato's ideas with Christian teachings.

The leading neoplatonist was a Florentine scholar called Marsilio Ficino. Plato said that pure love is a desire for beauty. Beauty, said Marsilio Ficino, is a reflection of the perfect nature of God, so if love leads to beauty it also leads eventually to God. When you tell someone today that you want a 'purely platonic' relationship, what you really mean is that you want a pure friendship the way Plato meant 'pure' – if you start adding lust or sex, the relationship becomes less pure, though more fun.

Now according to humanists, what is the most beautiful thing in Creation? Man. So Marsilio Ficino taught that to understand God you need to study Man, which is why Renaissance artists were so interested in anatomy and analysing how the body operates. The neoplatonists went on so much about how wonderful man is that the Church got worried. Where was God in all this philosophising?

The Birth of Renaissance Man

The neoplatonists (see preceding section) dreamed of creating the ultimate man – *Renaissance Man*. The ultimate Renaissance Man was a prince, because being a prince was clearly the recipe for creating the perfect ruler. So education Renaissance-style encompassed theology, philosophy, Latin and Greek obviously, other languages, rhetoric, history, mathematics, break for lunch, then music, dancing, wrestling, riding, fencing, all topped off with perfect manners.

Manners didn't just mean holding doors open: Manners meant being imbued with what the Italians called *virtú*, which is like the English 'virtue' but bigger. *Virtú* meant having the strength of character to grasp your fate and make the most of it. Rudyard Kipling's poem *If* ('If you can keep your head when all about you are losing theirs and blaming it on you . . .') provides an idea of what the Italians meant by *virtú*.

The Florentine writer Niccolo Machiavelli wrote about the sort of *virtú* a prince was supposed to have – or at least to *appear* to have – and Baldasar

Castiglione wrote a book of etiquette called *The Book of the Courtier*, teaching you how to treat everyone with perfect politeness and courtesy while keeping your real opinions strictly to yourself.

The Body Beautiful: Renaissance Art

What excited Renaissance artists about classical art was the way that it managed to reproduce the beauty of the human body in 3-D. A remarkable Greek statue of the priest Laocoön and his sons being dragged under by a sea serpent, all twists and turns and agonised biceps, turned up at just the right time. This sculpture made all those static kings and angels in medieval cathedrals look very boring.

Medieval artists wanted to go beyond the individual into the timeless nature of being, so medieval paintings and sculptures tend to show people all with the same sort of faces and poses. Renaissance artists were scornful of medieval art – they wanted to recreate creation itself.

The first statue that really created a stir was Donatello's statue of David, holding Goliath's sword and completely naked apart from a large hat. Donatello was using the image of the boy David to show the perfection of the human body. However, Donatello's pure motive didn't stop people seeing *David* as a rude statue, and wondering whether they shouldn't drape a cloak over him, at least when they had visitors.

Michelangelo's *David* showed a much more fully developed David in his full anatomical glory. (David was a sort of Florentine patron saint, in case you're wondering why everyone seemed to be carving him. You know, brave little lad standing up to the big guy and winning – just the sort of mascot for a small Italian state surrounded by more powerful enemies.)

So Much Art, So Little Time

I once heard of an American tourist who ran into the Louvre and demanded, 'Where's the Mona Lisa? I'm double parked!' If you want to see some of the art of the Renaissance, you'll need to plan things a bit better than that tourist.

Artists got commissions the length and breadth of Italy, so nearly every Italian town has a collection of Renaissance painting in its local art gallery. The three main centres of Renaissance art were:

✔ **Florence:** See the Uffizi gallery and the magnificent cathedral. The city fathers held a competition for someone to design a dome for the cathedral. The architect Brunelleschi won it by building up rows of overhanging bricks – simple really, but truly a great mind thought up this design. The runner-up, Ghiberti, got to design the panels for the enormous doors to the cathedral's baptistery, which are little masterpieces in bronze relief, showing scenes from the Bible in beautiful detail.

Some artists turned to Greek mythology, like Botticelli, who painted the famous *Birth of Venus* and various other good-looking young people lazing around in advanced states of undress – all in the name of art, of course.

✔ **Rome:** Check out the Vatican Museum, which you approach via an enormous queue. The popes seized the chance to put Rome at the cutting edge of European culture. Nicholas V and Sixtus IV created the Vatican Library, and Paul II set up the Vatican's first printing press. Julius II commissioned Michelangelo to paint the ceiling of the Sistine Chapel, and got Raphael in to decorate his private apartments. Raphael's painting of the School of Athens, with Aristotle and Plato in the centre, was daring subject to paint in the heart of the Vatican.

Michelangelo's *Pietà*, showing Mary holding the dead body of her son, Jesus, the *Pietà*, is still regarded as one of the most perfect pieces of sculpture in art. Michelangelo said that he didn't carve the stone, just that he found the shape which was already in the stone and brought it into the light.

✔ **Venice:** The two big Venetian painters were Titian and Tintoretto (real name Jacopo Robusti – 'Tintoretto' meant 'dyer', which may win you a pub quiz one day). Venice came to the fore a bit later than the other Italian cultural centres, mainly because while these cities were all being overtaken by war, Venice's geographical position put it out of the line of fire.

Leonardo

Leonardo da Vinci was quite simply the most remarkable man of his age, being a painter, musician, astronomer, engineer, and general visionary. Not all Leonardo's plans came to fruition: his giant horseman statue project never happened, and he never did work out how to fly. Leonardo's great mural in the Council Chamber of Florence faded before the councillors very eyes when he unveiled it – he hadn't realised quite how porous the wall was. In fact, relatively few of Leonardo's paintings have survived, though the ones that have certainly show his genius – just look at how people have enthused over every detail of the Mona Lisa.

Leonardo's greatest legacy lies in his notebooks. Unlike many of his contemporaries, Leonardo didn't draw much inspiration from classical art. Leonardo's strength lay in close observation, and he mastered human anatomy in order to portray the human body in a way that was absolutely true to life. Leonardo's insistence on learning from observation prefigured the basis for the great scientific revolution of the 17th century (see Chapter 15). In fact, Leonardo may even have worked out the very thing that would make the names of Galileo and Copernicus later – that the sun does not move. And, da Vinci wrote that fact with his left hand. Backwards.

Bang go the Middle Ages!

By the end of the 15th century armies were using gunpowder. Cannons kill a lot more people, so armies had to be a lot bigger. Cities had to pull down their old high walls and built new fortifications, with low bastions with thick sloping sides to absorb cannon shot. Doctors had to work out new treatments for bullet wounds and what soldiers wore also had to be rethought.

Historians call this period the Military Revolution because of its huge implications. And the place where all these boys' toys got to be tried and tested – and found to work very well – was Renaissance Italy.

Pope Paul II may have brought the printing press to Rome, but he banned the study of pagan ideas or rituals, and when the humanist scholar Bartolomeo Platina objected, he had him arrested and tortured. Paul's actions were a little sign that the humanists were not going to have everything their own way. (When Paul II died, Platina was given the job of writing his official biography, and I bet he enjoyed it.)

One Good Turn for Milan, 60 Years of War for Italy

The Italian Renaissance was killed off when Italy plunged into a long period of war. This war all started with a fairly typical Italian power struggle. Milan was being ruled by Ludovico Sforza, known as 'Il Moro' (the Moor) because of his dark complexion, on behalf of his young nephew, Gian Galeazza. The trouble was that Ludovico had become used to power and wasn't keen to give it up, even though his nephew had grown up and married a granddaughter of the king of Naples. The granddaughter urged her husband to get his act together and take power properly, and she got her granddad to agree to help.

Ludovico had to run for his life, but he wasn't a man to give up easily, so he went to have a word with his good friend King Charles VIII of France: Would Charles put him back on the throne of Milan? But what exactly, King Charles wanted to know, was in it for France? So Ludovico pointed out that since the king of Naples had helped get rid of him, perhaps King Charles might be interested in marching south and taking hold of Naples? King Charles was very interested, especially as his court was full of disgruntled Neapolitan nobles all begging him to come down and get rid of their appalling king. So in 1494, at the head of an enormous army with all the latest equipment, the king of France led his troops into Italy. This invasion was the start of 60 years of war that finally put an end the Italian Renaissance.

Bonfire of the vanities: Florence turns to God

Not everyone thought that France invading Italy was a disaster. A Dominican friar called Girolamo Savonarola, who had taken Florence by storm with his fiery sermons condemning loose living and decadence and predicting the end of the world any day now, welcomed Charles VIII as the instrument of God to purge Florence of its vanities.

Savonarola hated the Renaissance, with all its pagan gods and writers and its talk about the beauty of the human body. Filth, the lot of it! God was not fooled! When the Florentines sent the Medici packing, Savonarola took charge and turned Florence into a godly state, ruled by God's laws. Savonarola told the people of Florence to throw their fine clothes and ornaments and trinkets onto a great 'bonfire of the vanities' in the town square. Botticelli burned most of his paintings – there was no place for naked Greek gods in Savonarola's brave new Florence.

Savonarola also attacked the corruption and decadence in the Vatican. Doing so was a bad idea: Savonarola got himself investigated and excommunicated. Savonarola's excommunication got the Florentines scared. Were the people being led astray by a false prophet? Someone suggested that Savonarola should walk through fire to show that he was a real prophet, but he didn't show up to do so. So the Florentines turned on Savonarola, tortured him, and burned him in front of the cathedral. Well, I did say that Savonarola was a fiery preacher.

Charles VIII took Milan, put Ludovico on the throne, and headed for Florence. Piero de Medici had thoughts of trying to stop him, but the Florentines kicked the Medici out and set up a proper republic again, under a rather scary monk called Savonarola (see the nearby sidebar, 'Bonfire of the vanities: Florence turns to God').

Charles pressed on to Rome, marched his 30,000 heavily armed men past the Vatican – it took two hours – and headed down to Naples, where the king, who knew a hopeless cause when he saw one, abdicated and left his young son to sort it out. Thanks dad. In 1495, Charles VIII entered Naples, feeling very pleased with himself thinking that the invasion was all over.

In fact, the war had only just begun:

- ✔ **1495:** Pope Alexander VI teams up with Venice to form a big kick-the-French-out-of-Italy league, with King Ferdinand of Aragon (Spain) and the Holy Roman Emperor, Maximilian I. Even Ludovico of Milan joins in. However, the prostitutes of Naples entertain Charles's troops and give them all syphilis (only recently arrived from the New World). The French have to head back to France, where their wives await them.

- ✔ **1500:** New French king, Louis XII, takes Milan, throws the treacherous Ludovico into prison, where he dies, and divides Naples with King Ferdinand of Aragon. No, they didn't ask the Italian king of Naples first.

 ✔ **1503:** The Spanish drive the French out of Naples.

 ✔ **1508:** Pope Julius II forms a big international league to crush Venice. Why? The Italians all hated Venice.

 ✔ **1511:** Pope Julius II forms another big international league, this time to crush France. Amazingly, Venice joins in. Swiss drive French out of Milan, tidy the place up a bit, and put the Sforza family back in charge.

 ✔ **1515:** New French king, Francis I, comes marching in and blows the Swiss to smithereens with cannon in a two-day battle at Marignano. Francis drives the Sforzas out, makes himself Duke of Milan, and signs peace with the new King Charles I of Spain. *End of Round One.* (For Round Two, see Chapter 11.)

The Renaissance Heads North

The ideas that had been gripping Italy were now spreading to the rest of Europe. King Francis I of France invited Leonardo da Vinci to his court, but some very good home-grown north European painters were also in evidence, such as Albrecht Dürer and Hans Holbein, who worked in the new medium, oils. Hieronymus Bosch (a name you can't forget in a hurry) painted weird nightmare scenes that would have had Sigmund Freud reaching for the paracetemol, and Peter Breughel, who left saints and VIPs to the others and concentrated on beautifully-observed pictures of peasant life, which can still make you burst out laughing today.

However, the northern Renaissance's biggest contributions were in printing and theology. Johannes Gutenberg of Germany set up Europe's first printing press and the Germans, Dutch, and English became avid producers and readers of printed material. Much of what people read was about theology (see Chapter 10).

Plenty of royal courts and rich city states in northern Europe were eager to attract good artists-in-residence. The most magnificent of these places was the ambitious new state carving out a place for itself: Burgundy.

Burgundy may just mean a rather nice red wine to you, but in the 15th century it was the European state most likely to succeed. Burgundy had carved out a little empire along the border between France and Germany, and up in the Netherlands.

Because the Netherlands were one of the wealthiest trading centres in Europe, the court of Burgundy became a by-word for magnificence: Its Order of the Golden Fleece was the knightly must-have of the century. Burgundy's dukes dreamed of turning their duchy into a kingdom. The kings of France had other ideas, however.

The ups and downs of 15th-century Burgundy:

- **1415:** Henry V of England invades France. Duke John 'the Fearless' of Burgundy stays neutral, so French dauphin has him murdered. The new Duke, Philip 'the Good', fights on the English side. Philip's men capture Joan of Arc and his church court condemns her to death as a witch. So the epithet 'Good' depends rather on your point of view.

- **1467:** Philip's son Charles the Bold becomes duke. Charles tries to stir up a rebellion against his great enemy, King Louis XI of France. The plan doesn't work. Louis tries to do the same to Charles; Charles takes Louis prisoner and takes him to see the would-be rebels being disembowelled.

- **1473:** Charles tries to add to his collection of captured European monarchs by capturing the Holy Roman Emperor Frederick III but Frederick escapes. Louis XI and Frederick III are now determined to crush Burgundy.

- **1477:** Louis XI hires the Swiss to defeat Charles in battle. The Swiss do better than that – they kill him.

Louis XI took over the French part of Burgundy and nearly got the Netherlands as well. Luckily, the Dutch managed to marry Charles's daughter Mary to the Holy Roman Emperor's boy, Maximilian, just in time. From now on, the emperor protected the Netherlands and told the French to keep their grubby hands off.

Mary and Max had two children, Philip and Margaret. Both children married into the royal house of Spain. These marriages were the start of a link between the Netherlands and Spain and went on to have very big consequences in the 16th century.

The Reigns in Spain

Strictly speaking, 'Spain' was made up of different kingdoms: Portugal, Navarre, Aragon, and the biggest one, Castile. In 1469, in one of those weddings which occasionally make history, Prince Ferdinand of Aragon married Princess Isabella of Castile. The marriage didn't actually mean that their kingdoms were united, but Ferdinand and Isabella developed such a good working partnership that it might just as well have done. The couple imposed their authority in person, and they knew just how to divide and rule. Ferdinand and Isabella married their daughter Joanna to the handsome Duke of Burgundy, Philip of Habsburg, and their daughter Katharine (Katharine of Aragon) married into another up-and-coming dynasty, the Tudors. No, not Henry VIII but his big brother, Prince Arthur. (For what happened next, see *British History For Dummies* (Wiley).)

The fear of God: The Spanish Inquisition

After years of Muslim rule, Christian Spain had a large Jewish and Muslim population. Many of these people had converted to Christianity (they weren't given much choice) but many churchmen suspected that they continued to practise their old religion in private.

Isabella invited Pope Sixtus IV to set up an inquisition in Spain to find out exactly what was going on. The Spanish Inquisition, under its ruthless Grand Inquisitor, Tomas de Torquemada, didn't have to bother with bishops as it reported directly to the Crown. The Spanish Inquisition did use torture, but found that close questioning got better results. Those people found guilty of slipping back into their Jewish or Muslim ways were paraded in the streets and made to wear tall paper hats with slogans or pictures on them, rather like those poor people ritually humiliated in communist China. Then, the guilty were burned at the stake. The whole ceremony was called, without a shred of irony, an *auto da fe*, an act of faith.

The last crusade

In 1492, Ferdinand and Isabella wrapped up the story of the *Reconquistá* (see Chapter 7) and took Granada (the ruling dynasty in Granada were all at each others' throats, which helped). The Muslims of Granada were forcibly converted to Christianity and the Jews of Spain were thrown out. The Pope rewarded Ferdinand and Isabella by naming them 'the Catholic kings'. And while they were taking stock of their victory Ferdinand and Isabella had an unexpected visitor in the form of a young Italian sea captain, called Christopher Columbus, seeking their backing for an idea he had to sail to the Indies by heading west (for more on Columbus, see Chapter 11).

Isabella died in 1504. Isabella's throne passed to their daughter Joanna, but Ferdinand, who wanted to keep his son-in-law firmly in his place, didn't allow Joanna's husband, Philip, to become king of Castile alongside her. Philip bided his time, and made some friends among the Castilian nobles, who didn't like being told by an Aragonese who they could or could not have as their king.

Two years later, the Castilians rose up and threw Ferdinand out, though they could have saved themselves the trouble because Philip promptly died and Joanna went mad; she was always a bit on the edge, poor thing, but when she started carting Philip's body round with her in its coffin and refusing to let anyone take it away, even her dad could see that something wasn't quite right. And if Ferdinand couldn't see it, he could smell it.

Ferdinand ruled Castile as regent for his daughter until he died in 1516. Then, all those dynastic marriages came home to roost in a rather unexpected way.

A royal jackpot!

Joanna and Philip had a son, Charles, who now started inheriting royal titles as if they were in short supply. First, Charles became king of Castile (through his granny Isabella) and of Aragon (through his granddad Ferdinand). Charles was already Duke of Burgundy (through his dad, Philip of Burgundy), and soon he became Holy Roman Emperor (following his paternal grandad, the Emperor Maximilian). Charles was lord of all Spain's lands in the New World (through granny Isabella, Columbus's patron), and through his father's family he also inherited all the Habsburg family lands in central Europe, including Austria and a large chunk of Hungary. Oh, and not forgetting all the land in Italy that granddad Ferdinand had gained in those wars with the French. Charles had so many different kingdoms that knowing quite what to call him is difficult, though the history books usually refer to him by his title as Holy Roman Emperor: The Emperor Charles V. As you can probably guess, Charles features quite prominently in later chapters in this book.

Chapter 10

Reformation Ruckus

Christian Europe tore itself apart in the 16th century – not about territory or kingship, but about religion. The Reformation was intended to reform a Church that had got badly out of hand – but it became a battle between Catholics and Protestants, part of a cosmic war of Good and Evil, and at stake was their souls.

We Three Kings

Put the religious mayhem on hold for a moment and meet three new characters who all appeared on the European scene early on in the 16th century. These individuals were all young men, had all been educated in the approved Renaissance manner (captain of games, school prizes for French, maths, wrestling, and tapestry work) and were all crowned kings:

- **1509: Henry VIII of England.** Forget the fat man with the wives; he comes later. This king is a young, handsome Henry, sportsman, philosopher, warrior, married to Katharine of Aragon, who was aunt to Charles I of Spain.

- **1511: Charles I of Spain.** Katharine's nephew, quieter, rather more serious than Henry, and with a much bigger chin (the Habsburgs all had big chins, and as they interbred over the centuries the chins just got bigger). Charles was also Charles V of the Holy Roman Empire (see the following section).

- **1515: Francis I of France.** Definitely one of the lads. Enjoyed wrestling and jousting and slapping people hard on the back, though woe betide you if you did the same to him. Francis I should've carried a government health warning: Trusting this man can seriously damage your health.

So we meet at last

Generally, these kings had to rely on portraits and reports from ambassadors about what each was like (Well, your majesty, he has this *chin*...) but in 1520 Charles stopped off in England on his way from Spain to Germany and had a few days with Henry. Henry then crossed the Channel for a meeting with Francis in a venue so elaborate and magnificent — special decorated arches and pavilions were built and everyone dressed to dazzle — that the scene has gone down in history as the Field of the Cloth of Gold.

Tournaments, banquets, and even a royal wrestling match were held (which ended with Francis throwing Henry, leaving him with a serious fracture of the ego). Many discussions were held, with talk of eternal friendship and how France and England should stand firm against Charles, but as soon as they'd all packed up and gone home Henry met up with Charles again and signed an alliance — against Francis.

In 1519, the Germans elected Charles Holy Roman Emperor. Henry and Francis had put their names forward, too. Henry wasn't really expecting to win (Charles bribed the electors very handsomely), but Francis was badly put out and never really forgave Charles. Francis I didn't believe in losing.

Charles and His Many Royal Duties

Charles was King Charles I of Spain but the Emperor Charles V of the Holy Roman Empire. Charles was always very careful to use the correct title according to where he was or who he was talking to, but from now on I just call him Charles V. (See Chapter 9 for the low-down on Charles's many titles.)

Charles V took his royal duties very seriously. At first, Charles stayed in Burgundy (where he was duke) but the Spanish, tiring of having their king living at the other end of Europe, rose up in revolt. Charles was very understanding; after the revolt had been crushed and the leading rebels put to death, he decided that perhaps they had a point after all, so he packed his bags and moved to Spain.

In 1519, Charles met up with the German princes for one of their regular summits, known as *diets*, which that year was being held in the city of Worms. An extra item appeared on the agenda (or, better, on the menu). The attendees were going to have the chance to put some questions to someone who was rapidly becoming one of Charles's more celebrated subjects – Martin Luther.

The Dangerous Business of Criticising the Church

Martin Luther was a German monk with serious concerns about the state of the Church. Luther wasn't the first person to have these concerns by any means:

- **Fourteenth-century English reformer John Wyclif** argued that people don't need priests to forgive their sins or give them communion, and that they ought to be allowed to read the Bible for themselves, in English. Wyclif also denied the Pope's authority over the Church, and since this was the time of the Great Schism, with two different popes fighting it out, many people thought Wyclif had a point. (You can find out more about the Great Schism in Chapter 7.)

  Wyclif's followers, known as *Lollards*, were ruthlessly suppressed. The Church held a special Council at Constance which ordered Wyclif's bones to be dug up and scattered.

- **Bohemian reformer Jan Hus** followed Wyclif's teachings and also rejects the authority of the Pope. This move proved very popular with the Bohemians, who regarded Hus as a national hero. The Pope was less enthused and declared Hus excommunicated.

The Church had no intention of tolerating criticism. In 1415, Hus was invited to Constance to attend a General Council of the Church. This assembly was the same Council that ordered Wyclif's bones to be dug up and scattered. The Holy Roman Emperor offered Hus safe conduct to and from the Council but when Hus arrived the Council arrested him and burnt him at the stake. But the Church didn't have everything its own way. The Pope and emperor launched a crusade to stamp out the Hussites in Bohemia. The Bohemians fought back – and won.

New learning: New danger

In some ways, Hus's problem was that he was just a bit too early. The 'new learning' – Renaissance scholarship – only really took off after his death. Some humanist scholars were just as damning about the state of the Church as Hus had been (see Chapter 9 for more about the new learning).

A Dutchman, Gerrit Gerritszoon, better known as Erasmus, was the most important humanist scholar. Erasmus was a genuine European; he divided his time between Paris, Cambridge, Rome, Basel, and Louvain. Erasmus was a good friend of the English scholar, Sir Thomas More, and the two of them were scathing about the corruption in the Church. More's famous fantasy *Utopia* is not so much a description of a perfect society as a satire on imperfect ones, and Erasmus's *In Praise of Folly* lays into hypocritical popes and emperors. With popes and antipopes (rival claimants to the papal throne in the Great Schism. See Chapter 7 for the details) fathering children and going to war, they had plenty of material. (Antipope John XXIII, who had excommunicated Jan Hus, was rumoured to have seduced 200 women while he was a papal legate – papal leg-over, more like.)

The reformers

Apart from sexually-charged bishops, the reformers really had their sights on:

- ✔ **Simony:** Buying your way into ecclesiastical office.

- ✔ **Pluralism:** Holding more than one ecclesiastical post at once (and getting paid for both).

- ✔ **Absenteeism:** Holding a church post but not carrying out its duties. Also called *non-residence*.

- ✔ **General lack of education, vocation, or any sense of a spiritual life:** Drinking, gambling, fornicating, knowing next to nothing of theology or the scriptures – yes, this is the clergy we're talking about. Erasmus and the humanists thought there was some room for improvement here.

The Italian scholar Lorenzo Valla showed that there were mistakes in the Church's official version of the Bible, the *Vulgate,* so Erasmus set himself the task of producing a better version; his Greek New Testament soon became the standard text. Nevertheless, Erasmus and More remained loyal Catholics all their lives (More even died for his Catholic faith). But a new row was brewing in Germany about something more important than misbehaving monks or even the text of the Bible – this squabble was about how to get into heaven.

Roll Up! Roll Up! Climb the Stairway to Heaven

To medieval people, you had one big choice in life: Are you going to heaven or are you going to hell? The object of the game, the whole meaning of life, was not to go to hell.

Thanks to Adam and Eve, everyone was born with a serious stain on their soul known as *Original Sin*. Soap didn't shift the stain – you had to get the baby baptised. Baptism was so important that in an emergency you could even baptise your own baby without a priest. Make the most of that concession because for everything else you needed a properly paid-up priest if you were going to avoid those flames.

When you grew up and started committing your own sins, the sin became ingrained in your soul and had to be burned off after your death in a special furnace called *purgatory*. On Judgement Day, God looked carefully at your soul and if it didn't come up to scratch, down you went for good.

The trouble was that everyone committed sin: Were they all going to hell? Not if you stuck with the Church, you weren't. The Church ran a loyalty points system, known as *grace*. Grace counterbalanced your sins and earned you time off in purgatory. How to get this extremely useful quality? Easy: You went to mass or confession or received one of the other *sacraments* of the Church.

By 1517, the Church had come up with its most amazing special offer yet. Yes, folks, NO catches and NO small print: YOU can go STRAIGHT to heaven no matter WHAT you've done by buying an *indulgence*! A small flat fee could buy you a special pass through the pearly gates and into eternal bliss. 'I can't believe it!' said Herr Schmidt of Leipzig.

And then, the Church's offer got *even better*. For a limited season only, you could buy a special indulgence to get your deceased family and friends already in purgatory OUT of purgatory and INTO heaven! Free your friends, and leave your enemies to burn! Roll up! Roll up! When your penny in the copper plate rings, a soul from purgatory springs!

That was the slogan of John Tetzel, a Dominican friar who arrived in Germany in 1517 selling indulgences, which, not surprisingly, went like hot cakes. Martin Luther, who was teaching theology at the nearby University of Wittenberg, had already been agonising about how to get into heaven. Luther thought Tetzel was teaching dangerous nonsense, and he pinned up a set of 95 theses on the door of the university church saying so.

Now, privately, many churchmen agreed with Luther, but they all faced a rather important complicating factor – Tetzel wasn't making his claims up. Tetzel had a special commission to sell indulgences from Pope Leo X, who (though no one knew this at the time) wanted the money to rebuild St Peter's in the latest Renaissance style. So, if you attacked indulgences – and Luther had done just that – you were also attacking the Pope. Jan Hus challenged the Pope and look what happened to him.

Heavyweight theology championships

Luther's colleagues and students at Wittenberg University were initially surprised by his theses challenging Tetzel, but then rallied to his side. The allies' rivals at the University of Leipzig weren't so friendly and challenged Luther to a public debate against their champion theologian, Johann Eck. Doing so was dangerous. Eck wasn't going to waste time defending indulgences, he was going to press Luther on the much more important point – did Luther accept the authority of the Pope or not?

Luther accepted the challenge and fell right into Eck's trap: He said that indulgences were wrong and that the Pope had no power to issue them. 'Thank you very much, Dr Luther, you've been most helpful,' said Eck, and then went straight off to report to Pope Leo X.

The Pope sent a bull of excommunication off to Wittenberg by the next post. Luther burned the document in contempt, but he must have been at least a bit worried, as no one was supposed to help or shelter someone who'd been excommunicated – you got excommunicated yourself if you did – and you were meant to turn them over to the local magistrate for burning.

Luckily, Luther had a very useful protector. Luther's local prince, Frederick the Wise, Elector of Saxony, didn't like the Pope and he didn't like other people's universities trying to trip up his Dr Luther. Frederick had a word with the young man he had just helped elect as Holy Roman Emperor, Charles V. By rights, Charles ought to have been hunting Luther down as a fugitive from Church justice, but Charles decided to give Luther a fair hearing at the next imperial diet, to be held at Worms in 1521. Charles even offered Luther a safe conduct to and from the diet. Luther agreed.

Here I stand!

At the imperial diet, Luther was asked 'Did you write these books?'. 'Yes,' he said. 'Well,' said the diet, 'They've been judged heretical. Do you stand by them or have you changed your mind?' 'Er,' said Luther, 'can I get back to you on that?'

Luther came back to them the very next day. 'Yes,' he said, 'I wrote the books and I stand by every word,' and he explained why. Luther had discovered, thanks to a long dark night of the soul in his tower in Wittenberg, that the Church had got the route to heaven all wrong. You didn't need to do special things or gain grace to get past the pearly gates, you just had to believe in Jesus with all your heart. You got to heaven *'Sola fide',* as Luther called it in Latin – in English 'by faith alone'.

Charles V looked deeply sceptical, but Luther ended with a famous statement: 'Here I stand,' he said, 'I can do no other. God help me.' Charles stormed out of the meeting – he was a loyal son of the Church and didn't hold with this idea that you didn't need grace to get into heaven. Charles placed Luther under the ban of the empire, which meant that anyone was allowed to hunt him down, anywhere in Germany.

Luther went into hiding. Elector Frederick, who wasn't called 'the Wise' for nothing, had him intercepted on his way back from the diet and whisked away to a secret location, where he grew a beard and was known to everyone as 'Squire George'. George, er, Luther didn't just twiddle his thumbs, though, and went about writing a German version of the New Testament, and a whole series of pamphlets and letters in which he laid out his beliefs exactly:

- ✔ The Pope has no authority over the Church.

- ✔ You don't need sacraments. Only God can forgive sins – not priests.

- ✔ You don't really need priests anyway.

- ✔ Everyone must be able to read the Bible for themselves.

Curb Your Enthusiasm – The Radicals

In Wittenberg a group of rather wild visionaries had arrived from the German town of Zwickau and declared that the people must get rid of their princes and set up a proper kingdom of God, destroying all those idolatrous 'holy' statues and stained-glass windows.

A veritable orgy of icon and statue-smashing broke out and the whole town ran riot. Luther's friends and colleagues tried tutting very loudly and telling them all to settle down at the back, but to no avail – the town was fast slipping into anarchy. The situation got so bad that Luther came out of hiding and preached a special sermon on why God doesn't love a vandal, which did the trick. Luther threw the Zwickau prophets out of town.

One of the Zwickau prophets, called Thomas Müntzer, went around Germany telling the peasants that Luther's message was that if they read the Bible (which, of course, they weren't able to), they'd find that God wanted them to rise up against their rulers and stage a revolution. Luther was horrified, and rushed out a fierce pamphlet called *Against the Murdering Thieving Hordes of Peasants*, but he was too late to stop the peasants from rising up in a full-scale war against their princely rulers. The peasants lost.

In the town of Münster a group of radicals known as *anabaptists* (because they believed in adult baptism) took over the town and turned it into a godly republic. Sin was punishable by death (eek!) and private property was abolished. The self-appointed anabaptist 'King of Munster' revealed that polygamy was all right, though, and promptly took 16 wives (and had one wife executed for impertinence!).

The anabaptists were such a threat to the existing social order that the Catholic bishop of Munster and the leading Protestant prince, Philip of Hesse, buried their religious differences to join forces to crush them. The anabaptist leaders were tortured to death, and their bodies hung in a cage from the tower of the city church. A cage containing lights still hangs there today in their memory.

In 1529, Charles V met the princes at an imperial diet at Speyer. The royal gathering voted to uphold the decision that they had reached at the Worms diet to declare Luther an outlaw. However, some of the princes spoke up for Luther and issued a formal *protest* against the diet's decision – which is why Luther's supporters became known as *Protestants.*

Germany Prepares for Civil War

The Protestant princes joined together in the *Schmalkaldic League* and the Catholic princes formed the *Catholic League* to warn the Schmalkaldic League not to try any funny business. Germany was gearing up for civil war. It broke out in 1531:

- ✔ **1531–40:** Protestants have the upper hand. Luther says resisting your rightful monarch is against God's law, but then changes his mind and says resisting Charles V is acceptable. Charles is too taken up with fighting the French in Italy and the Turks to deal properly with the Schmalkaldic League.

- ✔ **1540:** Scandal! Leading Protestant prince, Philip of Hesse, is up on a charge of bigamy. Bigamy is a capital offence, so Philip's fate lies entirely in Charles V's hands. Then, the lusty Lutheran discloses he had wheedled none other than Martin Luther to agree to his bigamous marriage. Charles V licks his lips – as far as his chin will allow – he now has the Protestants at his mercy.

  Philip of Hesse agrees to leave the Schmalkaldic League and spend more time with at least one of his families. Other Protestants slip away and join Charles V.

- ✔ **1546:** Charles crushes the Schmalkaldic League at the Battle of Mühlberg.

And then Charles blew it.

Charles forgot the most important law of winning: Don't gloat. Charles announced plans to take power away from the princes and into his own hands. The princes, Catholic and Protestant, formed a league to oppose Charles. At the 1552 Battle of Innsbruck, the league beat Charles's army and very nearly captured him.

Sing yer heart out for the lads

Luther had a good ear for a tune, and he wrote some good, meaty hymns for belting out and making some noise with. Luther's biggest hit was '*Eine feste Burg ist unser Gott*', 'A mighty stronghold is our God', which Bach later used for one of his cantatas. The Lutherans sang their hymns in church, and they sang them marching into battle, too.

A compromise had to be worked out. Charles and the princes finally reached a solution in 1555, in what was called *The Religious Peace of Augsburg*. What it said was simple: *cuius regio, eius religio*, meaning 'whatever the religion of the prince, that will be the religion of his people.' So, if you had a Protestant prince, you were Protestant, but if your prince was a Catholic, so were you. The compromise worked.

Mind you, Charles V was so depressed about the solution reached by the Religious Peace of Augsburg (he didn't believe God wanted him to reach a compromise with heretics) that he abdicated, and went to live out his days in a Spanish monastery.

Luther married a nun called Katherine von Bora and settled down to raise a family.

A Rôle for the Swiss

The Swiss ran Europe's leading mercenary export business – Swiss guards still defend the Vatican to this day. A Swiss military chaplain, called Ulrich Zwingli, started a parallel reformation in Switzerland to Luther's reformation in Germany. In 1522, Zwingli was at a party in Zürich where a few slices of German sausage were passed round and Zwingli ate some. So what? So the party occurred during Lent, the season of penitence when the Church decreed that you were supposed to give up eating meat. When Zürich's Catholics denounced him, Zwingli led a coup and drove them out.

Zwingli's views on all these Church rules about what you could or couldn't do were pretty similar to Luther's , except for one important point. Luther held that Jesus's words spoken by the priest at communion, 'This is my body, this is my blood', meant more or less what they said – that *something* happened to the bread and the wine at that moment. Zwingli said that belief was nonsense – the bread and the wine might *represent* Jesus's body and blood, but that communion was still a slice of wholemeal loaf up there with a cupful of the local vintage.

Read all about it

The Reformation couldn't have happened without the printing press. University printers across Europe produced pamphlets and books setting out the new ideas about religion in language everyone was able to understand. Historians used to think that the Protestants had all the best printers, but more recently historians have shown that Catholics made just as much use of printing to oppose Protestant ideas: Not just books, but pages with pictures and little tabs to pull to make the pictures move. If you didn't like what you read in one pamphlet, you wrote another one in response – very good news for the printers' profit margins.

Zwingli ran Zürich as a *theocracy* – a kingdom ruled entirely by God's word, with a special court of morals to try people who had sinned. Some of the Swiss cantons followed Zürich's lead and became Protestant; others remained staunchly Catholic – after all, the Pope was an important client for their mercenary business.

In 1531, an army of 8,000 heavily armed Swiss Catholics marched on Zürich. Zürich was only able to muster about 2,000 men, but Zwingli got up and preached an inspiring sermon about how, with God's help, a small God-fearing army could defeat a godless army, however big that army was. The soldiers raised their voices in a hymn, and then marched out bravely to face the enemy in the Battle of Keppel, strong in the knowledge that God was on their side. They got slaughtered. One of the dead was Zwingli.

What Was Happening in the Rest of Europe?

Thanks to the printing press, news of Luther's quarrel with the Pope soon spread around Europe. Different parts of Europe reacted to the news in some radically different ways.

- ✔ **England:** Henry VIII pulled the English Church away from the Church of Rome and dissolved England's monasteries.

- ✔ **Denmark:** The German Hanseatic towns helped Christian III to impose Lutheranism on Denmark and Norway.

- ✔ **Sweden:** King Gustavus Vasa made himself head of the Swedish Church and forced the Swedes to accept Luther's ideas.

> ✔ **The Netherlands:** Strictly speaking, the Duchy of Burgundy, though the name was beginning to fall out of use. Charles V was Duke of Burgundy, and did what he liked there. What he liked was arresting Protestants. Charles's repression kept Lutheranism in the Netherlands firmly underground.

> ✔ **France, Scotland, and Switzerland:** All fell for the ideas of a new preacher on the scene, a stern-faced, long-bearded French reformer living and working in Switzerland who was all set to take over from Luther as Europe's No 1 Protestant reformer – John Calvin.

The French Revelation

Some of the top people in France were very keen on the new learning, including the king's sister, Margaret of Navarre; humanist scholars gathered at her court and had a fine old time discussing Erasmus's or Luther's latest writings before going in to a rather good dinner.

But the University of Paris, the Sorbonne, didn't like these new ideas one bit and said that the Lady Margaret was encouraging heresy and sedition. Francis I wasn't happy about these accusations against his sister and repeatedly told the Sorbonne to back off and apologise. Then, in 1534, a group of Protestant hotheads went round Paris pinning up posters saying that the Catholic mass was a snare and a delusion and that Christ was no more present in the bread and wine than he was in my old socks. Someone even pinned a poster to the door of Francis I's bedchamber in the Château of Amboise. Francis stayed calm. The king held a big procession with relics (just a few thorns from the Crown of Thorns – nothing too elaborate) and the consecrated communion host – and then he sat down to watch six Protestants being burnt to death. The Protestants had gone too far and had to get out of France fast.

Do you know where you're going to? I do!

John Calvin was one of the reformers who had to leave France in a hurry. Calvin had started off as a lawyer and never lost his lawyer's rather authoritarian approach to religion. Calvin headed for Basel in Switzerland, a nice safe Protestant town under a preacher with the impressive (though unpronounceable) name of John Oecolampadius.

While in Basel, Calvin wrote his most important book, *Institutes of the Christian Religion*. Most of the book was working through issues like how to organise your church and what happens in communion but what really made people sit up was what Calvin had to say about getting into heaven.

St Augustine had written about God deciding in advance who was going to get into heaven (you can find out about St Augustine in Chapter 5); Calvin took this idea a step further. Calvin said that even before you were born God had decided who was going to heaven and who was going to hell – it was *predestined*. So how you lived your life didn't actually matter; if you were one of the elect you were heading for bliss, and if you weren't you were heading for the heat, and you weren't able to do anything about it.

Welcome to Geneva, Dr Calvin. Why not stay over?

In 1536, Calvin was on his way to Strasbourg – another safe Protestant town – when he heard that there were troop movements up ahead and so went on a detour via Geneva. Geneva had just thrown out its bishop and declared itself independent of the local bigwig, the Duke of Savoy, but the local Protestant preacher, one Guillaume Farel, was having an uphill job trying to turn Geneva into a fully Protestant city like Basel or Strasbourg. Everyone kept arguing. Some people were happily smashing Catholic statues, others wanted the bishop back, and the city council was trying hard to impose its own authority. Farel, who didn't have much classroom control at the best of times, just didn't know what to do.

So when someone told Farel that the famous John Calvin, author of the *Institutes of the Christian Religion*, was staying overnight in the town, Farel was round there like a shot, asking if Calvin wouldn't mind staying on and helping turn Geneva into a godly city. Calvin decided that Geneva was where God wanted him to be, so he stayed.

Geneva, the City of God

Calvin wanted to turn Geneva into a true city of God, with a strong church keeping an eye on the people's morals and behaviour. Not everyone liked this idea. A party on the city council stood up to him at every turn, and when Calvin first outlined his plans they threw him out. Calvin was back within a couple of years, though. The city was still in turmoil and they wanted him to return and restore some sort of order – he came back, but on his terms.

A group of elders, all with long beards and even longer faces, governed Calvin's church by forming the *consistory*. Some of the elders sat on the city council as well, though Calvin himself never did. The consistory was elected by the congregation – okay, the male congregation. As well as overseeing the Church, the consistory also ran courts to deal with people who strayed from the straight and narrow. Punishments meted out were death for adultery (drowning for women, beheading for men), and fines or imprisonment for drunkenness or gambling. Not surprisingly, some of Calvin's fiercest opponents were innkeepers and card manufacturers.

Calvin had nothing but contempt for people who opposed him, calling them 'libertines'. Calvin referred to his most constant critic, a blunt-spoken man called Ami Perrin, as a 'Comic Caesar', which sounded a lot more scathing then than it does now. Above all, Calvin's Geneva was very intolerant, as the following events illustrate:

- ✔ **1551:** Visiting French Protestant Jerome Bolsec gets up and challenges a preacher who claims that Christ only died for the elect. 'Hello?' says Bolsec, 'In my Bible, Christ died for all sinners.' Preacher sends someone to fetch Dr Calvin, who promptly delivers a long sermon denouncing Bolsec and his heretical views. 'Ooh, we haven't had this much fun in church for a long time,' say the congregation. Bolsec finds himself on trial for his life, with Calvin leading the prosecution. Luckily for him, Geneva consults the other Protestant cities; some of them think he is guilty, while others don't. Bolsec is sent out of Geneva and told never to come back, though he probably didn't want to anyway.

- ✔ **1553:** A colourful character, one Michael Servetus, arrives in Geneva having escaped, in rather mysterious circumstances, from the Spanish Inquisition. Servetus argues against the idea of the Trinity and holds that Jesus cannot have been fully divine. Servetus is prosecuted (with Calvin doing his 'I put it to the jury' act again) and this time all the Swiss towns agree: Servetus is put to death.

- ✔ **1555:** Calvin drives Ami Perrin and the libertines – those who stood up for a modicum of freedom of speech – out of Geneva.

You may think that this stern, intolerant city where you weren't allowed to have fun was at the top of people's list of places to avoid, but you'd be wrong. Geneva became the centre of the Protestant Reformation, like Moscow for 20th-century communists. Calvin's doctrine of predestination was very comforting if you were trying to keep the faith under persecution – whatever they did to you, you *knew* that you were going to heaven and your enemies were going to hell. Also, Calvinists elected their own ministers so if your minister got arrested, you just elected a new one. Regular influxes of Protestant refugees arrived in Geneva, fleeing persecution in France, Spain, England, and the Netherlands.

One last (rather important) point

Calvin died in 1564. Calvin's successors went on to develop an idea that he had always been rather wary of, but that was going to have a big effect on Calvinism in the future. Should you obey an 'ungodly' (= Catholic) monarch? Calvin had been enough of a lawyer to say that yes, you should, but his followers increasingly thought that a good Christian faced with an ungodly monarch had a right – nay, a duty – to resist. Even to strike first. In the years to come, even Protestant monarchs were to find themselves increasingly threatened by this growing Calvinist 'doctrine of resistance'. And the monarchs decided to strike back (head to Chapter 11).

Chapter 11

Mass and Massacre: The Wars of Religion

· ·

In This Chapter

▶ Considering the Habsburg–Valois rivalry

▶ Understanding the Council of Trent and the Catholic Reformation

▶ Exploring the New World

▶ Witnessing a Revolt in the Netherlands and Wars of Religion in France

· ·

*T*he Reformation forced the Church to do some serious rethinking. Cardinals, bishops, and theologians met at the great Council of Trent to put the Catholic Church's house in order and revive its spiritual soul.

Meanwhile, Catholic Spain fought a long war against the Protestant Dutch and the French Crown organised the wholesale slaughter of French Protestants. Europe was in the grip of religious war, and in this war for salvation no holds were barred.

Charles V's Bad Dreams

The Holy Roman Emperor Charles V had a nightmare of all Europe falling for Luther or Calvin and their heretical ideas. Charles knew what was needed:

✔ **A General Council of the Church.** A big meeting of all the top brass was needed to take a good look at the Church and identify what needed changing.

✔ *Monarquia,* **or a United Kingdom of Europe.** This idea was the brain-child of Charles's Italian minister and adviser, Mercurino Gattinara. Charles liked this idea, but the different parts of his empire didn't. Gattinara died in 1530, and Charles let the monarquia idea die with him.

First Choose Your Pope – But Not Adrian!

In 1522, Pope Leo X died, so Charles persuaded the cardinals to elect his old tutor and friend, Adrian of Utrecht, Pope Adrian VI. Adrian was a great scholar and a genuinely holy man. Unfortunately, the cardinals didn't appreciate Adrian's crackdown on their *sinecures* (a sinecure is a job with good pay for no work – nice work if you can get it) Poor Adrian, he had a rotten time and died of illness after only a year in the job.

This time, the cardinals took no chances and elected Leo X's nephew, Giulio de Medici, who had been a cardinal since he was 13 and didn't believe in making cuts or praying too much. Giulio became Pope Clement VII, and Charles V gained an enemy. (For more on that consequence, see the next section.)

The Italian Job: Milan Is Mine!

Charles V and King Francis I of France were both determined to get hold of Milan, and anyone who stood in their way was going to get hurt.

- **1515:** Francis defeats the Swiss and takes Milan. *Advantage: Francis.*

- **1521:** Francis invades Navarre and the Netherlands. Charles beats him, and takes Milan back. *Advantage: Charles.*

- **1525:** Battle of Pavia: Spanish troops capture Francis and take him off to Spain as their prisoner. And on Charles's birthday, too. *Big advantage: Charles.*

- **1526:** Francis has to sign the Treaty of Madrid giving Burgundy back to Charles and making peace in Italy and the Netherlands. *Looking like match point to Charles. But wait.*

- **Still 1526:** Francis gets back to Paris, tears up the Treaty of Madrid (Ha! Suckers!), signs an alliance with the new pope, Clement VII, against Charles, and even – get this – signs an alliance with the Ottoman Turks. *Francis has levelled the score: Deuce.*

- **1527:** The infamous Sack of Rome: Charles's imperial troops, fed up because they haven't been paid, arrive in Rome, moodily trash the place, and take the Pope prisoner. *Oh, I say! Advantage: Charles.*

- **1530:** Charles is terribly sorry about capturing Pope Clement, but hey, Clement has to crown Charles officially as Holy Roman Emperor at Bologna. *Advantage and a very big smirk on his face: Charles.*

✔ **1536:** Charles invades southern France – which unites the French to chuck Charles out. *Advantage, feeling smug: Francis.*

✔ **1538:** Charles's men defeat the French and drive them out of Italy. In the Treaty of Nice, Francis gives up all his claims in Italy. *Game to the Habsburgs. New balls, please.*

Following in Father's Footsteps: King Henry II

Francis I died in 1547, but his son, King Henry II of France, carried on exactly where Francis had left off. This war was a grudge match: Charles had kept Henry and his younger brother hostage for three years as a guarantee of Francis's good behaviour, and Henry hadn't forgotten it.

Henry turned to Charles's enemies, the German Protestant princes (you can read all about them in Chapter 10). Henry promised to help them if he was allowed to pick up three rather useful fortresses in Lorraine, along the border with Germany: Toul, Metz, and Verdun. The princes agreed.

Henry and the princes combined were too strong for Charles. Charles had to make peace, so Henry got his fortresses. Even these events weren't the end of the war as Henry decided to have one last stab at invading Italy. Henry didn't quite make it to Naples, so he took Calais from the English instead. You win some, you lose some.

By 1559, both sides were exhausted and running very short of cash. Henry II and Philip II, Charles's son and successor as king of Spain, signed the Treaty of Cateau Cambrésis, and this time they kept to it. France kept Calais and the three fortresses, and the Habsburgs kept Italy. More importantly, the war was over at long, long last. Huge celebrations were held, including a tournament. Henry took part – and was killed.

This Pope Was Made for Talking: Pope Paul III

Alessandro Farnese became Pope Paul III in 1534. At first sight, Paul looked pretty much like his predecessors, being born into a rich Roman family, bishop at 20, cardinal at 25 (you sometimes get the impression that no one in the Renaissance College of Cardinals had actually started to shave). But then Paul had a midlife crisis and decided that if he was going to be a bishop and a cardinal, he ought to do it properly. So Paul went through the whole ordination process again, but this time for real, actually reading Augustine and Aquinas and saying his prayers as if he meant them. Paul appointed reformers to important positions in the Church and set up a special commission to look into whether changes in the Church were needed.

Just about everyone in the Church agreed that reform was necessary, but they had very different ideas about what form these improvements should take.

- ✔ Liberals like Cardinal Contarini or the English Cardinal Pole thought that if you talked nicely with the Protestants over tea and biscuits, you could work out a way round this little local difficulty.

- ✔ Hard-liners like Cardinal Carafa (remember that name because you meet him again in the following section 'The Council of Trent') thought that the Church had gone soft and needed a bit of firm discipline. Paul put Cardinal Carafa in charge of the Inquisition. He loved it.

The Council of Trent

Paul III finally decided to summon a General Council. Arranging this Council took some time because of all the fighting between the emperor and the king of France, but in 1542, Paul spotted a window and grabbed it. The Pope invited all the bishops, archbishops, cardinals, and universities of Europe to send representatives to a Great Church Council to be held at Trento in northern Italy (although called the Council of Trent, the event was not held in the English Midlands).

Some historians call the changes following the Church Council the *Catholic Reformation* – the Church reforming itself. Others see this event as the time when the Church launched its counter-attack – the *Counter Reformation*.

The Council had three sessions, with a rather important interruption in the middle:

- ✔ **1545–1547: First session: apologies, minutes, and matters arising.** Basically, the Council said that everything the Church said and did was right, but they weren't so sure about whether bishops really ought to visit their bishoprics (a diocese) at least once.

- ✔ **1551–1552: Second session: still on agenda item 3.** The Council sorted out the Church's position on Communion, but it still couldn't decide about those bishops and their bishoprics.

✔ **1555–1559: No Council: a four-year comfort break.** In 1555, Cardinal Carafa became Pope Paul IV. Paul IV thought there had been quite enough hot air spouted at Trent and he did not reconvene the Council. Paul had a big drive on discipline, and ensured that an increasing number of titles ended up on the Church's Index of Banned Books.

Paul IV genuinely wanted to reform Church abuses, and just went about it in a different way from Paul III. Paul IV died in 1559 and the reformers breathed a sigh of relief.

✔ **1562–3 Third session: AOB and date of next meeting.** This third session summed everything up in the definitive *Tridentine* (meaning 'from Trent') *Decrees*:

- *One single, uniform Latin Tridentine Mass for use throughout the world* – and every Sunday, too, not just Christmas and Easter. The Tridentine Mass remained unchanged until the 1960s.

- *A new improved translation of the Bible.* Note that you still need the Church to get into heaven. It is *not* predestined, whatever the Protestants might say.

- *Bishops should live in their bishoprics and check up on their clergy regularly.* And the Vatican will be checking to see that they've done it.

- *Clergy should preach a proper sermon every week* – and every diocese must have a seminary to train them in how to do it. (Preaching was the Protestants' trump card; thus, scoring well here was essential.)

- *BANNED: Selling relics, selling indulgences, priests' concubines.* Time to sell the double bed, Father.

The Tridentine Decrees were intended to make Catholicism a much more intense personal experience, instead of just a set of mechanical rituals. The Church started running off a printed Catechism, explaining what Catholics believe in a FAQ style; this text is still in use today. Catholics were to go to Confession more often, and really make a clean breast of things. To help people confess, Carlo Borromeo, the charismatic Archbishop of Milan, designed the confessional box, with a screen so you weren't able to see the priest's face clearly and he wasn't able to see yours – rather like Freud sitting behind his patients to help them to open up. If you really entered into the spirit of things you might become an ecstatic, like St Teresa of Avila or St Philip Neri, who used to go off into ecstasy for a couple of hours in the middle of mass – if you were wise you brought your sandwiches and something to read until normal service was resumed.

A Salvation Army with attitude

Ignatius of Loyola was a tough Spanish soldier who founded a special order of priests called the *Society of Jesus,* better known as the *Jesuits*, which he ran along the strict military lines outlined in his bestseller: *The Spiritual Exercises* – a sort of fitness manual for the soul. This text propounds firm discipline; regular and detailed confession; and excellence in everything, however lowly, because you were doing it For the Greater Glory of God.

The Jesuits have been called the 'shock troops' of the Counter-Reformation. They specialised in education, producing top-class academics and sending missionaries to India, America, and England. The Jesuits were so successful that their opponents began to accuse them of all sorts of strange and questionable practices: 'Jesuitical' came to mean, at least to Protestants, 'too clever by half' and 'not to be trusted'. Some Catholics felt that way about the Jesuits, too.

More Counter-Reformation popes

The Council of Trent was just the start of the story. The acid test came when the Church tried to implement the Tridentine Decrees. Overseeing that was down to the popes who were elected in the years that followed:

- ✔ **Pius V (1566–1572):** Hard-line former Inquisitor-General. Implemented the Tridentine Decrees but banned so many books most Italian printers shut up shop and moved to Germany. Quarrelled with Philip II of Spain and excommunicated Elizabeth I of England.

- ✔ **Gregory XIII (1572–1585):** Another hard-liner. Gregory was so delighted when he heard that 3,000 Protestants had been massacred in Paris he held a special service of thanksgiving. Best known for cutting ten days from the calendar: Protestant countries thought it was a Catholic trick and didn't adopt the Gregorian calendar for another hundred years.

- ✔ **Sixtus V (1585–1590):** Known as the 'iron pope'. Sixtus had thousands of bandits in Italy put to death and promised to bankroll the Spanish Armada, until he heard that it had sunk. Still, Sixtus did get the dome of St Peter's finished.

- ✔ **Urban VII (1590):** Caught malaria and died before he could be crowned.

- ✔ **Gregory XIV (1590–91):** Survived just long enough to ban betting on papal elections or the length of papal reigns and then died, just to annoy the bookies.

- ✔ **Innocent IX (1591):** Caught a chill and died.

- ✔ **Clement VIII (1592–1605):** Carried on implementing the Tridentine Decrees and very reluctantly allowed the French to tolerate Protestants.

I'm the King of the World!

When Emperor Charles V abdicated in 1556, his son Philip, inherited Spain and Spain's empire around the world. Philip saw himself as God's instrument on earth, so ruling a worldwide empire seemed only fitting. But how did the king of Spain end up with an empire that spanned the globe?

The Portuguese set sail

Prince Henry of Portugal, known as 'the Navigator', had set up a school of navigation back in the early 15th century and financed a number of Portuguese voyages to find a way to the East. The Portuguese wanted to undercut the Arabs in the highly lucrative spice trade (European food was so heavily preserved in salt that strong spices were needed to give it flavour). Portugal's Spanish neighbours, the kingdoms of Castile and Aragon, were fully engaged in fighting against the Muslims of Granada (Chapter 9 covers what this war was about) but when Granada finally fell in 1492, Queen Isabella of Castile received a visit from a young Genoese sea captain with an interesting proposal. This young man's idea was to sail west and reach the spice islands while the Portuguese were still trying to work a way round the southern tip of Africa. This sea captain's name was Cristobal Colon, but we know him as Christopher Columbus.

Columbus sails the ocean blue

Just about every film or TV version of Columbus's voyage shows him as a visionary who realised that the world is round when everyone else thought it was flat. That's wrong. By 1492, all learned opinion in Europe had come round to the idea that the world was round. The objections to Columbus's plan were about how long it was going to take and whether he would actually make it.

Queen Isabella decided to take the risk and provided Columbus with three ships, the *Niña*, *Pinta*, and the *Santa Maria*. Any lands that Columbus found on his voyage he was allowed to claim – and govern – for Castile.

Columbus didn't make it to the Indies (though to his dying day he believed he had); instead he landed in the 'West Indies', probably in the Bahamas. Although Columbus himself never landed on the American mainland, the Spanish settlers who followed him did, and Queen Isabella found herself with an overseas empire on her hands. Since the 'New World', as Europeans soon started calling these new lands across the sea, proved to contain substantial deposits of silver, this suited her just fine.

We come in peace – just kidding!

The Aztec and Inca Empires were massive, highly sophisticated civilisations, capable of advanced engineering and building and with large, well-trained armies; how on earth did the Spanish conquer them so quickly?

Weight of numbers cannot explain the conquest because Francisco Pizarro conquered Peru with 180 men and one ship. Capturing the leaders helped: Hernan Cortez captured Montezuma of Mexico and killed him; Pizarro kidnapped the Inca emperor, Atahualpa, got his people to fill a large room full of gold as a ransom, and then strangled him. Who said Pizarro had to play fair?

Historians have suggested many reasons for the Spanish success, including that maybe they brought diseases that the Indians weren't used to, or perhaps their arrival coincided with a prophesy of doom. The main reason was simpler. The Spanish had come looking for El Dorado, the fabled land of gold, and they would stop at absolutely nothing to get it. The Aztecs and Incas had simply never encountered such ruthless determination before.

For many years Columbus was celebrated as an American hero, the man who 'discovered' America . Historians nowadays emphasise the disastrous effects Columbus's landfall had on the Arawak and Carib peoples that he encountered in the New World. Within a generation of the discovery they had died out, from a combination of disease contracted from the Spanish, and the Spanish insistence on working them to death in their hunt for gold and silver.

East is east, and west is mine, all mine!

One day in 1493, Pope Alexander VI took a pen and divided the world. Spain was to have everything west of a line 370 leagues west of Azores, and Portugal got everything to the east. Spain got most of America (not Brazil, though, which fell east of the line), and Portugal got Africa, India, and the (east) Indies. The Portuguese soon started shipping African slaves off from their African possessions to work on their sugar plantations in Brazil.

In 1580, the Portuguese ran out of kings, so Philip II of Spain took over the Portuguese Empire, making him king of the world's first global superpower. (For more on Philip, see the next sections.)

The other Europeans weren't going to leave all these lucrative overseas territories to the Spanish. The French settled in North America; the English muscled in on the slave trade and ambushed Spanish bullion ships; and the Dutch took over the Portuguese spice trade. These actions weren't just about national rivalry or even getting rich quick: The English and Dutch were claiming the oceans for the Protestant religion. Europe's religious wars had gone global.

Just Put It in One of Philip II's Many 'Urgent Business' Piles

Charles V had spent all his time moving from one part of his empire to another, fighting wars or crushing revolts. Philip II wasn't going to make that mistake. Philip built a rather grim palace-cum-office block for himself near Madrid called El Escurial and he stayed there.

Philip had his fingers badly burnt early in his reign by a disloyal secretary called Antonio Perez, who tricked him into having a loyal official murdered and then stirred up a rebellion in Aragon. From then on, Philip's golden rule was to *trust no one*. Philip insisted on vetting every letter and every note coming in or going out, and he pondered long and hard on every decision. If you sent a letter to the king of Spain you might get a reply before you retired but you wouldn't bet on it.

You were in a worse situation if you lent Philip money – he went bankrupt *three times*. Calling in the bailiffs for the king of Spain wasn't an option, so his creditors lost their money, Philip borrowed from someone else, and his subjects found themselves with a big tax demand.

Triumph and disaster at sea

All the money that Philip was borrowing and not paying back was paying for war. Philip was the leader of Christendom, the Most Catholic King, as his title put it, and he took his duty to fight God's enemies very seriously – here was a man with 7,000 holy relics in his palace, after all.

The Turks were the most serious threat. Philip linked up with the Pope and the Venetians and in 1571, led by his half-brother, Don John of Austria, Philip's fleet crushed the Turks off Lepanto in Greece. Christian Europe went mad with joy. Philip was so worried about the Muslim threat that he banned Muslim dress and customs among the Moorish people of Spain, and when they rose up in protest, he crushed them without mercy and threw them out.

Things didn't go so well for Philip on the northern front. In 1588, Philip put together the great Armada to invade England, topple Elizabeth I, and take the throne of England. The Armada was sunk, partly by the English and partly by their weather. Philip took this defeat on the chin (like all the Habsburg clan, Philip had a good chin to take it on).

Keep it in the family

The Habsburgs believed in marrying within the family – there's no breeding like in-breeding – and Philip II's son, poor Don Carlos, was the result. Don Carlos only had four great grandparents instead of the usual eight (which tells you much of what you need to know) and he showed disturbing signs of taking after his mad great granny, Joanna 'the Mad' of Castile. He even started talking of running away to join the Dutch Revolt (see the 'Dutch courage' section for more on this). Philip had to have Don Carlos locked up, and he died in prison.

Great propaganda copy for Philip's enemies, who suspected Philip of killing his son; even in the 19th century Verdi's opera *Don Carlos*

shows the prince as a martyr for liberty, with his father egged on by the sinister (and blind – more spooky) Chief Inquisitor to murder him. Great music, bad history. The real Don Carlos threw himself into a cycle of hunger strikes and binge eating, which sounds like bulimia coupled with a death wish, and most certainly killed him.

Philip went through four marriages and a lot of dead children before the arrival of an heir who actually survived with a more or less normal mind. This child's mother was Philip II's fourth wife, Anne of Austria, who also just happened to be Philip II's niece. Philip II was said never to smile; looking at his home life you can see why.

Dutch courage

The Netherlands were all that was left of the old Duchy of Burgundy by the time the French and Spanish had finished fighting over it. The Netherlands was a collection of small city states, including some of the most important trading centres in Europe, like Bruges and Antwerp. The Netherlands hadn't been conquered by Spain, but they soon felt that the Spanish were treating them as if they had been, imposing taxes and interfering in the way they governed themselves and – most importantly – the way they worshipped.

The people of the Netherlands were inclined to be tolerant of different religions – religious persecution was bad for business – and they sent one of their leading nobles, Count Egmont, down to Spain to explain their toleration policy to Philip. Philip was preoccupied with the Turks at the time, so he nodded and said 'Fine, fine,' which Egmont took to mean that Philip agreed with the policy. Wrong!

The Iconoclastic Fury

In 1566, the Dutch Calvinists started smashing Church statues and pictures (which they saw as little better than pagan idols) in what became known as the *Iconoclastic Fury*. Philip's half-sister, Margaret of Parma, Regent of the Netherlands, restored order, but Philip, who was pathologically incapable of leaving things to the people on the spot, decided that the Dutch needed some very firm discipline. Philip sent the fearsome Duke of Alba north with 10,000 men and carte blanche to do whatever he thought necessary to stamp out the Calvinists.

Alba intended to teach the Dutch a lesson they wouldn't forget in a hurry:

- ✔ The duke's special *Council of Troubles* executes some 2,000 people and confiscates the lands of some 9,000 more. The Dutch call it the Council of Blood, and no wonder.

- ✔ The Council of Troubles executes Count Egmont and his colleague Count Hoorn. These people are well-respected noblemen and members of the Order of the Golden Fleece; even Catholic nobles are outraged.

- ✔ Alba imposes a new permanent tax, the *Tenth Penny*, which hits the Dutch where it hurts – in the pocket.

The Dutch Revolt

In 1572, the leading Dutch nobleman whom Alba had not been able to get his hands on, William of Nassau, Prince of Orange, declared war against Alba and his reign of terror. The Dutch Revolt was on.

William was known as William the Silent because everyone thought that he had lots of cunning plans up his sleeve, but he can't have been that cunning because the Duke of Alba was soon capturing every rebel town he came to. At Haarlem Alba went back on his word and massacred the entire garrison.

Although Alba was winning the war, his tough tactics were making the situation worse. And then Philip II's sluggish approach to paperwork finally provoked disaster:

- ✔ **1576: Philip II goes bankrupt.** His unpaid soldiers down tools and trash the nearest Dutch town, which just happens to be Antwerp, the most important trading port in northern Europe.

- ✔ **1578: Dutch Calvinists start smashing statues and windows in Catholic towns in southern Netherlands.** Catholic residents protest. 'Hmm. Religious divisions. Very interesting', think the Spanish.

- ✔ **1584: William of Orange is assassinated.** William is bumped off by a very cross Catholic monk. Philip II *almost* smiles.

- ✔ **1585: Elizabeth I of England agrees to help the rebels.** 'Right!' thinks Philip II: 'Time to deal with England once and for all.'

- ✔ **1588: Philip II launches the Armada to link up with the Duke of Parma and invade England.** Historians generally agree that the plan could have worked had Philip not interfered so much – but he did, and it didn't.

- ✔ **1596: Spanish Crown goes bankrupt again.**

- ✔ **1598: Philip II dies.**

- ✔ **1607: Spanish Crown goes bankrupt yet again.**

- ✔ **1609: Twelve-year truce is negotiated.** The Protestants of the northern Netherlands now become the Republic of the United Provinces.

Spain hadn't given up hope of getting the Netherlands back, though you may wonder what it wanted it back *for*. Another 40 years passed before the Spanish finally accepted the Dutch as an independent nation (see Chapter 13).

France's Wars of Religion

France was a Catholic country, but French kings were quite happy to support foreign Protestants against the Habsburgs (the *French* Protestants were the ones they couldn't stand). This religious conflict was entangled in a very bloody power struggle at court. Three groups vied for the upper hand:

- ✔ **Queen Catherine de Medici and her sons:** Catherine was Henry II's widow and Queen Mother to three kings of France, Francis II, Charles IX, and Henry III, but none of them was able to produce an heir.

- ✔ **The Guises:** Powerful and ambitious Catholic noble family led by the Duke of Guise. Strongly anti-Protestant. Catherine de Medici backed them at first and then rather wished that she hadn't.

- ✔ **The Protestants:** Admiral Gaspard de Coligny and the Bourbon family, Antoine de Bourbon the king of Navarre, his brother the Prince of Condé, and son Henry. The Bourbons were of royal blood and deadly enemies of the Guises, who weren't royal but wished they were.

French Protestants were known as *Huguenots*. Historians come up with different explanations for this title: The Huguenots may have been named after someone called Hugues (French for Hugh) or they may have got their name from a particular town. Whatever. Huguenot means French Protestant.

Episode 1: The turncoat

The only way for the Huguenots to follow their religion was to control the king, so Antoine de Bourbon came up with a plot to kidnap Francis II. The plot was discovered and Francis II died in any case. Francis's brother became King Charles IX, with Catherine de Medici as regent. But wily Catherine charmed Antoine de Bourbon into changing sides. When the fanatical Duke of Guise killed 30 Huguenots and started a war, Antoine fought on the *Catholic* side and was mortally wounded. As he lay dying, Antoine sent for both a Catholic priest and a Protestant minister – hedging his bets, you see.

Episode 2: Catherine's terrible revenge

Catherine had Condé executed for treason, which left only Gaspard de Coligny and young Henry of Navarre leading the Protestant side. Coligny joined up with Charles IX for a war with Spain ('I'm of age now, mother,' Charles pointed out to Catherine, 'and I'll do what I like'). When France lost the war, Catherine decided Coligny must die. Unfortunately, her assassins only wounded him. Catherine was afraid of what would happen when Coligny discovered who had tried to kill him, so she decided to stage a very grim cover-up.

Where do you hide a leaf? In a forest. Where do you hide a murder? In a massacre. On 24 August 1572, the eve of the feast of St Bartholomew, Catherine de Medici (probably) and the Guises (almost certainly) arranged the massacre of some 3,000 Protestants in Paris to cover up the murder attempt on Coligny. The English and Dutch were horrified. Pope Gregory XIII said a thanksgiving mass. And Philip II (or so his enemies said) smiled.

Episode 3: Henry versus Henry versus Henry

As a result of the massacre the Huguenots effectively declared themselves independent of the crown. When Charles IX died of tuberculosis, royal brother Number 3 became King Henry III and granted the Huguenots freedom to worship as they liked, anywhere outside Paris – anything for some peace. This declaration was alright with Henry of Navarre, who was now heir to the throne, but not with Henry of Guise. Henry of Guise had founded the ultra-militant *Catholic League* to campaign to get Protestantism stamped out in France whether Henry III liked it or not.

In 1588 on the *Day of the Barricades*, the Guises invaded Paris, defeated Henry III's men, and forced him to flee. Henry III retaliated by having Henry of Guise murdered.

Finally, on 1 July 1589, a mad monk came to see Henry III at the palace of Saint-Cloud and stabbed him to death. Doing so was silly really, because this action meant that France now had a Protestant king: Henry of Navarre.

Episode 4: Paris is worth a mass

Henry took the title Henry IV, but he faced enemies: but the Catholic League and Philip II.

At this crucial point, Henry IV played his masterstroke – he announced that he had converted and become a Catholic. A bit too convenient? Maybe, but Henry's plan worked.

Was Henry's conversion genuine, or a sign that he didn't take his religious loyalties seriously? Henry himself said, 'Paris is worth a mass.' Henry IV was crowned at Chartres in February 1594, entered Paris in state the following month, offered a pardon to anyone who had fought against him, and promptly declared a very popular war with Spain, which united the country – better than that – he won.

Epilogue

Henry IV tried to heal the wounds of the long Wars of Religion. He made a good peace with Spain, and issued the *Edict of Nantes*, which allowed Huguenots freedom to worship as long as they kept to certain places and did it out of the public eye.

Henry once remarked that his aim was to ensure everyone in France at least had enough to eat, so that every household had a chicken for the pot. Henry reorganised the laws, got France trading again, and had the roads seen to. But even Henry IV couldn't put the killing behind him.

In 1610, Henry married his second wife, Marie de Medici. The next day, a rather crazed Catholic schoolmaster, called François Ravaillac, came up to Henry and stabbed him to death. Assassination was fast becoming a central part of the French political system.

Chapter 12

Tsar Wars

*E*urope in the 16th century looked fearfully at the seemingly unstoppable force of the Ottoman Turks, who dominated the Mediterranean, conquered the Balkans and captured the mighty city of Constantinople. Meanwhile, a new and powerful dynasty was taking power in Russia and strong new states were emerging in Poland and the Baltic.

The Ottomans: New Improved Turks

In crusading times the Turkish top dogs were the Seljuk Turks, but in 1243 they were crushed by a terrible new enemy thundering down out of the East – the terrifying Mongol horde of Genghis Khan. Genghis Khan's hordes didn't stick around (well, they were nomads) but by the time they left, the Seljuks were finished as serious players. Into the power vacuum the Mongols left behind them led a Turkish tribe and its ambitious leader called Osman.

'Osman' comes out as 'Uthman' in Arabic (Turkish and Arabic are quite different languages), so this new Turkish empire became known as the *Ottoman Empire*.

In 1345 the Ottomans got a letter from the Christian Byzantine emperor, John VI Cantacuzenos asking for their help in dealing with a rival claimant to his throne. Were the Ottomans interested in coming?

European history is full of warlike peoples who get invited in to help and end up helping themselves. The Ottomans won the emperor's battles for him, and then spread all over Greece and the Balkans. No one was able to stop them:

✔ **1389: Ottomans crush the Serbs at Kosovo Polje.**

In 1989, to mark the six-hundredth anniversary of the Battle of Kosovo, Serb leader Slobodan Milosevic launched his bid to create a new Serb empire and so ushered in the Yugoslav civil war of the 1990s. Why do people only try to repeat the bad bits of history?

✔ **1393: Ottoman leader Bayezid conquers Bulgaria.**

✔ **1396: Bayezid crushes Crusaders.** King Sigismund of Hungary leads a crusade of Venetians, French, and Burgundians against Bayezid – and loses.

Bayezid is Mongol-mangled

Just when Bayezid didn't need it, the Ottomans' old enemies the Mongols came charging in again, led by the wily Timur the Lame – also known as Tamerlaine or Tamberlaine the Great. The Ottomans had made a lot of enemies so Timur, sensible chap, got in touch with them. When Bayezid squared up to Timur outside Ankara in 1402, half the Ottomans' allies suddenly changed sides – only the Serbs stayed loyal to him. Bayezid died a prisoner of the Mongols.

The Europeans were delighted to see their old enemy humbled. The Byzantine Emperor got together with the Venetians, the Genoese, and the crusading Order of the Knights of St John to force the Ottomans to hand over Thessaloniki. The Ottomans were in the throes of a bitter three-way civil war and couldn't hit back until Mehmet I restored order. His son, Murad II, turned his attention to Europe:

✔ **1430:** Murad II takes back Thessaloniki.

✔ **1440:** Civil war breaks out in Hungary, so Murad II invades.

✔ **1441:** Murad II invades Transylvania (yes, this place really exists) but is thrown out by the Hungarian warrior *John Hunyadi*.

I'm holding out for a (Hungarian) hero: John Hunyadi

The Ottomans were used to beating the Europeans so that Transylvanian defeat came as a shock. King Vladislav of Hungary was so encouraged that he thought the time had come for a new crusade, uniting all of Christendom, Catholic and Orthodox, against the Turks.

Dear mum, I am well, and if I behave myself, I could become prime minister

The Ottomans had a system called the *devshirme* ('collection') under which they took Christian boys from their families – about one in every forty – and brought them up to work for the Empire. No only sons were selected (not fair on the parents), no orphans (too badly behaved), no one too tall (too stupid) or too short (trouble) – this may be the only recruiting system in history where it paid to lie about your height. These lads went on to very good careers in the Ottoman civil service. Even slaves could rise to the top; the Grand Vizier (the Ottoman prime minister) was nearly always a slave. The sultans liked having a slave as Grand Vizier, as everyone was reminded that the Sultan was really in charge.

John Hunyadi was in charge of the campaign. Hunyadi marched through Serbia, and in 1444, the Crusaders and Ottomans faced each other at Varna, deep in Ottoman territory. The Hungarians spent a day blowing the Ottomans to bits with their cannon until, just when they thought everything was all over, King Vladislav snatched disaster from the gaping jaws of victory – he suddenly rode out on his own and got himself killed. Idiot! The Hungarians lost heart and the Turks, when they had stopped laughing, chased them from the field.

John Hunyadi had another go at beating the Turks four years later but lost at Kosovo – the Turks' lucky battlefield. Hunyadi did take Belgrade off the Turks a few years later, but died soon afterwards – from dysentery. Hunyadi is still a hero in Hungary today.

Mehmet 'the Conqueror'

If the Europeans thought that Murad II was bad news, they hadn't yet met his son, Mehmet II 'the Conqueror'. (See the section 'Bayezid is Mongol-mangled', earlier in this chapter, for more on Murad II.) No sooner had Mehmet come to the Ottoman throne than he went for the prize: Constantinople. The Byzantines appealed desperately to the West for help, but in 1453, the great Christian capital fell and the cathedral of Hagia Sophia became a mosque.

Next the Ottomans took Serbia (again), Athens, Bosnia, and Albania, invaded Hungary, Austria, Croatia, and even Poland. The Ottomans beat the Venetians at sea, raided Italy, and took the port of Otranto. It looked as if, within a generation or two, perhaps Europe would become a Muslim continent – worth bearing in mind when people talk a bit too airily of Europe's long Christian heritage.

Turkish rule wasn't necessarily as bad as people in the West thought. The Turks were very tolerant of different religions and under Islamic law protected religious groups could not be enslaved. Jews felt a lot safer under the Ottomans than they did under Christians, and with good reason.

Some of the sultans' most feared troops were their highly disciplined infantry, the *janissaries*. The janissaries were fiercely loyal to the sultans – and were all drawn from Christian families (see the nearby sidebar, 'Dear mum, I am well, and if I behave myself, I could become prime minister').

That magnificent man and his machinations: Suleiman 1

In 1520, Sultan Suleiman I came to the throne. The sultan's court at his famous *Topkapi Palace* was so glittering that he became known as Suleiman the Magnificent. Suleiman wasn't all show – he was a great law-giver and founder of schools. Suleiman was a contemporary of the Holy Roman Emperor Charles V and King Francis I of France – and he was going to play a complex diplomatic game with both of them.

Suleiman used to greet foreign ambassadors before the great gate to the Topkapi Palace. In French, which was to become the international language of diplomacy, the gate was the *Porte*, so the sultan's government became known as 'the Porte'.

Suleiman's great enemy was the Holy Roman Emperor Charles V (To find out more about him go to Chapters 10 and 11). Charles wanted to clear the Turks out of Hungary and the Mediterranean. Suleiman did not intend to give him the satisfaction on either front. In his first year as sultan, Suleiman took Belgrade, and two years later he took the island of Rhodes from the Knights of St John (to find out more about these crusading knights take a look at Chapter 7).

Francis I was itching for revenge for the way that Charles's men had captured him at Pavia in 1525, and Suleiman knew it. Suleiman and Francis started co-ordinating plans; in 1526 Francis I declared war on Charles V and Suleiman invaded Hungary. At the 1526 Battle of Mohacs, King Louis II of Hungary was killed and the new king, John Zapolyai, had to agree to act effectively as an Ottoman puppet. The Hungarians have never forgotten this indignity.

Charles V wasn't standing for this puppet arrangement; he marched into Hungary, sent John Zapolyai packing, and put his brother Ferdinand of Habsburg on the Hungarian throne. But John and Suleiman came back and Hungary became a sort of European wild-west frontier: forts, border raids, and Hungarians riding round saying 'Yep, a man's gotta do what a man's gotta do' – in Magyar.

Pirates of the Mediterranean

The Ottomans had a very useful ally – a pirate chief called Hayreddin Barbarossa who operated out of Morocco and Tunisia, attacking Spanish and Venetian ships.

Suleiman made Barbarossa Grand Admiral of the Ottoman fleet and when the Porte signed a formal alliance with France (which gave the rest of Europe's monarchs apoplexy over their breakfasts), Francis I allowed the Turks to spend the winter in harbour in Toulon. Barbarossa sank Charles's fleet and forced the Venetians out of their bases in southern Greece, and his successor, Dragut, kicked the poor old Knights of St John out of Tripoli and nearly took Malta off them as well.

The Spanish and Venetians finally defeated the Ottoman fleet at the Battle of Lepanto in 1571. This defeat didn't suddenly turn the tide of the war – the Turks took Cyprus the same year (the campaign features in Shakespeare's *Othello*), took Tunis back, and conquered Morocco – but the defeat did show that they *could* be beaten. The long slow years of Ottoman decline were about to begin.

Is this empire past its sell-by date?

Under the Byzantines, Constantinople had had a reputation for court intrigue and the Ottomans seem to have inherited it. One of Suleiman's wives, a nasty piece of work called Roxelana, had the Grand Vizier Ibrahim strangled after 13 years of loyal service and got her son-in-law appointed in his place. Roxelana framed Suleiman's own son (by another wife, of course) and persuaded Suleiman to have him strangled. People talked of the *Sultanate of Women* – it wasn't a compliment.

Alexander Nevsky's Ragtime Band

In 1240 the Swedes attacked Russia along the River Neva, but they were beaten by a young Russian prince called Alexander; he was given the name *Nevsky* after the River Neva in commemoration. Two years later Alexander Nevsky rode out to fight the German Teutonic Knights, met them at the frozen Lake Peipus, and sent them packing (Chapter 7 has the details about the Teutonic Knights. You can also head to the section 'Knights in White Satin' later in this chapter).

The Tatars invade

The Swedes and Teutonic Knights were small potatoes compared with the storm that was about to engulf Russia: in 1240 the Mongol Tatars of the *Golden Horde* swept down from the steppes of Central Russia and captured Russia's capital, Kiev.

The name 'Golden Horde' probably comes from the old Russian system of dividing the vast steppe lands into different 'colour' zones. The 'white' steppe lay in the west ('white' Russia comes out in Russian as *byelorussia*, which is the origin of the modern name *Belarus*); the 'blue' steppe was in the east; 'red' in the south; 'black' in the north; and 'gold' in the centre, which is where the Golden Horde based themselves.

This takeover was very good news for Moscow, then known as *Muscovy*. The Tatars liked Muscovy, partly on the divide-and-rule principle (use Muscovy to keep Kiev in its place), but mainly because they found out how good it was at tax collecting. Ivan I was so good at gathering money from his neighbours that the Tatars named him Grand Prince of Vladimir. (The Tatars also called him Ivan Moneybags, but that didn't sound quite so grand.)

A third Rome?

Under the Tatars, Muscovy grew in importance, especially when the Metropolitan (which means the head) of the Russian Church transferred his seat there. When Constantinople fell to the Ottomans in 1453 the Russians thought that it served the Greeks right. The Russian Church was the only genuine, real McCoy Christian Church left in the world, and they began to talk of Muscovy as the 'third Rome'.

And it's Muscovy coming up on the outside . . .

Could Muscovy be a new Roman Empire as well as a new 'Roman' Church? This idea certainly didn't seem a very likely outcome when the 15th century began: Poland and Lithuania were the big boys on the scene (to find out why, see the upcoming section, 'Double your country, double your fun'.) The Poles and Lithuanians crushed the Teutonic Knights and then turned on Russia, sweeping into Ukraine and even taking Kiev. The Russians badly needed a good leader and, as sometimes happens, they got one: Ivan III 'the Great'.

The (Russian) Declaration of Independence

Ivan took the idea that Muscovy was the third Rome, the successor to Byzantium, very seriously. Ivan married a Byzantine princess, Zoe Paleologos, adopted the old Byzantine double-headed eagle (to the Byzantines the symbol meant the eastern and western halves of the Roman Empire; for Ivan III it meant a pedigree to die for), and had rather convoluted charts drawn up to show that his family were descended from the Roman emperors themselves. Ivan's claim to kinship with the emperors was baloney, of course, but would *you* have dared tell him?

By now the Tatar Golden Horde was splitting up, and Ivan III hurried the process along in 1480 by publicly declaring Russia independent and then conquering most of it just to prove his point. Ivan waited until the very able Polish king Casimir IV was dead before launching his counter-attack on the Poles and Lithuanians.

But Ivan's most important step wasn't a war or a battle. A whole class of nobles, known as *boyars*, had plenty of land and didn't think that they needed to be loyal to the Crown (or to anyone else). On the other hand, a veritable army of lawyers and administrators were loyal but had no land. Ivan made these lawyers and administrators special grants of land (on two conditions – no dividing it up and no selling it) and hey presto! he had a new *nouveau riche* nobility, loyal to the Crown. Very useful.

Ivan the Terrible

The man who really benefited from Ivan III's policies was his grandson, Ivan IV, known to history as Ivan the Terrible. The moniker doesn't mean 'really bad' or even 'more than usually cruel' (though he was certainly that); it means 'awesome'. Ivan came to the throne when he was only 3 years old, and his childhood was spent hiding from his relatives who were all out to kill each other – or Ivan – and seize power for themselves. Not surprisingly, Russia's neighbours, the Lithuanians and the Tatars, thought 'Land-grab time!' and did their best to keep the chaos going while they took as much Russian land as possible.

In 1543, young Ivan, aged all of 13 years and his voice just breaking, gave orders to have one of the leading boyars, a man called Andrei Shuisky, arrested and thrown to the dogs. Literally – they tore him to pieces and ate him. Andrei Shuisky was the first man to learn what happened if you crossed Ivan the Terrible. And Shuisky was not the last.

Ivan had very simple wishes:

- ✔ Get proper respect for the Crown
- ✔ Retake the lands stolen by the Lithuanians and Tatars
- ✔ Make the boyars eat dirt

Ivan really stressed this I-am-a-descendant-of-the-Caesars routine. For his coronation in 1547, Ivan announced that he would be crowned with the very regalia used by the emperors of Byzantium, rescued from the fall of Constantinople (actually it had all been made specially by local goldsmiths).

Ivan was crowned not as grand prince or even as king but as a Caesar, or, in Russian, a *tsar*. The tsar summoned a great council of Russia's big cheeses called the *Zemsky Sobor* and asked those present how, given that Russia was now a lot bigger than Kievan Rus had ever been, the country ought to be governed. Being bright lads, they all said the best idea would be if absolute power lay in the hands of the tsar. Giving Ivan absolute power was sensible because he was clearly going to take it anyway.

Ta-ta Tatars!

Dealing with the Tatars was urgent; they were always launching raids into Russia and in 1571 they burned Moscow and made off with 150,000 Russian prisoners. Ivan reorganised his army, got hold of the latest guns, and promptly conquered two of the Tatars' three *khanates* (kingdoms), Kazan and Astrakhan, where all those rather nice coats come from.

Big celebrations followed these conquests. Ivan took the title 'Grozny' ('the Terrible') and built St Basil's Cathedral in Russia in thanksgiving. However, the third khanate, the Crimea, proved a lot tougher. Ivan's advisers kept urging him to go back and have another go at the Crimea, but Ivan decided to strike north and attack the Poles and Lithuanians in the Baltic. This plan was not one of Ivan's better ideas.

Trouble up north: The Poles and the Lithuanians

What Ivan was after when he set his eyes on the Poles and Lithuanians was Livonia – more or less modern-day Estonia and Latvia. Ivan's plan to attack in the Baltic wasn't a whim. The Livonians were doing everything possible to cut Russia off from contact with the outside world, even to the point of executing traders and travellers who were going there.

Unfortunately for Ivan, the Poles and Lithuanians were working very closely together under their king, Stephen Bathory, prince of Transylvania, a close ally of the sultan and good friend of the Crimean Tatars (see the preceding section).

All Ivan's attempts to take Livonia came to grief, and in 1582 he had to admit defeat. This defeat was good news for Livonia but very bad news for Russia.

My thousands of enemies say I'm paranoid

In 1564, Ivan suddenly announced that he was surrounded by traitors so he was abdicating. He would only come back on his terms:

- I execute anyone who I think has been plotting against me. No trials: just the hangings.

- I am dividing Russia in two. Part of it will carry on as before, but a huge area about half the size of Russia will be under my direct rule, subject to my laws and my orders.

Ivan the Terrible lives again

Stalin got Sergei Eisenstein (filmmaker to the murderous and despotic) to make an epic film about Ivan the Terrible. This film is very long and very slow, but if you sit through it (which was advisable in Stalin's day) you can see that Eisenstein has made Ivan into a wise old fox, cleverly outwitting the enemies who surround him, which is pretty much how Stalin saw himself.

The special zone was called the *Oprichnina*, or 'separate state' and Ivan ruled it with a rod of iron. Ivan set up a special police force, the *Oprichniki*, all dressed in black, to ride round (on black horses, naturally) sniffing out traitors. The Oprichniki carried a dog's head and a broom on their saddle to symbolise their job of sweeping out Russia's treacherous dogs. And like any good secret police, when they started looking for traitors, the Oprichniki found them – thousands of them.

We'll never know for certain, but Ivan seems to have had some sort of mental breakdown during that abdication business in 1564 and developed a paranoia about having enemies everywhere. Ivan even started executing members of the Oprichniki – he'd convinced himself that even they were plotting against him.

These purges virtually destroyed the power of the traditional Russian nobles, the boyars, which is why, when the Crimean Tatars launched their massive raid in 1571, they were able to get all the way to Moscow and burn the place (see the section 'Ta-ta Tatars!' earlier in this chapter). Ivan was profoundly shocked, and disbanded the Oprichniki. But Ivan had no one to blame for this destruction but himself.

The boyars are back in town

Ivan reorganised Russia's administration, gave it a new legal code, and broke the power of the corrupt provincial governors. Unfortunately, Ivan didn't make good provision for what was to happen after his death – he even killed one son in a fit of rage (though he was *very* sorry afterwards) – and the son he eventually handed over to, Fedor I, was only vaguely aware of which planet he was on. Fedor sensibly handed things over to his ruthless brother-in-law, Boris Godunov.

Everybody go serfing

In western Europe, peasants were busy setting themselves up as independent farmers, like those hard-nosed, penny-wise old smallholders you see in the 1986 film *Jean de Florette*. In Russia and eastern Europe things went the other way; the peasants were not allowed even to move off their land, never mind buy it. They became serfs, the absolute property of their masters – or, to put it another way, slaves. The peasants didn't like serfdom and raised many rebellions. The nobles always dealt with these uprisings harshly, severely scaring the peasants to stop them rebelling again. Even so, fear of peasant risings gave the Russian nobility sleepless nights for centuries.

When Boris died in 1605 Russia fell into chaos. Boris's son became tsar and then died, then someone got up claiming to be Boris Godunov's grandson Dmitri (who had actually died 14 years earlier), and the peasants rose up, and the Swedes invaded, and the Poles took Moscow until in 1613 the Russians chose Michael Romanov as their new tsar and he restored some order. The Russians call this period of mayhem 'The Time of Troubles', which shows a finely-tuned sense of understatement.

Knights in White Satin

In the Middle Ages some Baltic peoples, like the Prussians and Lithuanians, still held on to the old pre-Christian religion and the popes wanted them dealt with – preferably by convincing them of the revealed truth of the gospel, but, failing that, by military annihilation. The job went to Teutonic Order of the Hospital of St Mary in Jerusalem (see Chapter 7 for more on the crusading background of the Teutonic Knights).

The Teutonic Knights carved out a very nice little domain for themselves in north-eastern Germany, but then they got a bit greedy. The Knights widened their definition of 'heathen' to include orthodox Christians who, according to the Vatican, were almost as bad. Including orthodox Christians as targets of their crusade meant the Knights' invading Russia, and this invasion was the one that Alexander Nevsky defeated in the 1420s (see the section 'Alexander Nevsky's ragtime band', earlier in this chapter).

Focus on the Lithuanians

The Teutonic Knights gave up on Russia after their defeat by Alexander Nevsky and concentrated on the Lithuanians – though justifying crusading against them after they converted to Christianity was a bit difficult. Meanwhile, the

Knights branched out into trade (they did very well in Baltic amber and grain), ruled Prussia and Estonia with a rod of iron (they bought Estonia in 1346 from the king of Denmark – a bargain), and generally acted like any other north-European state.

However, the Teutonic Knights weren't any other state – to the kings of the region they were a wretched nuisance. In 1410, King Wladislaw II, Lithuanian king of the united Kingdom of Poland and Lithuania, crushed the Knights at the great Battle of Tannenberg. Every senior officer of the order, including the Grand Master, was killed. All over the region the Baltic kings and nobles were punching the air and saying 'Yesssss!'

The Germans never forgot Tannenberg and in 1914, they defeated a huge Russian army there at the start of the First World War. Because by then, Poland and Lithuania were both part of Russia, so you could say that this battle was revenge for what had happened to the Teutonic Knights – you could, and they did.

When Martin Luther started to preach wholesale reformation of the Church (see Chapter 10 for more on Luther) Albert of Hohenzollern, Grand Master of the Teutonics, rather liked what he heard and announced that the Order was closing down as a religious organisation. Albert did a deal with the Poles: Poland got West Prussia, the Hohenzollern family got East Prussia, and the Knights, in their new secularised form, got Livonia and Estonia. Everybody gets something – everybody's happy.

Albert had his eye on East Prussia's neighbour, the state of Brandenburg. A hundred years later, in 1613, Albert's dream finally came true. A marriage alliance joined the two states together as Brandenburg-Prussia, ruled by the Hohenzollerns from Berlin. Brandenburg-Prussia was the state that eventually became the Germany of Frederick the Great, the Kaiser, and Hitler.

Double your country, double your fun

Poland-Lithuania is one of those double names that only seem to exist in history books. The two states were very different: Lithuania had kept its ancient traditions and religion alive and only became Christian for its political advantage; King Casimir I 'the Great' had made Poland into a major European centre of learning and culture.

In 1386, Poland and Lithuania formed a marriage alliance to defend themselves against the Teutonic Knights. The states worked well together against the Knights, and then later against the Russians in the long wars for Livonia. In 1569, the union of the two countries was made official. Despite this union another up-and-coming state was the one that finally got Livonia (after all this trouble, you hope that Livonia was worth it): Sweden.

Princes of Denmark

In the Middle Ages, Denmark was the really important Scandinavian country. If you look at a map you can see why Denmark was so significant: the country juts out into the Baltic and controls the narrow passage (the Danish Sound – a geographical term, not a sixties' music fashion) that connects the Baltic with the North Sea. In effect, control of the Sound meant that the Danes could control all shipping and trade going in and out of the Baltic. Since the Baltic was one of the richest trading areas in Europe, this control was well worth having. The Danes' main rivals were the German merchants of the Hanse, who needed to pass through the Sound and weren't going to stand for anyone trying to stop them (see Chapter 8 for more on the Hanse).

Banner from heaven

The Baltic crusades against the pagan Prussians and Lithuanians (see the section 'Knights in White Satin' earlier in this chapter) offered the Danes a chance for expansion that was just too good to miss. In 1219, the Danes attacked pagan Estonia, but just when they thought they had won, the Estonians hit back and had the Danes at their mercy. At that moment, according to legend (and if you're in Denmark, you're well advised to believe this story), a red banner brandishing a white cross descended from heaven and a heavenly voice told them all to rally round it. The Danes won the day (you could say that flag saved their bacon), Estonia became a Danish possession – Tallinn, the Estonian capital, means 'Danish Castle' – and the red flag or *Dannebrog* (literally 'red rag') became Denmark's national flag, the oldest in the world.

Another day will come: King Valdemar IV

In 1340, the Danes got a new king, Valdemar IV (also known as Atterdag – 'Another Day' – because of his saying 'Another day will come'). Valdemar was a careful, cautious character. The Danish king sold Estonia to the Teutonic Knights, who had more use for it than he had, brought his overmighty subjects to heel, and left crusading to his rather effete neighbour, King Magnus II of Sweden.

What Valdemar did do, in 1361, was to invade the Baltic island of Gotland and take Visby, its capital. Gotland was the lair of a pirate syndicate known as the Vitalien brothers (Vitalien from 'victuals' – they stole foodstuffs from ships and sold them on at a profit; a sort of mafia-meets-the-co-op), and Visby was the headquarters of the Hanse.

By now, Valdemar was beginning to make powerful enemies. The Dane also fell out with the Teutonic Knights and the Dutch, and in 1370, the Dutch and the Hanseatic merchants joined forces to seize Copenhagen and force Valdemar to accept the humiliating *Peace of Stralsund*. Not only did Valdemar have to give up some of his ports to the Hanse, but the Hanse got the right of veto on his successor.

Three queens for the price of one: The Union of Kolmar

Valdemar's successor was his grandson Olaf (the Hanse approved of this choice and did not exercise their power of veto – phew). But then Olaf's father, King Haakon of Norway, died as well, so young Olaf found himself king of both Denmark and Norway. Then Olaf, never a strong child, died and his two thrones passed to his mother, Margaret. To cap it all, the Swedes, who had got very tired of Magnus II and his penchant for pretty stable boys, deposed him and invited Margaret to be their queen, too. Margaret said yes.

Margaret of Denmark was a remarkable woman, and she is nothing like as well known as she ought to be. In 1397, Margaret formed the *Union of Kolmar*, binding her three kingdoms into one, and arranged for her great-nephew, Boleslaw of Pomerania, to be her successor. Now, you cannot possibly have a Scandinavian king called Boleslaw of Pomerania (actually, whether you can have any job at all if you're called Boleslaw of Pomerania is debatable) so Boleslaw very sensibly changed his name to Eric. When Margaret died in 1412, her great-nephew succeeded to the three thrones as King Eric VIII.

Poor Eric VIII: perhaps he'd have been happier in Pomerania, because he didn't have a hint of his great-aunt's political nous. Eric started ruling Sweden and Norway as if they were Danish possessions, which was bound to cause trouble. The king ratcheted up the tolls on ships going through the Sound, which was virtually begging the Hanse to declare war on him. When Eric finally made peace with his enemies, the Danes, who couldn't stand the Swedes or the Hanse, were so disgusted with the Danish king for making peace with them that they staged a coup and got rid of him.

The Union of Kolmar wasn't smashed, but it had a bad crack down the middle. The only way that the Danes were able to hold the Union together was by force:

- ✔ **1471:** Swedish leader Sten Sture the Elder defeats Danish King Christian I and takes Sweden out of the Union of Kolmar.

- ✔ **1513:** Christian II of Denmark tries to force the Swedes back into the Union of Kolmar, but fails.

- ✔ **1517:** Christian II has another go at the Swedes and fails again, this time losing to Sten Sture the Younger.

- ✔ **1520:** Third time lucky. Christian II beats Sten Sture the Younger, kills him, and is crowned king of Sweden.

But Christian II hadn't finished with the Swedes yet – he wanted revenge for what had happened to his grandfather, Christian I. Christian II invited the Swedish nobility to Stockholm castle and had 82 of them taken away and executed – officially for heresy but in reality for daring to oppose him. This appalling massacre remains one of the most infamous moments in Swedish – or European – history and, just like Queen Margaret, it ought to be better known.

One Swedish nobleman was not present at the meeting and so escaped with his life. This nobleman's name was Gustav Eriksson of the House of Vasa. Gustav tried to start a rebellion against the Danes but everyone was too scared to join in, until Christian II started killing more Swedes: then men on skis caught up with Gustav and persuaded him to turn back. Gustav very cannily declared himself a Lutheran – he needed money and confiscating Church land was the quickest way to get it – and on 6 June 1523, he rode into Stockholm as King Gustav I Vasa of Sweden. Gustav's action was the start of a royal dynasty that was to lead Sweden to unimaginable triumph and power – and eventually to disaster.

Chapter 13

Absolute Power: The Sun King Rises

*E*urope had torn itself apart in religious wars in the 16th-century, and for its first 50 years 17th-century Europe did much the same. The carnage was so great that at the end of the war Europeans were desperate for a way to avoid falling into such destructive conflicts ever again.

The French seemed as if they might have the answer. King Louis XIV concentrated power in his own hands and reduced the mighty nobles of France to mere courtiers at his magnificent palace at Versailles. Most of Europe was soon doing likewise.

Give Me Liberties or Give Me Death

Seventeenth-century Europeans took the idea of *liberties* very seriously. Not liber*ty*: liber*ties* – special laws and privileges that had been given to their town or their state or even their family years ago, and which they fought to keep if these rights were threatened. A heavy price was paid for ignoring these laws and privileges – the English cut their king's head off.

You need to remember the importance of liberties because otherwise the ins and outs of 17th-century Europe don't make sense, especially if you're expecting everyone to line up along straight religious lines. Some people did fight for their beliefs, but others, known as *politiques*, put their religious loyalties to one side and acted purely on political grounds, even if this action meant supporting the 'other' religion against their own.

Trouble Brews in Germany

The Holy Roman Empire was still operating along the lines laid down by Charles V and the Protestant princes in the Religious Peace of Augsburg back in 1555: *Cuius regio eius religio* or 'Everyone follow the ruler's religion' (see Chapter 10).

Calvinist preachers in Germany believed that if your ruler was ungodly (meaning not a Calvinist) you shouldn't follow him; you should kill him. German Lutherans rejected Calvinism and its doctrine of *predestination* – the idea that whether you went to heaven or to hell was predetermined before you were born. Most German princes were Lutherans, but some important exceptions included:

- **Catholic princes:** Led by Archduke Ferdinand of Styria and the Duke of Bavaria.

- **Calvinist princes:** Led by the Elector Palatine (the Palatinate was in western Germany, around Heidelberg), who was prepared to help fellow-Protestants anywhere in Europe – that, as it turned out, ended up leading to a lot of trouble.

- **Politique princes:** Led by the Elector of Saxony, a wise old bird who kept his religion to himself and steered clear of both religious camps.

Rudolf's Mad Reign

When Charles V handed the empire over to his brother, Ferdinand I, in 1556, the Turks seemed about to overrun Hungary, so Ferdinand certainly wasn't looking for trouble in Germany. But in 1576, Ferdinand's grandson was elected Emperor Rudolf II. Rudolf was a staunch Catholic, brought up by Spanish Jesuits, much given to gazing at the stars and dabbling in the occult. Centuries of Habsburg inbreeding were coming to fruition – or, if you prefer, to a fruit cake. Rudolf was mentally unhinged and what mind he did have did not deal in compromises.

What's happening in Hungary? I must know!

After the Turks crushed the Hungarians at the Battle of Mohacs in 1526 there was permanent guerrilla war in Hungary between the Turks and the Habsburgs. The situation stayed more or less the same until the 1680s, when the Habsburgs and Poles finally began pushing the Turks slowly but surely out of Europe.

After a couple of major rebellions by the Hungarian nobles, the emperor agreed to respect their liberties, including their freedom of worship (a lot of them had turned Calvinist), and in return the Hungarians agreed to have a hereditary Habsburg monarchy. In 1687, the Hungarians crushed the Turks, virtually on the battlefield of Mohacs itself, and crowned the Archduke Joseph of Habsburg the first Habsburg King of Hungary.

Rudolf stamped out Protestantism in the Habsburg towns and then started on the countryside. In self-defence, the German Protestants formed an *Evangelical Union*. The Catholics formed the *Catholic League* in case the Evangelical Union started throwing its weight around. Just to make the situation worse, the Turks were on the march, the Hungarians were in open revolt, and Rudolf had shut himself away in Prague Castle and was refusing to speak to anyone. The Habsburgs held an emergency family council and delegated Rudolf's brother, Matthias, to take over until Rudolf was feeling more himself. Matthias was a reasonable sort of chap, and promised to respect the Religious Peace of Augsburg. But when Rudolf learned what his brother had been up to he went mad – well, even madder. 'Traitors!' he cried, 'I'm surrounded by traitors!' Rudolf died in 1612, not a moment too soon, and since, mercifully, he had no children, Matthias was elected emperor.

Matthias called a halt to the persecution, but in 1619 Matthias died and Ferdinand of Styria was elected Emperor Ferdinand II. Ferdinand believed that the only good Protestant was a dead Protestant and his reign was going to see a lot of them.

Bohemian Rhapsody: The Letter of Majesty

Trouble broke out in 1618, not in Germany or Hungary (see preceding section) but in Bohemia. The Bohemians were firm believers in religious toleration, but they stood by Rudolf, as their anointed king, against his more tolerant brother, Mathias. In return, Rudolf signed the *Letter of Majesty*, guaranteeing freedom of religion to Bohemia's Protestants.

Not surprisingly, Ferdinand II immediately started going against the Letter of Majesty and preventing Bohemia's Protestants from worshipping. The following year, however, the Protestants saw what you could call their window of opportunity.

The defenestration of Pra-aaaaaaghh!!

The crisis in Bohemia started when the Protestants began building a couple of new churches. 'You can't do that,' said the Bohemian government, known as the Deputies. 'Oh yes we can,' said the Protestants, 'The Letter of Majesty says so.' The Deputies gave a nasty little laugh and sent their troops round to arrest some of the Protestant leaders. This action got the Bohemian Protestants up in arms; the issue wasn't just about their religion, this was a matter of defending their liberties.

In May 1618, a group of Bohemian Protestants marched to the royal palace in Prague, grabbed two of the most hard-line Catholic Deputies, and threw them out of the window. This action is known as the *defenestration of Prague* ('defenestration' is a posh word for throwing something out of a window, though it seems an odd thing to have a special word for).

Throwing people out of windows was rather a Bohemian speciality. The Hussite Wars had started that way, and in 1948 Czech communists (probably) did the same to the democratic leader Jan Masaryck. (You'll find the Hussite Wars in Chapter 10 and post-war Czechoslovakia in Chapter 23.) The Deputies landed on a dungheap, which left them with a hefty dry-cleaning bill but no broken bones. This act of open defiance meant war – Catholics against Protestants.

The Bohemian Protestants sent a round robin (a circular letter) to all the Protestant rulers of Europe: 'Help wanted to defeat vengeful, fire-breathing Catholic monster.' Unfortunately, the rulers' responded, 'You're on your own, matey' – all except one, Elector Frederick of the Palatinate that German Calvinist ruler who saw himself as a Protestant International Rescue (see the section 'Trouble Brews in Germany'). On 26 August 1619, the Bohemian Estates deposed Ferdinand and elected Frederick of the Palatinate King of Bohemia. Different countries in Europe now started to take a close interest in Bohemia's troubles:

- ✔ **England:** Frederick of the Palatinate was married to James I's daughter and James, with his unerring instinct for backing a loser, decided to send English troops to help his son-in-law.

- ✔ **Spain:** The 12-year truce with the Netherlands (see Chapter 11) was due to expire in 1621 and a strong war party in Madrid wanted a return match. Crushing an anti-Habsburg rebellion in Bohemia was a nice way to get some practice in before the big fight in the Netherlands.

✔ **Germany:** The Catholic League didn't want Spanish troops all over Germany, so they put an army together under the formidable Count von Tilly and offered to crush the Bohemians for Ferdinand before the Spanish arrived.

Frederick didn't stand a chance. In 1620, Tilly demolished the Bohemians in the *Battle of the White Mountain* near Prague, and Frederick fled to the Netherlands with a price on his head. Meanwhile, the Spanish invaded the Palatinate and the Netherlands. Game, set, and match to the Habsburgs.

Ferdinand II overplays his hand

Ferdinand II had won the war, but now he lost the peace. He executed 27 Bohemian nobles, confiscated land and property and sent some 30,000 Protestant families into exile, shouting after them 'And don't come back!'

Worst of all, Ferdinand took Frederick's lands and electoral title and awarded them to the Catholic Maximilian of Bavaria. Now, most German princes thought Frederick had deserved everything he got, but taking his title and giving it to someone else set a very alarming precedent. Who would be next?

Ferdinand II was making a lot of Protestant enemies just when an old and formidable rival of the Habsburgs, Cardinal Armand Jean Duplessis, Duke of Richelieu, was looking for a strong anti-Habsburg Protestant ally.

Cardinal Richelieu, the sharpest mind in France

The French had never forgiven the Spanish Habsburgs for winning those long wars for control of Italy back in the 16th century (see Chapter 11). Cardinal Richelieu, chief minister to King Louis XIII, wanted those Italian lands back, though this move was complicated because the Spanish had the Pope on their side. Richelieu simply hired Protestant Swiss mercenaries and went on the offensive (a French Catholic Cardinal hiring Protestant mercenaries to fight against the Pope and his Catholic allies – certainly the action of a *politique* putting his religion on one side!).

Unfortunately, the Spanish came back again so Richelieu needed an anti-Habsburg ally. King Christian IV of Denmark seemed keen. Was Christian prepared to take on the Holy Roman Empire?

Bring it on, you Protestants!

Ferdinand II had found a very useful ally, a Bohemian Catholic called Albert von Wallenstein, and he was in the mood for taking on the Protestants. Ferdinand told Wallenstein to head north and help Tilly drive the Danes and Swedes out of north Germany and generally turn the area Catholic. Together Wallenstein and Tilly destroyed the Protestants and forced Christian IV of Denmark to sign a humiliating peace treaty, with all the usual clauses about returning Church property and sending Protestants into exile. Sweden was next on the hit list.

Sweden's Martial Kings

Sweden had finally become independent from Denmark back in 1523 (Chapter 12 has all the thrilling details), but since then, things had gone rather pear-shaped. One king had gone mad and had had to be deposed (and probably poisoned), and Queen Catherine, who was married to King John III and clearly wore the trousers, was doing her best to turn Sweden Catholic.

Sweden is mine, Sigismund!

Catherine was just grooming her son, Sigismund, to be a good Catholic monarch when he got an invitation to go off and be king of Poland (being invited to be king of Poland was a sort of occupational hazard for European royalty). Sigismund said yes, but when John III died in 1592, he came back to Sweden to claim the Swedish crown as well. 'Oh no you don't,' said the Swedish Protestants, led by Sigismund's uncle, Charles of Södermanland, 'You can be king of Poland or king of Sweden, but not both.'

Sigismund wasn't giving up either kingdom, so from 1592 to 1604 – *12 years* – a civil war raged in Sweden between Sigismund III and his Uncle Charles. Charles won, capturing Sigismund at the 1598 Battle of Stångebro and had every member of Sweden's royal Council who had supported him executed in what became known as the *Bloodbath of Linköping*, which goes to show that the Protestants were just as murderous as their Catholic enemies.

It's war, Charles!

In 1611, King Christian 'I-can-drink-you-under-the-table' IV of Denmark declared war on Sweden. Charles IX, who was not a well man, challenged Christian to a duel, but he was so upset by Christian's reply – 'Drop dead, granddad' – that he had an apoplectic fit and did.

Sweden did very well out of Charles's death. The new king was Gustavus Adolphus, the 'Lion of the North', and one of the greatest figures Sweden has produced in its history. Until ABBA, of course.

Gustavus Adolphus – Protestant superhero

Gustavus Adolphus, Charles IX's replacement, was a remarkable man. First Adolphus won the war with Denmark that had so shocked Charles IX (see preceding section), and then he got a very good settlement (plus most of Finland and Livonia) from Russia and another out of Poland. Gustavus married the daughter of the Elector of Brandenburg, which made him a sort of honorary German Protestant prince and just the man the other princes had been looking for to put Emperor Ferdinand II in his place. Gustavus Adolphus had very wisely seized the port of Stralsund, enabling him to invade Germany by sea, and in 1630 he left Sweden in the hands of Chancellor Oxenstierna and did just that.

Europe's religious conflict now moved north to Germany and the Baltic:

- ✔ Gustavus Adolphus conquers Pomerania and Stettin along the north German coast. Cardinal Richelieu, thinking 'this is more like it', writes to Gustavus Adolphus and asks if he needs any extra cash.

- ✔ Ferdinand II gives in to pressure from the Catholic princes (who were terrible snobs and didn't like being led by a Bohemian upstart) and sacks Wallenstein. Tilly is now commander-in-chief of the imperial forces.

- ✔ Tilly takes the city of Magdeburg and massacres the population. The Protestants want Tilly dealt with, and fast.

- ✔ The Big Match: Gustavus Adolphus against Tilly at the Battle of Breitenfeld. Gustavus Adolphus wins and takes the Palatinate.

- ✔ Gustavus Adolphus beats Tilly again, at the River Lech, and kills him. Ferdinand II starts writing a very grovelling letter to Wallenstein.

- ✔ Wallenstein digs in at Nuremberg, and Gustavus Adolphus only just forces him back. In December 1632, the two armies meet at the Battle of Lützen. The Swedes win – but Gustavus Adolphus is found in a ditch, shot through the head.

After Gustavus Adolphus died, Wallenstein got into secret talks with the Protestants and the French about putting him on the throne of Bohemia. Ferdinand II got wind of this plan, sacked Wallenstein, and had him assassinated.

I want to be alone

Gustavus Adolphus's daughter Christina was only five when her dad was killed, and she became king (yes, king) of Sweden. All sorts of stories have been told about Christina: how she dressed in men's clothes – well, she was a king – and that she was secretly a lesbian. Christina was certainly secretly a Catholic.

In 1654, Christina abdicated and retired to Rome, though it's a funny sort of retirement if you arrive in state dressed as an Amazon.

Christina had a go at regaining the throne, but the Swedes didn't want her, and neither did the Poles, which was strange because they weren't usually so fussy.

Greta Garbo, who was Swedish herself, played Christina in a famous Hollywood silent film, all dark looks and darker lighting. Christina's story makes a great film, but in all honesty, the Swedes were probably better off without her.

Not So Fast, Ferdinand II! It Is I, Richelieu!

Historians debate about just how devastated Germany was – and if you were lucky enough to live outside the immediate war zone you were probably able to carry on more or less as normal – but the people caught up in the fighting suffered terribly. But if the German people hoped for an end to the fighting, they had reckoned without Cardinal Richelieu of France. Richelieu announced that France was putting all the German Protestant princes under its protection, declared war on Spain, and sent French troops in to drive the Spanish out of Germany, Italy, the Netherlands, and anywhere else they might find them.

The brilliant young French commander, the Prince of Condé, beat the Spanish and the imperial troops along the Rhine, in the Netherlands, and in Italy, until in 1643 at the Battle of Rocroi, aged only 21, he virtually destroyed Spain's long history as a military power.

The following year the two sides started peace talks. The Protestants met at Osnabrück and the Catholics at Münster (the atmosphere was still too frosty for them to meet together) and in 1648, amid great international rejoicing, they signed the *Treaty of Westphalia*, which brought the *Thirty Years' War* to an end.

The treaty's terms were the usual mixture of give and take. Sweden got some land in northern Germany and France got some land along the German border, the United Provinces (the new name for the Netherlands) and Switzerland were to be independent, and the German princes were to have the final say in new laws for the Holy Roman Empire.

While you were all busy killing each other. . .

The Thirty Years' War coincided with the English Civil War and Charles I's execution. Plenty of leaders and rulers died in the continental wars, but the English were the only ones who put their king on trial and condemned him to death. This action created a terrible shock throughout Europe and determined Europe's monarchs, especially the king of France, to make sure that never again would an anointed king be so completely at the mercy of his own subjects.

But the real result of the war was much simpler: from now on, the premier state in Europe was France.

Did You Really Think France Was Finished?

France seemed as though it would never recover from the terrible bloodletting of the 16th-century Wars of Religion (see Chapter 11 for details), but thanks to Henry IV and his able chief minister, the Duke of Sully, the country enjoyed a period of peace before religious hatred reared its ugly head again.

Henry was assassinated in 1610. Henry's son, now Louis XIII, was only 8 years old so his mother, Queen Marie de Medici, ruled the country as regent. Marie was a hard-line Italian Catholic, and she brought a gang of like-minded Italians led by Concino Concini to Paris to help her harrass Huguenots (French Protestants). Eventually, Marie de Medici's persecution plans were stopped by her son, King Louis, who in 1617, at all of 15 years old, locked his mother up in the Château of Blois, had Concini murdered (and his wife burnt as a witch, if you please), and Richelieu sacked. Marie escaped and a short, sharp civil war took place between mother and son, with Richelieu acting as honest broker between the two of them until, in 1620, Marie's troops were beaten and she had to make peace.

In 1620, the Huguenots gathered in their stronghold at La Rochelle on France's Atlantic coast and declared an independent Protestant state. Richelieu crushed them mercilessly. From now on, Richelieu ran France.

He's the finest swordsman in France. Arrest him!

Richelieu's loyalty was to the French Crown and he was willing to fight anyone, Protestant or Catholic, who threatened it. Richelieu had all non-essential forts and castles demolished (which is why so many French *châteaux* are palaces rather than castles) and he also banned the nobles' favourite sport, duelling.

Imagine banning whisky in Scotland – the reaction to the ban on duelling was the same. The young Count de Montmorency-Bouteville deliberately fought a duel outside Richelieu's window, just daring the Cardinal to have him arrested. To everyone's amazement, not least the Count de Montmorency-Bouteville's, Richelieu did arrest him, and both the count and his opponent were executed. Clearly, Richelieu meant business.

Marie de Medici loathed Richelieu, and she felt that he had far too much power in his hands. The queen, Anne of Austria, blamed him for turning her husband away from her. (In fact, Louis XIII probably preferred men, but what girl wants to hear that?) The two queens decided to take the cardinal on.

The French court now saw a power struggle between Richelieu and his enemies:

- ✔ **1626:** Henri de Talleyrand-Périgord, Count of Chalais, is arrested and executed for plotting against Richelieu. The plot also implicates the queen, Anne of Austria, and the king's uncle, Gaston, Duke of Orleans.

- ✔ **1630:** 11 November, the 'Day of the Dupes'. Marie de Medici has a blazing row with Richelieu in front of Louis about Richelieu's policy of going to war with Catholic countries. 'Him or me, Louis,' she warns him, 'Choose!' Louis is just about to dismiss Richelieu when he thinks, 'No,' and dismisses his mother instead. Marie has to go into exile, and the rest of Richelieu's enemies have to run for their lives.

- ✔ **1632:** The Duke of Montmorency, Governor of Languedoc in south-western France, rises in rebellion. On Richelieu's advice, Louis XIII promises to uphold the region's liberties but crushes the rebellion and executes the duke. Richelieu is amassing an impressive tally of noble heads.

Richelieu died in 1642, and Louis XIII died the following year, which was unfortunate because his son, Louis XIV, was only 5 years old. This time Anne of Austria took charge with Richelieu's successor, Cardinal Mazarin. No one could have guessed, but that 5-year-old boy would eventually cut all the nobles of France right down to size. But not quite yet.

All for one?

The Three Musketeers (who, for musketeers, seem to have spent an awful lot of time sword-fighting) and the famous *Man in the Iron Mask* were originally written by the 19th-century writer Alexandre Dumas, who was always a bit coy about where he had got his ideas from.

Historians have since discovered that, although the stories are fiction, the characters are based on real people. A real d'Artagnan existed, Aramis, Athos, and Porthos were based on three genuine musketeers called d'Aramitz, de Sillègue d'Athos, and Portau, and they did indeed have a run-in with Cardinal Richelieu's guards.

The Man in the Iron Mask really existed, too, though historians think that the mask was probably made of velvet (a bit kinder on the face, agreed, but couldn't he have just torn it off?). In the story, the man is the twin brother of Louis XIV, locked away because he has a better claim to the throne; in the Hollywood film he *is* Louis XIV, and his brother has taken his place.

Sorry to disappoint you, but the chances of either version of the story being true are tiny. So many people were present at royal births that the chance that a twin could have been born without an awful lot of people knowing was non existent.

With frondes like these, who needs enemies?

Little Louis XIV spent his childhood in constant fear of being kidnapped or killed by rebellious nobles in a series of disruptions known as the *frondes*. In French, a *fronde* is a child's catapult; the term suggests that the French nobles were behaving childishly, though there was nothing childish about the danger posed by the frondes.

The frondes started with the Parisians protesting against royal officials and setting up street barricades, thus starting what was to become a cherished Parisian tradition. The queen and little Louis fled the capital in fear of their lives – kidnapped and assassinated kings in France weren't a rarity.

Soon the nobles joined in the frondes, led by the Prince de Condé. The queen had to keep running from one not-so-safe château to another, bundling little Louis (who was getting less little now and beginning to take note of what was happening) into coaches in the middle of the night to keep one step ahead of Condé and the *frondeurs*.

Eventually, Louis solemnly declared himself to be of age (he was only 13, but he was the king), cut the powers of the Paris *parlement*, and sent a royal army off to deal with Condé. In 1652, Louis re-entered Paris in great state and formally took charge, to a general sense of relief all round. His men beat Condé, though Condé was such a good general that Louis kept him on (he turned out to be very useful). Cardinal Mazarin ran the country until he died in 1661, when Louis XIV took over for real.

Louis XIV takes charge

When he was 18, Louis XIV took part in a court entertainment known as a *masque*, a mixture of dance, drama, and music, which often carried an allegorical message. For his costume, Louis dressed up as the sun, and liked the look so much that he adopted the sun as his personal emblem and became known as the *Sun King*: the radiant giver of life and warmth around whom the whole world revolves – you get the idea.

But of course, you can only have one sun in a universe, as Louis's minister of finance, Nicolas Fouquet, found out to his cost. Fouquet invited Louis to his magnificent château, Vaux-le-Vicomte. Unfortunately, all the finery just made Louis think Fouquet had got too powerful, so he sent his guards back to Vaux-le-Vicomte to carry Fouquet off to jail. But not before Louis had taken the names and addresses of Fouquet's architect and landscape gardener – Louis had a little building plan of his own: Versailles.

Versailles

Versailles was designed to show the king at the heart of France.

Three great avenues converge on the great Place d'Armes at the front of the building (though one of them is a stump, only there for show, to balance the other two), and the palace itself is designed to take your breath away. Louis engaged the greatest architects of the day, Louis Le Vaux and Jules Hardouin-Mansart. The latter's masterpiece was the great Hall of Mirrors, a glittering hall of crystal that must have seemed like fairyland to people at the time.

André Le Nôtre designed the grounds, including the great Grand Canal outside the windows, and a forest studded with glades containing classical statues and fountains. Incidentally, bear in mind that 17th-century fountains were impressive works of engineering and the fountains at Versailles were bigger and faster than any in Europe.

Later, when Louis's second wife, Madame de Maintenon, said she'd like somewhere to go and be on her own, Louis had a little palace built for her in the grounds called the *Grand Trianon*, which for most people would be a perfectly acceptable full-time palace. This building was Louis's idea of a garden shed.

Versailles, not Paris, was the centre of power now. Louis made the French nobles come to him in Versailles, where no angry local mob could be called on.

Louis instituted an elaborate system of court ritual, with strict rules about how many steps you were allowed to take and what you were allowed to wear and even how to knock on a door (you didn't – you scratched, discreetly). The nobles fell over themselves fighting for the honour of holding the king's wine glass and pouring the royal wine from the royal bottle (ignoring the whispers of 'It's not fair! The king said I could do it!'). Court fashion was very expensive – another very effective way of keeping the aristocracy under control.

Versailles was a glittering centre of courtly etiquette and the setting for a flowering of French literature and music. It was also a ruthless exercise in *absolute monarchy.*

Fabulously absolute

Louis's rule was based on the relatively new idea that the king had absolute power. The French cleric Jacques Bossuet taught that absolute monarchy was all part of God's plan – Louis was so pleased that he made him Bishop of Meaux and tutor to his eldest son, the Dauphin.

Louis built up an efficient and loyal new nobility of lawyers and administrators who owed their titles and position to him, and not to their family pedigree. He could also issue a *lettre de cachet*, which allowed him to send anyone to prison for anything at all without any sort of trial. Absolute monarchy was another word for elegant tyranny.

Louis XIV gathered a glittering array of artists and writers to Versailles:

- **Lully:** Court composer. Poor chap died when he smashed his foot with his spiked conducting stick and the wound turned septic.
- **Couperin:** Court organist and composer. Conducted from the harpsichord, sensible chap.
- **La Bruyère:** Philosopher and social commentator. More fun than he sounds.
- **La Fontaine:** Best writer of fables since Æsop.
- **Molière:** Playwright and comic actor. His *Tartuffe*, which satirised holier-than-thou Catholics, went too near the knuckle and was banned for years.
- **Racine:** Writer of great tragedies on classical themes, like *Phèdre* and *Britannicus*. A bit heavy.

Louis was married to the Spanish princess, Maria-Theresa, yet he also had a mistress, Madame de Montespan, who carried herself as if she held an official position – which she more or less did. When the king seemed to go off her, Madame de Montespan dabbled in black magic and poison to try to get him back again. But the Madame's plan became public knowledge amidst enormous scandal, and resulted in no fewer than 34 executions. Truly, life was never dull at Versailles.

While you're living it up, some of us are starving

The other side of Louis XIV's France was not so glittering. Increasing hunger and unrest were evident in France towards the end of the Thirty Years' War (see the earlier sections in this chapter), and since France's ingenious system of taxation meant that the people with least money paid most, the situation didn't get any better. Serious tax riots broke out in 1662 and the king's response was to privatise the tax-collection system in what was called the *General Tax-Farm*, which just meant that unscrupulous characters could put taxes up even higher and pocket the difference. This tax was going to make for a great deal of trouble in the end. Meanwhile, the 1690s and 1700s were years of terrible famine in the land of the Sun King.

L'eglise c'est moi – I am the Church!

Attached to Versailles was a big chapel royal with a very elaborate pew for the king. The courtiers' pews didn't face the altar but faced the king. Louis XIV saw religion as a means of enhancing his own position and prestige. The king insisted on appointing French bishops himself and he didn't want the Pope interfering in the way that the French Church was run.

On the other hand, Louis did want the Pope to clamp down on a small Catholic sect called *Jansenism*, after its founder, a Dutch theologian called Jansen. The Jansenists were a strange bunch; they believed that you got to heaven through God's grace and not through any good things you may do in your life (which was exactly what Luther said) and they accepted the idea of predestination (which was what Calvin said), and yet they insisted that they were loyal Catholics. (Refer to Chapter 10 for more on what Luther and Calvin said.)

In 1709, Louis closed down the Jansenist community at Port-Royal near Paris, and in 1713, right at the end of his life, he persuaded Pope Clement IX to condemn Jansenism as heresy.

Louis XIV's most important religious act, however, was to have much wider and more serious consequences. Egged on by his secret new wife, the staunchly anti-Protestant Madame de Maintenon (who had been governess to his illegitimate children – Louis had a curious sense of morality), in 1685 Louis revoked the 1598 *Edict of Nantes*. That was the edict issued by Louis's grandfather, Henry IV, which had allowed French Protestants freedom of worship. Protestant pastors had 15 days to leave the country.

The whole Huguenot community threw some things into a bag and sought refuge in Protestant countries like England and the Netherlands, where they made an important contribution to the economic life of their new homelands.

Louis was declaring war on Protestant Europe, just when Protestant Europe was entering its period of greatest strength.

Part V
Europe Rules the World

The 5th Wave   By Rich Tennant

"The troops are in place, we have the area surrounded, but the maitre'd says we still need a reservation before he can seat us all at the same table."

In this part . . .

In the 18th and 19th centuries, Europe did what no other continent had ever done: it dominated the entire world. Europeans learned how to use their scientific knowledge to make huge technological advances that put them far ahead of any other peoples. Gradually Asia, South America, the Pacific, and finally Africa were all drawn into the European system of production and control.

As European technology became more advanced, so Europeans experimented with new ideas about how they should be governed. In this part you'll see how the 18th century threw up some important new thinking about the human condition – and how it came to a head, for good or ill, in the French Revolution.

As Europe grew up, so a new force emerged from the French Revolution and began starting some revolutions of its own: nationalism. By the end of the 19th century Europeans were keenly aware, and proud, of their different nations, and eager to proclaim their own nation the greatest of all. Meanwhile, a German intellectual called Karl Marx was sitting quietly in the British Museum working out the basics of the creed that would blow the 20th century apart.

Chapter 14

The (Almost) Irresistible Rise of France and Russia

*T*he second half of the 17th century saw King Louis XIV of France embark on a series of wars of conquest aimed at making France the dominant power in Europe. When Louis made his move to put his grandson on the throne of Spain, with control of all Spain's worldwide empire, it seemed that Louis had all of Europe at his feet. Meanwhile, in the East, Russia's powerful neighbours, Poland and Sweden, were on the way down just as Russia was on the way up under its dynamic new tsar, Peter I 'The Great'. Europe was moving painfully into the age of the great power and the modern state.

Spain's Decline – It's Terminal

King Philip III of Spain was a lazy character who liked to put things off till *mañana*. His son Philip IV was a much wiser character than his father (but then, most people were), but the real power behind the throne was the great Count-Duke Olivares, Duke of San Lúcar. Poor old Olivares, he really believed in Spain and tried everything possible to make her a great power again. Olivares taxed the nobility, clamped down on corruption, and got Spain involved in the Thirty Years' War, hoping they'd get the Netherlands back (take a look at Chapter 13 for more on the Thirty Years' War).

Unfortunately, the Dutch fought back, Spain went bankrupt, the Catalans staged a major revolt against the Crown and Portugal, knowing a sinking ship when it saw one, declared itself independent.

Tilting at windmills

Miguel Cervantes's *Don Quixote* is a sad story about a rather dotty old man who makes a fool of himself riding round the Spanish countryside thinking that he's a chivalrous knight in armour, not realising that those days are long gone. In a famous passage, Don Quixote even mistakes a row of windmills for giants and charges at them with his lance.

In a sense, Cervantes was describing Spain itself. Spain had been the greatest power in Europe, possibly in the world, but by the 17th century, the country seemed tired and weak, its glory days long gone. Spain was threatened by enemies a lot more deadly than windmills.

A Golden Age in Holland

For the Dutch, in contrast to Spain, the 17th century was their Golden Age. Trade had never been better; they seized most of the Portuguese possessions in Asia and Africa and set themselves up as a world-wide trading empire. The main trading rivals of the Dutch were the Swedes in the Baltic and, increasingly, the English, so they went to war with both of them and did really rather well – especially when they sailed up the Medway and attacked the English fleet.

In fact, the main problems facing the United Provinces, to give Holland its proper name, were internal ones. Should Holland be a republic ruled by the States-General, the Dutch parliament, or should the country be a monarchy ruled by the House of Orange? The republicans were able to retain control until their leader, the *Grand Pensionary*, Jan de Witt, declared war on Louis XIV and got beaten.

In 1672, an angry mob tore de Witt and his brother to pieces and Prince William of Orange took over as *Stadtholder* or head of state. Holland was now a monarchy, and Louis XIV had gained a formidable enemy.

England on the Up

In addition to Holland, the other power clearly on the way up was England. The English had recently executed their king, Charles I, overthrown the monarchy, and declared a republic under Oliver Cromwell at the head of a highly professional army (for more details on what the English had been up to, see *British History For Dummies* (Wiley)). The other European powers soon started doing business with Oliver Cromwell. Louis XIV signed an alliance with Cromwell against Spain, and the Dutch soon found that Cromwell's navy was just as strong as his army when they went to war with England in 1652.

In 1660, the English invited King Charles II back from exile in Holland and set up the monarchy again. Charles was going to have to work with parliament (he'd get no taxes otherwise) but nothing was going to make him like this arrangement. Louis XIV reached a secret deal with Charles: Louis kept Charles supplied with money and Charles tried to keep England on France's side. A trade war between England and the Dutch suited Louis XIV's purposes just fine.

Expanding Overseas

The Dutch had taken over most of Portugal's empire in Africa and the East – they even held Brazil for a time – the French had established settlements in Quebec and Louisiana, and the English had set up colonies in North America, Canada, and India. The English got hold of Bombay in 1662 when Charles II married a Portuguese princess, Catherine de Braganza, and she brought it as part of her dowry, which certainly beats a half-share in the family carpentry business.

For many years historians wrote about Europeans 'taking' vast areas of overseas territory, or even passing them around between themselves as wedding dowries. Nowadays, historians are much more aware that these diplomatic bargains had enormous, and often disastrous, consequences for the people who actually lived in these lands the Europeans were casually acquiring and exchanging.

These countries were able to expand overseas because they took care to build up their fleets. Louis XIV's minister, Colbert, virtually created the French navy single-handedly, and in England, Samuel Pepys (who deserves to be much better known for this than for his diary) did the same. These men were all working to a theory called *mercantilism*, which held that only so much wealth and trade existed in the world, so you needed to get as much of it as possible into your own hands. Colonies existed to trade with the mother country and with no one else. This theory made sense in the early days but the principle made for trouble as the colonies grew up and wanted to choose their own trading partners.

Hold It Right There, King Louis XIV!

Louis XIV was used to winning his wars, especially against the Dutch, whom he regarded as a rather impudent, upstart little people. *Hegemony* means dominating everyone and telling them what to do. The term sums up Louis's war aims rather well.

In 1686, the Austrians, Swedes, Spanish, and Germans – just about everyone, in other words, who had reason to fear Louis XIV – got together at Augsburg and formed the *League of Augsburg* to try to stop him. At first Louis just laughed and invaded the Palatinate (the area of Germany closest to the French frontier); he devastated the area so badly that it turned the whole of Germany against him. Everything seemed to be going Louis's way when his arch-enemy and leading light in the League of Augsburg, William of Orange, staged a dramatic and quite unexpected *coup* – he invaded England.

The invasion of England was unusual because parliament had actually invited William over, to replace Catholic King James II, who had turned out to be a disaster. James fled to France, and William of Orange was now King William III of England, with the combined military and naval forces of England and Holland at his disposal. That gave Louis something to think about.

If judged only by the outcome of battles, then Louis did very well in the *War of the League of Augsburg* – his fleet even controlled the English Channel for a time – but winning battles is not the same as winning a war. When the war was over in 1697, everyone gave back the bits and pieces they had taken, but the main message was clear: Louis XIV had been stopped. And if Louis had been stopped once, he could be again.

Who's the Prince Most Likely to Succeed (to the Spanish Throne, That Is)?

Just because Spain had been going through a bad patch, no one actually thought that it was finished as a European power. (See the section 'Spain's Decline – It's Terminal' earlier in this chapter, for more on Spain's problems.) That was why, as the 17th century drew to a close, everyone started paying particular attention to the rapidly deteriorating health of King Charles II of Spain.

The players

Charles had no children, so the big question was who going to succeed him. Three main candidates were in the running:

- **Archduke Charles of Habsburg:** Younger son of the Holy Roman Emperor Leopold I; therefore, not likely to be elected emperor (not impossible, though). Archduke Charles was acceptable to most of Europe except France.

- **Louis, the dauphin:** Eldest son of Louis XIV and heir to the French throne. The idea of a single Bourbon on the thrones both of France and of Spain gave Louis's opponents conniptions.

- ✔ **Prince Joseph Ferdinand of Bavaria:** Prince Joseph at least was half-Spanish and was also a grandson of the Holy Roman Emperor. Unfortunately, Joseph was only seven. Even more unfortunately, in 1699 the prince died.

Charles announced his own heir: Philip, Duke of Anjou, the younger grandson of Louis XIV who was not *very* likely to inherit the French throne as well – though at the rate members of the House of Bourbon suddenly started dying of smallpox, you couldn't rule it out.

Then, on 1 November 1700, Charles II of Spain died. Louis gave a big sigh, said that the situation was most regrettable, and then presented his young grandson to the Spanish ambassador with the words, 'Behold your king!': 17-year-old Philip of Anjou was now King Philip V of Spain, which effectively meant that Spain had become an annexe of France. Louis declared, with a glint of triumph in his eye, 'The Pyrenees have ceased to exist! Heh heh heh.'

The War of the Spanish Succession

The other powers of Europe, England, and the Holy Roman Empire, were never going to tolerate Louis XIV effectively annexing Spain like that, and would fight Louis and Philip to get a Habsburg on the Spanish throne. This *War of the Spanish Succession*, lasted 13 years and spread all over Europe. Louis was up against two of the greatest military commanders of the 18th century, the Austrian Prince Eugene of Savoy and the British commander, John Churchill, Duke of Marlborough:

- ✔ **1704: Battle of Blenheim.** Marlborough marches across Europe at lightning speed and defeats the French in southern Germany. The defeat is so heavy, only Madame de Maintenon, Louis XIV's queen, dares break the news to him.

- ✔ **1706: Battle of Ramillies.** Marlborough nearly gets himself killed but drives the French out of the Netherlands, while Prince Eugene of Savoy drives them out of Italy.

- ✔ **1706:** Archduke Charles is crowned King Charles III of Spain at Madrid.

- ✔ **1708: Battle of Oudenarde.** Marlborough and Prince Eugene defeat the French again. Louis is prepared to give up his claims to Spain and make peace. The allies have won. However, the allies want Louis to send French troops in to drive Philip V out of Spain, which he declines to do, so the allies haven't won after all, and the war starts again.

- ✔ **1709: Battle of Malplaquet.** Marlborough wins, but at horrific cost in lives (estimated at 30,000). Everyone is wondering whether this war will ever end.

- ✔ **1711: Archduke Charles becomes Holy Roman Emperor.** However, the British don't want Charles to be both emperor and king of Spain any more than they want Philip of Anjou to be both king of France and king of Spain. So Britain pulls out of the war.

- ✔ **1712:** The Austrians and Dutch throw everything they've got at the French. Instead, the French win, at the Battle of Denain. Everyone wants to talk peace now.

The war ended with the 1713 *Treaty of Utrecht*. The treaty said:

- ✔ Philip of Anjou is to be King Philip V of Spain, on condition that he renounces all claim to the throne of France. (And why, you might well ask, couldn't they have thought of that in the first place and saved a lot of trouble, money, and lives?)

- ✔ Austria is to get all Spain's possessions in Italy: Milan and Naples, plus Sicily as a bonus.

- ✔ Austria is to get the Spanish Netherlands, also known as Belgium. ('Oh well', thought the Austrians, 'if we have to.')

- ✔ Britain is to get Gibraltar and Minorca in the Mediterranean, and Newfoundland and Nova Scotia in Canada.

- ✔ The Dutch get nothing much; the French – apart from getting their man on the Spanish throne – get even less.

Sunset in the West: Exit Louis XIV

The end of Louis XIV's reign was a miserable period for France. The peasants of the Cévennes staged a long revolt, and thousands froze to death in the terrible winter of 1709, even in Versailles.

Not that Versailles was immune to tragedy: Louis's son, the dauphin, died of smallpox in 1711 (not that he was any great loss, by all accounts), and the same outbreak carried off the dauphin's son and daughter-in-law and two of their sons. Smallpox would've killed their youngest son, too, if his governess had not refused point blank to have him treated by the same incompetents who had seen to all the others.

So by the time Louis XIV died in 1715, mocked by writers and satirists for his absolute style of government and largely unloved by his poor, hungry, cold, and exhausted people, his only heir was his 5-year-old great-grandson, Louis XV. What a come-down for the once-splendid Sun King.

Handover to Hanover

In 1714, the British monarch, Queen Anne, died. The English were determined not to have the Stuarts back at any price as long as they remained Catholic, which meant that they had to go right back up the family tree to find a Protestant heir. They found Queen Anne's first-cousin-once-removed, Elector George of Hanover. This German prince now became King George I of Great Britain.

However, this regime change also meant that the kings of France, and anyone else opposed to the British, could always keep the British government awake at night by offering shelter and support – and sometimes an army – to the Stuart pretender to the British throne and to his supporters, the *Jacobites*. Which is exactly what the French court did.

The Nobility of Poland-Lithuania Invite Us into Their Beautiful Home

Poland-Lithuania had been a big-shot player in the 17th century, dominating eastern Europe and the Baltic, but this alliance had one big weak point; the Polish nobles wouldn't give an inch on any of their liberties, which made the situation very difficult for any Polish king wanting to modernise the country.

In 1655, Poland's enemies all attacked in what is known officially as the *First Great Northern War*, but to the Poles is simply 'the Deluge'. The Russians and the Cossacks attacked from the east, and the Swedes attacked from the north (just to show how awkward the Polish and Lithuanian nobility were, some of them helped the invaders!). Poland was crushed, and afterwards, a number of Polish and Lithuanian nobles decided to slip away and offer their services to the Russians.

The one bright spot in this otherwise grim piece of Polish history was the heroic defence of the monastery of Jasna Góra, home of the famous ikon of the 'Black Madonna'. The Poles were so delighted by their success here, which they put down to the Madonna's prayers, that King John II Casimir declared Poland dedicated specially to the Virgin Mary. When John Paul II was elected the first ever Polish pope in 1978, he put an M for Mary on his personal coat of arms.

John Casimir tried desperately to make the Poles see sense and set up a hereditary monarchy; if they didn't, he said, Poland would simply be carved up by her neighbours. The nobles of the *sejm*, the Polish parliament, took no notice and John Casimir gave up in despair, abdicated, and went to live in France. Casimir didn't live to see his prophesy come true, but it did.

In 1674, the Polish *sejm* elected a remarkable man as king, John III Sobieski. Sobieski was a born fighter, with just the right sort of thick moustache that Poles admire on their leaders.

In 1683 the Turks had one last go at taking Vienna – not, to be fair, as serious a go as their attacks in the 16th century (see Chapter 12 for more details about these), but they did at least get to Vienna and Emperor Leopold I didn't seem to have much idea of what to do about the situation. John Sobieski came charging to the rescue and defeated the Turks in a great pitched battle outside Vienna that became famous throughout Europe – a big painting of it hangs in the Vatican.

After Sobieski died in 1696, the *sejm* invited a foreigner, Augustus II Elector of Saxony, to be king, largely because the tsar of Russia told them to. The Poles didn't really warm to the new king. In the end, however, Augustus – and Poland – fell victim to the Poles' old enemy and rival, another power that, had anyone but known it, was on its way out – Sweden.

Sweden: All Seems Fine

Sweden had played a dominant role in the Thirty Years' War and seemed set to dominate the Baltic region for the foreseeable future. King Charles X had joined in the 'Deluge' attack on Poland (see the section 'The Nobility of Poland-Lithuania Invite Us into Their Beautiful Home', earlier in this chapter) and had kicked some Danish ass.

Charles X died of pneumonia in 1660, when his son, Charles XI, was only 4 years old. Charles XI's uncle, Magnus de la Gardie, ran the country for him and rather carelessly got into a war with Brandenburg-Prussia, the Netherlands, Denmark, and the Holy Roman Empire – the sort of silly mistake anyone could make. Charles XI, who had grown up a bit by now, managed to salvage a bit of national honour by beating the Danes (the Swedes didn't mind losing to other nations but they hated losing to the Danes).

Thereafter, Charles XI steered clear of war, sensible fellow. Charles set about a thoroughgoing reform programme, rooting out corruption, confiscating unnecessary extra palaces (including his uncle Magnus's ones), setting up an efficient and honest civil service (thereby proving that it can be done), and taking personal control of the Swedish Lutheran Church. All in all, Charles XI was a very able king – pity he had to die aged only 41 of stomach cancer. Charles's son, aged only 14, became King Charles XII (in kings' names, the Swedes didn't like surprises).

The Odyssey of King Charles XII

Charles XII spent most of his reign, wandering round Europe having one incredible adventure after another until, like Odysseus, he finally arrived home in disguise. Unlike Odysseus, the young king's story doesn't have a happy ending.

The Baltic region's trouble spot was Livonia, more or less modern-day Estonia and Latvia, which was well positioned for trade and war and which everyone in the region wanted. The Swedes had managed to get hold of Livonia in the 16th century. In 1700, Augustus II of Poland decided to grab Livonia. The Polish king got in touch with Frederick IV of Denmark and the two launched a sudden unprovoked attack on the Swedes. This action precipitated the Second Great Northern War.

Charles XII set out from Stockholm and thrashed the Danes, which made the Poles quietly pull out and go home. But at this point, a new player enters – the remarkable Russian tsar, Peter I. Peter wanted Livonia for Russia, and by way of a starter he sent a huge Russian army (Russia tended to run to huge armies) to seize the important Livonian port of Narva on the Gulf of Finland.

Charles XII, still only 18 years old, rushed to Narva to raise the siege and save the day. The young king found some 50,000 Russians in good, strongly fortified positions in front of Narva; Charles XII had about 8,000 men completely whacked after their march (if you like, try taking the 000s off to get an idea of the odds: 50 strong, fresh Russians against 8 tired Swedes). Charles attacked. In a snowstorm. Incredibly, the Swedes broke through the Russian lines, the Russians panicked and by evening thousands of Russians, including almost all their cavalry, had drowned in the river trying to escape. And that, thought Charles, wiping his hands, is that.

Beware hubris!

Charles XII's victory at Narva was so stunning that it went to Charles's head – he was still only a teenager after all. Charles reckoned that he could sort out the whole Baltic region himself, and that he needn't worry about the Russians – he'd only have to say boo, and they'd run away home to mummy.

Charles decided to deal once and for all with Sweden's old rivals, Poland-Lithuania; he marched in, took Warsaw, and told the *sejm* to depose Augustus II, and elect a puppet who would do as Charles told him, called Stanislas Lesczynski. The *sejm* agreed. Charles even invaded Augustus's native Saxony and forced him to recognise Stanislas Lesczynski officially as king of Poland. Only then, rather belatedly, did Charles turn his attention to what Tsar Peter I was up to.

Peter never made the mistake of underestimating Charles. The Russian tsar was afraid that Charles was going to head north, through Livonia, which was exactly what all Charles's advisers were urging him to do. Charles, however, decided to go straight for Peter's jugular – he would invade Russia and seize Moscow.

Charles's plan was simple: A quick campaign, take Moscow, make Peter I grovel, and then head home for a well-earned rest and a sauna. Which just goes to show that Charles XII hadn't begun to understand Peter. Peter ordered all the crops along Charles's line of march to be destroyed, so the Swedes found absolutely nothing to eat. All the Swedes had to fall back on was Charles XII's enormous self-confidence; the Swedish camp was full of people muttering 'If I hear one more story about how he won the Battle of Narva . . .'

Peter caught up with Charles at the town of Poltava and virtually destroyed his army. Charles spent much of the battle laid out on a stretcher thanks to a wound in his foot that had gone septic, but, incredibly, he still managed to escape. With a small band of followers, the Swedish king headed south and successfully reached Turkish territory. The sultan was rather alarmed by this unexpected and rather dangerous royal guest; he even had Charles placed under very courteous and comfortable arrest for a short time.

Charles decided he'd better get back to Sweden as soon as possible (the sultan certainly agreed with him on this point) and he set off in disguise, riding right across Europe in just two weeks. Charles got back just in time; the Russians had taken Livonia, the Poles had overturned Charles's puppet-king Stanislas Lesczynski and put Augustus II back on the throne, and just about every enemy the Swedes had ever had was ganging up for an attack on the vital Swedish port of Stralsund. Charles took command at Stralsund – to no avail; his enemies were too strong and Charles had to make a quick escape from Stralsund shortly before it fell to Peter and his allies.

And Sweden goes out of the European cup

In 1718, Charles XII was at war again, this time invading Norway. Unfortunately, Charles was in the trenches besieging the town of Fredriksten when a musket ball hit him in the head and killed him.

Charles's sister Ulrika took over and set about negotiating a peace deal with Peter I. Peter, who was in no mood to compromise, demanded nearly all of Sweden's lands on the southern shore of the Baltic – meaning the end of Sweden as a major European power. Ulrika signed.

A Deadly Game of Russian Roulette

Russia spent much of the 17th century trying to recover from the chaos that followed Ivan the Terrible's death (check out Chapter 12 for more on Ivan and why he was so terrible). The Romanov dynasty managed to impose a bit of order, and Tsar Alexis I found time to conquer the Ukraine and introduce some modernisation into the Church, but serious problems existed:

- ✔ The imperial guards, the *streltsy*, had far too much power, rather like the Praetorian Guards in ancient Rome (which was only fitting since the tsars saw themselves as the new Caesars. Chapter 4 fills you in on the original Caesars and their guards).
- ✔ Alexis's two sons, Fedor and Ivan, were very sickly and weak-minded.

When Fedor and Ivan's mother died, Alexis married a younger woman called Natalya, who gave birth to a healthy baby boy whom he called Peter (perhaps not surprisingly, questions were continually raised throughout Peter's life about who his father really was). Alexis's first family were not amused.

Alexis died in 1676 and handed over to first sickly son, Fedor III. Fedor didn't do much ruling; he left that to his sister Sophia. Sophia wanted her father's second family cut right out of the picture. So, Sophia had Peter and his mother sent away from the court.

When Fedor III died in 1682 without naming a successor, Sophia prepared a very bloody coup to ensure that the throne passed to second sickly son, Ivan; she egged on the streltsy to hack Natalya's family and friends to pieces. Peter, still only 10, was so terrified that he developed a nervous tic, which he had for the rest of his life. Peter and Natalya had to settle for the boy being joint tsar alongside his half-wit half-brother Ivan V, with dear half-sister Sophia as regent; Peter and Natalya were just thankful still to be alive.

Peter takes charge

Peter grew into a big, hearty, heavy drinking young man, happiest downing vodka with the common soldiers. Sophia decided, a bit late, that she really ought to have him killed, but the guards all rallied to him and instead he had her packed off to a convent. Peter carried on for a few more years with poor old Ivan V, but in 1694, he took over on his own and proceeded to turn Russia upside down.

I say! The tsar of Russia has trashed my house!

No one knew quite what to make of Peter's foreign tour. Officially, he was travelling incognito as 'Peter Mikhailov', and he spent much of the time in Holland and England living and working as a common shipwright, getting hands-on experience and learning all he could about ships and sailing. Peter gathered detailed information about the Swedish defences in Livonia (which was handy, since he was planning to attack them) and in Holland he learned anatomy and dentistry; his poor courtiers had to let him pull their teeth when he got back. Peter was puzzled by the corsets the women wore in Prussia and thought German women must have very tough ribs.

In London, Peter stayed in the house of the eminent writer John Evelyn in Deptford, and left the place a wreck – the floors and windows were smashed to pieces and covered in vomit, the doors and curtains had been burned and the paintings were full of bullet holes. Peter insisted on pretending to be one of his own servants in Vienna, even though Emperor Leopold knew perfectly well who he was. When the tsar went home everyone gave a sigh of relief.

Travel broadens the mind

In 1697, Peter astounded his court by announcing his decision to leave the country and lead a Great Embassy to western Europe.

Peter wasn't going to be sitting through boring official banquets – he was going to learn practical skills and information. Peter visited the Baltic, Prussia, Holland, England, and Austria and was just getting ready to go to Venice when he received serious news from Russia; the streltsy were in rebellion and plotting to put Sophia on the throne.

Peter rushed back to Russia, and his vengeance was terrible. Peter had hundreds of the guards tortured and executed, even cutting off some of their heads himself. Then, Peter started torturing and exiling their wives and maidservants; some of them were buried alive. Sophia lost all her privileges and titles and had to become a nun.

While he was at it, Peter divorced his wife the Empress Euxonia and sent her off to a convent too, poor woman; not because she'd done anything wrong but because he thought she was too boring and, well, *Russian* after all the western European beauties he'd seen on his travels. Euxonia wasn't even allowed a maid to go with her and was denied contact with their little son, the Tsarevitch Alexis.

The tragic fate of Prince Alexis

Peter and his son Alexis were completely different characters, and Alexis grew to fear and hate his father. Alexis continually disappointed Peter, who bullied and beat him mercilessly. When Alexis dared to criticise some of Peter's reforms, though, he fled to Austria and asked the Austrian emperor to protect him, but Peter tricked him into coming back. Then Peter had his own son arrested, imprisoned, and tortured to death.

Peter was determined to modernise Russia and make it more western:

- ✔ **No beards:** The tsar thought that they were a symbol of old-fashioned superstition: after all, people only wore them because the Church told them to. Peter met the leading boyars (members of the aristocracy) and cut their beards off himself.

- ✔ **No kaftans:** Western dress only. Russian costume carried a hefty fine.

- ✔ **Western calendar:** Peter introduced the Julian calendar, ironically just as the rest of Europe was moving to the more accurate Gregorian one. Russia finally caught up in 1918.

- ✔ **News:** Peter introduced Russia's first newspaper and kept a close eye on what went in it.

St Petersburg

In 1703, Peter founded a new capital, St Petersburg. The city was built in the wetlands on the Gulf of Finland, and designed by Venetian, French, and German architects – anybody except Russians in fact. The result was breathtakingly beautiful, an 18th-century masterpiece.

St Petersburg was open to trade and ideas from the West, and Peter expected his court to adopt western dress and etiquette. The tsar had brought hundreds of experts and craftsmen back with him from his Great Embassy and he set them to work creating a large Russian fleet. Peter was making Russia a power to be reckoned with, and St Petersburg was its shop window.

Building a city on water isn't easy, and some 30,000 people died making Peter's dream come true, just like the slave labourers who died building Stalin's underground and canal systems (see Chapter 22 for more on Stalin). But then, in Peter's eyes, these people were there to live and die for their tsar – which was also pretty much Stalin's view. Not surprisingly, Stalin regarded Peter the Great as one of his role models. The other was Ivan the Terrible.

Peter built a palace for himself a few miles outside his capital. He thought this plan would give the tsar extra security and, in a way, it did. In the Russian Revolution of 1917, the palace was where the Bolsheviks imprisoned his descendant, Nicholas II (see Chapter 21).

Viennese Whirl

The Austrian Habsburgs had proved tough fighters in the War of the Spanish Succession (see that section earlier in this chapter for details) and had done well out of the peace settlement. As the Habsburgs basked in all this glory, their capital, Vienna, was fast becoming a lively, happening city, the centre of European art, music, and culture.

The only fly in the ointment was the thorny question of the succession. Archduke Charles, who became Emperor Charles VI in 1711, had a daughter, Maria Theresa. There was nothing to stop a woman inheriting the Habsburg lands, but there was nothing to say that the rest of Europe would necessarily stand for it.

Charles didn't want the family lands divided up, so in 1713 he drew up a document called the *Pragmatic Sanction*, which said: 'I accept that the Habsburg lands should be undivided and that Her Imperial Highness Princess Maria Theresa of the House of Habsburg should inherit them all on the death of her father, the Emperor Charles VI' and sent it round to all the nobles and crowned heads of Europe with the instruction 'Sign here, please'.

Crossing Charles VI was unwise, so nearly everyone did sign the Pragmatic Sanction, but not all of them felt bound to keep their word after he'd died. The succession to the Spanish throne had provoked a very bloody war at the start of the 18th century; the Austrian succession was about to do the same.

Chapter 15

Seeking Enlightenment

Historians often date modern history from the 18th century, not just because this period was of the American and French Revolutions, but because at this time a fundamental change took place in the way people *thought*. Writers of the moment felt that they were emerging from a period of darkness and ignorance into the light of knowledge and reason. The Enlightenment was to have huge consequences, not just for philosophy and science but for politics and the way people were governed – both then and now.

Faith or Reason?

The roots of *Enlightenment* thinking go back a long way before the 18th century. The humanist scholars of the Renaissance had insisted on going back to the original texts of the ancients rather than simply accepting traditional teachings, and by the 17th century this habit of looking and thinking for yourself had spread to observational science.

The 16th-century Polish scientist Nicholas Copernicus had noted that the earth appeared to go round the sun and not vice versa, and a hundred years later the Italian astronomer Galileo Galilei was able to demonstrate from his own observations and from mathematical calculation that Copernicus had been right. This discovery was not welcome news to the Church, which had always taught the Biblical story that the earth was the centre of Creation and the sun merely a sort of light switch placed by God in the heavens so he could see what Adam and Eve were getting up to.

Galileo got into trouble with the Inquisition (though he probably wasn't tortured, as people believed for a long time), but the Church couldn't turn back the way scientific thinking was going; close observation and deduction with precise mathematical calculation were rapidly replacing faith in the classical authors. Might they even replace faith in God?

France produced three thinkers who had a particularly profound impact on European thought:

- ✔ **Michel de Montaigne, 1533–1592.** Montaigne pointed out that peoples in other lands had developed perfectly good codes of morality and ethics. Who was to say which set of values was better than any other? And why should anyone impose their values on other people? Well, quite.

- ✔ **René Descartes, 1596–1650.** Descartes, a philosopher and mathematician, argued that, if you start from the basic point that you know you exist, or, as he put it, 'I think, therefore I am', you can actually *prove* the existence of God by applying reason and mathematics. Descartes's ideas (known as Cartesian philosophy) lasted well into the 18th century and formed the basis for the Enlightenment cult of *Reason*. However, Descarte's idea of a mathematical proof of God didn't last; religious people didn't like basing faith in Reason, and those who believed in Reason increasingly tended not to believe in God.

- ✔ **Blaise Pascal, 1623–1662.** The mathematician Pascal agreed with Descartes on the importance of mathematics, but didn't think that you could apply reason and logic to areas of faith and emotion. 'The heart has its reasons,' he said, 'which Reason knows not.'

This French thinking was all very fine and theoretical, but over the Channel the English were up against hard practicality. When English politics slid into civil war in the middle of the 17th century, two English philosophers in particular tried to work out what the situation all might mean:

- ✔ **Thomas Hobbes, 1588–1679.** Hobbes reckoned that people are pretty brutish, and you need a good strong state, possibly a single ruler with absolute power, to keep them in order.

- ✔ **John Locke, 1632–1704.** Locke took a rather more optimistic view of human nature and reckoned that people are born equal, with no in-built sense of right and wrong. We are the result of what we observe and experience as we go through life; no one is 'naturally' any better than anyone else.

These philosophers' thoughts ran counter to commonly accepted attitudes of 17th-century Europe, when people were born into 'better' or 'lower' families every day. If Locke (and Montaigne) was right, then by what *right* did nobles claim to be of 'higher' birth than peasants? And by what *right* did they hold their lands and wealth while others, just as 'well' born as they were, had nothing? The implications of Locke's thinking were enormous and revolutionary.

Bewitched?

Belief in witchcraft seemed to take a much deeper hold in the 16th and 17th centuries, just when the Renaissance and the Scientific Revolution were developing the practice of reasoned observation and argument.

Witches were supposed to exercise magic powers, which they gained from consorting with the Devil and used to harm their neighbours.

Suspected witches were thrown into rivers; if you sank, then you were all right (and yes,

they'd haul you out), but if you floated, then God's pure water was spitting out the spawn of Satan and you'd hang.

Witchcraft trials began to die out in the 18th century, though cases still cropped up even into the 19th century. Belief in witchcraft is a reminder not to place too much faith in reason and logic – people often prefer magic and fear.

The Militant Middle Classes

The growth of the middle classes was the main factor that distinguished the 18th century from its predecessors. Through trade, through the professions, and increasingly through industry, the middle classes were growing in numbers and in wealth, especially in the big trading nations such as Britain, France, and the Netherlands.

However, in much of Europe political power was reserved for the aristocracy; in many countries you weren't allowed by law to rise to top positions unless you had the right aristocratic pedigree. To the aristocratic mind this situation was how things had always been and that was the end of it. The power of the aristocracy didn't *need* to be defended or explained, any more than you needed to make excuses for the fact that grass is green or Tuesday follows Monday.

But to the growing middle classes this situation wasn't good enough. These people increasingly challenged the reasoning that excluded them from political power. The middle classes got their ideas from a new generation of increasingly radical philosophers and thinkers:

✔ **Baron de Montesquieu, 1689–1755.** Montesquieu wrote about the origin and development of laws and legal codes, showing that they had evolved over time and that no set of laws could in any way be called 'natural' or 'pre-ordained'.

✔ **Voltaire (François-Marie Arouet), 1694–1778.** Voltaire attacked the absurdity and inconsistencies of contemporary society with such delicious wit that, ironically, he became very popular in the pampered and privileged aristocratic circles he was criticising. Voltaire's most famous work was *Candide*, an extended fable about a naive young lad

> who trusts in the assurances of his teacher, Pangloss, that 'All is for the best in the best of all possible worlds' despite abundant evidence in their travels that it is anything but.
>
> ✔ **Jean-Jacques Rousseau, 1712–1778.** This rather gloomy Swiss philosopher built on Locke's idea that people are born equal, except that, of course, in reality they're not: 'Man is born free but everywhere he is in chains.' Rousseau argued that inequality was not only unnatural and wrong, but ultimately inefficient. Rousseau believed in handing more power over to the people.

Encylopaedia Spells Trouble

The 17th century had been the period of the great scientific revolution, when Isaac Newton defined the laws of motion that govern the operation of the physical world around us (for more on Newton see *British History For Dummies*). Soon, those with enough time and leisure developed a mania for gathering what was called 'useful' knowledge and information and publishers began producing multi-volume encyclopaedias to meet the demand.

Nowadays, we think of encyclopaedias as somewhere to do some quick fact-checking for homework or a quiz, but the 18th century had a rather higher opinion of them; these books set out to be a collection of *Everything There Is To Know About Everything In The World in Space* – quite a claim. When the French writer Denis Diderot was asked to edit a new French edition of an English *Cyclopaedia* by Ephraim Chambers, he took this information-gathering an important step further, however. Chambers's *Cyclopaedia* could just as easily have been called 'Well I never, that's actually quite interesting'. Diderot wanted to produce something rather more practical than a list of interesting facts. So, the writer contacted every leading *philosophe* in France and together they produced the *Encyclopédie*, a collection of analytical essays analysing and attacking a whole range of issues including the power and influence of the Church, the injustice of the French social system, the claims of European civilisation to superiority, even the basis for monarchy.

The *Encyclopédie* consisted of 17 volumes, appearing over a 30-year period from the 1750s to the 1780s. The French authorities were fully aware of the dangers of the *Encyclopédie's* implications, and they continually tried to ban it and arrest its authors (not a hazard the editors of *Encarta* face on a daily basis).

Diderot was offered a way out of all this persecution by the French authorities from a rather unusual source. The Empress Catherine II of Russia wrote and asked if he would like to come and live at her court in St Petersburg. The empress was looking for someone to give her good advice on how to rule her people well, and because she exercised absolute power, the chance of Diderot's ideas actually being put into practice was very likely. Interested? Diderot went.

Large earthquake in Lisbon – faith in Creation shattered

On 1 November 1755, the city of Lisbon was almost destroyed in a catastrophic earthquake and tidal wave. Lisbon's elegant buildings crumbled into rubble and something like 40,000 people were killed. If you believed in a benevolent God who had created the world and who looked favourably on man's efforts to create a civilised, harmonious society, then how on earth were you able to explain this act of appalling destruction? For those who believed that this world was the best of all possible worlds, the destruction of Lisbon took a lot of explaining; others found their faith in God running very low.

Principals with Principles: The Enlightened Despots

Catherine II of Russia was one of a number of European monarchs who were interested enough in the ideas of the Enlightenment to want to see if they could apply them to practical politics. This style of monarchy became known as *Enlightened Absolutism* or, if you disapproved of it, *Enlightened Despotism*.

In Russia, it's mayhem at the top as usual

Peter the Great had made a rule that each tsar should choose his own successor. The idea was to ensure some stability and avoid the risk of having a child tsar. Peter's plan didn't quite work.

Peter's widow, Catherine I, and his grandson, Peter II, only reigned for a couple of years each. Peter's niece, Anne, was completely controlled by her lover, Johannes Biron, who instituted rule by terror. When she died, her 4-month-old great nephew became Ivan VI. That was when Peter the Great's feisty daughter Elizabeth overthrew Biron and had little Ivan VI locked up. Elizabeth took the throne herself.

Elizabeth's heir was going to be her nephew, Peter. Peter wasn't one of imperial Russia's great brains. In 1745, Elizabeth married Peter off to another German, Sophia-Augusta of Anhalb-Zerbst, who quickly adopted her new country and dropped her old one. Sophia-Augusta took a more Russian name, Catherine, and set about making friends among the imperial guards (she had learnt quickly). When Elizabeth died in 1762, Peter became Tsar Peter III, but it was painfully clear that he wasn't any happier as tsar than he had been as prince. So Catherine put him out of his misery. Catherine hatched a plot with her lover, a handsome young guards officer called Gregory Orlov, and he and his brother burst in on Peter and strangled him. Catherine became empress in her own right, as the Empress Catherine II.

Catherine the Great

Catherine was a fascinating woman, a real bundle of contradictions. The empress had a string of lovers among the imperial guards (this perk must've worked wonders for recruitment), and historians think that she probably married her most steady one, Prince Gregory Potemkin. Catherine corresponded daily with the French *philosophes* on the most scientific and rational way to govern, and she set the French philosopher Diderot up in proper style when he arrived, with all his books and papers and a little hermitage where he could work (see the section 'Encylopaedia Spells Trouble', earlier in this chapter, for more on this philosopher).

In 1767 Catherine reordered Russia's system of law and administration along the more rational lines laid down in Montesquieu's *Spirit of the Laws*, namely that prisons were to improve their inmates and make them useful citizens rather than just slamming them up and throwing away the key. She reduced the number of executions and even put an end to torture. Catherine founded schools, and laid down exactly what privileges Russia's nobles did and did not enjoy.

Voltaire was so impressed with the empress that he hailed her as Catherine the Great and the name has caught on, at least among historians (see the earlier section 'The Militant Middle Classes' for more on Voltaire).

Catherine was no bleeding-heart liberal, though. The empress had no intention of ending Russia's system of serfdom, which kept millions of peasants tied to the land as slaves, even though human rights and an end to slavery were pretty basic Enlightenment beliefs.

Catherine had her Enlightenment principles sorely tested in 1773 when a Cossack called Yemelian Pugachev led a massive peasant rising, claiming he was Catherine's husband, Tsar Peter III (which seemed unlikely since Pugachev clearly had a brain). The uprising lasted for two years before Pugachev was finally cornered and brought to Moscow in a cage. Catherine had the peasants executed in their thousands (what was that about fewer executions?) and Pugachev himself was hanged and cut into quarters. But the executioners waited till Pugachev was dead before chopping him up – no torture, remember? (Given Pugachev's gruesome end, you could argue that Catherine was a *sort* of bleeding heart liberal.)

Tsarina of Spin

In 1787, Catherine organised a little river trip down to the Crimea, which her troops had seized from the Turks and Tatars. This jaunt was a big propaganda exercise, with triumphal arches and garlands and happy smiling people waving from the river bank. Catherine made sure to invite as many foreign dignitaries as possible; even the Austrian emperor, Joseph II, came along for part of the way. The idea was to show Russia spreading European civilisation forward, into the barbarous lands of the south, though in fact the region was far from settled and peaceful. The river trip was organised by Potemkin, and to this day the Russians speak of a 'Potemkin village' to mean a good looking façade put up to hide a mess.

Catherine ruled Russia for 34 years, 1762–1796 – no mean feat for a Russian ruler. Catherine's enemies made up all sorts of exaggerated stories about her love life – though with her succession of toy boys, exaggeration wasn't really necessary. The story that she died in the act of copulation with a horse is, I'm happy to say, entirely untrue (the truth is much more boring – she died of ill-ness) though this tale still gets repeated – as its inventors doubtless intended.

Prussia's Brandenburg Concerto

The old territory of the Teutonic Knights in northern Germany had become the small state of Prussia ruled by the Hohenzollern family. In 1613, Prussia joined up with the Electorate of Brandenburg to become the medium-sized German state of Brandenburg-Prussia.

In theory, Brandenburg-Prussia belonged to Poland, but Frederick William, the 'Great Elector', declared Prussian independence in the 17th century, and ever since, the Brandenburg-Prussians had been operating very successfully as a middleweight power, with a powerful military nobility known as the *Junkers*.

King Frederick William I prized soldiers, and kept a regiment of giants whom he loved to inspect (they were so conspicuous they'd have been no good on the battlefield) and even sent agents around Europe to find extra tall men to trick or kidnap into his army. The king made his son Frederick's life a misery; Prince Frederick also liked soldiering, but he enjoyed reading and music, too. When Prince Frederick and his best friend Küstrin tried to escape to England, they were caught and the king made Frederick watch his friend being put to death.

Frederick succeeded his father as king of Prussia in 1740. Frederick II proved one of the most remarkable monarchs of his time – and he was up against some stiff competition. Frederick II was a great friend of Voltaire, and built a delight-ful little palace for himself at Potsdam, to escape from all the paperwork and play Bach on his flute, sometimes with the great man there to accompany him.

Prussia Invades Silesia

The Holy Roman Emperor Charles VI died in 1740. Charles VI had done his best to ensure a smooth hand-over to his daughter, Maria Theresa, by getting everyone to sign his *Pragmatic Sanction* (see Chapter 14) and promising to accept her, but when the time came to the actual succession, a lot of German princes began studying the carpet and saying that they were very sorry to hear that the emperor was dead, but of course they couldn't promise anything.

Frederick II went rather further than doubting Maria Theresa's position as empress. The Prussian king sent his troops into Silesia, a coal-rich Polish province that belonged to the Habsburgs. Maria Theresa was furious, and the rest of Europe was rather taken aback: Prussia wasn't exactly a major power, so this move was very cheeky of Frederick – and was even more cheeky when he hung onto it. Maria Theresa was speechless with rage.

The War of the Austrian Succession

Maria Theresa had more problems than just invading Prussians. Charles Albert of Bavaria declared himself Holy Emperor Charles VII. Maria Theresa can be Queen of Hungary and Bohemia, Charles said, generously, but that's it. Maria Theresa was livid, and the way events developed didn't exactly improve her mood:

- ✔ **1741: France declares war on the Habsburgs.**

- ✔ **1742: Britain, already at war with Spain, sends money to help Maria Theresa and declares war on France and Prussia.**

- ✔ **1743: France and Spain form the Bourbon Family Compact and swear to fight Maria Theresa and her allies to the death.** *Zut alors! Olé!*

- ✔ **1745: The Emperor 'Charles VII' dies.** The emperor's demise rather defeats the point of the war.

Honours were more or less even between the British and French; the British had defeated the French in Germany, and the French had won a big victory at Fontenoy. More importantly, the two countries had also fought in their overseas colonies; the British had taken the French settlement of Louisbourg in Canada and the French commander Dupleix had captured the British base of Madras in southern India. The involvement of the colonies is why you can call the War of the Austrian Succession the *real* First World War.

In the 1748 *Treaty of Aix-la-Chapelle* which ended the war, Maria Theresa's husband Francis became Holy Roman Emperor and she ruled Austria and the Habsburg lands. Everyone gave everything back that they'd seized, which makes you wonder why they took them in the first place. Everything, that is, except for Silesia. Maria Theresa was determined to get it back if it was the last thing she did.

The Seven Years' War

The peace established by the Treaty of Aix-la-Chapelle didn't last. The war really started again in 1755 when the French and their native allies ambushed a British force under General Braddock in the Ohio valley in North America. When the conflict broke out in Europe, it was known as the *Seven Years' War*, but in America and India, the fighting had never really stopped.

Now the conflict involved Austria and France against Britain and Prussia – the British and French still on opposite sides, you see. Britain's William Pitt the Elder and France's Duke de Choiseul actually planned this one as a world war – the winner really could take it all.

On the European front, Frederick II was in serious trouble when the Russians joined in against him. By 1762, the situation looked like curtains for Frederick and his little Prussian state, when suddenly he heard that his arch-enemy the Russian Empress Elizabeth had died. The new tsar was Peter III, who adored Frederick . Russia pulled out of the war, Prussia was saved, and the participants all met in Paris to draw up a peace treaty.

As the allies were closing in on Berlin in 1945, Hitler heard that US President Roosevelt had died. Hilter's propaganda minister, Goebbels, said the situation was like that of Frederick the Great and the Empress Elizabeth all over again, and Germany was saved. It wasn't.

The 1763 *Peace of Paris* said that Prussia was to keep Silesia, but otherwise, the overwhelming winner was Britain. The British had taken Quebec from the French and defeated them in India at the Battle of Plassey. Under the treaty terms, Britain kept all of Canada and nearly all of India. Suddenly, Britain had become a European and world power of the first rank.

Enlightenment Europe

Enlightened rule did not always mean peaceful rule:

- ✔ **Denmark:** Count Struensee centralises the government, liberates the serfs, reforms the legal and administrative system, and brings in religious toleration. Unfortunately, Struensee's way of enforcing liberty is so brutal that the Danes overthrow him and execute him in 1772.

The Jesuits: Your handy local scapegoats

In 1773, Pope Clement XIV finally gave in to intense international pressure and dissolved the Society of Jesus, the Jesuits. Enlightenment thinkers hated the Jesuits because they represented the intellectual wing of the Church, and European rulers, even Catholic ones, wanted them out of the way so that they could control the Church more effectively.

The Jesuits' fate was sealed far away, in South America. The Society had set up some very successful missions working with the native peoples of the Brazilian rainforest, and were operating virtually as an independent state, protecting the native peoples from the Spanish and Portuguese who wanted to carve the area up and enslave them.

The Spanish and Portuguese piled the pressure on Pope Clement, until Clement gave in. The Pope dissolved the Jesuits, closed their schools and colleges, and the Spanish and Portuguese moved in on their South American missions. The film *The Mission* depicts how this change in policy affected the relationships among the Jesuits, natives, and colonists.

- ✔ **Italy:** Leopold of Habsburg, Grand Duke of Tuscany (1765–1792) and later the Emperor Leopold II (1790–1792) is a model ruler; good reforms, fair trials, no torture, and he tells the Pope to keep out of Tuscan internal affairs.

- ✔ **Portugal:** Country is ruled by the ruthless Marquis de Pombal since King Joseph I (1750–1777) can't be bothered. Pombal is certainly very efficient but he is also intolerant and bloodthirsty. Pombal makes many enemies and Queen Maria I (1777–1816) finally sacks him.

- ✔ **Spain:** King Charles III (1759–1788) reforms the law, encourages business, and kicks the Jesuits out.

- ✔ **Sweden:** King Gustavus III (1771–1792) abolishes torture and reforms the laws. Gustavus also goes to war with Russia and loses, which is silly. The Swedes overthrow the king in a *coup*.

Please Don't Give Joseph II Ideas

When she wasn't fighting the rest of Europe for her throne or for Silesia (see the section 'Prussia invades Silesia', earlier in this chapter), Maria Theresa was actually quite a good ruler. She improved the army and the tax system, which brought in much needed revenue, and she had the roads mended and generally made herself useful. But Marie Theresa died aged 63 in 1780 and handed the throne over to her son Joseph II, who had been waiting in the wings with increasing impatience.

Joseph wanted radical, even revolutionary change, and he was going to improve people's lives whether they wanted him to or not. Joseph's wide-ranging reforms included:

- No more serfdom, at least not on Habsburg lands.

- No more monasteries unless they run schools or hospitals; otherwise they're a waste of good space. We need more parish churches, though, so no one has to walk more than an hour to get to one.

- Cut those religious holidays and processions – they take up valuable working days.

- We need more schools, but we don't need so many universities. Turn all but the most important ones into schools again. And while we're at it, professors are paid too much: See to it.

- Coffins are a waste of good wood. Everyone is to be buried in a bag (one each, that is, not one big one).

- No feather beds; simple straw is good enough for the emperor and should be good enough for everyone else.

- Centralise! Centralise! Centralise! No need for different governments when you've got a perfectly good one in Vienna that can oversee every-thing. As long as everyone does everything in the same way, you only need one central government.

That last reform caused ructions. In Belgium, they were so angry at having everything dictated from Vienna that they rose up in rebellion in 1789 and declared independence. (Ironically, some people at the end of the 20th cen-tury felt the same way about Brussels.)

Joseph II wanted scientific rules for everything, including music. The emperor had Mozart composing for him, but paid him a pittance and once memorably told him he had written 'too many notes'.

But Joseph's most serious legacy was his obsession with spies. Joseph felt sure that his officials were trying to frustrate his plans, so he set up an elabo-rate secret police service and set them to keep an eye on everyone – and on each other, of course. The secret police was unaccountable to anyone except the emperor himself. His police may not have been the legacy that Joseph II would have chosen to leave to posterity, but they're the feature of his reign that lasted longest – 19th- and 20th-century Europe got to know secret police forces only too well.

Poland Polished Off

Once-mighty Poland simply disappeared from the map in the 18th century.

In 1764, Frederick II and Catherine II both agreed to let the Poles elect Stanislas Poniatowski as their king; because he was one of Catherine's many former lovers (how did she keep track of them all?), she thought that he would more or less do as he was told.

Stanislas tried to introduce lots of changes, but he found himself blocked by the Polish nobles, so Catherine sent him troops to help bring the Polish nobles to order. That action angered the Poles, who appealed to France for help against this blatant Russian interference and before you knew it Poland had fallen into anarchy and the Russians, French, Austrians, Prussians, and Turks were all threatening war.

At this point, Frederick II proposed to the Austrians, and then to the Russians, that carving up Poland between them would solve matters and avoid a war that no one wanted. No more Poland – no more problem. Frederick was not the last German leader to come up with that little scheme (see Chapter 22).

What followed is known as the *Partitions of Poland*. You could also call it 'Murder of a Nation':

- ✔ **1772, First Partition:** Russia, Prussia, and Austria take great chunks of Polish territory. Poland loses about a third of its land and population. The Polish *sejm* (parliament), suitably bribed, agrees to the loss.

- ✔ **1793, Second Partition:** King Stanislas Poniatowski draws up a constitution for Poland with a hereditary monarchy and no foreign influence. The Russians don't like this idea, and they like it even less when the Poles start corresponding with the revolutionaries in France. Prussia and Russia carve off more land, just to protect the Poles from the French Revolution, you understand.

- ✔ **1795, Third Partition:** Poles stage a nationalist uprising under Tadeusz Kosciuszko, a veteran of the American Revolutionary War. Russia, Prussia, and Austria crush the revolt and carve up the rest of Poland between them. Poland will not be an independent state again until 1918.

The American Revolution

The British were very proud of their parliamentary system, which they thought offered a much better guarantee of liberty than relying on the whims of a monarch, no matter how enlightened.

However, one important English group disagreed profoundly. This group argued that parliament was just as oppressive and tyrannical as any king, if you happened to live on the other side of the Atlantic. When the British government started imposing taxes on the American colonies in the 1760s, the colonists thought that their basic rights as Englishmen were being trampled on. In 1775, a group of colonists on Lexington green fired on British troops looking for an arms cache, and started a war.

The Europeans were fascinated by what appeared to be a breakdown in the fabled English parliamentary system – the Americans certainly didn't encourage any of the enlightened despots to introduce such a legislative body.

Unlike enlightened despots, who could rule as well or as badly as they pleased, Thomas Jefferson and Benjamin Franklin, had the enviable task of designing a whole new country along Enlightenment principles. When Franklin arrived as American Minister at Versailles, wearing his own hair and plain clothes (none of those fancy wigs and ruffles), he caused a sensation; here was a child of nature, a messenger from the land of forests and log cabins where Man could go back to the basic principles of life, just as Rousseau had said he should (see the earlier section 'The Militant Middle Classes', for more on Rousseau's ideas). (Actually, Franklin was a highly sophisticated political operator and wouldn't have lasted five minutes in the forest, but hey.)

After a good many more skirmishes on land and sea with the colonists and their French allies, Britain had to sign the Treaty of Versailles in 1783 recognising the United States as an independent country. The Spanish had taken advantage of the war to attack Gibraltar, but without success, and the French, although they had helped the Americans win, came out of the war with nothing but a very heavy bill to pay for their involvement.

France on the Brink

Eighteenth-century France seemed to be prospering. First the Duke of Orleans and then the Duke of Bourbon acted as regent for little Louis XV, until in 1726, he took over for himself.

Louis XV was lazy, and left government to his old tutor, Cardinal Fleury. Louis spent his time showering gifts on his mistresses, first Madame de Pompadour and later Madame du Barry, which wasn't such a good idea because the French Crown was rapidly going bankrupt. The nobility of France were exempt from paying taxes, and they weren't likely to start in the near future. Every time one of Louis XV's ministers came up with a scheme for increasing revenue by taxing the nobles, the nobles squashed the idea. Meanwhile, France kept going to war, so the debt just got worse.

As well as the uncooperative nobility, Louis faced opposition from the *parlements*. The parlements were regional law courts, which enjoyed the right to register royal decrees for their areas – so if they didn't approve, the decrees didn't apply there – and they increasingly used their powers to frustrate any attempt by Louis XV's ministers to introduce any reforms that might infringe their rights or liberties.

The result of this stalemate between Crown and nobles was that France was about the only major country in the 18th century that didn't try out a new approach to government and wasn't able to introduce a package of reforms. When change finally came, it had to be forced through. By revolution.

Chapter 16

France Catches a Cold – and We're All Still Sneezing

The French Revolution is where modern history began. The Revolution started as a struggle for human rights against a bankrupt and corrupt monarchy, but soon the French revolutionaries instituted rule by terror. Napoleon tried to instil order by imposing military rule, which certainly brought stability but did nothing for human rights. Nevertheless, the ideals of the revolution have inspired people to our own day.

The French Have Problems, Problems . . .

The king of France in 1789 was Louis XVI, the well-meaning, rather plodding grandson of Louis XV and married to a vivacious Austrian princess, called Marie Antoinette, with whom he had virtually nothing in common. Louis was keenly aware that the French people had problems; he just wasn't too sure what they were.

Marie Antoinette

Marie Antoinette was brought up in the glittering Habsburg court of Vienna. She had a little farm built in the grounds of Versailles where she and her friends went to play at being shepherdesses. At a time when real shepherdesses couldn't get enough to eat, her play farm was more than a little insensitive. A well-known story tells how when someone told Marie Antoinette that the people of France had no bread to eat, she airily replied 'Well then, let them eat cake. Ha ha ha!' There's no evidence that she ever said anything of the kind, but the fact that the story was doing the rounds shows what people were prepared to believe of her.

Marie Antoinette was supposed to have been having a lesbian affair with the Countess of Polignac (not true), and to have ordered a fantastically expensive necklace made of 647 diamonds and then tried to evade paying for it (not true either). People called her 'the Austrian bitch' (okay, not to her face). This hostility towards Marie Antoinette did not help a monarchy that was soon going to need every bit of public sympathy it could get.

One for You, Five for Me: Privilege

The whole French social system was based on the idea of *privilege*. Privilege means, in effect, a 'private law', which only applies to you and no one else. The French nobility had privilege in spades; they got all the top posts in the government, the law, the army, the navy, the church – you name it.

Without the right birth you weren't *allowed* to reach the top, however good you were. So a whole class of highly educated and well-qualified people of middling or humble birth existed whom the system stopped from ever reaching the top. Not surprisingly, many of these people went on to become leaders of the French Revolution.

The biggest privilege by far was that the nobles didn't have to pay taxes. Everyone else had to pay a poll tax and a salt tax and a tenth tax and even a tax-in-kind when they had to go and work on the roads. Finance minister after finance minister tried to show the nobles exactly why a better idea would be if they shouldered their share of the tax burden. No dice. If a finance minister tried to force the issue, the nobles forced the king to sack him.

A country cannot carry on with an economic system like this indefinitely. The French Crown had never recovered from the cost of the War of American Independence (see Chapter 15), and at some point, the money was going to run out. That point came in 1789.

The Estates General to the Rescue!

King Louis decided the time had come to summon the *Estates General*. The Estates General was a gathering of representatives of the ancient *estates* of France. The estates were based on the medieval idea that three types of people existed:

- ✔ **First Estate:** Those who prayed – the Church
- ✔ **Second Estate:** Those who fought – the nobles
- ✔ **Third Estate:** Er, everyone else

Don't get the idea that the Third Estate were 'the peasants' or 'the workers'; it included everyone who wasn't either a clergyman or a noble. That accounts for a lot of people, including many who were wealthy and educated. A clergyman called the Abbé Sieyès wrote a popular pamphlet called 'What is the Third Estate?' and decided that that this council was the proper representative of the French people.

1+1 = trouble

The Estates General was due to meet at Versailles in May 1789. Everyone started getting their robes fitted, and royal officials dusted off old etiquette books to find out how the meeting was actually supposed to work. The Third Estate said that because it was easily the biggest section of the population, it ought to have more representatives, so Louis let them have double the number of each of the other two estates.

Let me help

Louis XVI got rather carried away with the excitement of calling the Estates General by inviting all the people of France to write to him with their problems and worries – and they did. Hundreds of *cahiers de doléance* – grumble sheets – flooded into Versailles. Some of these sheets had been written up by clerks and were full of the latest enlightenment phrasing – 'the freeborn people of this region groan under the weight of an oppressive and archaic fiscal régime' – but the ones which came directly from the people were full of complaints like 'My neighbour's pig keeps running onto my land so could Your Majesty kindly put him in prison or failing that, can I eat his pig?'

Louis had raised people's expectations far too high, and they were bound to be very disappointed. Disappointing people in this way is never wise, and can be downright dangerous.

Came the big day and the proceedings hit a snag. The courtiers who had been reading up on the rules announced that the three estates would meet and vote separately. That meant that the other two estates could always out-vote the Third Estate, no matter how many deputies it had. Uh-oh.

Do you realise who we are?

The Third Estate had all read Sieyès's pamphlet (see the section 'The Estates General to the Rescue' above). 'We're not the *third* anything,' they said, 'We're the Nation.' They also reckoned that the time had come for the Nation to take a hand in government. The king tried locking them out of the meeting hall, but they simply marched to a nearby indoor tennis court and called on the other estates to come and join them in a new *National Assembly*. Then the king sent a courtier to tell them to disperse, but their leader Count Mirabeau (a rather louche nobleman elected to the Third Estate – the Second Estate wouldn't have him) thundered at him to get lost; no one dismissed the representatives of the Nation. As tends to happen when people get carried away by excitement, events now took on a momentum of their own:

- ✔ The Night of 4 August 1789. In a highly emotionally charged scene, the nobility of France give up all their titles and privileges – including their tax exemption. Nobles who don't feel quite so emotionally charged get out of France fast.

- ✔ The National Assembly declares that all land belonging to the Church is to be nationalised and sold off. The money is to be used to launch a new paper currency called the *assignat*.

- ✔ The National Assembly issues the *Declaration of the Rights of Man and of the Citizen* laying down the basic rights to which every Frenchman is entitled. This document becomes the basis for everything that then follows.

Rights for all (well, nearly all)

In theory ,the Declaration of the Rights of Man applied to all people, but a lady called Olympe de Gouges pointed out that it didn't seem to apply to women (she was right – it didn't). Unfortunately, Olympe was a royalist, so she ended up on the guillotine, where she at least had equal rights with everyone else.

The African slaves in France's Caribbean colony of Saint-Domingue (Haiti) also thought the Declaration sounded good, so they rose up and set up a republic under their leader, Toussaint l'Ouverture. At first, the revolutionary government in Paris was all in favour, but later it changed its mind. Napoleon even sent an army to Haiti to re-impose slavery. Toussaint died in prison in France.

Fear and Looting in the Country

When people are frightened they do strange things. A severe bread shortage developed in 1789 because the previous year's harvest had been destroyed in the mother of all thunder storms. Now all sorts of wild rumours started flying around about an army of vengeful nobles killing peasants and burning their homes.

The panic-stricken people attacked châteaux the length and breadth of France, taking particular care to burn any old manuscripts in case they said something about how much tax they owed (researching medieval France is still difficult today because so much evidence was destroyed in the Revolution).

To the Bastille!

People in Paris were scared that the king was going to do something drastic when they saw cannons pointing down at them from the top of the Bastille, the enormous fortress that towered over the working class parts of the city.

The Bastille was a symbol of the king, his taxes, the nobles, and everything else that made being poor in 18th-century France such misery.

On 14 July 1789 – still France's national holiday – the poor of the city gathered every weapon they could find and attacked the Bastille, to free its political prisoners (they'd all been moved out long ago, though seven lunatics were in residence). The crowd massacred the guards, stuck the governor's head on a pike, and demolished the place stone by stone. (The man who oversaw the demolition did a very handsome trade afterwards in guaranteed genuine Bastille bricks.)

The poor people of Paris were known as the *sans culottes*, which means 'without breeches' – no, they didn't go round bare-legged, they wore good honest trousers instead of fussy embroidered breeches and silk stockings. The sans culottes were to play a key role in the Revolution.

Go get him, girls!

In October 1789 a huge crowd of women sans culottes marched out to Versailles, armed to the teeth and in no mood for talking. The women cut Louis's guards to pieces, burst into the palace, and chased Marie Antoinette screaming through the royal apartments until they finally ran into Louis. The women wanted bread ('Don't even *think* of saying it, Marie Antoinette') and they wanted the king, queen, and National Assembly to come back with them to Paris. The women sharpened their knives and pitchforks meaningfully and, not surprisingly, the king agreed to go.

Join the club

People from all over France gathered in special debating clubs in Paris, such as the *Jacobins*, so-called because they met in an old Jacobin convent, and the more radical *Cordeliers*.

The Jacobins started off as the more moderate group; but radicals joined the Jacobins as well, like Louis Saint-Just and Maximilien Robespierre. Eventually they threw the moderates out. These club radicals wanted to get rid of the king and set up a republic. Eventually, the Jacobins and Cordeliers were to take over the government and direct the Revolutionary Terror.

Louis XVI gets one last chance . . .

The National Assembly elected a special assembly to draw up a new French constitution. Eventually, the assembly decided to have a constitutional monarchy, more or less along the lines of the English system. That system of government meant keeping the king, and also meant that the king had to play along with the idea.

Louis promised to co-operate, but secretly he hated this new constitution. He was particularly shocked at the way French bishops and priests were now to be elected by the people and controlled by the state. When the Pope condemned this new *civil constitution of the clergy*, Louis decided that the time had come to get out.

. . . and blows it

At the dead of night, Louis and his family crept out of Paris and headed for the Austrian frontier. Unfortunately, as a means of escape the royal family had chosen a huge, very noticeable coach which couldn't go very fast.

'He went that-a-way,' said half the peasants of eastern France. The royal family were stopped at Varennes, near the border, and sent back to Paris, where huge crowds lined the route in ominous silence. 'I told you so!' said the more radical elements in the National Assembly, 'You can't trust a king. What we need is a republic.' Apparently, Marie Antoinette's hair turned white during the flight to Varennes, which is hardly surprising.

This Means War! (and Terror)

In 1792, the ruling group of hotheads, called *Girondins* because many of them came from the Gironde region in the south west, came up with a bright idea to unite the country. 'Let's have a war!' they said.

La Marseillaise

When the Germans were closing in on Paris, troops from Marseilles marched up to the capital singing a stirring new song to give the Parisians courage. The tune was originally called the Song of the Army of the Rhine, but is now universally known, after the people who first sang it, as the Marseillaise. The song was written by a young officer called Joseph Rouget de L'Isle, and for my money it sounds a bit disjointed, by going off at a tangent halfway through and seems to need a whole movement to resolve the tune. However, the French lapped it up, and the Marseilles can still bring a tear to the eye when sung in the film *Casablanca*.

The idea was to attack Austria and Prussia, take over Belgium (which belonged to the Austrians who really wouldn't miss it), and spread a bit of revolutionary fervour among the neighbours.

Unfortunately, the French weren't able to get their army together, so while they were all trying to work out which end of the musket the ball went in, the Austrians and Prussians made mincemeat of them, had a quick beer, and headed for Paris. The German commander, the Duke of Brunswick, sent a message to Paris telling them that he'd better find the king safe and well. Bad idea:

✔ The French got their act together and beat the Austrians at the Battle of Valmy, beat them again at Jemappes, annexed Belgium, and declared that they would come to the aid of any oppressed peoples wanting to be free. The war was far from over.

✔ The Parisian sans culottes ran through the city prisons killing everyone they found, burst into the Tuileries palace, massacred the king's Swiss guards (recruiting royal guards must have been a thankless task in those days), and hauled Louis and Marie Antoinette off to prison. France was now to be a republic, ruled by an elected *National Convention*.

✔ The Convention put Louis on trial, and by a narrow majority, condemned him to death. On 21 January 1793, Louis XVI was executed by guillotine, more or less on the site of one of the fountains in the Place de la Concorde.

✔ France declared war on Britain and Holland, and the French commander-in-chief, General Dumouriez, defected to the Austrians. The Convention declared a state of emergency and brought in strict new security regulations – they were called the Terror.

The Duke of Brunswick probably wished he'd kept his mouth shut.

Dr Guillotin's useful device

The guillotine has a grim reputation, but Dr Guillotin invented the device as a much more speedy and humane way of execution than hanging or chopping with an axe. Educated people in France had enormous faith in machines and technology, so they regarded a machine that could confer instantaneous and painless death as a great blessing for mankind. One story says that Dr Guillotin was himself guillotined, but it's not true. However, Louis XVI did make some helpful suggestions about the shape of the blade, and he did get the chance to try out his own ideas in practice.

Rule by Terror

A special Committee of Public Safety was appointed by the Convention to run the Terror (and the people who sat on the committee were the world's first official terrorists – terrorists don't just undermine governments, they can run them, too).

The idea behind the Terror was to turn France into a nation of informers in such a way that no one would dare even to think, let alone act, against the Revolution. Under the *Law of Suspects* you could be arrested on anyone's say-so, even anonymous tip-offs, and when you were hauled up before the *Revolutionary Tribunal* you weren't allowed a defence lawyer. This system was a great way to pay off a personal grudge, and many people did.

The Convention even tried to use the Terror to control the economy. Under the *Law of Maximum*, bakers and grocers were executed for charging too much. Every day, ordinary people (far more of them than of aristocrats, though the Convention did execute Marie Antoinette as well) were taken in *tumbrils* (carts) through the streets to the guillotine. Special *Representatives on Mission* went to the provincial cities to seek out public enemies, and they took their guillotines with them.

Revolt in the provinces

Terrible scenes took place in the French provinces. The Terror was so severe in Lyons that the city was even re-named No-Name, and hundreds of people were drowned in specially-designed barges on the river.

The city of Toulon opened its port to a British fleet until a young artilleryman called Bonaparte drove the British out again.

Does anyone know what day it is?

The revolutionaries changed everything. No more Monsieur and Madame; everyone was 'Citizen'. Christianity was abolished and replaced with a goddess of Reason and a wonderfully daft cult of the Supreme Being, which required Robespierre, the Jacobin leader, to go through the streets in very silly fancy dress.

The revolutionaries even introduced a new calendar, with a ten-day week, years numbered from the start of the republic rather than the birth of Christ (so 1792–93 was Year I, 1793–94 Year II, and so on) and twenty months named after the seasons: windy, snowy, rainy, hot, flowery, corny, and so on. This system made the maths easier, but the calendar sounded like the seven dwarfs.

In the Vendée region of western France, a romantic young nobleman called Charette led a popular rising against the revolutionary government. The government ruthlessly crushed the revolt, including using mass drownings at Nantes, which is comparable to 20th-century 'ethnic cleansing'.

One girl from Normandy managed to give Paris a taste of provincial thinking. The girl's name was Charlotte Corday, and in July 1793 she travelled all the way to Paris to see Jean-Paul Marat, one of the more ruthless members of the Committee of Public Safety (and that's saying something). Marat was having a special bath for his nasty skin complaint and didn't want to see Charlotte, but changed his mind when she revealed that she had a nice juicy list of traitors for him. She stabbed him.

Charlotte Corday was proud of her actions. The revolutionaries regarded her with horror and regarded Marat as a martyr in the cause of liberty. Historians have generally had more sympathy for Charlotte Corday than for Marat. After all, Marat was responsible for thousands of deaths; that he met a bloody death end too seems like justice.

Off with their heads – and theirs – oh, and theirs

With all the killing going on, a macabre little power game began:

- ✔ The Jacobins blame the Girondins for putting the country in danger with their silly games of soldiers, and have them all guillotined.

- ✔ Jacobin leader Maxim Robespierre decides that all this Supreme Being business is causing unnecessary trouble and has the radicals who put the idea forward rounded up and guillotined. (They were known as the *enragés*, but that day they were more likely the *gobsmackés*.)

Born to be French

In 1768, France bought the island of Corsica from the republic of Genoa. The following year, a son was born to the Buonaparte family of Ajaccio, christened Napoleone. Thanks to that deal the year before, Napoleone was born a French subject and not a Genoese Italian. Napoleone's name was Frenchified into Napoleon Bonaparte and the rest, as they say, is history.

✔ Georges Danton, the people's darling who organised all those prison massacres (see the section 'This Means War! (and Terror)' earlier in this chapter) and was carefully pocketing large sums of money for a rainy day, suggests that maybe enough people had been guillotined now? 'So!' declares Robespierre, 'You must be an enemy of the Revolution!' Danton and his pals are rounded up and guillotined.

✔ Robespierre goes to the Convention and says that many more enemies of the people need to be executed, and some of them are sitting in this very room. While Robespierre pops out of the room (what was he thinking of?) the Convention decide that the time is now or never – Robespierre and his associates are arrested and guillotined in what becomes known, after the revolutionary month when it happened, as the *Thermidor coup*.

Historians have long been deeply divided about the Terror. Some historians accuse others of using the Terror as an excuse to condemn everything the Revolution achieved, while other historians see the Terror as the model for the dictatorships of the 20th century.

By 1797, the French had beaten all their enemies and redrawn the map of Europe, and the areas they hadn't annexed had either made peace with them or been turned into French puppet states. Only Britain remained.

Er, Thank You, General Bonaparte, We'll Take Over from Here

The new government of France was called the Directory (French: *Directoire* – the only government ever to give its name to a pair of frilly knickers, which were in fashion at the time). This government was a strange affair, deliberately designed to keep power in older hands and away from the sort of young hotheads who had run the National Convention. However, the young person who gave the Directory its biggest headache wasn't in politics; or rather he was, but he shouldn't have been. Young General Bonaparte had just won a brilliant campaign against the Austrians in Italy. Afterwards, he dictated the peace treaty of Campoformio with them: France got to keep Belgium and set up a string of puppet states in Italy, and in return the Austrians got to keep Venice.

Normally generals leave peace treaties and diplomacy to the politicians – what if Napoleon's little foray into politics gave him ideas? The directors needed to think of something to keep him busy, and ideally a long way away – and then Bonaparte suggested just the thing himself: Egypt.

Napoleon has a cunning plan

Napoleon's plan was to conquer Egypt, plant French revolutionary ideas about liberty and equality in this rather backward and oppressive part of the Muslim world, and cut Britain off from India at the same time. Napoleon even had dreams of leading a French army of liberation all the way to India itself.

Napoleon wanted his Egyptian expedition to be a voyage of discovery and learning, so he brought scientists, archaeologists, botanists, and mathematicians with him to discover the Orient and explain the mysteries of the East to the West. This was to be no ordinary war of conquest, but rather a meeting of two worlds. The expedition slipped past the British naval blockade, stopped off to take the island of Malta from the old crusading Order of the Knights of St John, and then sailed for Egypt.

In words that are now famous, Napoleon addressed his men before what he termed the Battle of the Pyramids: 'Soldiers! From the heights of these pyramids, forty centuries look down at you!' before presumably adding, 'Charge!' The French took hold of Egypt, examined Egypt's flora and fauna and sketched its ancient monuments. And then suddenly everything went horribly wrong.

The British admiral Horatio Nelson sank Napoleon's fleet in Aboukir Bay. Napoleon abandoned his men and headed back to Paris.

Meanwhile, back in Egypt Napoleon's men died of plague, and the British landed and took Egypt for themselves. The Egyptian campaign ended in a disastrous defeat for France and a living hell for the men who were there, but that didn't stop Napoleon listing the Egyptian campaign as one of his great victories.

Napoleon takes charge

Back in Paris, Napoleon and his brother Lucien overturned the government, and set up a Roman-style *Consulate*. Two of the consuls had to be elected, as in Roman times, but Napoleon was First Consul for life, which had rather sinister overtones of the way Julius Caesar used to operate (Chapter 4 gives you the details). After some royalists had tried to assassinate him, Napoleon declared himself emperor. Which was almost *exactly* how Julius Caesar operated.

For many people across Europe, Napoleon seemed to offer the only hope that someone was actually able to govern a country successfully along the lines of the Rights of Man. But as Napoleon took more and more power into his own hands, and started placing his family on the thrones of Europe, his foreign admirers began to lose faith in him. Napoleon's drive towards personal rule is the main reason why historians usually cite 1799, the date of Napoleon's *coup*, as the end of the Revolution.

At last, a bit of law and order

Napoleon always considered that his best work was in governing France, based on:

- A free and fair constitution (with ministers chosen by Napoleon, all power in Napoleon's hands – you get the idea)

- Guaranteed rights for all (except women – they were kept strictly under male control)

- Freedom and liberty for all (and just to guarantee this liberation, Napoleon introduced strict censorship of the press and an extensive secret police network)

- A clear legal code

Would he like Spain or Holland for his birthday?

Napoleon made his brother Louis king of Holland (the Dutch quite liked him), his brother Jerome king of Westphalia in Germany, and big brother Joseph king of Spain. Napoleon annexed the papal states (and locked up the Pope) and made his little son the king of Rome. The emperor hoped that replacing the royals with his own family would unite the peoples of Europe along the principles of the Rights of Man. Napoleon's action united Europe all right – against him.

The Napoleonic Code was exported to other parts of the world, and is still the basis of French law and the legal systems in South America and even Louisiana to this day.

Napoleon's wars

Napoleon fought so many battles, you can easily get a little confused. Below is a handy guide:

- **1799–1802: Napoleon beats Austria** – *just* – at Marengo (1800) but can't get at Britain, so in 1802 the two countries sign a truce. No one expects the truce to last.

- **1803–1805: The truce doesn't last.** Napoleon defeats the Austrians again, once at Ulm (1805) and then he defeated them and the Russians, at Austerlitz (1805), his greatest victory. The British destroy the French and Spanish fleet at Trafalgar (also 1805).

- **1806–1807: Napoleon destroys the Prussians** at Jena (1806) and the Russians at Eylau and Friedland (1807) – he now controls the whole continent.

- **1806: Napoleon's cunning plan, the *Continental System*,** closes every port in Europe to British ships.

- **1807: The British hit back** by blockading any port joining the Continental System, so now no one can trade with anyone. Britain is the largest manufacturing power in the world. Who will crack first?

- **1808: The Spanish stage a massive anti-French rising.** Britain sends an army to help the Spanish (and the Portuguese, because they join in too) and the *Peninsular War* drags on for six long years, draining France of men and morale.

- **1812: Napoleon invades Russia** and captures Moscow. The Russians promptly burn the city down, so that Napoleon and his men have to retreat. Most of them die on the way. Napoleon gets in a nice warm sledge and dashes off back to France.

- **1813–1814: Everyone joins in for the kill.** The Russians, the Prussians, and – a bit cautiously – the Austrians defeat Napoleon and what's left of his *Grande Armée* at the Battle of Leipzig. Napoleon has to retreat to France and surrender. He is sent to the little island of Elba, just off the Italian coast and told to stay there.

- **1815: Napoleon escapes from Elba and returns to France.** The allies act fast. The British under Wellington and the Prussians under Marshal Blücher defeat Napoleon at the Battle of Waterloo.

How does it feel now you've lost the war?

After Waterloo, Napoleon tried to throw himself on the mercy of the British, his most consistent and – he hoped – generous enemies, but London wasn't interested. Napoleon was sent to St Helena, a God-forsaken spot hundreds of miles off the coast of Africa. He whiled away the time dictating a highly inaccurate version of his life story and hiding from the guards, to make them think he'd escaped again and give the British governor heart failure.

Controversy rages about Napoleon's death. The French like to think that the British poisoned him, possibly with arsenic in the wallpaper (though if so, why didn't it kill anyone else?). The latest evidence is less dramatic but rather more likely: Napoleon died of cancer.

The Bourbons Are Back

The great powers of Europe had to decide who was going to rule France. It couldn't be Napoleon or any of his family (they'd only just exiled him), it certainly couldn't be a republic (what, bring the guillotine back?), so that just left, er, the Bourbons.

So in 1814, Louis XVI's brother, the Duke of Provence, came home from his comfortable exile in England and took the throne as King Louis XVIII. After all that trouble, France was a monarchy again. Had all the bloodshed been worth it?

So, Why Was the French Revolution So Important?

Historians point out that much of what we take for granted – democratic government and the idea that everyone should have equal rights – really started with the French in the 1790s. The 1789 Declaration of the Rights of Man is the basis for both the United Nations and the European Declarations of Human Rights. Quite simply, after 1789 Europe was never the same again.

Chapter 17

Grime Wave: Europe Gets Industrial

I'd better tell you straight – this chapter's got industry in it. Don't worry, it's not a long slog through all the different inventions in the textile industry – although concerned with industry, this chapter isn't really about industry but about *power*. Changes in industry led to other sorts of power: economic and ultimately, political power. This chapter is about how, early in the 19th century, Europe produced a new sort of power game with different players and who won.

A Touch of Romanticism

People in the 18th century weren't very keen on emotions; they preferred reason and the intellect. The idea was that these would free people from the tyranny of religion and superstition. Unfortunately, the French Revolutionary Terror, when thousands of people were guillotined throughout France, had been conducted along perfectly rational principles: if you're not for us you must be against us, and if you're against us you must die (refer to Chapter 16 for more about the French Revolution and the Terror).

The Terror provoked a strong reaction against that kind of cold logic, and a desire for a more human kind of leader. The new thinking was all about letting your human feelings and emotions out and this belief was called *romanticism*.

Romantic Germans

The Germans embraced Romanticism with great enthusiasm. The poet Johann Wolfgang von Goethe created an unlikely role model in the figure of young Werther, who gives in to his feelings and kills himself most romantically – which started quite a fashion for suicide. Young Ludwig van Beethoven was another keen romantic, refusing to brush his hair and breaking all the strict rules of classical composition so as to allow his emotions free range. The romantic painter Karl Caspar Friedrich specialised in rather mysterious images like his evocative painting of a solitary traveller looking down from a mountaintop at the awesome power of nature. Friedrich's paintings are often full of tall, unnaturally thin trees and ships – usually symbolising death.

Ooh, Napoleon, I've come over all funny

The ultimate romantic hero was Napoleon.

Napoleon generated emotion; his soldiers loved him and they didn't mind showing it. When Napoleon abdicated and went into exile they were all in floods. Not only the French found Napoleon's romantic image irresistible; the Poles were devoted to him, because he actually formed them into something like a nation again, and the Germans fell under his spell too. The Prussians had prided themselves on their military prowess ever since Frederick the Great's day (go to Chapter 15 for more on Frederick), so when Napoleon picked up their army, swung it round his head, and marched into Berlin through the Brandenburg Gate, the Prussians set in motion a huge programme of reforms, in administration, law, and education, to try to turn themselves into a more modern nation along French lines.

Romanticism gains force

This cult of romanticism reached its peak in the fashion for gothic tales of the supernatural or grotesque. A group of English writers got together on a dark and stormy night and told each other creepy stories, of which the most famous was Mary Shelley's tragic tale of a German scientist's ill-fated experiment to create a human being, *Frankenstein*. That Dr Frankenstein harnessed electricity to give life to his creature is significant; the romantics were fascinated with electricity, the most elemental of natural forces. The novel also shows that in those days, scientists were seen as romantic hero figures, harnessing the awesome power of the elements, and not as wild-haired nerds.

Is It Me, or Is It Getting More Crowded?

Of all the things that made the 19th century different from all the centuries that had gone before, the most important by far was the simplest: many more people were around. The population of Europe increased massively – by more than double – and overwhelmingly these people lived in cities.

This population explosion wouldn't have been possible if the English hadn't worked out a much more efficient method of feeding people. I know things like three-crop rotation and seed drills may not be your idea of fun, but they were the basis of 19th-century industrial power.

Full steam ahead

The steam engine was probably the most important invention since the wheel. Steam engines work by heating water, and they use huge quantities of fuel. Wood burns too quickly, so steam engines used coal. Suddenly, all the areas of Europe with rich coal seams found themselves being turned upside down as everyone scrambled to buy up the land and sink very profitable mine shafts: northern France, southern Belgium, the Ruhr area of Germany, Bohemia (the modern-day Czech Republic but then ruled by Austria), and Silesia, now in Poland but then in Prussia, all became important industrial regions thanks to their coal reserves. In fact, the country with no coal mines stood in grave danger of being left behind in this new industrial century.

Industrialism spreads

After the war against Napoleon, engineers and entrepreneurs from all over Europe flocked to Britain to study the latest ideas and techniques.

Belgium was the first continental country to industrialise – it had lots of coal and was geographically close to Britain. France industrialised in the north and around Paris.

The Italians built railways in the north, but the Pope thought that they were inventions of the devil and wouldn't allow them into the areas he ruled in the centre of Italy, which simply helped the north of Italy forge ahead from the rest, which remains the case to this day. (You can see why Italians thought Mussolini was a miracle maker when he made the trains run on time.)

The Germans sensibly arranged themselves into a free-trade zone called a *Zollverein* (customs union); most Europeans were only too happy to slap heavy taxes on foreign goods whenever times got hard, which didn't help the flow of trade. The Germans developed their main industrial base along the river Rhine, with Hamburg as their main international port.

The Austrians and Russians were a bit more cautious: Vienna, Moscow, and St Petersburg all became industrial cities with good railway connections, but the rest of their empires remained largely untouched.

Rage Against the Machine

The Romantics were appalled at this big industrialisation drive. (For more on the Romantics, see the section 'A Touch of Romanticism', earlier in this chapter.) These people hated what industrialisation was doing to the countryside, and especially to the traditional pattern of life. The Romantics kept up the idea that man's natural place was in the country, through writing and painting, which is why in due course city dwellers took off for the country whenever the chance arose – and then complained about the smells and the noise when they got there.

The Romantics did have a point about the way industry was changing life. Since human beings first emerged from Africa they'd always been governed by the sun and the seasons; you worked in daylight and slept at night.

Steam engines, however, didn't need to sleep or hibernate; these machines could keep going all night, and factory owners with an eye to their profits made sure that they did. So the simple country folk who wandered in looking for work found themselves up against a completely new phenomenon – the night shift. You didn't get up at dawn or cock-crow or when the church bell sounded; your movements were governed by the factory bell, and your shift might start well before dawn.

You no longer sold the things you made or negotiated a rate for your labour; you took the wage that the factory owner offered or you got out – and if you weren't happy to take that rate of pay, plenty of others were. Workers needed to live near their factories, so the factory owners threw up cheap – very cheap – housing; no need to waste money on sanitation or light or space, or any of the things that the owners made very sure that they had for their own houses. Railways changed things even more. The need to keep trains to time meant that for the first time in history everyone had to keep the same ways of measuring time.

The unacceptable face of capitalism?

Friedrich Engels was a young man making his way in his father's cotton business in Germany in the 1840s when his father sent him over to Manchester, the centre of the international cotton trade, to pick up some tips. Engels did learn a lot about the business, but he learned even more about its human underside, and he was appalled. Engels visited the slum areas of Manchester and other industrial cities, and saw people living ankle-deep in excrement, or dying in dirty hovels with no light or sanitation. He wrote an influential book called *The Conditions of the Working Classes in England,* which described everything he'd seen in graphic detail.

Engels met up with another German living in England, Karl Marx, and together they produced a pamphlet called *The Communist Manifesto,* calling on the workers to stage a revolution and take control themselves. Marx and Engels were most disappointed – and surprised – when the workers didn't revolt.

With railways you were able to transport coal much more quickly than you could with carts or canals, which meant that you could supply many more steam engines, and transport the goods they helped produce. Industrial towns threw up veritable forests of chimney stacks, all belching smoke and coal dust into the atmosphere.

Railways also carried food supplies, which meant that farmers even in quite remote places could have their livelihood affected by foreign food coming into the country and carried inland by rail. You can easily get an idea of the miserable lives of people in industrial towns, but life could be just as hard in the countryside.

I'm A-getting Outta Here: Emigration

The changes brought about by the industrial revolution meant that 19th-century Europe became a continent on the move – and the railways and steamships gave Europeans the means to move a lot further than ever before. Europeans could go to the cities looking for work, and they did – France's mines were often worked by people who had taken the train from Poland – but they could also save up to buy a steerage ticket to go and seek a new life overseas.

Emigration was a constant undercurrent to European history for most of the 19th century until the final decades, when it suddenly became a flood, especially to the United States. By then, most of the agricultural land in the West had been taken, so the emigrants of the 1880s and 1890s were mostly heading for city life, in the poor districts of New York or Chicago. Even so, emigration offered them the chance to escape from oppressive governments – many immigrants to America were political radicals, or Russian Jews escaping from violent anti-Semitism – or from even worse poverty at home.

More Than a Touch of Class

Before long, people realised that the new industrial system was producing two new and quite distinct types of people:

- ✔ The bourgeoisie, or middle classes (sometimes divided into the bourgeoisie and the lower- or petit-bourgeoisie)
- ✔ The proletariat, or working classes

The bourgeoisie: Power to the right sort of people

Bourgeois is a French word meaning town-dweller. In the days before industry, the people based in towns were either professionals, like lawyers or doctors, or merchants, trading in food or cloth – that is, things actually produced in the countryside.

By the 19th century mill-owners and factory-owners, who had sometimes started from quite small beginnings, were becoming rich enough to buy themselves smart new townhouses and start rubbing shoulders with the nobs. These industrialists had money, and a whole army of bankers, accountants, stockbrokers, and insurance brokers to help them get even more, but these people were still – to use the French phrases – *parvenus* (newcomers, upstarts) or *nouveaux riches* (new rich, as opposed to the 'proper' rich). The middle classes were NQOTD – Not Quite Our Type, Darling.

The middle classes tended to be dynamic characters, at the cutting edge of technology, and they often didn't have much respect for the old ways of doing things.

The discreet charm of the petit bourgeoisie

As European industry expanded, a growing army of clerks and office workers grew to service it. These people often came from poor backgrounds and the wages they earned weren't going to change that – think of Bob Cratchit in

Dickens's novel *A Christmas Carol* – but at least they weren't working on the factory floor. This group became known as the *petit bourgeoisie* or lower middle class.

The lower middle classes lived in the new suburbs of the great cities, they dressed smartly, and always went to church on Sundays and for a stroll in the park in the afternoon. They tended to be very conservative in their views – their position was too vulnerable for them to be anything else. Radically-inclined painters and writers used to mock the petit bourgeoisie mercilessly for their poor taste and their obsession with appearances, but in their quiet way these people kept the industrial system ticking over, and in that sense, you could say that they were the most powerful of all the new industrial classes.

What about the workers?

Servicing the whole structure of 19th-century society was a vast army of workers known as the *proletariat*. These people worked in the factories and lived in the slums. The middle classes were always rather nervous of the working classes and used to regard them as savage beings, scarcely human. Sometimes, 19th-century sociologists conducted studies of working class life, rather like anthropologists studying a remote tribe.

The workers performed a wide range of functions:

- ✔ They worked in factories and mines.
- ✔ They laid railway tracks and worked the railways that ran on them.
- ✔ They sailed cargo vessels and unloaded them in Europe's rapidly expanding docks.
- ✔ They built houses and dug sewers.
- ✔ They ruined their eyesight in badly-lit sweat shops sewing fashionable dresses and hats that they could never afford to buy on their meagre wages.

The best way to get a picture of the great cities of 19th-century Europe is to think in terms of cities in the developing world today. There, you have the smart, up-to-date areas with nice flats and flashy cars, and round the corner, or even on the street outside, are the poor, living in shanty towns or sleeping on the pavement among the filth. You can see this scenario in Mumbai or Rio de Janeiro today, but in the 19th century you could see this same setting in London or Paris or Vienna.

Two nations for the price of one

Benjamin Disraeli, during his days as a novelist, articulated the idea that the rich and the poor were two separate nations, with nothing in common. Others thought much the same thing: When Lenin was in exile in London he and his wife used to like to go for strolls in the evening looking through the windows of rich houses (you can imagine the people inside calling out 'I say, do you mind?') and then wandering through the poor streets just round the back (where the reaction was probably much the same).

Most major cities had a working class area where the rich didn't go, and vice versa. Most

European cities built tenement blocks which housed different classes of people under one roof; the working-class poor in the cellars, well-off families in the big apartments, not quite so well off people on the next floor up, and penniless artists and writers starving up in the top-floor garrets. But although all these classes of people might all be under one roof, they had separate entrances and different rules, and had very little to do with each other.

At the start of the 19th century the workers didn't really have a separate sense of identity, but as the century wore on they began to be more conscious of themselves as a class. Although they were often illiterate, workers were able to have an idea of what was going on in the world from those who could read, or from the idealistic young middle class people who came to make speeches.

Telling it like it is

Nineteenth-century writers and artists played an important part in opening the eyes of the middle and upper classes to the ghastly conditions that poor people were living in. In Britain, Dickens and Mrs Gaskell wrote about the lives of the poor in London and Manchester, while in France, Victor Hugo's famous *Les Misérables* is about an escaped convict who, despite improving himself and the lives of the poor people around him, is pursued relentlessly by the police.

Emile Zola wrote *Germinal* about an angry strike amid the grinding poverty of life in the mining

districts of northern France. Some of the most atmospheric pictures of poverty in Victorian London were drawn by a French artist, Gustave Doré.

People's main reaction to this poverty was to set up special relief funds or to support church missions to the poor, but gradually the idea that the state should provide for these people began to take shape. The Germans set up a system of National Insurance in the 1880s, and other countries gradually followed suit.

Marx and Sparks

Karl Marx was a German intellectual who spent much of his life in England reading economic reports and studies trying to figure out exactly what made the world's richest and most advanced economy tick. Marx never did finish his work, but the first volume of his massive work *Capital* came out in 1860, which really made the sparks fly.

Marx thought that just feeling sorry for poor people or giving to charity, wasn't doing enough; you had to ask yourself *why* they were poor, and that also meant asking why the rich are rich, and what the connection is between the two.

Marx reckoned that the difference wasn't just that the rich had more money than the poor, but that they had more power, and that they had more money *because* they had more power and not vice versa (you are following this, aren't you?) And the reason that the rich had more power was because – wait for it – they *owned the means of production*. Which just goes to show that Marx had very clever ideas but he had a lot to learn about snappy catchphrases.

Marx's thinking went like this: In the middle ages, everything came, directly or indirectly, from the land: food, cloth, shelter, and just about everything else. Land was the means of production – and the lords owned it. Nowadays, however, most of what we need to live comes from factories, and the middle classes own them. Hence *they* own the means of production and hold real power.

But, although the means of production belongs to the rich, you don't actually see them doing any producing. The people who actually did the producing were the working classes, and they got paid a pittance.

Marx reckoned that the working classes would eventually wake up to this reality and say 'Hang on, why am I working myself into an early grave in order to make him rich?' Much better to work for yourselves and share the profits out equally. Marx called this idea *communism*.

Marx thought that this conflict between classes for control of the means of production went right through human history, and some historians agree with him. Laying emphasis on class struggle means that other areas of conflict, such as religion or nationalism, appear to be less important, or even irrelevant. Other historians reject Marx's analysis and say that class conflict was no more important in than other factors in history.

Easy as A1, B3, C2

The German sociologist Max Weber felt that Marx was thinking too simply. Instead of just identifying the middle classes and the workers, Weber felt that Marx needed to recognise that all sorts of differences within these classes existed, to do with social status and hierarchies, and that these differences really mattered.

Lumping shopkeepers and bank clerks together as the petit bourgeoisie was all very well, but *they* didn't like that way of thinking; the clerk wanted to be like his boss, not his butcher, and the butcher was certainly not welcome in the bank clerk's smart front room.

The working class usually didn't want to show proletarian solidarity – they wanted to strike it rich and hot foot it out of there. Weber's social categories have proved very useful to modern advertisers, who have come up with all sorts of clever ways to take the workers' minds off any idea of seizing control of the means of production.

I tell you, it will happen! One day . . .

Marx and his followers always insisted that the revolution would happen come what may. In the ruthless world of the free market, anyone who can't compete goes under, until the whole market is dominated by a mere handful of jealous competitors. The day will inevitably come when the capitalist system implodes, and then a revolution will take place in the streets. And so indeed there was, though not quite where or how Marx expected it.

Marx was naturally expecting that revolution would happen in the most industrialised countries, like Britain, France, Germany, or the United States. Marx wasn't entirely wrong – there *were* revolutionary groups in all of these countries, and there was a major communist rising in Paris in 1871. But Marx didn't anticipate that governments in these countries would make enough concessions to the workers – better housing, sickness and old age benefits, education and healthcare, and so on – that the workers wouldn't necessarily *want* to smash the system.

It was Russia, which was about the least industrialised of the major European states, that had the first successful workers' revolution, though the Russians had to come up with a specially altered version of Marxism called *Marxism-Leninism* in order to explain it (and in Chapter 23 you can find out how).

That's Progress

Perhaps not surprisingly, 19th-century Europeans were great believers in progress. They realised that all this prosperity they enjoyed had a very nasty underside, but they had tremendous confidence that science and technology were the best, indeed the only, means to improve life and carry mankind forward.

Sociologists like Claude de Saint-Simon reckoned that science was the only way of improving society – and he died in 1825 when he hadn't, as it were, seen nothing yet. The French philosopher Auguste Comte even argued that 19th-century Europe represented the highest conceivable stage in the history of the development of humankind.

Scientific technology on display

The highpoint of the belief in science came right in the middle of the century in 1851, when the British staged the Great Exhibition in the Crystal Palace. The idea was to open people's eyes to the possibilities that science had created in their lives, from the latest domestic gadgets to innovative machines for the workplace or the farm. The exhibition was very popular with visitors, who seem to have gone along in a 'what-will-they-think-of-next?' frame of mind.

After the success of the London exhibition, other cities around the world held their own, all designed to show off the latest in technology and, of course, to show how advanced the host city was. In 1889, the Universal Exhibition in Paris unveiled Gustave Eiffel's famous tower, though no one's yet found a very convincing use for it.

Science and (lack of) civilisation

Nowadays, we too have a strong faith in technology, so you may be tempted to go along with the sort of thinking prevalent in the 19th century: If so, remember some of the other aspects of the nations who exhibited their wares so confidently in 1851.

At the time of the Great Exhibition the Russians still kept most of their population in slavery (and so, in the South, did the Americans); the British had just presided over a famine in Ireland that caused the death of an estimated one million people; and the French, as well as carrying out a brutal policy of destruction and oppression in the southern Sahara, had only recently shot some 1,500 Parisian workers and students without any form of trial after a rising against the government. Technological advance is a very good thing, but history doesn't suggest that change has anything to do with advances in ethics or standards of behaviour.

If it doesn't clear up in a week, come back and see me again

Medicine was one area where science really did seem able to make a difference. Over the course of the 19th century, European scientists made huge advances in combating diseases that had, er, plagued Europe for centuries. A few highlights:

- **Louis Pasteur:** Well known for finding a cure for rabies and coming up with a way of purifying milk, but Pasteur's main importance was in identifying the theory of contagion and working out that you could use vaccination, originally developed to combat smallpox, on a much wider range of diseases.

- **Robert Koch:** Identified the cholera and syphilis bacilli; thereby, not only making the development of cures possible, but proving conclusively that diseases are spread by germs and not, as many people still believed, by bad air.

- **Joseph Lister:** Introduced the idea of disinfecting equipment with carbolic acid in order to combat germs and prevent infection. Lister's students used to gleefully intone 'Let us spray' before starting work.

- **Marie Curie:** With her husband, Pierre, she discovered radium, and developed the world's first X-rays. Marie won Nobel prizes for both physics and chemistry. Not bad for a girl who started as a penniless student from Poland.

Developments in medicine weren't just big breakthroughs by famous scientists. Hospitals became safer, more professional places, staffed by properly trained nurses, and even more were created after Henry Dunant founded the Red Cross in 1863. Underneath all this activity – literally – cities were developing proper sewer and drainage systems. Paris was so proud of its sewers that you can still take a boat tour in them, and the Vienna sewers provided the setting for the climax of the Carol Reed film *The Third Man*.

Religion: I'm right and you aren't right

Faith in progress doesn't mean that the 19th century was somehow less religious. In fact, in some ways the 19th century took its religion more seriously than the two centuries on either side of it. European missionaries went all over the world, teaching, setting up hospitals, and spreading the gospel; the Catholic Church set up bishoprics in parts of the world it had previously kept out of, including Britain and its colonies, Canada, and the United States.

The vision thing

In 1858, a young French girl called Bernadette Soubirous from Lourdes in southern France announced that she had seen the Virgin Mary in a vision. Some people were sceptical, but Bernadette stuck to her story and added that the vision had told her 'I am the Immaculate Conception', which seemed an odd thing to have made up, since this notion was a rather complex bit of Catholic belief that was still being worked out inside the Vatican. (The Immaculate Conception says that the Virgin Mary was born without original sin.)

Lourdes became the centre of a huge pilgrimage cult, which is still going on today, associated in particular with miraculous healing of the long-term ill. Just when faith in science seemed to be making religious faith redundant, here was religious faith, even faith healing, making a strong come-back. This renewed faith was a sign that science wasn't having everything its own way, even in the 19th century.

In time, Bernadette would leave her name to half the female population of Ireland, while Lourdes would leave its name to Madonna's daughter.

Pope Gregory XVI did all he could to keep progress out of Italy. Gregory's successor Pius IX issued the *Syllabus of Errors,* which explained very clearly that

- ✔ The Pope was right in all matters.

- ✔ You, too, could be right if you agreed with him.

- ✔ If you disagreed with him you must be wrong by definition (see the first bullet).

Just in case there was any further doubt on the matter, in 1870 the Pope declared the doctrine of *papal infallibility,* which said that on matters of doctrine and morality he could not err. This decision was a controversial move; the idea had always been that such matters should be decided with all the cardinals and bishops in a General Council, though since this doctrine was itself declared in a General Council (known as Vatican I) this policy was a bit difficult to argue with – it usually is, with people who have declared themselves infallible.

Pope Pius IX's strong line provoked *anticlerical* reactions in France, Germany, Austria, and Holland (even in Rome quite a few anticlerical people tried to get their revenge on Pius by attempting to push his coffin in the river during his funeral procession).

Mr Darwin's Interesting Ideas

In 1859, Charles Darwin published his book *The Origin of Species*, which argued that species adapt to their environment and that the best fitted tend to survive while the least fitted die off. Darwin called this process 'natural selection'. Exactly *how* species adapt, and how such changes pass from one generation to the next, Darwin didn't know, though scientists immediately began trying to find out.

This book may not sound very controversial, but it challenged the whole basis of religious belief in creation and in a God who oversees the development of all living things. *The Origin of Species* doesn't deal with mankind, though Darwin wrote another book called *The Descent of Man* in which he made his thoughts clear that humans evolved from the apes. This theory of evolution provoked huge controversy in the Church of England, and the arguments soon spread to the rest of the world.

The Pope put *The Origin of Species* on the Index of banned books (though any Catholics who read it in secret, hoping to find the smutty bits, were going to be sorely disappointed). Ironically, the most important work in support of Darwin's ideas was carried out by a quiet Austrian Catholic monk called Gregor Mendel, who experimented with peas to show how changes and mutations could be passed through the generations.

Socialists and anticlericals tended to regard Darwin as a hero; they were particularly keen on him later on in Soviet Russia. Darwin's ideas got badly distorted, however, especially in the famous phrase 'survival of the fittest', which he himself never used. Later on, the Nazis would use a simplified version of Darwin's view to justify their belief that only the 'fittest' among the different ethnic groups should be allowed to survive. (Head to Chapter 22 for more about the Nazis).

Chapter 18

Building Nations

. . . .

In This Chapter

▶ Redrawing the map of Europe at the Congress of Vienna

▶ Launching revolutions across Europe

▶ Uniting Italy and Germany as nation states

. . . .

*T*he idea that really changed Europe in the 19th century was *nationalism*, the idea that people of the same nation live under the same flag with the same government. Nowadays, most people are used to the concept of nationalism, but that hadn't been the way of things before the French Revolution – and for most of Europe, that wasn't the way of things after the Revolution, either.

The 19th century saw many revolutions and wars with people trying to shake off foreign rulers and set up their own nation states. Unfortunately, even when they succeeded, creating nation states didn't stop all the fighting; next thing you knew, each nation wanted to show that it was better than every other nation. So people can be surprised to find out that the original idea of nationalism was that it would spread peace and justice and liberty. Something, clearly, went badly wrong.

What Was So New about the Idea of a Nation?

Before the French Revolution (take a look at Chapter 16), what mattered was not which nationality you were, but who ruled you. For example, the people of Belgium were ruled by the emperor of Austria, hundreds of miles away in central Europe; the Poles had to get used to being ruled by the tsar of Russia, the emperor of Austria, or the king of Prussia, depending on which bit of Poland they lived in; the Greeks and everyone else in the Balkans were ruled by the sultan of Turkey; the Irish were ruled by the king of Great Britain, the Norwegians by the king of Denmark, and the Italians were ruled by a whole string of different rulers including the Pope, the king of Sardinia, the king of Naples, the duke of Parma, and the grand duke of Tuscany. That was how the situation was, and – allowing for changes in borders and personnel over the centuries – that was how things had always been.

Then the French revolutionaries came along, saying that people should be allowed to rule themselves within their own 'national' boundaries, which might well be very different from the ones drawn up by their rulers. So the French overturned their neighbours' rulers and redrew the map of Europe broadly along national lines. I say broadly because Napoleon always operated along one very simple line: French interests come first. If it was in France's interests for you to get a national state, then you got one; if not, you didn't.

I Don't Know: You Liberate People, and Then They Want to Rule Themselves

When the French started invading the rest of Europe and imposing French domination (or, if you prefer, 'overturning despotic rule and spreading the benefits of liberty and the Rights of Man'), they encouraged those people to rule themselves and live in perfect harmony and concord. What actually happened was rather different:

- ✔ **Spain, 1808–14:** The French invade and set Joseph Bonaparte up as king of Spain. The Spanish people stage a massive rising against him, and wage a murderous guerrilla campaign, killing every French soldier they can find.

- ✔ **Russia, 1812–13:** The French invade and capture Moscow. The Russian people burn the city down, force Napoleon to retreat, and wage a murderous guerrilla campaign, killing every French soldier they can find.

- ✔ **Germany, 1813:** The French arrive back after the Retreat from Moscow. The German people wage a murderous guerrilla campaign, killing every French soldier they can find. (Are you sensing some kind of theme here?)

Napoleon's Europe

Napoleon overturned Europe's rulers and redrew its borders along more rational lines, but somehow French national interests kept getting in the way:

- **France:** Like the old kings of France, the revolutionaries thought that France should have her 'natural frontiers', which meant taking over a huge swathe of German land as well as Belgium and Holland, northern Italy, and even Rome.

- **Germany:** Germany was made up of hundreds of different states, all with their own rulers and their own customs barriers. Napoleon got rid of most of them, closed down the Holy Roman Empire, and arranged the rest into what he called the *Confederation of the Rhine*, with French laws, a French-style constitution, and French leadership.

- **Poland:** Napoleon set up a Polish state called the *Grand Duchy of Warsaw*. The Grand Duchy was much smaller than Poland used to be, had no access to the sea, and Napoleon insisted that it should do as he said. The Poles were still delighted and were loyal fighters for Napoleon ever after.

The French also created a series of so-called republics in other parts of Europe: the Batavian Republic in Holland, the Helvetic Republic in Switzerland, the Cisalpine, Ligurian, and Parthenopean Republics in Italy. Each republic had its own flag and constitution, but they were French puppet states and everyone knew it.

This idea of trying to draw up 'natural' national boundaries was rather like the way some African countries, after they became independent, tried to overturn the artificial national borders the Europeans had drawn for them in the 19th century (head to Chapter 19 for the details) and to reassert their old tribal boundaries. Both times, engineering borders ended up with a lot of people getting hurt.

That's Quite Enough Popular Nationalism for One Century

In 1814 the great powers got together in the *Congress of Vienna* to settle Europe's boundaries. The settlement rearranged the map of Europe but steered clear of the idea of nation states:

- **France:** Got her Bourbon kings and her old frontiers back, and she was expected to stick to them.

- **Belgium:** The allies took Belgium away from Austria (which is not exactly just round the corner from Brussels) and gave it to Holland. The idea seemed good at the time, though soon led to trouble (see the section 'Belgium for the Belgians' below).

✔ **Germany:** The allies didn't bother reviving the Holy Roman Empire or all those titchy German states (see the section 'Napoleon's Europe' earlier in this chapter); instead, they just brought back the big ones, like Bavaria and Saxony, and grouped them all together in a sort of club called the *Germanic Confederation*, which looked suspiciously like the old Holy Roman Empire. The Confederation was even chaired by the Austrian Habsburgs. 'This is just like old times!' the Austrians said, as they settled back into what they enjoyed most (apart from eating very sticky cakes) – telling the rest of Germany what to do.

The Prussians had fought well against Napoleon (including at the Battle of Waterloo) so in return they got the Rhineland along France's eastern border. Gaining the Rhineland meant that, for the first time, Prussia was no longer just interested in looking east; she was an important power across the whole of Germany.

✔ **Italy:** No one thought of Italy as a country – least of all the Italians. 'Italy' was a region, a geographical expression like Scandinavia or the Balkans, as the Austrian foreign minister, Count Metternich, put it. (See next section for more on the count.) The allies re-established most of Italy's kingdoms and principalities, including the large state in the centre ruled by the Pope, with two important exceptions. Lombardy and Venice in the north were to be ruled directly by the Austrians, who were also to keep an eye on the rest of Italy.

✔ **Poland:.** The Poles had stayed loyal to Napoleon, so no one had much sympathy for them. Poland was divided up and most of it went to Russia.

Count Metternich is watching you

The Austrians seem to have come out of the Congress of Vienna with a lot of responsibilities; they were going to be supervising Germany and Italy as well as ruling their own lands, which included Hungary, Bohemia, Slovakia, Slovenia, and Croatia.

All of this responsibility suited the Austrian foreign minister, Count Clemens von Metternich, just fine. Metternich *hated* revolution and revolutionaries; he had seen the rebellion when the French arrived in his native Rhineland, and he never wanted to see it happen again. So the count set up a system of spies and agents to keep an eye on nationalist and liberal groups and report back to him. In 1819, Metternich gathered all the German rulers together in the very pleasant spa town of Carlsbad and got them to sign a set of decrees introducing censorship of the press, bans on political meetings, and keeping a close eye on radical students and their teachers. These decrees became known as the *Metternich System*.

All together now: The Concert of Europe

The French wars had begun in 1792 and they didn't end until 1815, which meant that a whole generation had never really known a time of peace. The leaders of Europe decided to work together to make sure that this fighting never happened again. From now on, whenever a crisis arose, they would hold a big summit meeting, or *congress,* to agree on what to do – or as Metternich would say, to decide whose turn it was to crush without mercy any outbreak of revolutionary activity anywhere in Europe the moment it happened. The European leaders called this arrangement the *Concert of Europe* – it wasn't very harmonious.

The Concert of Europe was soon in business, crushing risings in favour of constitutional government in Spain, Portugal, Piedmont (northern Italy), and Naples (southern Italy). The British, who rather liked revolutionary nationalists as long as they weren't Irish, protested and refused to attend any more congresses, but the Austrians, Prussians, and Russians took no notice; they had already set up a special *Holy Alliance* to defend Christian Europe against the ravages of nationalism and free speech. This disharmony between Britain and the other great powers makes the only thing that they all agreed on rather ironic, which was supporting a group of revolutionary nationalists in the 1820s – in Greece.

Europe's Age of Revolution

The first half of the 19th century saw a series of revolutions across the continent as the peoples of Europe – or rather, the middle classes – tried to establish constitutional government and national boundaries.

Oh, all right, the Greeks can revolt, I suppose

Ever since Constantinople fell to the Turks in 1453 (head to Chapter 12 for more about that cataclysmic event) Greece had been a province of the Ottoman Empire.

However, Tsar Alexander I of Russia had a dream of leading a great union of all the Orthodox Christians of Europe, and that meant creating a free and independent Greece. Russian agents got to work, and in 1821 the Greeks rose up against the Turks.

The Turks may have been an empire in decline but they had some very efficient troubleshooters in the form of special forces called Bashi-Bazouks and Janissaries, who shot first and asked questions later. The Turks also called in help from the tough *pasha* (ruler) of Egypt, the wily Mehemet Ali.

All across Europe people got out their best Greek-style china and decorated their drawing rooms with Greek motifs in sympathy with the rebels, while the romantic poet Lord Byron actually went out to Greece and got himself killed. Rather more practically, the Russians sent troops and a British, French, and Russian fleet sank the Turkish and Egyptian fleet in Navarino Bay. Result: one (okay, rather smaller than nowadays) independent Greece.

If anyone asks, we're charcoal burners

Many people in Europe were unhappy at the way their old rulers came back after 1815, just when they thought that they'd seen the back of them. In Naples, in southern Italy, the people got a particularly unpleasant branch of the Bourbon family, and all over Italy, Austrians were making the fact that they were boss very clear. Most Italians just shrugged and got on with making the pasta, but some followed the age-old Italian tradition of taking to the woods and setting up a secret society.

The best known (which surely rather defeats the purpose of a secret society, doesn't it?) were the *Carbonari* (not to be confused with carbonara – a rather nice sauce for pasta), which means charcoal burners, because they met deep in the heart of forests. The Carbonari went in for strange initiation rites and secret handshakes and all the other paraphernalia of secret societies; they also staged revolutions, in Naples in 1820 and in the northern state of Piedmont the following year. The Carbonari didn't manage to overturn any governments or get any constitutions accepted (the great powers and their congresses saw to that) but they just went back to the woods, rolled up a few more trouser legs, and bided their time.

Belgium for the Belgians

Meanwhile, by 1830 the Belgians had had quite enough of being ruled by the Dutch and decided that the time had come to declare independence. Instead of trying to stop them, the British and French sent ships and men to help the Belgians, with the result that by the terms of the 1839 Treaty of London, Belgium became an independent country, internationally guaranteed, free to make as many waffles and put as much mayonnaise on its chips as it liked.

In 1914, the Germans invaded Belgium and the British declared war, upholding the Treaty of London. The kaiser couldn't understand why the British were prepared to go to war 'for a scrap of paper', which in British eyes just confirmed everything that they thought of him.

To the barricades!

Every few years, 19th-century Europeans felt the need to drag lots of furniture into the street, build it up into a barricade, and stage a street battle. The idea was usually to persuade the local ruler to grant a constitution. Sometimes the tactic worked – for a time – and sometimes it didn't. Two major years of revolution took place: 1830 and 1848.

Round One: 1830

The state of play in 1830 looked like this:

- **France:** The French rise up in revolt and the House of Bourbon gets overturned *again*. But the Parisians don't get another republic; instead they get the genial duke of Orleans, from another branch of the royal family, who becomes *King Louis Philippe I.* Louis Philippe promises to grant a constitution and generally be an all-round nice chap.

- **Germany:** Inspired by the French example, the Germans raise barricades in Saxony, Brunswick, Hesse-Cassel, and Hanover, and they all get a nice, liberal constitution. So wrecking granny's best sofa was worth all the effort.

- **Italy:** The Carbonari stage risings all over northern and central Italy: Parma, Modena, and in the papal state. The Austrians send their troops in and soon put a stop to all that nonsense. The Carbonari go back to the woods, muttering under their breath and wondering whether the pasta's ready.

- **Poland:** Major rising in Warsaw, which drives the Russians out for a while. However, the Russians come back the next year and show the Poles no mercy; the short-lived Polish republic is crushed.

Intermission

In the interim (and don't forget that no one *knew* that an even bigger year of revolution was coming), a number of European states had become much more heavily industrialised, so even more people were wanting a few changes. The 1840s were very bad years – this period was the time of the Irish famine, and bad harvests and food shortages occurred all over Europe (for more on the terrible Irish Famine see *British History For Dummies* by me, Sean Lang, and *Irish History For Dummies* by Mike Cronin (both Wiley)). The French had got bored with Louis Philippe I, and Metternich seemed to have been keeping his beady eye on Europe for ever. Well, not for much longer.

Round Two: 1848

In February 1848, the Parisians staged yet another revolution (they were getting rather good at rising up in rebellion) and turfed out Louis Philippe. This time, a republic would be created, but they couldn't decide if it should be a nice, moderate middle-class affair with tea and cakes, or a proper socialist workers' republic.

The rest of France quickly grew tired of these violent Parisians and elected Louis Napoleon Bonaparte, nephew of the great Napoleon Bonaparte, as President of the Second Republic to restore a bit of order. (In case you're keeping count, the First Republic had been set up back in the *first* French Revolution. You can find out about it in Chapter 16.) Louis Napoleon quickly arrested his opponents, had a number of them shot without trial, seized complete power for himself, and in 1852 shut down the Second Republic entirely. Instead, Louis Napoleon set up a (second) empire with himself as Emperor Napoleon III and got himself a massive approval rating from the people of France.

If you're wondering what happened to Napoleon II, he was the little son of the great Napoleon and his Austrian empress Marie Louise. Little Napoleon II was known to the French as *l'aiglon*, the little eagle. As a child, little Napoleon briefly became king of Rome, but after his father was sent into exile, the lad grew up as an Austrian nobleman. He never actually became Napoleon II, but the Bonapartes liked to claim that he had been Napoleon II *really*.

All the other revolutions involved Austria directly or indirectly:

- **Austria:** Workers and students stage a revolution in Vienna and send Metternich packing. The retarded in-bred emperor, Ferdinand I, agrees to everything the rebels demand (a constitution and no more serfdom), and abdicates in favour of his nephew, Franz Josef.

- **Bohemia:** Big rising in Prague. The Austrian field marshal, Windischgrätz, demolishes Prague, and crushes the Czech revolution.

- **Italy.** The Italians rise up led by the very romantic Giuseppe Mazzini. Just about all Italian rulers grant constitutions as soon as the trouble starts, even the Pope.

Creating a united Italy proves more tricky. King Charles Albert of Piedmont reluctantly agrees to help, but the Austrians crush the Italian nationalists without mercy, except for Rome, where the republic is defended by Giuseppe Garibaldi.

Louis Napoleon of France, fresh from crushing the French republicans, (see preceding section) sends French troops to capture Rome, destroy the republic, and restore the Pope. Garibaldi flees; his wife is killed and dies in his arms.

✔ **Germany:** Revolution in Prussia; through gritted teeth King Frederick William IV has to agree to grant a constitution and support a united Germany. The Germans then elect a special Parliament of the whole German Nation, which meets at Frankfurt and spends the next 12 months arguing over what to do next. The Frankfurt Parliament finally decides to go to war with Denmark to get hold of two German states, Schleswig and Holstein, though the king of Prussia has to do the fighting for them. War ends in a tie. King Frederick William then sends his troops to Frankfurt and closes the Parliament down.

✔ **Hungary and Croatia:** The Hungarians declare independence from Austria, but they're not happy when Croatia promptly declares independence – from Hungary. The Austrians link up with the Croats (along 'My enemy's enemy is my friend' lines) and they invade Hungary together. Then the Russians come barging in and crush the Hungarians before they can give any of the Russians' subject peoples any dangerous ideas about freedom or independence.

Never mind: Just think about selling your memoirs

Once the revolutionaries were in exile, they became celebrities. Many revolutionaries fled to England (which was also where their old enemy Metternich had fled to – just think of the chat show possibilities). The American minister in London even hosted a revolutionaries-in-exile dinner, with Mazzini, the Hungarian leader Louis Kossuth, the French republican Ledru-Rollin, the Russian socialist Alexander Herzen, and Garibaldi all swapping anecdotes and hoping for better luck next time (Alexander Herzen called the event a red dinner hosted by the defender of black slavery).

The undoubted star was Garibaldi, who had already had a pretty exciting life: he'd been a sailor, a revolutionary in Brazil, and a maths teacher (okay, that bit wasn't quite so exciting). After the Roman Republic collapsed in 1849, Garibaldi fled to New York, worked in a candle factory, and captained a Peruvian ship to China. Then Garibaldi went to England, where he fell in love with a rich widow called Mrs Roberts and had a very enjoyable time visiting Newcastle.

These revolutionaries didn't just live for pleasure, though; they were all working on plans to get back home and have another go at overturning the government.

Historians still argue about what to make of the 1848 revolutions. Some see them as a crucial turning point even though they failed; others see them as a sign that the middle classes couldn't organise a revolution for toffee and that the only truly revolutionary force were the workers.

Well, Napoleon III, What Next?

Napoleon III spent so much time and effort getting to the top that he wasn't sure what to do when he got there. The emperor's main idea, apart from cultivating possibly the silliest moustache of the 19th century, was somehow to be as glorious and successful as Napoleon I, but since Napoleon I had gained his success by invading almost every country in Europe, achieving this status was easier said than done.

Napoleon III did invade Russia in the Crimean War (for more about this shambolic episode, see Chapter 19) and he certainly liked to *act* as though he dominated Europe. He even invaded Mexico and made a rather hapless Austrian archduke called Maximilian emperor of Mexico, but he had to pull out quickly when the United States threatened to enforce the Monroe Doctrine (which said that no one was allowed to invade anywhere on the American continent except the USA). The Mexicans put Maximilian against a wall and shot him. All in all, if Napoleon III got in touch with one of his foreign policy schemes, you were better off pretending that you weren't in.

At home, Napoleon III ruled like a benevolent despot; there was no freedom of speech, but there was work, and food in the shops. He also commissioned Baron Haussmann to demolish most of Paris and build it up again in a new style with nice wide boulevards and lots of sharp corners. Next time you're strolling down an elegant Parisian street bear in mind that the boulevards are so wide to make them more difficult to barricade, and they're so straight, with such sharp angles, to allow artillery to fire down them.

Honey, 1 United the Italians

Mazzini and Garibaldi did get their united Italy, though not quite in the way they intended. In fact, nothing happened in the way anyone intended:

> ✔ **1858: Bomb misses.** Italian nationalist Felice Orsini throws a bomb at Napoleon III as a punishment for crushing the Roman Republic ten years earlier, and misses. Orsini then makes such an impression at his trial that Napoleon III decides to see what he can do for Italy. Though not before Orsini is guillotined in prison.

- ✔ **1859: Secret plot goes wrong.** Napoleon III hatches a secret plot with the prime minister of Piedmont (northern Italy), Count Camillo Cavour, to attack the Austrians and drive them out of northern Italy. Piedmont is to get northern Italy and give France Nice and Savoy as a thank you present.

Unfortunately, the Austrians fight them to a standstill, Napoleon III pulls out, Piedmont has to make peace fast, and everyone blames everybody else.

This war was so bloody that a new colour dye, magenta, was named after one of its battles because it's the colour of dried blood. A Swiss businessman, Henry Dunant, was so appalled at what he witnessed at the other battle, Solferino, that he was inspired to found the Red Cross.

- ✔ **1860: Cunning plan goes wrong.** Garibaldi comes up with an idea for sailing south with a thousand men and invading Sicily. 'Good,' thinks Cavour, 'he'll get himself killed and we'll be shot of one revolutionary nuisance.' Unfortunately, Garibaldi sparks off a popular rising in Sicily, crosses over to the mainland, overturns the government, and heads north to invade the papal state to drive out the Pope. A loud clang is heard from Cavour's office as his jaw hits the floor, followed by a stream of language which modesty forbids me to translate.

- ✔ **1860: Unification of all Italy – well, almost all.** Cavour and King Victor Emmanuel II of Piedmont get their army together quickly and move south to stop Garibaldi before he can provoke an international war to save the Pope. In a very emotional and romantic scene Garibaldi hands his conquests over to King Victor Emmanuel, who is now king of all of Italy. Well, all except Rome, where a large French garrison is guarding the Pope, who's sulking and demanding his kingdom back. Oh, and Venice, which is still in Austrian hands. Not forgetting Nice and Savoy, which had both gone to France.

Viva Verdi!

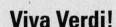

Giuseppe Verdi was a great supporter of Italian unification. The composer's Chorus of the Hebrew Slaves from the opera *Nabucco*, which is all about how they long to be free and a nation once again, became a nationalist anthem.

The Austrians were puzzled to see 'Viva Verdi!' chalked up on the walls, and thought that this act was just a sign that the Italians appreciated his operas. What the Austrians didn't realise was that it stood for *Vittorio Emanuele Re D'Italia* – Victor Emmanuel, king of Italy.

No one got what they wanted from the unification of Italy. Cavour wanted the north but ended up with all of the south; Garibaldi and Mazzini wanted a republic and ended up with a kingdom – they also wanted a united Italy but ended up without Rome or Venice; Napoleon III had wanted to humiliate the Austrians in Italy just as his uncle had done (check out Chapter 16) but had found it was a lot harder than it looked.

Bismarck: One Part Blood, Three Parts Iron

The German liberals had made a very respectable attempt at the title for Most Spectacular Failure of the 1848 Revolutions; they'd got constitutions granted all over Germany, and set up a parliament for all of Germany, and then blown it, mainly because they couldn't actually agree on whether Germany included Austria.

Reasons for including Austria:

- ✔ Austria has always been part of 'Germany'
- ✔ Austria has *ruled* Germany since the Middle Ages
- ✔ The Austrians make all those rather scrummy cream cakes

Reasons for not including Austria:

- ✔ The time is ripe for someone else to take over the leadership of Germany, and the Austrians will never allow someone else to be in charge
- ✔ Austria rules a huge area of non-German lands, like Hungary and Croatia

In 1863 the Prussians got an ambitious new chief minister, Otto von Bismarck. Bismarck had noted that the reason the 1848 revolutions had all failed was because the military had always stayed loyal to the regimes, so he immediately started building up the Prussian army. When the Prussian parliament refused to accept his military spending plans, Bismarck simply spent the money anyway. Then the chief minister started training his army in the best way possible – in action.

Bismarck worked very closely with Field Marshal von Moltke, the Chief of the Prussian General Staff (the military planning department) to prepare a series of short sharp wars:

✔ **1864: War with Denmark.** The king of Denmark ruled two small German states called Schleswig and Holstein and German nationalists were determined that he shouldn't. Prussia and Austria both declared war, defeated the Danes, Prussia got Schleswig and Austria got Holstein. The Austrians went home to coffee and cakes thinking what a nice chap that Otto von Bismarck was.

✔ **1866: War with Austria.** The Prussians crushed the Austrians and the south German states that were fighting on the Austrian side at the Battle of Sadowa and signed a remarkably generous peace treaty – all within six weeks. Bismarck shut down the Germanic Confederation and set up a new *North German Confederation* – no Austrians allowed.

Bismarck wasn't known as the *Iron Chancellor* for nothing. In fact, Bismarck always said that he unified Germany through blood and iron. Now the time had come to plan the big one: War with Napoleon III.

The Franco–Prussian War

In 1870, Spain suffered a *coup*, and the Spanish needed a new king. Wilhelm I of Prussia suggested one of his young relatives (the royal houses of Europe were always sending younger sons and nephews off to be king of somewhere else). However, Napoleon III didn't want a German king on both his borders, so Wilhelm very politely withdrew the suggestion. End of story? Not yet.

The French ambassador came to see Wilhelm at the rather nice spa town of Ems, and asked him, ever so politely, to promise never again to try and get one of his relatives on the Spanish throne. Wilhelm, who was a man of honour and didn't like having his intentions doubted, told the ambassador, with utmost politeness, that he had withdrawn his offer, and the matter was closed. Oh, no, it wasn't. Wilhelm sent a telegram about the exchange to Bismarck back in Berlin, and Bismarck, who knew an opportunity when he saw one, edited it to make it look as if Wilhelm and the French ambassador had had a blazing row and released the telegram to the press. The Germans were furious, the French were outraged, and Napoleon III declared war.

Historians usually condemn Bismarck for doctoring the 'Ems telegram', and they're right, but Napoleon III and his ministers were to blame, too. You don't *have* to declare war, however rude you think a telegram might be.

Bismarck and von Moltke had been planning for this war for a long time, down to the smallest detail. The Germans tore into France, cooped the French army up inside a whole series of cities, captured Napoleon III at the Battle of Sedan, and then camped down to besiege Paris. The German army brought out their heavy guns and bombarded Paris.

Eventually, in 1871, after an epic siege of four months, with less and less food (everyone claimed to have eaten a part of the elephant's trunk in the zoo), Paris surrendered. The Germans held a victory parade down the Champs Elysées (revenge for Napoleon's victory parade down Unter den Linden in Berlin – go to Chapter 16) and in Louis XIV's great Hall of Mirrors in Versailles, they proclaimed a new united German *Reich* (empire) with King Wilhelm I as its first emperor. And Bismarck, of course, as the Reich's iron chancellor.

The peace terms were very harsh: France had to pay Germany an *indemnity* (fine) of 5 billion francs and the German army would occupy the country until the fine was paid. The French would also have to give up two border regions, Alsace and Lorraine, to the Germans. The French were devastated.

Napoleon III spent a couple of years as a prisoner in Germany and then went into exile in England; he was buried in Farnborough Abbey. Years later, in 1919, the French got revenge for 1871 by making the Germans sign the humiliating Treaty of Versailles in the same Hall of Mirrors where the Germans had proclaimed their empire. But see Chapter 22 for that story.

Part VI
Europe Tears Itself in Two

The 5th Wave · By Rich Tennant

©RICH TENNANT

At the Treaty of Versailles, Britain, France, Italy and the United States established that Germanys colonies be taken from her, that they be excluded from the League of Nations, and that they pay reparation for World War I. (Additionally, several lunch and dinner bills were charged to their account by the "Big Four".)

I think I'll start with the escargot, and then I'll have the Coq au Vin...

In this part . . .

The 20th century began with Europe divided into two armed camps and the Balkans tearing themselves to pieces, and that's pretty much how the century ended too. The 20th century was when Europeans and their problems sparked the most destructive wars the world has ever seen. In this part you'll see how Europe's statesmen proved unable to solve the continent's problems without going to war with each other. You'll also see the terrible consequences for the ordinary people of Europe, bombed from the air, herded into concentration or labour camps, and divided by an ideological barrier that Churchill aptly termed an Iron Curtain.

Yet, Europe learned (some) lessons from the years of war, and the 20th century ended with a determined effort to create a democratic, united continent. The idea of a European Union wasn't new: The Romans had tried for it, and so had Charlemagne and Philip II. Would the new Europe be more successful than the old? This part will help you decide.

Chapter 19

Europe's Age of Empire

*T*he second half of the 19th century is when history really begins to feel modern. The clothes and the transport begin to look more familiar – give or take the odd top hat or bustle. This is the age of newspapers and commuters and package tours and radio communications. It was also a time of tremendous opportunity and adventure in Africa, which the Europeans were in the process of carving up between them (the opportunity and adventure were all for Europeans, I need hardly add). Some Europeans lived in unbelievable luxury, but others lived in equally unimaginable poverty. So this was an age of kings and socialists. They tended not to get on.

Carnage in Paris

In 1871, Europe's whole shape and future changed. In this year, the Germans defeated the French and declared themselves a new empire. And during this year the French slaughtered each other in the streets of Paris.

Paris felt that the rest of France had let her down in the Franco–Prussian war (Chapter 18 has more on this event). The Parisians had withstood a terrible siege through the winter of 1870–1871, and not a single French soldier had come through from outside to help. Now, the French government had agreed that the Germans were to march down the Champs Elysées and occupy Paris until a full treaty was signed. The Parisians felt humiliated and angry, but not with the Germans – with the French.

The President of France's republican regime was Adolphe Thiers. Thiers was a hard-liner who knew that the rest of France had had enough of Paris trying to dictate what sort of government they should have. The time had come to put the Parisians in their place.

No sooner had the fighting against the Germans come to an end than Thiers commenced military action against Paris:

✔ **18 March 1871:** Thiers sends troops into Paris under two generals to remove the Parisians' cannons, up on the hills of Montmartre. The Parisians resist and hang the generals – and also keep the cannons. Thiers prepares to attack. The Germans, who were stationed outside the city, helpfully show his men the best places to fire from.

✔ **28 March 1871:** The Parisians elect a revolutionary government called the *Commune* and defy Thiers to do his worst. The Commune takes hostages, including many priests, and people start digging up the cobbled paving stones to build barricades.

✔ **21 May 1871:** Thiers sends in troops. Bitter house-to-house fighting results in more Parisians killed than in the war with the Germans, and destroys whole areas of the city. After a week of fighting, Thiers's forces finally crush the communards, most of whom are put up against a wall and shot.

Both sides were utterly ruthless. The government troops shot prisoners, and the communards shot hostages, including the Archbishop of Paris.

Socialists and communists regarded the communards as martyrs. When the Russians put Yuri Gagarin into space in 1961, he took with him three socialist symbols: A book by Marx, a book by Lenin, and a flag from the Paris Commune. (See Chapters 17 and Chapter 21 for more on Marx and Lenin.)

Judging by the way they voted in the 1871 elections, the French people wanted a monarchy. But which monarch? Two choices were on offer:

✔ **Bonapartist?** No one wanted Napoleon III back (he had led them into a disastrous war with the Germans which you can read about in Chapter 18); his son, the Prince Imperial, was a nice lad but a bit young.

✔ **Bourbon? Orleanist?** The Bourbons were the old kings of France, and the Orleanists were their cousins, but they weren't on speaking terms; the duke of Orleans had sat on the tribunal that sent Louis XVI to the guillotine. The idea was to give the crown to the only surviving Bourbon, the Count de Chambord; then the monarchy would pass to the Orleanists. Unfortunately the count insisted on restoring the old royal flag, white with three gold fleurs-de-lys. Even the most royalist French dug their heels in about giving up the tricolour; it was like expecting them to work in August. So the French had to make do with a republic – their third – and hope that this third time really would be lucky.

Montmartre

The outbreak of killing in Paris in 1871 came as a terrible shock. The French decided to build a great white basilica high on the Butte of Montmartre, where the killing had started, as a way of asking God's forgiveness for all Paris's sins. The basilica was dedicated to the Sacred Heart of Jesus, *Sacré Coeur* in French, and from its position high on the hill, it still dominates the whole city.

There was a bit more to this basilica than met the eye. The French Church was trying to get its

old power back – it hadn't forgotten what the Commune did to the Archbishop of Paris – and building Sacré Coeur was a useful part of the propaganda campaign. A permanent prayer vigil has been held in Sacré Coeur ever since it was built, which is handy because Montmartre is also the site of the famous Moulin Rouge and Paris's red light district, so there's plenty of sin to forgive – so I'm told.

The French Try a Republic . . . Again

France had tried being a republic twice before, and no one knew for certain whether this third attempt in 1871 would work. In 1877, President MacMahon even dissolved the National Assembly and called elections hoping – wrongly, as events turned out – that the French would vote monarchist. However, the French did miss having a glamorous military figure at their head. Step forward dashingly handsome war hero, General Georges Boulanger, appointed Minister for War in 1886. The French people decided that he was just the sort of man to stand up to Bismarck, the German chancellor.

French President Jules Grévy thought that Boulanger was a dangerous nuisance who badly needed to stop playing soldiers and grow up. In 1888, Grévy had Boulanger removed from office and sent him off to take charge of the garrison at Clermont Ferrand (a second-rate provincial town), which was about the right level for him.

The Parisians were so upset that they lay down in front of Boulanger's train to stop him leaving, and everyone was expecting him to march on Paris and stage a coup. And then – Boulanger got cold feet and ran off to Brussels with his mistress. The French were deeply shocked – why *Brussels*? In the end, Boulanger's mistress died and he shot himself on her grave. The French were having a republic, and they'd have to accept it.

Church versus State

The French Church hated the republic. A cult of the Sacred Heart sprang up to pray for France to be saved and to bring back a proper Catholic king. The republic decided to hit back. Priests lost all their privileges, such as exemption from military service. Above all, the government kept religion right out of the classroom, because they saw schools as a battleground for reducing the influence of the Church in French society as a whole.

The idea of keeping State and Church strictly separate became deeply ingrained in France. In 2004, President Jacques Chirac made it illegal for Muslim girls to wear the Islamic headscarf in schools. Other countries were horrified, but the French said that they were maintaining an important principle that they had held to for over a hundred years.

A touch of scandal

The third French republic developed a rare talent for political scandal. First, President Grévy's son-in-law turned out to have been earning a tidy sum selling honours and medals, and then the French company that was trying and failing to build the Panama Canal went bankrupt amid revelations of wholesale bribery and blackmail. A number of the shady characters in the Panama scandal were Jewish, which only served to add fuel to the most serious crisis of all: the Dreyfus case.

The Dreyfus case began as a straightforward miscarriage of justice. In 1894, Captain Alfred Dreyfus was found guilty of passing military secrets to the Germans, and when he refused to do the decent thing and shoot himself, the French government had him shipped off to Devil's Island, a notorious penal hell hole in French Guyana.

But the leaks didn't stop. Soon it became clear that the evidence against Dreyfus had been forged and that the real traitor was a Major Esterhazy, but the French military courts refused to accept that they'd made a mistake. The whole country was split, into *Dreyfusards* (left-wingers and intellectuals) who said that Dreyfus was innocent and that the army should own up, and *Anti-Dreyfusards* (conservatives, the army, and the Church) who said that the others were trying to undermine the army and everything France stood for and that Dreyfus was Jewish anyway so what did it matter? The novelist Emile Zola wrote a famous newspaper article called *J'accuse!* (I accuse!), which pointed the finger at the politicians and military who had conspired to keep an innocent man in jail. Dreyfus took 12 years to clear his name; France took a lot longer to recover.

Africa Scrambled

Europe's wholesale take-over of 19th-century Africa began with the British and French:

- ✓ **1814:** Britain takes South Africa from Holland at the Congress of Vienna. When Britain abolishes slavery in 1833, the Dutch settlers clear out in the *Great Trek* to enslave the local population and carry on living in the style to which they'd become accustomed.

- ✓ **1830:** France invades Algeria. Eventually it even makes Algeria a part of France itself; a special part, ruled by a military governor where hardly anyone had the vote.

- ✓ **1869:** Suez Canal opens, designed by French engineer Ferdinand de Lesseps. The European powers are suddenly very interested in Egypt.

- ✓ **1881:** France takes over Tunisia. Even better: The Italians had wanted it for themselves and were now having a tantrum.

- ✓ **1882:** Major anti-European rising in Egypt. Britain sends a military force, which crushes the rising and takes over the whole country – all on behalf of the Egyptian government, of course.

Suddenly, everyone decided that what they needed most in the world was a large chunk of Africa. A big conference took place in Berlin in 1884–1885 to try to divide the continent up so everyone got their fair share (except the Africans, of course).

The French, who were incensed at the British take-over of Egypt, took over most of west Africa to make themselves feel better; the British spread north from South Africa and got Kenya in the east and Nigeria in the west; the Portuguese piled back into Angola and Mozambique; and Germany took Togo and Cameroon in the west, Tanganyika and Zanzibar (more or less modern Tanzania) in the east, and South West Africa (Namibia). This situation was like one of those mad land-grabs in the American west; it became known as the Scramble for Africa.

Imagine for a moment that things had been the other way round, and all the different African nations had divided Europe up between them and made the Europeans work in the fields as slaves in their own land. That scenario is what the books really mean when they say things like 'France took over Senegal' or 'Belgium took over the Congo'.

The official reason for Europeans wanting all these African lands was to open Africa up to the benefits of trade and to rescue the Africans from slavery, but the *real* reason was simply to get hold of Africa's natural resources without having to pay for them.

Death in the sun

The arrival of a European expeditionary force in the neighbourhood usually, though not quite always, spelt disaster for the local African people:

- ✔ **Zulu War 1879:** British launch an entirely unprovoked attack on the Zulu kingdom. Zulus wipe out a British army column at Isandhlwana before the British get their act together and virtually annihilate the Zulu kingdom.

- ✔ **Matabeleland 1893:** British raiders launch an entirely unprovoked attack on the Ndebele kingdom. This time the British have cavalry, cannon, and five Maxim machine guns. Ndebele are slaughtered; the survivors can look forward to a life of forced labour under British rule.

- ✔ **Ethiopia 1896:** Italy invades the Christian kingdom of Ethiopia, but bungles the main battle, at Adowa. The Italians are forced to pull out and Ethiopia remains a rare independent African nation until Mussolini finishes the job in 1936 (see Chapter 22).

- ✔ **German South West Africa 1904:** Herero and Nama people put aside years of rivalry and rise up against German rule. The Germans respond by trying to exterminate them, by shootings, starvation, and hard-labour camps. Two years later, the people of German East Africa rise up too, believing that a special charm will turn German bullets to water. The Germans destroy the rebels' crops and upwards of a quarter of a million starve to death.

Heart of Darkness: The Belgian Congo

The novelist Joseph Conrad set his famous novel *Heart of Darkness* in the Belgian Congo. The darkness wasn't the Africans or their way of life, it was the appalling tyranny visited on them by King Leopold II of Belgium.

Leopold enlisted the explorer Henry Morton Stanley (the man who 'found Livingstone') to help him take over a vast area of central Africa based on the River Congo, which became Leopold's personal property. Leopold turned the Congo into a vast slave-labour camp for the production of rubber. To force the people to work, the Belgians burned their villages, shot their women and children, and cut the hands off anyone who tried to resist. Such an outcry occurred that Leopold was forced to hand 'his' Congo over – no, not to the Congolese; to the Belgian government. Nearly 50 years later, the Belgians finally got round to giving a few of the Congolese the vote.

A bloody nose for the British

The biggest war in Africa was between the British and a people who were able to shoot back: the Boers. The Boers ('farmers') were descendants of Dutch settlers who had arrived in South Africa back in the 17th century. These people had two republics of their own, the Transvaal and the Orange Free State. The British coveted their neighbour's land, especially when that land turned out to be rich in diamonds.

The British high commissioner in South Africa, Lord Milner, was pretty obviously planning an invasion, so in 1899 the Boers decided to get their retaliation in first and invaded British territory. The Boers cooped the British up in three townships, including Mafeking where the British commander was Colonel Robert Baden-Powell, who went on to found the Boy Scouts movement and impose long shorts and woggles on a hitherto happy world.

The British managed to regain the initiative and defeat the Boer armies, but the Boers turned to guerrilla warfare, and the British responded by burning crops and clearing the population into concentration camps. These actions forced the Boers to surrender, but the revelations of disease and starvation in the camps shocked public opinion around the world. The other Europeans already sympathised with the Boers, and this event made them even more anti-British.

Cathay not-so-Pacific

The Europeans didn't restrict themselves to 'colonising' Africa. The French took over South East Asia – Vietnam, Cambodia, Laos – and the British, French, and Germans (and the Americans) helped themselves to islands in the Pacific and small bases in China. Even areas like South America, which appeared to be made up mainly of independent states, depended so heavily on European trade and investment that they were virtually European colonies – 'informal empire', as historians say.

Malaria

Two advances enabled the Europeans to take over Africa: steamboats, which carried them along Africa's rivers deep into the interior; and quinine, which kept them safe from malaria when they got there. The British scientist Ronald Ross showed that malaria was carried by mosquitoes; and therefore, you could eradicate the disease by exterminating them. Ross won the Nobel prize, which upset the Italian Giovanni Grassi, who said that he'd proved the relationship between malaria and mosquitoes himself.

Germany on the Up

The German Chancellor, Otto von Bismarck, wanted to shape the country in his own military and authoritarian image. Bismarck had a very good working relationship with the emperor, Wilhelm I – they just shouted at each other – and an even better one with all the Liberals in the Reichstag, the German parliament: he ignored them. Germany's big advantage was that the country was rapidly overtaking Britain to become the most advanced industrial nation in Europe. German merchants wanted to get hold of raw materials as well – which is why they put such pressure on Bismarck to start grabbing colonies in Africa. But Bismarck wasn't really all that interested in Africa; he thought that Germany's main enemies were a bit closer to home – the German Socialist Party and the Catholic Church.

1 fought the Pope and the Pope won

Bismarck introduced a whole set of anti-Catholic laws, stripping Catholics of their civil rights and even throwing Catholic priests into prison. Pope Pius IX sent a special letter telling German Catholics that they didn't have to obey the new laws. Bismarck saw this action as a rerun of when the medieval Emperor Henry IV had had to beg for the Pope's forgiveness at Canossa (see Chapter 7); he declared it a *Kulturkampf*, a cultural battle for Germany's soul, against an un-German enemy within.

Bismarck soon realised that most people sympathised with the persecuted Catholics and in any case, the Catholic Church was just as anti-socialist as he was, so fighting over the matter was silly. Bismarck waited until Pius IX had died and then called the Kulturkampf off.

Reds under the beds

Bismarck decided that socialism was much more dangerous than Catholicism. After all, socialists actually did talk about staging a revolution and overturning Europe's monarchs. Right on cue, there were two assassination attempts on the kaiser.

Without a shred of evidence, Bismarck said that the socialists were responsible and got a law passed through the Reichstag closing the Social Democratic (socialist) Party (SDP) down.

But Bismarck wasn't able to ban the SDP in the Reichstag itself, because of parliamentary privilege, so a bizarre set-up resulted in which SDP candidates could stand for election but the SDP itself couldn't officially exist. Not officially existing didn't stop the SDP increasing its vote year by year, however.

Keeping in with the neighbours

Bismarck's great nightmare was that the French would manage to put together a great anti-German coalition to get revenge for the way the Germans had humiliated them in 1871. So Bismarck set up a series of alliances with Russia and Austria, to keep France isolated. This took some doing because these two nations didn't trust each other further than they could spit.

An *alliance* is an agreement between two or more states that they will help each other if one of them is attacked by a third party. Peacetime alliances were not unknown, but they were not the norm until Bismarck made alliances the whole basis of European diplomacy.

And then Wilhelm II decided he wanted to play, too.

Yes, thank you, I'll take over from here

Wilhelm became kaiser in 1888 and immediately decided that Bismarck's proper place was in the history books. Wilhelm wanted Germany to have its 'place in the sun' and when Bismarck snorted at the idea, Wilhelm sacked him.

'Dropping the pilot' was how the British magazine *Punch* saw the situation: Bismarck had steered Germany through the difficult waters, and now Wilhelm was going to take her into the open seas. *Punch's* image was appropriate because Wilhelm wanted a massive navy to challenge Britain's supremacy. In fact, Wilhelm seemed to positively relish annoying the Brits:

- ✔ **1895:** British irregular (in other words, totally illegal) force invades the Transvaal state in South Africa and is rounded up by the Transvaal police. Wilhelm sends a telegram of congratulations to President Kruger of the Transvaal saying, congratulations and next time you want to kick the British up the backside, here's my number.

- ✔ **1908:** *Daily Telegraph* publishes conversation with Wilhelm, in which Wilhelm says that he's England's friend, and the English must be insane not to see it. Wilhelm says that he saved the English from the devious Russians during the Boer War and that the English will be very pleased to have the German navy alongside them when the Japanese get nasty. German foreign minister holds his head in his hands while Russian and Japanese ambassadors ask sternly if they might have a word.

These events tell you that diplomacy was not exactly Kaiser Wilhelm II's strong point.

Collective Insecurity

By the 1890s, all the great powers were feeling the need for an ally. In 1894, the French did what Bismarck had always been afraid they would do and signed an alliance with Russia.

In 1904 the British and French decided that the time had come to kiss and make up. King Edward VII made a very successful visit to Paris (where he'd already had plenty of experience of kissing and make-up) and the two governments signed a strange sort of agreement they called an *entente cordiale* – a friendly understanding. Was the friendly understanding an alliance? The kaiser decided to find out:

- ✔ **1905:** Kaiser Wilhelm visits Morocco and warns the French to keep their paws off it. The British stick firmly by the French, and at the special summit conference held the next year at Algeciras to smooth things over, all the other powers agree that France and Spain can run Morocco between them if they want to. Which the two countries proceed to do.

- ✔ **1911:** The Germans send a gunboat to Morocco to protect 'vital German interests' from the dastardly French who were taking over the country. The British warn the Germans in no uncertain terms to keep off or there'll be trouble.

The Anglo–French *entente* looked very like an alliance.

Russia Works Out Which Century It Is

Ever since Peter the Great's time (check out Chapter 14), the Russians had been trying to decide whether they ought to do things the western way, which meant introducing a few basic human rights, or whether they ought to turn their back on the West and do things the traditional Russian way. Tsar Alexander I (1800–1825) was a complex character who tried to do both. In Russia, the tsar kept power firmly in his own hands, but in Poland, he allowed his brother the Grand Duke Constantine to introduce a constitution with fair trials, a free press, and, above all, a separate Polish army.

Liberals in the rest of the Russian Empire were, understandably, rather envious, and when Alexander died in 1825, a group of hot-headed young officers known as the *Decembrists* (because their revolt didn't last longer than December 1825) rather foolishly tried to get Grand Duke Constantine put on the Russian throne instead of his more hard-line brother, Grand Duke Nicholas. No one supported the Decembrists, least of all Grand Duke Constantine, and Nicholas, now Tsar Nicholas I, had the ringleaders hanged and the rest carted off to Siberia.

Poland seizes its chance – and blows it

Nicholas I thought that constitutions and civil liberties were a dangerous left-over from the French Revolution. The tsar began to censor the Polish press and accidentally-on-purpose forget to summon the Polish parliament.

In 1830, the Poles rose up in revolt. Unfortunately, the Poles couldn't decide whether to go for full independence or just a form of home rule, and while they were still arguing about the situation, the Russian army arrived and crushed them.

In 1863, the Poles had another go at revolt. The outcome was even worse, as the Russians simply got the Polish peasants to turn on their masters. Poland disappeared from the map – from now on, the country was known as 'the Administrative District of the Vistula'.

Alexander II: Tsar Liberator

Nicholas I's gung-ho foreign policy got Russia into trouble. In 1854, Russia found itself at war with France, Britain, and the Turks in the Crimean War, and lost. Nicholas I died during the war and the new tsar who would have to clear up the mess was his young son, Alexander II.

Alexander decided that the reason Russia had lost was because the country was still stuck in the old ways, with an army of serfs and Cossacks up against the most industrially advanced powers in Europe. Serfdom had to go. In 1862, Alexander issued his decree emancipating the serfs – as he pointed out to a group of sceptical Russian nobles, to free them peacefully from above was better than waiting for them to do emancipate themselves rather less peacefully.

Although Alexander became known as the Tsar Liberator, he wasn't giving the serfs complete freedom:

- Peasants had to live in villages called *mirs*, which owned the land collectively and decided how to farm it. The farming method chosen tended to be the same as they'd always used; no going organic or setting up a B&B.

- The peasants had to pay for their freedom in an annual tax called *redemption payments*. This tax was not universally popular – at all.

Don't get the idea that emancipation was a scam, though; it changed Russia profoundly. For example, now that landlords no longer had the power to decide disputes between 'their' serfs, Russia needed to develop a proper legal system, with trial by jury. New local councils were set up, called *zemstva*, which built hospitals and primary schools, and the army eventually got a complete overhaul.

All of these changes took time, though, and not all Russians were prepared to wait. Here are a few of these would-be revolutionary Russians:

- **Nihilists:** Strictly speaking 'believers in nothing' (Latin *nihil* = nothing), they wanted to tear down everything in tsarist Russia and start afresh.

- **Social Democrats:** Socialists who wanted Russia to be ruled by the working class, but that meant waiting for the country to get a bit more industrialised first – which looked like being a long wait.

- **Populists:** Middle-class students and intellectuals who didn't know one end of a cow from another but believed that the future of Russia lay with the people who did. In the 1870s, hundreds of them set out for the countryside to preach revolution to the peasants, who listened a bit, and promptly turned most of them over to the police. After that, the Populists decided to try a new tactic: terrorism.

Boom! Why does my tsar go boom?

A special secret group of the Populist movement called the *People's Will* started to set traps for Alexander II. The group thought that the tsar had let the people down by not following up emancipation with a proper constitution for Russia. Most of the plotters got caught (including the older brother of one Vladimir Ilyich Ulyanov, better known as Lenin), but in 1881 they got lucky and blew Alexander II up with a bomb. Ironically, the tsar had just that moment agreed to a constitution for Russia. The new tsar, Alexander III, put the constitution straight in the bin.

Wider still and wider – Russia, that is

Russia had been expanding into Turkish territory the 18th century: Nicholas I called Turkey 'a very sick man' and was obviously hoping to move in soon and take over completely. The question of what would happen to Turkey was known as the *Eastern Question*.

The Russians had their eye on two areas in particular:

- ✔ **The Balkans:** The area of southern Europe including Romania, Bulgaria, Greece, and Serbia. These people were Slavs and Orthodox Christians, so they looked to Russia as a big brother they could call on to protect them from the Turks.

- ✔ **Central Asia:** Persia (modern Iran), Afghanistan, and the Caucasus region – all the areas between Russia and the north-west frontier of British India. The British thought that the Russians might carry on through to India, and British and Russian secret agents along India's north–west frontier spent a happy century spying on each other in what became known as the 'Great Game'.

Russia's difficult relationship with Turkey caused a lot of friction with the rest of Europe:

- ✔ **1833: Treaty of Unkiar Skelessi.** The pasha (ruler) of Egypt invades Turkish territory. Tsar Nicholas I sends troops in to save the Turkish sultan from the Egyptians; in return Turkey signs this treaty saying that it will never turn to anyone else for help or let anyone else go through the narrow Dardanelles straits into the Black Sea. The other European powers are deeply alarmed.

- ✔ **1854–1856: Crimean War.** British and French troops capture Russia's Black Sea naval base, Sevastopol. Under the peace terms at the end of the war, Russia is not allowed any warships on the Black Sea.

- ✔ **1870.** Russia puts her warships back on the Black Sea during the Franco–Prussian War, while no one's looking.

- ✔ **1877–1878.** Russia sends troops to stop the Turks massacring the population of Bulgaria and the British send troops to stop the Russians turning Bulgaria into a puppet state. The situation looks like war until the *Congress of Berlin* works out a compromise (a smaller Bulgaria) and everyone can go home.

Buy Austria, Get Hungary Free!

The Austrians had been Europe's top nation before revolution broke out all over their empire in 1848 (Chapter 18 covers this).

In 1867 the domain changed its name to the Dual Monarchy of the Austrian Empire and the Kingdom of Hungary, or Austria-Hungary for short. The Hungarians decided, sensible people, that the moment when Austria had just been hammered by Bismarck and the Prussians in 1866 was the ideal time to demand a separate government.

The *Ausgleich* (Compromise) of 1867 was hammered out by the Austrian government and the Hungarian diet (parliament). The Compromise said that Hungary was to be a separate kingdom with full powers for its diet (which was to be housed in a rather handsome riverside building based on the Houses of Parliament in London), but the details were incredibly complex. Some ministries were to cover both countries and some were to be separate; a joint parliament was to exist that met one year in Vienna and the next year in Budapest, but they were never to meet together. Even the emperor – who was emperor of Austria but king of Hungary – didn't know if he was coming or going.

Austria-Hungary looked cumbersome, but it worked surprisingly well. The two parts traded with each other on favourable terms, and the other national groups, like the Bohemians or the Croats, usually managed to get enough concessions, like being able to use their own languages, to keep them happy.

Serbia: A Small State, Thinking Big

The Serbs had won their independence from the Turks in 1878 – achieving this autonomy had been a bit difficult because the different Serb leaders kept murdering each other – and now they thought that what southern Europe needed was a big Slav state with the king of Serbia at its head. The Russians were keen on this plan (fellow Slavs, you see), but the Turks and Austrians and Hungarians weren't. The Serbs were particularly interested in the little province of Bosnia-Herzegovina, which had a mixture of Serbs, Croats, and Muslims, and which Serbia wanted for itself. For a time, the Turks looked like they might give Bosnia-Herzegovina to the Serbs, but in 1908 the Austrians marched in and took the province over themselves.

By the 1910s everyone was expecting a war between these different ethnic groups to break out in the Balkans. They were right. (See Chapter 20 about the war to end all wars.)

Chapter 20

The War to End All Wars – Doesn't

*B*efore 1914, Europe was still a 19th-century continent, with kings and emperors and soldiers in fancy dress; by 1918 most of that – including most of the kings and emperors – had gone and wouldn't be coming back. The Great War was the crucible on which modern Europe was forged, which was a very painful process.

One Big Happy Family

Queen Victoria and Prince Albert of Great Britain had nine children in 17 years. The couple married these offspring into half the royal houses of Europe, so that by the 1880s, just about all Europe's monarchs were related to each other, even kings of places like Norway, Greece, and Romania.

The Russians were related to the British royals twice over: Tsar Nicholas II was related through his grandmother, and his wife, Alexandra, was Queen Victoria's granddaughter. Nicholas and Alexandra spoke English together at home, and called each other 'hubby' and 'wifey'. Yuk.

The German connection was less syrupy but more worrisome. Queen Victoria's eldest child, Princess Victoria, had married Crown Prince Frederick of Prussia, heir to the throne of Germany. The idea was that together they would introduce an English-style monarchy and make Germany less militaristic, but Frederick was ill and died of cancer shortly after he came to the throne.

Kaiser Wilhelm II

Princess Victoria and Crown Prince Frederick's son, Kaiser Wilhelm II rejected his parents, enthusiastically encouraged by his wife Dona, who couldn't stand the English. Wilhelm loved his grandmother Queen Victoria dearly, but he deeply resented his uncle Edward VII, and thought that the English wanted to keep him and his country firmly under their thumb. When Wilhelm was in English mode he was all tweeds and 'Fine weather, dontcha know?', but when he was in an anti-English mood, which was increasingly common after 1900, he would blame the English for everything that had ever gone wrong in Germany.

In the navy

Wilhelm's dream was to have a huge German fleet, big enough to challenge Britain's Royal Navy. The German navy minister, Admiral von Tirpitz, was already drawing up plans, and soon the two countries were launching ships as fast as they built them. In 1906, Britain upped the ante by launching HMS *Dreadnought*, which was heavy and fast enough to win a fight, but the Germans just switched to building Dreadnoughts as well. Both sides calmed down a bit by 1913, but by then they both had large fleets and were just itching to try them out in a real live war.

General von Schlieffen's Cunning Plan

The Germans had always been scared of having to fight a war on two fronts: against France in the west and Russia in the east. General von Schlieffen, Chief of the General Staff (the army planning department), came up with the answer. Schlieffen said:

- There are more Russians than Germans and Russia is pretty big. Therefore the war with Russia is likely to last longer.

- *But* the Russians couldn't organise their way out of a paper bag and will never be ready in time. That gives us time to deal with France first.

- If we come at France through Belgium, where they won't be expecting us, we can surround Paris and knock France out of the war in a matter of weeks. Then we'll have a quick evening out at the Folies Bergères and set off for the Russian Front.

Schlieffen's idea was all based on careful planning, using the railways to get the troops where they needed to be fast. The generals had such faith in the plan that they didn't want anything to stand in its way – such as a peace initiative or an attempt to solve things through diplomacy instead of by war.

Barney in the Balkans

The Turks had conquered the Balkans back in the Middle Ages (find out more on the Turks in Chapter 12).

Serbia and Bulgaria each wanted to eject the Turks and set up – and lead – a big, independent Slav state. Balkan politics became a four-way power-struggle between the Serbs, Bulgarians, Austrians, and Turks:

- **1908: Coup in Turkey.** Turkish army officers, the *Young Turks*, seize power and put some much-needed backbone in the Turkish government. The Austrian government annexes the province of Bosnia-Herzegovina. The Serbs are hopping mad (they wanted it themselves).

- **1912: First Balkan War.** Bulgaria, Serbia, and Greece launch a huge attack on Turkey. The Turks lose nearly all their European land.

- **1913: Second Balkan War.** Serbia and the other Balkan states attack Bulgaria. Bulgaria loses lots of land. Bulgarians are now *really* angry. The Serbs throw a big party and crack anti-Bulgarian jokes.

Don't mess with the Austro-Hungarian empire

The Serbs hadn't forgiven the Austrians for taking over Bosnia-Herzegovina in 1908, and they were determined to get their hands on the province by fair means or foul. Simultaneously, a hard-line Austrian group wanted to deal with Serbia once and for all. This group was led by the heir to the throne, the Archduke Franz Ferdinand.

To celebrate their wedding anniversary on 28 June 1914, Franz Ferdinand and his wife decided to visit Sarajevo and inspect the Austrian troops stationed in Bosnia. June 28 was also the anniversary of the 1389 Battle of Kosovo, the most sacred day of the year for Serbs, so Franz Ferdinand was really rubbing the Serbs' noses in it.

The Serb terrorist group, the Black Hand, rose to the occasion. A young Black Hand member called Gavrilo Princip, jumped up on the running board of the archduke's car and shot the archduke and his wife. Dead.

The Austrian government checked with Berlin. The kaiser said that Germany would stand shoulder to shoulder with the Austrians whatever they decided to do. Having sent this diplomatic time bomb off to Vienna without consulting anyone (well, okay, he had a short stroll in the park with the war minister), the kaiser got on his yacht and went on holiday.

The Austrians had what they needed, and sent an ultimatum to the Serbian government in Belgrade, saying:

- This assassination was all your fault; you should keep your murdering terrorist gangs under better control. (This accusation held some truth – some people high up in the Serbian General Staff had known all about the affair.)

- You will immediately stop the Serbian press saying anything against Austria.

- You will immediately sack anyone who has ever said anything against Austria – and we will give you their names.

- You will allow the Austrian police into Serbia to look for the rest of the Black Hand gang who did this, and you will let them arrest whomsoever they please.

- You will accept these terms within 48 hours, or else.

This ultimatum was tantamount to saying, 'From now on, you are an Austrian colony. Sign here.' The Russians told the Serbs, 'Yes, we'll support you, but don't go to war if you can possibly avoid it – *please.*'

So the Serbs backed down, and said to Vienna, 'We accept everything – except, can we just talk over that bit about letting your police in?'

Every government in Europe breathed a sigh of relief, even the kaiser: crisis over. Every government, that is, except one. The Austrians declared war on Serbia.

After that declaration of war, things happened very fast:

- **28 July: Austria declares war on Serbia.**

- **30 July: Russia mobilises its troops – calls them up, sends them to the frontier.**

- **31 July: Germany tells Russia to send its troops home, or there'll be trouble.**

- ✔ **1 August: Germany declares war on Russia.** The Germans immediately start putting the Schlieffen Plan (see the earlier section 'General von Schlieffen's Cunning Plan') into operation, so France mobilises its troops and sends them off to the German frontier.

- ✔ **3 August: Germany declares war on France and sends troops pouring into Belgium.** Britain tells Germany to clear out of Belgium fast or there'll be trouble.

- ✔ **4 August: Britain and her empire declare war on Germany.** This is now a worldwide war.

It'll All Be Over by Christmas

People really did think this confrontation would only be a short war; after all, all the other wars in recent history had only lasted a few months, and no one expected this one to be any different. Right from the start, the Germans' plan of winning the war quickly began to go wrong. The Russians had got their act together and were ready in three weeks, instead of the six or seven that the Germans had confidently predicted they would need.

Second, the German generals were nervous about the Schlieffen Plan (see the section earlier in this chapter) and didn't send all their men through Belgium, so the Belgians and the British were able to hold them up at Ypres and Mons and put them off schedule.

Even so, the Germans were getting perilously near Paris when the French managed to stop them at the Battle of the Marne. The Germans fell back a bit and then got their spades out and dug. Soon, to everyone's bafflement, the whole war in the west consisted of a long line of parallel trenches that ran all the way from the Swiss border to the English Channel.

Sorry, guv, I don't do battles south of the river

When the French finally managed to stop the Germans at the Battle of the Marne, an officer called Colonel Nivelle had the bright idea of commandeering 600 Parisian taxis to move troops up to the front quickly. Later, the French were so relieved at winning the battle and saving Paris that this episode of the 'taxis of the Marne' passed into legend, and you can still find books that tell the story as if the whole battle was fought by taxi. In fact, this episode involved only a few troops in one part of the battle, but the idea of such a bold attack caught hold of French imagination.

The Russians Are Coming

The Russians were really excited about going to war. The Russian army was so vast that people compared it to a steamroller that would simply crush anything in its path through sheer weight of numbers.

This view of the Russian army did hold some element of truth. The Russians got their troops together much more quickly than anyone had expected, marched into eastern Germany, and walked all over the German army. But then two new German commanders arrived to take charge, General Hindenburg and General Ludendorff.

General against general

The German Generals Hindenburg and Ludendorff put some backbone into their men and hit on a plan for stopping the Russians, based on a very interesting piece of intelligence: The two Russian commanders, General Rennenkampf and General Samsonov, couldn't stand each other. So, if one of the generals got into difficulties, the other one would almost certainly leave him to stew in his own juice. Just to make the situation even better (for the Germans), the Russians didn't have enough code books, so their radio operators had to send all their messages in clear. All the Germans had to do was listen in and keep a Russian dictionary handy.

The Germans lured General Samsonov into four days of battle near Tannenburg, where the Slavs had once crushed the Teutonic Knights (see Chapter 12 for more on this incident). The Germans certainly got their revenge for that ancient defeat; some 70,000 Russians were killed or wounded in the 1914 Battle of Tannenburg, and the Germans took 100,000 prisoners. General Samsonov was so devastated that he shot himself. Then Hindenburg and Ludendorff closed in on General Rennenkampf in the marshy lands of the Masurian Lakes and forced him to turn tail and clear out of German territory.

All quiet (eventually) on the eastern front

The war in the east just consisted of the Russians acting on the defensive and not being very good at it. In 1916, the Russian General Brusilov did break through the Austrian lines by the simple means of attacking without pounding the enemy lines in advance with thousands of artillery shells, which was just a rather noisy way of saying 'Guess what, we're going to launch a surprise attack just as soon as this shelling stops'. Brusilov captured a quarter of a million men and advanced some 200 miles behind Austrian lines, but then he ran out of ammunition and had to turn back, which, frankly, was the Russian supply system all over.

Trenches in the West

In the west, the fighting was all being done from a whole network of deep trenches in parallel lines.

The problem with the trenches was that they turned the normal rules of war on their head. The generals had grown up with the idea that you won the war by attacking the enemy – hard. But with trenches and barbed wire, the defenders were the ones who had the advantage; all you had to do was position a few machine guns, and you could mow the attackers down before they got anywhere near your front line. The generals kept trying to think of clever ways round this one:

Bright idea: Flatten the enemy's trenches with bigger and bigger shells so no one's left alive to fire back.

Result: The whole ground gets covered in craters, and the enemy simply sit down at the bottom of their dug-outs until the shelling stops. (Not such a bright idea, then.)

Bright idea: Flatten the enemy's trenches with shrapnel shells to cut their barbed wire.

Result: You can't cut barbed wire with shells, even shrapnel ones.

Bright idea: Poison gas.

Result: The Germans first used gas in 1915. The allies protested but privately the allies were thinking 'Now *that's* a good idea'. Sometimes the gas helped one side break through, but as often as not the wind changed, so the vapour just drifted back into the people who had launched it.

It really *could* be quiet on the western front

Most people have the picture of life in the trenches as a hell on earth, and conditions were at times, especially when it rained and the ground got churned into mud by shellfire. The mud was so thick and liquid that if you fell in, you could drown. When the big guns opened up over the troops was certainly hellish; the noise was so loud that the guns could be heard in England, and the men under the bombardment went mad with the stress and fear.

But the situation wasn't like that all along the line of trenches all the time. Quiet sectors and quiet times existed, and soldiers on both sides took a live-and-let-live policy whenever possible. The most famous occasion was on Christmas Day in 1914, when British and German soldiers met in no-man's-land between the trenches and had a game of football, though the generals were so horrified that they made sure it never happened again.

Bright idea: Tanks.

Result: The British tried these machines out in 1916 at the Battle of the Somme, and scared the life out of the Germans. But tanks were very slow and kept breaking down. By the end of the war, both sides had built some more reliable tanks that didn't need pit stops every 200 yards, but they couldn't win the war on their own.

Bright idea: Er, that's it.

Winston's winning wheeze

In 1915, Britain's First Lord of the Admiralty, Winston Churchill, came up with an idea that looked really rather clever – on paper: Send a huge allied force through the Black Sea into Russia so that the Germans can be squeezed from both sides.

The plan was to send a naval force to seize the Dardanelles, which is that very narrow passage of water in Turkey that controls the way in or out of the Black Sea. Then an allied army would land, march up to Constantinople and take it off the Turks in time for tea.

Unfortunately, the ships ran into a string of Turkish mines which sank a third of the allied force. Instead of staying and sweeping the mines, the allies withdrew to have a think. The Turks very sensibly poured troops into the area in case the allies came back, and a month later, in April 1915, they did.

This time the allies landed troops on the Gallipoli peninsula, but the Turks, who could defend their own country as well as any other nation, fought back so hard that the allies were never able to advance inland from the beaches.

In January 1916, in the only part of the campaign that did go according to plan, the allies pulled out.

The Gallipoli campaign is best remembered for the large numbers of Australian and New Zealand troops that took part. The area where the troops landed is still known as ANZAC Cove (from ANZAC – Australia and New Zealand Army Corps). Nowadays, many Australians feel very bitter about the Gallipoli campaign, thinking that the campaign showed Australian troops paying with their lives for the stupid decisions of British generals. You can get a good idea of that way of looking at the action in the film *Gallipoli* with Mel Gibson, which is a brilliant and very accurate portrayal of the battle, though very unfair on the British commanders.

Death struggle at Verdun

General Erich von Falkenhayn had a rather different plan from Churchill's nip-round-the-back idea to win the war for Germany. In 1916 von Falkenhayn launched an attack on the French fortress city of Verdun.

Verdun was an ancient city with an important part in French history. This city was where Charlemagne's sons had divided his empire between them (see Chapter 6). Falkenhayn thought that the French would pour men in to defend Verdun, and then he would be able to rain shells down on them till he had bled France dry. At first, the Germans caught the French off-guard; one fort even fell to a single German soldier. The French did exactly as Falkenhayn had hoped they would: French President Aristide Briand sent General Pétain to defend Verdun at all costs. Pétain issued a defiant message: 'They shall not pass!' and started pouring men into Verdun. The road to the front become known as the Sacred Way, because it led so many men to their deaths.

Despite these losses, the French held on to Verdun, and even retook the forts the Germans had taken. Now the Germans had to pour more and more men into the attacks as well, and soon they were losing at the same rate as the French. After 300 days of the most appalling slaughter, the Germans gave up.

The French had won, but at such a fearful cost that the big joint attack on the German lines that the allies had been intending to launch in the summer of 1916 would now have to be a mainly British affair. This attack was due to take place in northern France, along the river Somme.

Slaughter on the Somme

The idea behind the Somme was very simple: The allies would open up with the biggest artillery bombardment in history – the shelling would last a *week* and would (or so the generals said) utterly destroy the German trenches. Then the British would get out of their trenches and simply walk over to the German lines.

The reality of the Somme was rather different. The bombardment didn't destroy the German trenches, and when the allies started walking across no-man's-land they found that the shelling hadn't destroyed the German machine guns, either. The Germans mowed the British down in their thousands; the British lost 60,000 casualties on the first day alone. The battle dragged on until the autumn, but at the end of it the allies had merely advanced their front line a few miles. Like the French at Verdun, the Somme left the British exhausted and shocked, and not much further forward than they were at the start.

Crimes of war

When the Germans invaded Belgium, all sorts of stories circulated in the allied press about German soldiers raping women, bayoneting babies, and murdering priests and nuns. The worst stories were almost certainly made up or else blown out of all proportion, but we now know that the Germans did indeed carry out atrocities in Belgium. The Germans were convinced – wrongly – that a Belgian civilian resistance movement was shooting German soldiers in the back. The Germans did shoot and deport civilians, and they burned down villages and even the library of the University of Leuven. The soldiers said that they acted in self-defence; the Belgians, who had shown themselves capable of the same atrocities in the Congo, remembered the German actions rather differently.

Death in the mud

In 1917 the new French commander, General Nivelle, came up with another plan to smash through the German lines and be in Berlin by Christmas. When this plan came to grief like all the others, the French soldiers decided that they'd had enough – they would defend their trenches, but they weren't taking part in any more stupid attacks. The French soldiers were being sent forward like lambs to the slaughterhouse; one body of troops even went into battle baa-ing like sheep, which shows that whatever else they were losing, the French hadn't lost their sense of sarcasm. So, the British were the ones who launched the year's big attack, near the little Belgian village of Passchendaele.

Passchendaele became a nightmare because a mixture of heavy shelling and torrential rain turned the battlefield into a quagmire. In this battle you made sure that you didn't fall into the liquid mud because men drowned in it; the Germans also used mustard gas in this attack, which doesn't just choke your lungs but can penetrate clothing. The Canadians did actually capture the village of Passchendaele, or what was left of it, resulting in a small bump in the allied front line, which the Germans could then shell from three sides – and they did.

Coming Full Circle: Serbia and Salonika

By September 1915, the Germans, Austrians, and Bulgarians were licking their lips and closing in on Serbia for the kill.

The British and French sent an army to Salonika in Greece, which was cheeky of them because Greece was neutral. King Constantine of Greece, who was Kaiser Wilhelm's brother-in-law, kept telling them to clear off, but they took no notice. Unfortunately, the Austrians, Germans, and Bulgarians then invaded Serbia, and the whole Serb army had to escape by sea, which rather defeated the purpose of going to Salonika in the first place. Then the allied forces started dying of dysentery and malaria. Eventually the allied forces in Salonika did manage to defeat Bulgaria and knock her out of the war – so maybe the effort was worthwhile.

Italy Finally Joins In

The Italians were allied to Germany and Austria-Hungary but they got a better offer (mainly of land after the war) from the British and French, so in 1915 Italy declared war on her allies and declared herself allied to her enemies.

Italy's change of allegiance didn't do her much good. The Italians spent two years advancing ten miles into Austrian territory, and then at the 1917 *Battle of Caporetto* the Austrians and Germans cleared them out and sent them running for home. The Italians did win an important battle at Vittorio Veneto right at the end of the war, though they had a lot of British and French help, and the Austrians were surrendering anyway.

War with the Turks

Winning at Gallipoli wasn't a fluke for the Turks (see the earlier section 'Winston's winning wheeze' for more on this campaign); in 1915 they trapped a British and Indian force at Kut-el-Amara in Mesopotamia, as Iraq was known in those days (though the British soldiers just called it Mess Pot, which turned out to be about right). In the end the British had to surrender, and thousands of prisoners died in Turkish hands.

What happened in Armenia was even worse. Armenian troops helped in a successful Russian attack in the Caucasus, and started killing Turks. The Turks decided to take a terrible revenge; they ordered the entire Armenian population to be deported, and some 700,000 of them died of starvation and thirst when the Turks force-marched them through the desert.

The Turkish government and some Turkish historians vigorously deny that what happened to the Armenians was an attempt at genocide, though the overwhelming weight of opinion among historians in the rest of the world is that, that is exactly what happened.

The British carried on fighting the Turks, in Mesopotamia and in Palestine. In 1916 the Arabs rose up in revolt against the Turks under Sheikh Hussein of Mecca and the famous British officer T. E. Lawrence – 'Lawrence of Arabia'. Lawrence was good at blowing up trains and inspiring revolts but a bit naive in politics. Lawrence genuinely thought that the British and French would let the Arabs set up independent states after the war, and as long as the Arabs needed to think that in order to fight against the Turks, that's what the British and French let them think.

War at Sea

After all that fuss before the war about building battleships (see the earlier section 'In the navy' about Dreadnoughts) , when the war actually came submarines were what proved crucial. The British used their fleet to blockade Germany's ports, which caused terrible hunger and hardship by 1918. The Germans tried to do the same back, using U-boats. In 1915 the Germans sank the British passenger liner *Lusitania*, which had sailed from New York with a number of American passengers. Americans were appalled; but they didn't know that the *Lusitania* was secretly carrying weapons for Britain.

The big showdown came in 1916, when the British and German fleets met up off the Danish coast at Jutland. The British forced the Germans to turn back, but when the battle began the British found, to their horror, that their ships had an unfortunate tendency to blow up. Obviously the British couldn't take the ships back to the shop and demand their money back, so the Germans managed to slip away back to port. Jutland proved a very bad day for the British, though it shook the Germans, too. The Germans kept their fleet in harbour from then on, and when the order finally did come to sail out and fight one last battle, right at the end when the war was clearly lost, the German sailors refused to budge.

You Win Some, You Lose Some (Allies, That Is)

In April 1917 the United States declared war on Germany and her allies. The Americans had had it up to here with German U-boats sinking American cargo ships, and now the German government was engaged in some crazy plot with Mexico to invade Texas. Enough already! said US President Woodrow Wilson (though not in so many words – he was too well spoken) and declared war.

In February 1917 the Russians rose in revolution and overturned the tsar. (You can find the full details of all these events in Chapter 21.) To the relief of Russia's allies, the new Russian government stayed in the war and even launched a massive attack (which failed). In October 1917 the Russians had a *second* revolution. Russia's new leaders were Lenin and the Bolsheviks, and their line was simple: Make peace at any cost – so they did. In March 1918 Russia signed the Treaty of Brest-Litovsk and pulled out of the war.

How It All Ended

The German High Command did some quick calculations and decided to make one last all-out attack in the spring of 1918, before the Americans started arriving in large numbers. In March 1918, the Germans stormed through the British lines on the old Somme battlefield (see the section 'Slaughter on the Somme' above) and raced towards Paris. But the German soldiers soon ran out of steam and started to retreat.

In August, the British launched a shattering tank attack, and American troops were now arriving in large numbers. The Germans started surrendering, also in large numbers; they wanted out of the war. The German generals told their government to start talking peace terms fast or the whole country would collapse.

Austria-Hungary literally did collapse. All its different nationalities, Czechs, Slovaks, Hungarians, Croats, Slovenes, and Poles, started declaring independence – even the German Austrians declared a republic. The Austrian Emperor Karl I was left with nothing to do but abdicate and get out fast.

Kaiser Wilhelm of Germany wasn't quite so sensible; he virtually had to be ordered to abdicate by Field Marshal Hindenburg and Admiral Scheer. Germany became a republic, and the new government, seeing that the Americans were offering very reasonable peace terms, decided to take them up. Germany signed an armistice and the shooting stopped at 11.00 on 11 November 1918.

Whose Fault Was the First World War?

Historians have spent ages arguing about who was to blame for the First World War. One popular British historian, called AJP Taylor, believed that the First World War was just one of those things that no one wants but still happen, like road accidents. In the 1960s a German historian called Fritz Fischer said that if you looked at what the Germans had actually been planning before 1914, it seemed as if they had indeed been intent on a major war in or around 1914, which was all part of a drive for world domination. They're all still arguing about it.

Make warfare history

None of the nations went into the war thinking that this conflict would end all wars, yet that was how everyone was describing the affair by the time the fighting ended. Partly this view was taken because the experience had been so terrible that people *hoped* that this war would be the last one ever. US President Wilson had grand plans for a League of Nations to solve the world's problems peacefully, so maybe the Great War would indeed prove to have been the war that ended war.

Dream on; the very peace settlement that Wilson and the other allied leaders were so busy negotiating in Paris was what would make another, even more terrible war virtually certain.

Chapter 21

Revolution in Russia

The Russian Revolution was one of the most important events in world history – it changed everything. For the first time, a country was going to try and completely remodel itself along the lines that Karl Marx had laid down (Chapter 17 tells you what those lines were). Communism was meant to bring in freedom and equality, yet Communist Russia was soon devastated by civil war and famine, and became a ruthless one-party dictatorship. This chapter reveals why.

A Tsar Is Born

Tsarist Russia was an *autocracy*. That meant that the tsar had complete authority to rule as he liked. Russia had no written constitution, no parliament, and no elections. The most Russia stretched to was a few elected local councils and a more or less fair system of justice that Tsar Alexander II had introduced (see Chapter 19 for more on the remarkable Alexander II). So when the tsar's grandson, little Prince Nicholas, was born in 1868 he was brought up to believe that one day he would be the all-powerful tsar of all the Russias, just like his grandfather. And then Tsar Alexander II was blown up by a bomb.

Nicholas's father now became Tsar Alexander III, and in the new tsar's view, Alexander II had paid the price for being too soft. To Alexander III, the Russian people were like cattle: docile enough if you treated them firmly, but very dangerous if you didn't. (This wasn't such a strange idea: Russian land was actually *measured* in people – 'souls' as they were called – rather as you might describe a field or a farm by how many head of cattle it had.) So Alexander III immediately applied the brakes; freedom of the press was denied, only the right sort of people were allowed to vote in the local elections, and a tough new secret police force was introduced to keep an eye on everyone – the *Okhrana*.

Let's lynch the usual suspects

The tsar was supposed to be God's representative on earth, so murdering Alexander II seemed like declaring war on God. The Russians looked round for someone to blame, and picked on Russia's Jews.

No evidence shows that the assassination of Alexander II was a Jewish conspiracy. But then, anti-Jewish hysteria seldom worries about such things as evidence.

The Russians started organising attacks, known as *pogroms,* on the Jewish communities in towns and villages – not just a bit of stone-throwing and name-calling, but properly co-ordinated attacks, burning homes, rounding people up and lynching them. The police sat back and watched, or else charged in to beat up any Jewish people who dared to defend themselves.

Many Russian Jews decided to clear out while they still could, packed their bags and headed for America, which, of course, suited the other Russians just fine. If you've ever seen the film *Fiddler on the Roof* and wondered what that was all about, well, now you know.

Full steam ahead

Alexander III might not have liked modern ideas, but he wasn't blind; he knew that Russia had to industrialise fast or it would go under. Thanks to his finance minister, Sergei Witte, who poured state money into industrial enterprises, in the space of the 1890s Russia changed from being a backward, peasant country, to being one of the fastest-growing economies in the world. The only trouble was that the industry was concentrated in just two cities: Moscow and St Petersburg.

Russian workers by 1900 were living and working in some of the worst conditions in Europe: long shifts, overcrowding, and an industrial accident rate to make your hair stand on end. These conditions were very interesting if you were in one of the groups campaigning for change in Russia:

- ✔ **Liberals:** (Also known as Constitutional Democrats or CDs, which comes out as *Kadets* in Russian.) They wanted a democratic constitution with an elected parliament, political parties, and all the rest of it.

- ✔ **Social Revolutionaries (SRs):** The political wing of the *People's Will*, the terrorist group who had blown up Alexander II. The SRs could never agree among themselves, but they knew two things: one, power in Russia lay with the peasants, if you could only get them to realise it, and two, terrorism works.

➤ **Social Democrats:** These were the Marxists. This group all agreed that change in Russia had to come from the industrial workers in Moscow and St Petersburg. There was only one problem: Marx had specifically said that a country had to be fully industrialised before you could pass on to the workers' revolution. But Russia wasn't fully industrialised. So should the Social Democrats be working for revolution at all?

Losing is the new winning

In 1903, the Social Democrats met in London. The big debate at the meeting was over whether anyone could join the Social Democratic Party, or whether the party ought to be more of an exclusive private club. The vote was 28 to 23 in favour of Yuli Martov, who thought that the party should be open to anyone.

Leader of the losers was Vladimir Ilyich Ulyanov, now going by the code name Lenin. Lenin was all in favour of power to the workers, but he didn't want them actually running things; he wanted to keep power in the hands of a small elite group of people.

Lenin never let a little thing like a democratic vote change his mind. When a group of seven members walked out in a huff about a completely different issue, leaving Martov with 21 supporters and Lenin with 23, Lenin renamed his followers the Majority Party, *Bolshevik* in Russian, and he called the others the Minority Party, *Menshevik*. In fact, the Bolsheviks were almost never in a majority, but what did that matter? Lenin's party had the *name*. (Imagine getting up and saying 'Vote for us! We're the Minority Party!' Well, quite.)

Lenin argued that Russia was a special case because the country was so big – so it should have a workers' revolution even though most of the country was still farmed by peasants. Lenin called this theory *Marxism-Leninism*. (You could try this idea yourself: It is right that normally I should share this cake, but I am a special case because I am so big. I call my theory *Findism-Keepism*.)

While Alexander III's Okhrana was on their tail (see the section 'A Tsar is Born', earlier in this chapter, for more on the tsarist secret police), these groups were either doing time in prison, in hiding or in exile. But then in 1894, Alexander III died and his son became Tsar Nicholas II. Nicholas said that he would carry on ruling exactly as his father had, but he was far too nice to rule properly (kings who get overturned usually are). Nicholas was a devoted family man, and he loved animals – it's sounding bad already, isn't it?

A Little War . . .

In 1904 the Russian government decided to go to war with Japan.

The quarrel was all about who should control Manchuria and Korea; the Japanese thought they should, and the Russians, who hadn't just built the Trans-Siberian Railway from Moscow to Vladivostok for nothing, rather thought *they* should. In January 1904, the Japanese attacked the Russian base of Port Arthur in Korea, and the *Russo–Japanese War* was on.

Some historians think that the Russo–Japanese War was all a clever plot by the hard-line Russian interior minister, von Plehve, to give the Russians something to take their minds off their troubles at home. We'll never know because the Social Revolutionaries blew him up.

The Russo–Japanese War did not go *quite* as the Russians had planned:

- ✔ **January 1904:** Japanese trap a huge Russian army inside Port Arthur, sink some Russian ships, and keep the rest cooped up in harbour.

- ✔ **October 1904:** Russians send their Baltic fleet round to the other side of the world. On the way, the Russians encounter the Hull fishing fleet, which they immediately assume to be Japanese torpedo boats (very common in Hull, as you no doubt know). Russians open fire, sink a trawler, kill two seamen, and cause a major international incident with Britain.

- ✔ **December 1904:** Port Arthur surrenders to the Japanese.

- ✔ **February 1905:** Japanese run rings round Russians at the Battle of Mukden. Russians think, 'Just you wait till the Baltic fleet gets here.'

- ✔ **May 1905:** Russian Baltic fleet arrives and Japanese immediately sink it at the Battle of Tsushima. Noisy celebrations heard in Hull.

The outcome of this war did not help the mood in Russia, which only needed one more disaster to spill over into revolution. So, on 9 January 1905, Nicholas II provided them with one more disaster – a really big one.

Sunday, Bloody Sunday

The trouble started with a massive strike in St Petersburg at the end of 1904; just about every worker in the city was out on the streets demanding food and a better way of life. Then a radical priest, called Father Gapon, had an idea.

Gapon was a firm believer in the tsar, and he didn't want the workers to start listening to the socialists. So Gapon suggested a huge march, all very respectable, lots of hymns and icons, to go and see the tsar, or the 'Little Father' as people used to call him. When once Nicholas II knew how bad things were, said Father Gapon, he would be bound to do something.

So the workers all got ready on the morning of 9 January, put on their Sunday best – women and children, too – and went off to see the tsar. Nicholas wasn't at home, but Father Gapon was right; the tsar, or at least his men, did do something. The guards opened fire, straight into the crowd. By the end of the day, 200 people were dead, and some 800 wounded. Those marchers weren't the only ones who died that day; the people's faith in their Little Father died, too.

This is a revolution, isn't it?

The incident on 9 January started things moving. More and more workers came out on strike, including on the railways, which virtually paralysed the country. The workers set up a big elected council in Petrograd, called the *Petrograd Soviet*, to run the strike, and soon soviets were set up in other cities as well.

The Petrograd Soviet wasn't just a strike committee; the council became a sort of alternative government. The Petrograd Soviet was run by the Mensheviks, led by Leon Trotsky (you can find out about the Mensheviks in the earlier section 'Losing is the new winning').

The peasants were joining in the protest, too. The poor were still paying those redemption payments that had come in when serfdom was abolished (Chapter 19 explains those), and they'd had enough of this state of affairs. So the peasants grabbed a pitchfork and went out to trash every noble or land-lord's house they could find. Doing so didn't get the payments cut, but the peasants felt a lot better afterwards.

Just to add to the fun, Russia's other nationalities, the Finns, Balts, Georgians, Ukrainians, and Poles, all started demanding self-rule as well – and got it, in some cases. 'If things go on like this, we'll have a revolution on our hands,' Nicholas told his ministers. 'Er, this *is* a revolution, sire,' they replied.

Battleship Potemkin

In 1905 mutiny broke out on the battleship *Potemkin* stationed at Odessa on the Black Sea. The incident started when the captain had one of the men shot for complaining about the food, the crew rose up, shot the officers, and headed into port to try to start a revolution.

Lots of people gathered to see what was going on, but then Cossack soldiers appeared and started shooting into the crowd – which was becoming quite a habit in Russia. Some 2,000 people were killed, and the *Potemkin*'s crew had to seek asylum in Romania.

Sergei Eisenstein made an epic film about this incident, which includes the famous sequence where the Cossacks gun down the crowd on the Odessa steps, though in reality the mutiny wasn't quite such a big event as the film suggests. Still, this event says something about Russia in 1905, where you could kill 2,000 people and wound 3,000 more and no one thought that this kind of mindless massacre was that big a deal.

Oh, all right, then, you can have a parliament

In response to the revolution, first Nicholas tried playing stern and inflexible, and then he tried offering a special parliament that could make suggestions that he might possibly listen to if he had nothing better to do and which was to be elected by two men and a very right-wing dog. Not good enough.

Eventually, in October 1905, Nicholas saw sense and announced that a properly elected parliament would be established, called a *Duma*. Everyone breathed a sigh of relief.

Just don't call it a constitution

The rules for this new Duma (or parliament) were called the *Fundamental Laws*. These laws were a constitution really, but Nicholas didn't want to call them that in case people got the idea that Russia was no longer an autocracy. The Fundamental Laws said that the Duma has full, unlimited powers to pass all the laws in Russia; but, except that:

- The tsar could veto any law
- The tsar could dissolve the Duma whenever he likes and rule on his own
- The tsar could appoint his chums as ministers
- The tsar could make alliances, go to war, and order the armed forces around entirely as he likes

As you can see, Russia was not exactly a fully democratic constitutional monarchy.

Setting up the Duma did not exactly usher in a period of stability and peace:

- ✔ **1906: First Duma meets.** Starts demanding a proper constitutional monarchy, so Nicholas dissolves this Duma and appoints a tough new prime minister called Peter Stolypin.

  Stolypin had thousands of critics of the government arrested and hanged. Latest sardonic joke in Russia: The hangman's noose is 'Stolypin's necktie'.

- ✔ **February 1907: Second Duma elected.** Calls for all land in Russia to be nationalised. Nicholas and Stolypin close it down. Nicholas thinks, 'This constitutional monarchy business is easier than I thought.'

  Stolypin then rigs the electoral system to give more votes to the rich.

- ✔ **November 1907: Third Duma elected.** This parliament is quiet and conservative and will do whatever it is told. Surprised?

- ✔ **1911: Stolypin is assassinated.** Surprised?

Ra-Ra Rasputin

Gregory Rasputin was a most unorthodox Orthodox monk, whose personal philosophy was that in order to gain of forgiveness you should give God more things to forgive. In Rasputin's case, this philosophy meant throwing himself into all-night orgies of sex and drink and then feeling rather sorry for his actions in the morning, which sounds like ordinary student life to me.

Rasputin had a reputation as a faith healer, which is why the Tsarina Alexandra summoned him to the palace to see to her son, the little Prince Alexis, who was haemophiliac and subject to violent fits. Rasputin was the only one who could calm him down and stop the internal bleeding – we still don't really know how he mastered this control. The tsarina was overjoyed, and invited Rasputin back to the palace many times. The whole imperial family fell under his spell, including Nicholas, who wouldn't hear a word against 'Our Friend' and even listened to his advice about ministerial appointments.

Eventually, a group of dissolute young Russian aristocrats led by Prince Felix Yusoupoff, invited Rasputin round for a bite to eat and poisoned the cake, but to their horror, Rasputin ate it all up and asked for seconds. Then Felix's gang tried shooting him and whipping him with chains and eventually managed to throw him in the icy river. And all the time they were trying to murder Rasputin, these young aristocratic assassins played ragtime music on a gramophone. And you think the fights in *James Bond* look contrived.

Rasputin wasn't the reason the Russian revolution happened, but he was a very good example of why the revolution *needed* to happen.

Russia Goes to War and Gets a Revolution

In 1914, Nicholas II went to war with Germany and Austria-Hungary. After a promising start (you can read all about it in Chapter 20), the war began to go disastrously wrong. Nicholas announced that he was taking personal charge of the army as Commander-in-Chief, which was all very noble of him, but just meant that from now on the buck for everything that went wrong – not just military defeats, but simple things like the men having to fight without sufficient food or equipment – stopped firmly at his personal door.

By 1916 troops were deserting en masse, and the commanders found that stopping them was impossible. In February 1917, strikes and riots broke out in Petrograd (they'd re-named St Petersburg to make it sound less German) and Nicholas sent a message to the local commanders to stop the disturbances in the capital. Nicholas's intervention was too late. This was revolution, and this time the people wanted him out.

A very provisional government

Nicholas II agreed to abdicate and hand over power to a committee of members of the Duma, who would look after things until they were able to hold proper elections and draw up a constitution; that's why this committee was called the *provisional government*. Everyone thought that from now on they would all have enough to eat and life would be sweetness and light. Then reality set in:

- ✔ **Problem 1: Who is in charge around here?** The provisional government was very middle and upper class; its leader was a nobleman called Prince Lvov. The workers started electing their own councils – 'soviets'. The Petrograd soviet met in the same building as the provisional government and even started issuing orders to the army. Not surprisingly, the provisional government got rather fed up with this, and wanted to know just who was in charge of Russia. So did everyone else.

- ✔ **Problem 2: Peace or war?** Most Russians just wanted peace, but the provisional government reckoned that with their new revolutionary zeal the Russians could overwhelm the Germans and Austrians, march into Berlin and Vienna, and then they could have the mother of all victory parties back in Petrograd. That was the plan, at any rate.

Hi, Comrades, I'm home!

Lenin was still cooling his heels in Zurich when he heard the news that revolution had broken out in Russia. Lenin travelled back thanks to a secret deal with the Germans and arrived at Petrograd's Finland Station in April 1917. Lenin got off the train and immediately made a speech. 'Don't faff around with the provisional government!' he declared, 'All power to the soviets!' Then Lenin issued a sort of Bolshevik manifesto, which said that if they were in power, they would give people bread, land, and, above all, peace.

Some people liked what Lenin said, but many were suspicious and thought that he was a German spy – after all, the Germans had smuggled him into the country. In any case, the country had only just set the provisional government up and wanted to give this arrangement a chance to show what it could do – which actually turned out to be not very much.

So much for Plan A

The man in charge of the plan to win the war was the ambitious new minister for war in the provisional government, Alexander Kerensky. Kerensky fancied himself as a new Napoleon, especially when he became prime minister in July 1917 and launched the long-awaited Kerensky Offensive.

The Russians advanced a bit – those who hadn't already headed for home, that is – found an abandoned store of booze and decided to give the war a rest and get paralytically drunk instead. Then, the Germans moved in for the kill. Kerensky's offensive cost about 400,000 Russian lives.

After the failure of the Kerensky Offensive, the Russian troops wanted nothing more to do with the war. The men were only going to support someone who promised to make peace, and that meant the Bolsheviks.

What this country needs is a spot of discipline

One man decided that the time had come to restore a bit of order and discipline: General Kornilov, a Russian general of the old thrash-'em-and-flog-'em school. Kornilov decided to march on Petrograd, turf out the provisional government, and take charge. The general nearly managed to take control – but the Bolsheviks saved the day by forming armed units called *Red Guards*, and inundating Kornilov's men with propaganda telling them not to overturn the revolution. When Kornilov gave the order to charge he looked round and found the soldiers had all gone. When the general had finished shouting and spluttering the Bolsheviks took him away and put him under house arrest.

Lenin decided the time had come for the Bolsheviks to take power themselves.

Red October

Lenin and the Bolsheviks had taken over a rather posh ladies' college called the Smolny Institute as their headquarters for planning their coup – Russia's second revolution in a year. The Menshevik leader, Trotsky, who had been heading up the Petrograd soviet, came and joined the Bolsheviks, and did most of the detailed planning for the attack on the Winter Palace, the tsar's old riverside home where the provisional government was meeting. The idea was to start with a red signal lamp and a great salvo of artillery, but they couldn't find a lamp and the cannons missed. The Bolsheviks did manage to fire a blank shell from the cruiser *Aurora* (which means 'dawn' very appropriately).

Paintings and films of the October Revolution show huge crowds climbing the gates and fierce gun battles in the corridors, but in fact there wasn't much fighting, mainly because most of the provisional government's men had gone off to get a bite to eat. Kerensky had slipped away, but the Bolsheviks found the other ministers and arrested them all. And that was that; the Bolsheviks were in charge.

The two revolutions of 1917 are known as the February and October Revolutions because that was when they happened according to the old Julian calendar Russia was using at the time. Later, when Russia switched to the Gregorian calendar, the dates of the two revolutions fell in March and November. Some history books call them that, but most stick to the old dating: February and October.

Handbags away and fix bayonets

The troops most fiercely loyal to the provisional government – in fact, by the end, just about the only troops loyal to the provisional government – were the Women's Battalion of Death, a group of women volunteers who had seen enough of men deserting from the front and wanted to show them what women could do. These women were fierce fighters, and Kerensky thought that seeing them would help inspire the men to fight more ferociously. Unfortunately, the men reasoned that if the government was relying on women to fight for them, things must be even worse than they first thought. The women shaved their heads in order to look like men, which gives the rather surreal impression that the provisional government was being defended by Sinead O'Connor.

We'll Have None of That Democracy Nonsense Here

The provisional government had arranged for elections to a special parliament to draw up a constitution for Russia, a Constituent Assembly. Lenin wasn't very keen to let these elections go ahead because he reckoned that the Bolsheviks would lose – he was right, too. But the other Bolsheviks thought that they couldn't start off by *cancelling* elections, so Russia went to the polls and elected a Constituent Assembly.

Sure enough, the biggest party by far was the Social Revolutionaries, who didn't see why an upstart little group like the Bolsheviks should think that it had the right to run the country. But when the Assembly gathered, Lenin filled the place with armed men, turned the members out of the building, and closed the assembly down. 'We will now proceed,' he said, 'to construct the socialist order.' Which meant: Hold tight, this is going to get bumpy.

Peace at any price

Lenin immediately sent Trotsky to negotiate terms with the German high command. Trotsky spun the Germans out for months with highly intellectual arguments – 'When you say "Germany" do you mean the essential concept of "Germany-ness" in the fullest sense of the word' – until the Germans reckoned, rightly, that he was padding things out until the Germans staged their own revolution. So the German high command said that if Trotsky didn't sign a treaty the war was on again. Lenin was worried that the Germans might reach Petrograd and restore the tsar, so he told Trotsky to sign.

By the terms of the *Treaty of Brest-Litovsk* Russia gave up a vast area of land, including Finland, Poland, Ukraine, the Baltic states, Belorus, and the whole Caucasus region. Lenin said that losing this land didn't matter; the important thing was to stop the war.

This means (civil) war!

Lenin and the Bolsheviks had many enemies, known as the Whites (the Bolsheviks were the Reds) and by 1919 they were all gathering their forces. For the next three years Russia was plunged into a terrible civil war, with famine and the most appalling atrocities.

In the white corner . . .

. . . were a number of different groups with very different aims:

- ✔ **Different commanders, with their own different ways of doing things:** *Admiral Kolchak* (the others agreed that he could be in charge), *General Denikin*, and down in the south *Baron Wrangel*.

- ✔ **British, French, American, and Japanese forces:** All helping to overturn the Bolsheviks and wondering why.

- ✔ **The Social Revolutionaries:** They hated the Bolsheviks for what they did to the Constituent Assembly. An SR called Fanny Kaplan shot Lenin and nearly killed him.

- ✔ **The Greens:** Russian peasants who attacked soldiers on both sides.

- ✔ **The Czech Legion:** A group of Czech soldiers who were trying to head home to an independent Czechoslovakia via the Far East and the United States. They got into quarrels with the Bolsheviks, and had to shoot their way out – which they were rather good at.

- ✔ **The Nationalities:** Meaning the Finns, Poles, Estonians, Lithuanians, Latvians, Ukrainians, Georgians, and all the other non-Russian people of the Russian Empire, who seized this golden opportunity to declare their independence from Russia.

In the red corner . . .

Against the groups listed in the preceding section, the Bolsheviks had the Red Army, made up of thousands of soldiers and sailors but not many officers to lead them (the Whites had no shortage of officers, but not so many men for them to lead). Their commander, Trotsky, was an intellectual, with no military experience whatsoever, but he turned out to be a formidable commander.

The secret of the Reds' success was the creation of *commissars*, political officers attached to every unit, to make sure that everyone knew what they were fighting for and to keep an eye on – and shoot, if necessary – anyone who showed any sign of slacking or changing sides, including the officers. Most Red Army men were far more scared of their commissars than they were of the enemy – which, of course, was the whole idea.

Reds against Whites

Initially the Whites looked as if they would easily win the civil war; but the Whites couldn't agree among themselves, and quickly alienated the ordinary people in the areas they took over. The allies began to withdraw. By 1921, the only White force left in the field was Baron Wrangel's Cossacks down in the south. The Whites had to evacuate by sea, and the civil war was over.

The end of the tsar

The tsar and his family were being held in a large house near Ekaterinburg, where the local Bolsheviks were keen to shoot them. The Czechs were closing in on Ekaterinburg, and Lenin was worried in case they rescued Nicholas and used him to rally support against the Bolsheviks. Lenin gave the go-ahead, and on the night of 16 July 1918, the whole imperial family, and their servants, were gathered together in the cellar of the house and shot.

For many years afterwards people believed that Princess Anastasia had somehow escaped the massacre and made her way to the West. We now know that the American wasn't the Russian princess; the bones have been found and DNA-tested – Anastasia died in the massacre like all the rest of her family.

I say, which end of this spade does one use?

The Bolsheviks introduced strict communist principles right from the start. Under a system called *War Communism*, all industry, banking, and business was taken out of private hands and private property was abolished.

If you've seen the film *Doctor Zhivago* you'll know that the big houses of the rich were opened up to poor families, and the rich – rapidly becoming the former rich – had to do menial work for a living. But what Russia needed wasn't titled road sweepers, they needed food – and getting that meant taking a very tough line with the peasants.

War Against the Peasants

The Bolsheviks never liked or trusted Russia's peasants. They didn't believe the peasants were or ever could be a revolutionary class.

Lenin created a special secret police service, the *Cheka* (from its Russian initials, which sound like Che-Ka), under his old Polish comrade, Felix Dzerzhinsky. Dzerzhinsky set up mounted Cheka patrols with orders to go into the countryside and confiscate any food they found. The peasants retaliated by destroying their crops, or killing their livestock and poisoning the carcasses. Then the Cheka went rounding people up and shooting them, either to make others tell them where the food was hidden, or as a reprisal for food that had been destroyed. What food the Cheka did find, they took off to the cities, so the peasants weren't able to plant food for the following year.

Food was short in the towns, but in the countryside the people were faced with famine. Historians estimate that some *five million* people starved to death in the famine of the civil war years in Russia. Cases of peasants who resorted to cannibalism were reported.

The Bolsheviks hushed up details of the famine (except the cannibalism, which they used to discredit the peasants). This cover-up worked; most people have never even heard of the event.

The most important protest against the cruelty of War Communism came from the sailors of the Kronstadt naval base in Petrograd. In 1921 they called for an end to food requisitioning and to the Cheka's campaign against the peasants. The government's response was ruthless. Trotsky personally ordered the Red Army to storm the naval base. The rising was crushed and the leaders were executed.

Would You Buy a Used Economic Policy from This Man?

After years of revolution and civil war, famine was rife in the countryside, the population in the cities had fallen dramatically, and the Russian rouble was virtually worthless.

In response to these problems, Lenin got up and announced a *New Economic Policy (NEP)*. The NEP said that peasants and small businesses could go back to operating privately, for profit – which, as some rather shocked comrades pointed out, is what is normally known as, er, capitalism. But Lenin insisted on this policy, with the result that: (a) Russia was soon full of flash characters called *nepmen* offering you a special deal, guv', just for you, I'm robbing meself, really I am; and (b) food began to reappear in the shops.

In 1922, Lenin had a series of strokes, and it was clear that he wasn't going to be around for much longer. The Bolsheviks all sent Get Well cards and made feverish plans to take over once he was dead. Everyone assumed that Trotsky would be taking over when Lenin died, but the Party General Secretary, Joseph Stalin, had other ideas. When Lenin finally died, on 24 January 1924, the stage was set for a spectacular, and very bloody, power struggle.

Chapter 22

Europe Goes to Extremes

· ·

In This Chapter

▶ Examining the Treaty of Versailles

▶ Introducing Mussolini and fascist Italy

▶ Understanding Hitler's Germany and Stalin's Russia

▶ Investigating the Spanish Civil War and the Munich Crisis

· ·

*A*fter the First World War, everyone thought that the world was entering a new era of peace and prosperity. The economic slump of the 1930s knocked those dreams on the head; unemployment and soup kitchens seemed set to be on the scene for the foreseeable future. Many people in Europe gave up on the traditional political parties and turned towards some of the new, dynamic extremist political groups, such as the communists, who were busy building up the Soviet Union, Hitler's national socialists, or Mussolini's futuristic fascists.

The Yank Is Coming – and So Are His Fourteen Points

By 1919 the European powers were broken and exhausted; the Russian, German, and Austro-Hungarian Empires had all collapsed, and the Turkish Empire seemed about to follow them. The war seemed to everyone a product of the old European way of doing things: Secret diplomacy, and upper-class politicians and generals sending the ordinary people of Europe to their deaths. Europe needed someone fresh with big new ideas – US President Woodrow Wilson.

League of Nations – fine in theory

When Wilson first proposed the idea the League seemed to hold out real hope for the future; especially among ordinary people. As well as its grand headquarters in Geneva, the League had local branches where people were able to discuss world events and promote the idea of world peace through world unity, known as *Collective Security*. The idea was that creating a peaceful world was everyone's responsibility, not just the responsibility of politicians and statesmen.

The League of Nations established some fundamental principles of international law and reforms in areas such as support for refugees, famine relief, safety at work, and safety at sea which have lasted to the present day. But the League was based on the idea that all reasonable people want peace; it couldn't cope with the unreasonable people who preferred war.

Wilson was a Democrat, and a history professor with a firm and abiding belief in the problem-solving capacity of Woodrow Wilson. Wilson thought that if you redrew the map of Europe along lines of *national self-determination*, the people would have nothing to go to war about. Wilson put his ideas down in his famous *Fourteen Points*, in January 1918. Europe's frontiers were to be completely redrawn along national lines, freedom of navigation at sea was to be introduced, and instead of lots of alliances there was to be a special organisation called the *League of Nations*, which would settle any problems between states.

Not Very Blessed Peacemakers: The Paris Peace Conference

The Paris Peace Conference of 1919 began to go wrong right from the start. Holding the event in Paris wasn't such a good idea; doing so meant that the French chaired the meetings, and they were just itching for revenge on the Germans.

Most of the business was conducted by the 'Big Three', President Wilson, the French Prime Minister Georges Clemenceau, and the British Prime Minister David Lloyd George. Wilson said that he wanted to create 'a just and lasting peace'. That ideal was always going to be a little bit difficult:

 ✔ The French wanted to crush Germany so she could never threaten her again.

 ✔ The Poles were demanding a huge area of eastern Europe, including all of Ukraine.

- The Romanians, Czechs and Yugoslavs were all demanding land from Hungary and threatening violence if they didn't get it.

- The Hungarians were in the middle of a communist revolution and wondering if anyone was going to recognise their new government (no one did).

- The Serbs, Romanians, and Greeks were all demanding big chunks of Bulgaria.

- The Italians were demanding big chunks of Yugoslavia.

- No one seemed very interested in President Wilson's League of Nations.

Eventually, the Big Three (Wilson, Clemenceau, and Lloyd George) agreed on a new map of Europe. This map looked very different from the old one because a lot of new states were now where the old Austro-Hungarian Empire had been, such as Hungary, Czechoslovakia, and Yugoslavia. A huge new independent Poland also emerged, with a corridor to the sea which cut part of Germany – East Prussia – off from the rest of the country.

The dictated Treaty of Versailles

The allies presented their terms to the German delegation at the Paris Peace Conference of 1919 and told them that if they didn't sign, the war was on again. The signing was due to take place in Louis XIV's great Palace of Versailles on 28 June, the anniversary of the assassination in Sarajevo that had started the war in the first place (see Chapter 20 for details).

The Germans had trouble finding anyone who wanted to go and sign the treaty; in the end, they just sent the foreign minister and the minister for transport. The two Germans walked up the staircase flanked by the French guards so that the men felt as if they were prisoners. The men were shown into the great Hall of Mirrors, where Bismarck had proclaimed the German Empire back in 1871 (see Chapter 18 for more on Bismarck); the French were really rubbing their humiliation in. With great dignity, the two men signed the treaty, then sat quietly while the allied representatives signed and collected autographs.

When news of the treaty was announced, Berlin went into mourning. When you see what the Treaty of Versailles said, you'll see why:

- Germany will give Alsace and Lorraine back to France, and bits of land to Belgium, Denmark, Lithuania, and Czechoslovakia, and a huge area of land to Poland. Germany will hand the port of Danzigover to the League of Nations and Poland can have free use of the docks. No you can't have it at weekends.

- Germany will hand over the Saaraland, on the border with France, to the League of Nations (which meant, in effect that the French would run it). No German troops will pass west of the River Rhine. Ever.

- ✔ The German army is to be no bigger than 100,000 men (which is tiny, believe me), with no tanks, poison gas, or aeroplanes; the navy is to have no ships that won't fit into hand baggage and no, repeat, no submarines.

- ✔ Germany accepts that it was to blame for the whole war and is to pay *reparations,* either in cash or in industrial goods and materials, to France and Britain for all the cost of the war.

- ✔ All Germany's colonies in Africa and Asia are to be handed over to the League of Nations who will then give them to Britain and France to look after.

- ✔ Germany and Austria may not join together as one country. National self-determination is only for good countries who don't start horrible nasty wars.

- ✔ Germany accepts the League of Nations but is not allowed to join it.

The Germans were aghast at the terms of this treaty. They called the Treaty of Versailles a *Diktat*, a dictated peace, and longed for revenge.

Don't think you're getting away with it, either

Germany's allies had to sign similarly harsh treaties, giving up land to their neighbours, accepting limits on their armies and a whacking great bill for reparations. The Hungarians were so outraged by their treaty, the Treaty of Trianon (these treaties were all signed in rather nice French châteaux in the Paris suburbs) that they kept little samples of earth from all the provinces they had lost and hung them in the streets as a constant reminder of the allies' injustice.

ON THE ONE HAND

We woz robbed

One of the reasons that the Germans were so outraged by the Treaty of Versailles was because they just couldn't bring themselves to accept that they had lost the war. The Germans thought that because the allies hadn't actually crossed into Germany by the time the war ended, the result had somehow been a draw, but that they'd been 'stabbed in the back' by traitors in Berlin and – guess what's coming? – their Jewish friends.

This theory was very comforting (unless you were a socialist or Jewish, or both) and you can still find people who believe it to this day. But the theory isn't true. The German army wasn't stabbed in the back in 1918; it was beaten to its knees.

This Turkey's not for stuffing

The Turkish delegation travelled out to Sèvres, where the porcelain comes from, and signed a treaty that gave all their non-Turkish lands (like Palestine, Syria, Iraq, and Arabia) to the League of Nations (not, of course, to the Palestinians, Syrians, Iraqis, or Arabians), and gave Thrace and Smyrna to Greece.

The Ottoman government, what was left of it, signed the treaty, but then a group of tough Turkish army officers led by General Mustafa Kemal seized power, kicked out the sultan, and tore the treaty up.

Kemal set up his base at Ankara, deep in the Turkish heartland, and dared the Greeks in Smyrna to come out and grab some more Turkish land, if they were hard enough. The Greeks did dare, but Kemal beat them into a kebab, took back Smyrna, and even started talking about invading Thrace.

The British prime minister, Lloyd George, sent reinforcements to Chanak on the Dardanelles to keep them out. The allies thought they'd better do a deal with this tough-talking Turk. At Lausanne in Switzerland, they agreed that Turkey could keep Smyrna, and even that Greece should give the Turks the eastern half of Thrace. 'Result!' thought the Turks; the Greeks' thoughts were unrepeatable.

Mustafa Kemal declared Turkey a republic, and was elected president in 1923. The president changed his name to Kemal Atatürk, or 'Father of the Turks', and turned Turkey into a secular, western-style republic.

The League of (Some) Nations

In theory, the League of Nations would resolve all international disputes. This idea was called *Collective Security;* unfortunately, the idea turned out to be not very collective and anything but secure.

- Germany wasn't allowed to join as a punishment for having started the First World War, and the Soviet Union wasn't allowed to join as a punishment for being communist.
- The United States Senate was afraid of getting dragged into more overseas disputes, so it refused to join the League.
- The League could only back its decisions with economic sanctions, which might hurt but only in the long run.

The League managed to resolve a number of territorial disputes in its early days, but it soon hit problems.

- ✔ **1920:** Poles seize Vilna from the Lithuanians. When the League tells them to give it back the Poles come over all deaf and take no notice.

- ✔ **1923:** Lithuania seizes the German port of Memel and refuses to give it back.

  That same year, the Turks attack the Greeks in Smyrna and take no notice of the League of Nations; the French march into the Ruhr area of Germany and take no notice of the League of Nations; the Italians bombard the Greek island of Corfu and take no notice of the League of Nations.

You're probably beginning to see a pattern here.

The Italians: Fuming at Fiume

The Italians had been expecting great things from the peace conference, and were most put out when they didn't get them. The Italians particularly wanted the port of Fiume on the Adriatic, not because they needed it particularly – they already had the port of Trieste – but because they didn't want Yugoslavia to get it.

While the allies were still debating the issue, an eccentric old nationalist poet, called Gabriele d'Annunzio, got a group of men together and seized Fiume himself. The League took until 1921 to get him out of there, and even then, they gave most of the town to Italy.

I'm the leader!

Italy was deeply divided. The country didn't have a strong government, but it did have a growing communist party and a new party called the *fascists* led by an ex-socialist called Benito Mussolini.

By 1922, such serious street fighting was breaking out between the communists and the fascists – not just fist fights, but barricades and guns – that Italy seemed to be sliding into civil war. So, in October Mussolini decided to stage a spectacular *coup*. He called it the March on Rome.

In fact, Mussolini got on a train to Rome (with a return ticket in case it all went wrong), and asked the king very politely if he could be prime minister. Mussolini promised to clear up all the street fighting, which was a bit rich, seeing that he was behind most of it in the first place. The king said yes, and Mussolini promptly went out and proclaimed himself *Il Duce* – the Leader of Italy.

How to get away with murder

The socialist leader in the Italian parliament, Giacomo Matteotti, had a few things to say about Mussolini, and he said them so well that a group of fascists kidnapped and murdered him. Everyone thought that Mussolini had ordered the murder (and he probably had) but instead of resigning he came up with a rather ingenious argument:

- ✔ I didn't kill Matteotti, but
- ✔ I am morally responsible for his death, and therefore
- ✔ I should have full powers to ensure this sort of thing never happens again.

Incredibly, Mussolini got away with this audacious argument. Parliament gave him full powers, and fascist Italy became Europe's first *totalitarian dictatorship*.

All this, and the trains run on time, too

Mussolini wanted his fascist rule to transform Italy into a new, futuristic state, including:

- ✔ **A corporate state.** Mussolini banned trade unions; workers did whatever the bosses told them to.

- ✔ **Battle for Births.** Mussolini gave out special medals for mums and imposed a special tax on bachelors, to provide the soldiers of tomorrow.

- ✔ **Land reclamation.** Mussolini drained the malaria-infested Pontine marshes near Rome, which was one of the few engineering projects the Romans hadn't been able to achieve, and built lots of new houses there.

- ✔ **The Lateran Treaty.** Mussolini struck a deal whereby the Pope could have the Vatican City as his own little separate state, and in return the Church would stop denouncing the Italian state and tell people to support Mussolini.

- ✔ **Trains, planes, and automobiles.** Mussolini built smart new motorways, started building an air force so big, he said, that it would blot out the sun, and, as everyone knows, he made sure that the trains ran on time. (Actually only the tourist trains ran on time, but hey, it was a start.)

Is it a bird? Is it a plane? No, it's the Italian prime minister

Mussolini used every trick in the book to make himself appear a superman. The prime minister sat in a vast study, so you had to advance about 5 miles to meet him, and when you got there you sat in a low chair so he could tower over you.

Mussolini left the lights on in his study all night, to make it look as if he was working late for his people (whereas in fact he liked to turn in early). Italians learned a special catch phrase: 'Mussolini is always right!'

Above all, Mussolini liked to pose as a macho man of many parts, driving sports cars, riding horses, playing with a lion cub, playing the violin, and fathering a nice big family. He was forever stripping to the waist and showing off his pecs. Mussolini's idea was that a people was like a body: it needed exercise to be healthy. And the best sort of exercise was war.

Can We Play Dictators, Too?

Other countries were very impressed with Mussolini. By the 1930s, Portugal, Yugoslavia, Hungary, Austria, Poland, and Romania were all fascist-style dictatorships, and fascist movements existed in France, Belgium, Holland, Ireland, and Britain. Mussolini's biggest fan, however, was the new dictator of Germany, Adolf Hitler.

Germany's nightmare years

At the end of the First World War Germany fell apart. The kaiser fled and communists, monarchists, and militarists all started fighting for power. The street fighting in Berlin grew so dangerous that the new government decamped to the pleasant little spa town of Weimar, which is why the German republic between the wars is often known as the Weimar Republic.

The man with the unenviable job of trying to sort out all this mess was Friedrich Ebert, a socialist MP who now became the first ever president of Germany.

Ebert's first task was to restore order, but with what? The army was being cut right down, thanks to the Treaty of Versailles and in any case many soldiers hated the Weimar republic.

So did the Freikorps, gangs of ex-soldiers who were parading through the streets in their old uniforms, and often with their old weapons, looking for communists to beat up. The Freikorps murdered the Spartakist (communist) leaders, Karl Liebknecht and Rosa Luxemburg when they tried to launch a *coup*, or *putsch* to use the German term. Having a bit of order was all very well, but to maintain this order President Ebert had to rely on a homicidal bunch of former servicemen with fanatically right-wing views, which was slightly worrying.

Sure enough, next up was the Freikorps' turn to try to seize power. In 1920, a right-wing army doctor called Kapp got a group of *Freikorps* together and staged a *putsch*. Instead of defending the government, the army sat back to watch the fun, and Kapp was only stopped because the workers all came out on strike and brought the country to a standstill.

You dig 16 tons – and I'll take them home with me, thank you

The French were insisting on those reparations payments (see the earlier section 'The Treaty of Versailles: A dictated peace' for the low-down on this form of retribution). Normally, these payments took the form of a percentage of Germany's industrial production, especially coal. But Germany was having trouble feeding its own poor and unemployed, So in 1923, President Ebert asked the French for a breather. 'Aha!' said the French, 'so you're going back on your treaty obligations, are you?' and promptly sent the French army to take command of the Ruhr, the German industrial region.

The Germans were outraged by this French action. The government told the workers to go on strike and bring the Ruhr to a complete halt. The French tried to force them to go back to work, and the situation got very nasty, with shootings and killings. But even worse was to come.

For a fistful of dollars, you should get a cup of coffee

In 1923, with German industry at a standstill, the German mark collapsed. Inflation is one thing, but the mark was losing value by the hour. The Germans did the worst thing you can do in that situation: they printed more money, in bigger and bigger denominations – a million marks, a billion marks, a billion trillion zillion marks. The situation just got silly; you could stuff a suitcase full of banknotes, but the value of all this money would only buy you a cup of coffee or a tram fare. The country had gone mad.

Eventually, a new German chancellor, Gustav Stresemann, restored a bit of order; he called in all the old banknotes, issued proper ones, got the Ruhr back to work, kept the French sweet, and even negotiated a deal on reparations payments. Germans were able to breathe again, and even start having fun; if you've seen the film *Cabaret* you'll know the sort of fun they had.

Stresemann died in 1929 just before his great achievement in building up Germany's economy and international position came crashing down again. The American economy collapsed in the famous Wall Street Crash, and because America's money was keeping most of Europe going at that time, so did the European economy. All of Europe was hit, but Germany was hit worst of all. People had just about had enough of politicians, and they turned to a new party that promised to shake things up a bit: *the Nazis*.

Springtime for Hitler

Adolf Hitler didn't found the Nazi party, but he liked what he heard, signed up, and soon became the party leader.

In 1924 Hitler tried to launch a *putsch* from a beer hall in Munich, but the police and army stayed loyal to the government and the putsch failed. The Nazis were given a slap on the wrist by the courts and sent to very comfy cells in Landsberg Prison, where Hitler spent the time putting his ideas down in a turgid book called *Mein Kampf* ('My Struggle', which accurately describes the experience of anyone attempting to read it). Hitler promised that if ever he got to power he would

- tear up the Treaty of Versailles
- provide full employment
- get Germany 'living space'

'Living space' meant extra territory that the German people needed, though quite why they needed this territory Hitler never really explained. The Germans would get living space in Poland and Russia. The Poles and Russians, said Hitler, were *untermensch* – sub-humans. Hitler also loathed communism, so crushing Russia would very conveniently destroy communism's heartland. Hitler often said that communism was a Jewish plot to destroy western civilisation; however, he also said that capitalism was a Jewish plot to destroy western civilisation. These contradictory opinions show that Hitler didn't know much about Jews, capitalism, communism, or western civilisation.

Bad times for German Jews

Gradually, the Nazis made life increasingly difficult for Jews; they were sacked from universities and the civil service, and people began to shift their custom to non-Jewish shops or services. Children were taught to beware of Jews, and many towns and villages put up signs saying that Jews were unwelcome. The Nazis kept close tabs on people, so that they knew exactly who *was* Jewish: Jews had to take an extra name, Israel for men and Sara for women, and later they had to wear a large yellow star in public. Those brave souls who protested were beaten up or sent into concentration camps; not surprisingly most German Jews decided to obey the law and hope for the best.

In November 1938, the Nazis organised a mass attack on Jewish shops and businesses all over Germany. The party smashed so many shop windows that it became known as *Kristallnacht*, the night of broken glass. The Nazis were also secretly gassing mentally ill people, until the Catholic Church protested. The Nazis had learnt their lesson – not to refrain from gassing people, just to make sure that no one found out.

For most of the 1920s no one took much notice of the Nazis, but when the economy collapsed after 1929, increasing numbers of people turned to them. In 1932, the Nazis became the largest party in the Reichstag, and in January 1933 President Hindenburg, holding his nose (he was a field marshal, Hitler was a corporal), appointed Hitler chancellor.

Hitler immediately set about dismantling the Weimar Republic and pulling Germany out of the League of Nations. A young Dutch communist burned down the Reichstag building in March 1933; the Nazis said that this move was a communist plot to take power, and started arresting labour leaders or socialist MPs. In 1934 Hitler even massacred a whole group of his own Nazi supporters, who, he thought, were getting too dangerous. The situation sounds pretty grim, doesn't it?

But if you weren't a trade unionist or a socialist or a Jew or a gypsy or a homosexual or any of the other groups the Nazis disapproved of, you could have quite a good time in Nazi Germany. Free holidays were provided for the workers, and Hitler did get Germany back to something like full employment, by the simple task of rearming as fast as he could. For many Germans the 1930s became a golden period, when they were able to put the bad times behind them and look forward with confidence.

Whatever Happened to Leon Trotsky?

Before Lenin died in 1924 (see Chapter 21 for the full story of this Russian leader) he dictated a secret testament to his wife about who should take over after he'd gone. Everyone assumed that his successor would be his right-hand man Leon Trotsky, but Lenin said Trotsky was a bit arrogant. But Lenin really put the boot into the Communist Party general secretary, Josef Stalin: he said that Stalin was rude and ill-mannered, couldn't be trusted to use power properly.

You'd have thought that character testimonial would've stopped Stalin's career in its tracks, but Stalin put on his best behaviour and the other soviet leaders thought that maybe comrade Lenin had been a little harsh. The leaders didn't like Trotsky, and they were worried that he might use the Red Army to seize power for himself. Gradually Stalin gained the upper hand in the great struggle for power.

As general secretary, Stalin kept files on every party member – he was even nicknamed 'Comrade Card Index'. At the big party congresses that made all the important decisions, nearly all the delegates in the hall had been hand-picked by Stalin. Trotsky didn't stand a chance. Trotsky had to watch as his ideas were voted down and condemned, and in 1927, he was thrown out of the Communist Party and of the Soviet Union.

Stalin's Russia

Once he had got rid of Trotsky Stalin promptly stole Trotsky's ideas and said that Russia needed to modernise. All Russia's old-fashioned villages had to be replaced by large collective farms, getting their orders from the centre.

The official paintings of *collectivisation* showed happy peasants in sunny fields reading the latest cheery missive from Moscow, but the reality was very different. The peasants resisted in the only way they knew how – by holding back their food produce.

Stalin accused the peasants of being *kulaks* – rich peasants living very well thank you while everyone else starved – and said that he was going to eliminate them as a class. He just about did. The secret police, the NKVD (previously known as the Cheka; see Chapter 21) went round the villages, confiscating food and leaving the peasants to starve; some 15 million people died. And Stalin hadn't finished yet.

Stalin launched a series of *5-year plans* to build heavy industrial plants from scratch. Central planning, GOSPLAN, sent out ever-crazier quotas that factories had to fill; these quotas were impossible to comply with but death if you didn't, so people just lied about their production figures, or else bribed their way out of trouble. The result was that to this day no one really knows exactly how much Russia was producing in the 1930s.

But Russia was also a country living in fear. In 1934 Sergei Kirov, the popular party boss in Leningrad (formerly St Petersburg) was murdered, and Stalin responded by arresting many thousands of people. These arrests were called the *purges*, and no one was safe; even leading Bolsheviks were put on trial in Moscow on fantastical charges of treason. Stalin's assassins even murdered Trotsky, in exile in Mexico. You could be accused of anti-soviet activity for almost anything and sent to work in slave labour camps known as *gulags*. Historians still don't know exactly how many millions died during this period.

No Pasaran! Fascists versus Communists

In 1936 the Spanish elected a left-wing government called the *Popular Front*, which covered everyone from people who occasionally glanced at the *Guardian* to out-and-out anarchists. An ambitious army general, called Francisco Franco, got an army together in North Africa, landed in Spain, and declared war on the Popular Front.

People came from all over the world to fight in Spain. Left-wing sympathisers joined the *International Brigade*, to fight for the Spanish republic; Mussolini sent troops to help Franco and Hitler sent an air squadron, the Condor Legion. Appalling atrocities were committed, for example the Condor Legion's bombing of the town of Guernica on market day – which was an early example of what air power could do.

The republicans called out defiantly 'No Pasaran!' – 'They shall not pass!' – but the fascists did. By January 1939 Franco had taken the last republican stronghold and made himself *caudillo* – dictator – of Spain.

How to Win Land and Intimidate People: The Anti-Comintern Pact

The Japanese, Germans, and Italians, who all joined up in an anti-communist alliance called the *Anti-Comintern Pact,* had worked out just how to get the various bits of land that they wanted – simply take it.

The British and French knew that they weren't anything near strong or united enough to stop the dictators. Called *appeasement,* the British and French policy has had a very bad press. Appeasement didn't mean giving in to dictators, but the policy did mean trying to find a peaceful settlement. Unfortunately, with these dictators, giving in was the only peaceful settlement they understood.

Any idea that appeasement would restrain the dictators and safeguard world peace soon proved sorely mistaken:

- ✔ **1931: Japan invades Manchuria.** League of Nations protests. Japan leaves the League of Nations.

- ✔ **1935: Italy invades Abyssinia (Ethiopia).** League of Nations imposes sanctions, though not on oil. Italy leaves the League of Nations.

- ✔ **1936: Hitler moves troops into the Rhineland.**

- ✔ **March 1938: Hitler takes over Austria.** This move seems very popular with the Austrian people. Britain and France shrug their shoulders and decide to accept the situation – they don't really have much choice.

- ✔ **September 1938: Hitler demands the German-speaking parts (the Sudetenland) of Czechoslovakia.** Hitler, Mussolini, French Premier Edouard Daladier, and British Prime Minister Neville Chamberlain meet at Munich and Chamberlain persuades Hitler to take the Sudetenland without starting a war. Everyone breathes a sigh of relief. Except the Czechs.

- ✔ **March 1939: Hitler takes over the rest of Czechoslovakia.** Hitler now starts demanding the Polish 'corridor', the land cutting off East Prussia and Danzig from the rest of Germany. Britain and France decide to have a word with Stalin.

- ✔ **August 1939: Nazi-Soviet Pact.** Germany and Russia agree to carve Poland up between them.

- ✔ **September 1939: Germans invade Poland.** Britain and France declare war on Germany. Soviet Union invades Poland. Germans and Russians carve Poland up between them, and the Germans start looking out their maps of France.

Chapter 23

World War to Cold War

· ·

In This Chapter

▶ Watching the Second World War unfold in Europe

▶ Collaborating with or resisting the Germans

▶ Ending the Second World War and starting the Cold War

· ·

The Second World War and the Cold War that followed on afterwards subjected Europe and its citizens to some of the darkest days in its history. People have always had the capacity to commit acts of terrible evil and cruelty, but they had never before had the means to perpetrate them on the scale of the atrocities of the middle years of the 20th century. This period was the age of the gulag and the extermination camp, of aerial bombing, and nuclear confrontation. One false move in Europe, and the world could be brought to an end.

Lightning War: Blitzkrieg

When the Germans invaded Poland in September 1939 (refer to Chapter 22), they were working on the principle of *blitzkrieg*, 'lightning war'. The idea was to use tanks and aircraft to tear right through the enemy's defences, destroying their airfields, spreading panic among the civilians, and clogging the roads with refugees so the enemy forces couldn't advance.

This conflict was *total* war; the old distinctions between military and civilian no longer counted. Workers in factories were just as vital for the war effort as soldiers at the front, so they were just as legitimate targets.

Warsaw held out heroically, and only surrendered when the Russians attacked from the east. The Germans and Russians divided Poland up between them, and the Germans sat back, feeling very satisfied with themselves.

Hitler spoke of a 'new order' for Europe under German rule, and the Poles immediately got an idea of what this new regime might mean. Polish Jews were rounded up in specially-sealed ghettos in the cities, and the Germans began selecting ordinary Poles to work in their slave labour plants.

Massacre in the woods

In the eastern zone of Poland, in 1940, the Russian secret police (the NKVD) shot some 10,000 Polish officer prisoners of war in Katyn Forest, near Smolensk. These prisoners were middle-class professionals, the sort of people who would lead Poland after the war, and the Russians, who were thinking in terms of running the country themselves after the war, wanted them dead.

For years, the Soviet Union denied the murders and said they that had been carried out by the Germans. The truth wasn't revealed until the era of glasnost, in 1991, when Mikhail Gorbachev and Boris Yeltsin finally publicly admitted that the Soviet Union had been responsible.

A Phoney War in the West

Through the winter of 1939–40 the British and French sat behind the French ultra-modern defence system, the *Maginot Line*, wondering what would happen next. Things were so quiet, people called this period the Phoney War. Then, in the spring of 1940, Hitler finally attacked.

Hitler didn't strike in the west; his troops poured north, into Denmark and Norway. The allies rushed troops to Norway but they had to pull out, lick their wounds, and leave Norway to its fate.

In London the criticism of the failure in Norway was so strong that the Prime Minister Neville Chamberlain resigned and was replaced by Winston Churchill. However, the very day Churchill took office, the Germans struck again; this time they were invading Belgium and Holland, and bombing Rotterdam flat. Then they turned on France.

The SS

The SS *(Schutzstaffel)* were originally a small elite police force under Heinrich Himmler; they acted as Hitler's bodyguard. However, Himmler was ambitious, and gradually the SS grew in power and influence, organising the round-ups of Jews and running the concentration camps.

The SS became a state-within-a-state, with its own semi-independent army, the *Waffen-SS* (fighting SS), and working closely with the Nazi secret police, the Gestapo. During the war many non-Germans volunteered to serve in some of the SS foreign battalions. Nothing summed the Nazi terror up better than the SS.

Free France fights on

One French officer who managed to escape to England in 1940 was General Charles de Gaulle. De Gaulle refused to accept that France was out of the war, and he organised the other French troops who had got away into a special fighting unit called *the Free French*. De Gaulle issued a radio call over the BBC saying that France had lost a battle, but she had not lost the war. Stirring stuff, and the Free French became an important fighting unit, but at the time hardly anyone heard De Gaulle's appeal.

France was no more prepared for blitzkrieg (see the earlier section 'Lightning War: The Blitzkrieg' for a definition of this tactic) than any other country. The Germans tore through France and trapped the British and large numbers of French in a pocket around the port of Dunkirk. The British improvised an evacuation plan and managed to get most of their men off the beaches and into boats, but they had to leave all their tanks and heavy guns behind. The French declared Paris an Open City – meaning that the city wouldn't defend itself – and the Germans marched in. The unthinkable had happened: France had fallen.

Game Over. Isn't it?

Hitler had no quarrel with Britain now that he had beaten France, and was quite happy to make peace on generous terms. The German leader wanted to get on with planning the big campaign – the invasion of Russia.

To everyone's surprise, Churchill's government rejected the idea of a peace deal out of hand and vowed to fight on, even though the British didn't seem to have much to fight on *with*.

Hitler gave orders for *Operation Sealion*, the invasion of Britain. But first the Germans would need to control the skies above the Channel.

Battle over Britain

Hermann Goering, commander of the German air force, the *Luftwaffe*, thought that he could knock the Royal Air Force out quickly. But the RAF had built up their strength, and had fighters that could match the Germans'; the Luftwaffe also switched from attacking airfields to bombing London, which was terrifying for Londoners but gave the RAF a chance to recover.

By September 1940 it was clear that the Germans were not going to win the 'Battle of Britain', as it was called, and Operation Sealion was called off.

Bombs and U-boats

The Germans couldn't invade Britain, but they could bomb it. The Luftwaffe launched an intensive night bombing campaign against Britain's industrial cities: the *Blitz*. The German air force bombed Coventry so hard that 'to Coventry' in German came to mean to annihilate a city.

The British bombed German cities back. By 1943 the British were launching massive raids; in the worst cases, like the bombing of Dresden in February 1945, they created a 'firestorm', a hurricane-force wind that whipped up the flames to the point where people were incinerated. Fierce arguments still take place about how justified bombing was: The bombardment didn't hit industrial production nearly as much as people thought, and some people see the bombing of cities as a war crime.

The Germans were also using their U-boats to starve Britain of food and supplies. Britain depended on imports, so this damage to the supply chain was crucial. The British imposed strict rationing at home and a convoy system at sea. Gradually, thanks in large part to the work of their secret code-breakers at Bletchley Park, the British were able to anticipate the Germans' moves and come up with better anti-submarine devices. Later in the war, when the Americans developed long-range aircraft that could seek out U-boats far out in the Atlantic, the game was up for the Germans.

Hitler's New Order

Europe was having to adjust to life under German occupation. People had to carry new passes and papers, and, needless to say, the people most immediately affected were Europe's Jews.

Plenty of people in all European countries were only too happy to help the Germans. In Norway, Vidkun Quisling created a Nazi puppet state; thousands of Nazis in Belgium and Holland helped arrest Jews and volunteered to join the SS; in France, a special pro-Nazi police force, the *milice*, hunted down Jews and resistance fighters; the French police rounded up thousands of French Jews, including children, locked them in a cycling stadium and sent them off to the concentration camps.

The Germans relied heavily on imported labour and tried to persuade people to volunteer to go to work in Germany. Worst off were the thousands of people the Germans arrested and sent to work as slave labourers for German companies with no pay whatever. Many of them were worked until they died.

Does anyone know which side we're on?

France was in a particularly painful position. The Germans occupied the north and west of the country, including Paris and the whole of the Atlantic coastline, but southern France was a separate state, ruled from the little spa town of Vichy by a national hero, Marshal Pétain.

Pétain said that France must collaborate with the Germans, and that those who didn't were traitors. What were good patriotic French people to do?

Many French people chose collaboration with the Germans because of the British decision to sink the French Mediterranean fleet in the port of Mers-el-Kebir in Algeria in 1940. The British were genuinely afraid the Germans might get hold of it – but this act was a great propaganda *coup* for the Germans wanting to portray Britain as France's enemy.

Resistance is futile!

Resistance was a very risky business. For every German the resistance killed, the Germans would take hostages and shoot them until the culprits were handed over. Not surprisingly, people often preferred to betray members of the resistance rather than see more innocent people shot.

Some of the most heroic resistance came in less violent forms. In the Netherlands, the workers staged a massive strike in protest against deportations of Dutch Jews; in Denmark, where the Germans had naively thought that they would be welcomed as fellow Aryans, the Danes managed to smuggle all but a handful of the country's Jews out of the country to neutral (well, officially neutral) Sweden. In both cases, the Germans responded by cracking down without mercy.

Put Russia on hold – something's come up

In 1940 Mussolini attacked Greece, but the Greeks, with British help, kicked him out again; you may have read about or seen these events in *Captain Corelli's Mandolin*. The British defeat of Mussolini in Greece encouraged the king of Yugoslavia to get rid of his pro-German ministers and join up with the British.

If the Germans didn't act quickly, they would have a whole new battle front in the Balkans. Hitler gave the order, and in March 1941 the Germans launched their blitzkrieg ('lightning war') against Yugoslavia and Greece, and sent troops to help the Italians fight the British in North Africa.

The Germans quickly conquered Greece and Yugoslavia, and turned the tables on the British in North Africa, but things soon proved more complicated. The North African campaign swung to and fro like a pendulum. In Yugoslavia, the Germans found that they were up against the *Chetniks*, a very active resistance movement led by a Serbian royalist, Drazha Mihailovic. The Croat militia, the *Ustashe*, enthusiastically helped the Germans fight back. Later resistance was taken over by the communist partisans, led by Josip Broz, codenamed Tito.

This little excursion to the Balkans delayed the German attack on Russia, which would not now be wound up before winter set in – and in Russia that could be fatal.

Operation Barbarossa

Hitler codenamed his June 1941 invasion of Russia *Barbarossa*, after the great medieval German emperor and Crusader. Hitler saw the invasion as a modern crusade against barbaric Russian communism, and he encouraged people from all over occupied Europe to come and join in. The Russians had no idea the Germans were coming and the Red Army collapsed; the Germans took many thousands of prisoners. The Germans regarded Russians, like all Slav people, as sub-human, so these prisoners were made to live and die as slaves in German labour camps.

The Germans overran Ukraine and the Baltic states (where the people welcomed them as liberators from the hated Russians); one group headed north for Leningrad; one group headed for the rich lands of the south; and one group headed for the ultimate prize: Moscow. Special units – *einsatzgruppen* – travelled through Russia killing and destroying whole villages to make space for German settlers.

Hero City Leningrad

The city of Leningrad endured a terrible siege of over two years' duration. During the winter of 1941, 3,000 people starved to death in Leningrad – *every day*. Bodies were left lying in the street, because no one had the strength to move them. People were reduced to eating wallpaper paste and carpenter's glue. But the Russians managed to keep up a supply line across the frozen Lake Ladoga, despite the Germans' attempts to shell it and break the ice.

Stalin (who actually hated Leningrad and always subjected it to the worst purges) gave the city the title 'Hero City' in honour of its brave stand, and the composer Dmitri Shostakovitch wrote a Leningrad symphony, which he conducted during the siege. The siege of Leningrad is one of the epics of modern history, and ought to be better known.

For many years, people claimed that these atrocities were all the work of the SS, and that the German army kept its hands clean. However, plenty of evidence shows that the German army in Russia committed murders and atrocities every bit as bad as those of the SS.

Before the Germans could reach Moscow, the weather changed. First rain, then mud, then snow, then ice, and then more snow. The Germans didn't have proper winter clothing, and had to start collecting woollens back home to send to the lads at the front.

The Russians were properly padded; they were getting their breath back, too. The Russian people had managed to move heavy plant machinery out of the factories in the Germans' path to sites beyond the Urals, where they fixed the machines up again and started production. Sometimes, these 'factories' were just machines sitting in a field, but they worked; the Russians were able to turn out tanks and aircraft at an impressive rate.

Then, Stalin let his crack Siberian troops loose on the Germans, and for once the Germans were the ones who didn't know what had hit them. The Germans were forced back, and Moscow was saved.

Stalingrad

In 1942, the Germans planned a major offensive towards the Caucausus oilfields, to cripple the Russians and make Germany self-sufficient in oil. The Germans would need to take the city of Stalingrad, however.

The Germans got trapped in bitter fighting in Stalingrad. The sensible response would've been for the Germans to pull out and press on to the oilfields, but Hitler ordered General von Paulus to hold fast to every inch of ground. Stalingrad was reduced to rubble. Finally, in January 1943, von Paulus surrendered. The failure to hold on to Stalingrad was the biggest German defeat of the war so far, and this disaster was all Hitler's fault.

In 1943, the Germans and the Russians fought the biggest tank battle in history, the Battle of Kursk. The Russians won, thanks to their latest tank (the T-34 for any anoraks looking in), which proved tough, fast, and deadly. The Germans lost so many tanks and men that they were never able to launch another offensive in the east; from now on they had to stage a fighting retreat all the way to Berlin.

The Holocaust

The Germans had been taking action against the Jews since they came to power in 1933. In January 1942, a group of leading Nazis met at a very smart house in Wannsee, a rather nice Berlin suburb and devised what they called – and always remember that this term is a euphemism (that is, it's not really saying what it means) – the *Final Solution of the Jewish Problem*. The Nazis were going to kill Europe's Jews. All of them.

The Final Solution was very simple; every Jew in Europe was to be rounded up, put on a train, and sent off to one of a network of special extermination camps in Poland, where they would be gassed. Some 6 million Jews were killed in these camps between 1942 and 1945. The most notorious camp was Birkenau, part of the vast Auschwitz complex. More typical were much smaller places like Chelmno, Belzec, or Treblinka: a fake railway station (to calm people's nerves when they arrived), an administrative building, and a gas chamber. No prisoners' barracks or dormitories – these facilities weren't needed.

Don't forget that thousands of ordinary people were involved. The cattle wagons the prisoners were herded into had to be booked with railway companies, firms were contracted to supply the barbed wire or the gas chambers or the ovens. People filled in order forms for gas crystals, or simply delivered the guards' beer, food, and cigarettes. All of these people played their part in helping one of the greatest crimes in history to happen.

We're Going to Have Real Problems If We Win

Japan was desperate to attack Europe's colonies in Asia and seize their raw materials, especially oil, but the United States would certainly try to stop Japan if they did. So the Japanese decided to strike first and cripple the United States fleet at Pearl Harbor (for more on this see *World War II For Dummies* by Keith D. Dickson (Wiley)).

The allied leaders, Churchill, Roosevelt, and Stalin, soon starting meeting to discuss how to fight the war and what should happen afterwards. The leaders had some very different ideas:

- ✔ Churchill wanted to restore the British Empire and stop Stalin from taking over Europe.

- ✔ Roosevelt wanted the British Empire to collapse, and didn't think that Stalin wanted to take over Europe.

- ✔ Stalin wanted to take over Europe.

The leaders divided Europe into 'zones of influence': the Russians would have the eastern half, and the British and the Americans (and the French! shouts General de Gaulle through the keyhole) would get the western half.

In 1941, the British and Americans signed the *Atlantic Charter*, saying that the war was for freedom and democracy in all lands. Stalin hadn't signed this charter, which was just as well, because he didn't believe in freedom and democracy in any lands. If and when the allies won the war, these differences between the allies were going to become serious.

Second front now!

The Russians wanted the allies to open a second front against Germany, in the west. Opening a second front was easier said than done, but the Russians thought the western allies were holding back on purpose, so that they'd be so worn down by fighting the Germans that they wouldn't be able to stop the Americans taking over the world after the war.

At first the western allies launched an invasion of Italy. The Italians were delighted and rose up to overthrow Mussolini, but then the Germans invaded as well and held the allies down in a long, slow, difficult campaign. Eventually, after months of planning, the British, Canadians, and Americans landed on the beaches of Normandy on D-Day, 6 June 1944, to start the liberation of France and of western Europe.

Get Berlin!

The British were keen to push forward to Berlin, before the Russians got there; Eisenhower, the American supreme allied commander, was more cautious and wanted to advance along a much broader front. If the Russians got to Berlin first, why did this matter?

The British staged a massive airborne invasion of Holland; they hoped to cross the Rhine and race ahead into Germany. Unfortunately, the British got cut to pieces by the Germans at Arnhem, and the plan failed.

The Germans took terrible revenge against the people of Holland for the help they gave the allies during the Arnhem campaign. The German forces arrested hundreds of people and sent them to concentration camps; they also held back food supplies. The winter of 1944 became known as the 'tulip winter' because the Dutch were reduced to eating bulbs from the tulip fields. The Dutch have never forgotten this terrible time.

The Russians under Marshal Zhukhov were the ones to finally take Berlin. The Germans fought fiercely (they were terrified of what would happen to them if they fell into Russian hands, and bearing in mind how they'd treated the Russians, they were quite right to feel scared) and the Russians had to fight street by street.

Hitler had retired to an underground bunker, where he imagined that he still had huge armies to command and looked over big models of cities he'd build when he'd won the war. Eventually, with the Russians fighting in the streets overhead, Hitler married his long-term sweetheart, Eva Braun, and as a special wedding day treat, they killed themselves. The SS burned the bodies to stop the Russians getting them (the remains turned up many years later, in a box in Moscow) and on 7 May 1945 Germany surrendered.

Some Germany for you, and some Germany for me

The allied leaders had worked out how to divide Germany at their conference at Yalta in the Crimea at the start of 1945: Germany was to be split in four – the north for Britain, the south for the United States, a doggy bag along the Rhine for the French, and the whole of the eastern half of the country for Russia.

The allies were going to divide Berlin in the same way, even though the city was right in the heart of the Russian zone. The leaders met up again at Potsdam, where US President Truman (Roosevelt had died) ever-so-casually mentioned to Stalin that the Americans had got the atom bomb and were going to use it on Japan. Which meant: 'Don't get clever and think that you can do what you like in Europe, buster, 'cos we can blow you to kingdom come and back again.' Stalin, who had his troops over the whole of eastern and central Europe, and who already knew about the atom bomb thanks to his spies, wasn't too worried by this veiled threat.

Time to Sort This Mess Out: Marshall Aid

Europe in 1945 was utterly shattered. Whole towns had been reduced to rubble, thousands of people had been displaced, and the allies had been discovering to their horror just what had been going on in the Nazi concentration and labour camps. That Europe would ever walk again seemed impossible.

The Americans decided to step in. They set up a commission led by US General George C. Marshall to look at what was needed and provide US money – *Marshall Aid* – to make the plan happen.

The Soviet Union was suspicious of the Americans' offer of aid; they reckoned that US money would mean US control, so they very politely told the Americans that they could manage, thank you. The Soviet Union also said that all the countries under their control could manage, too.

The court of history

The allies captured a number of leading Nazis, including Hermann Goering, and put them on trial at Nuremberg on charges of planning and waging aggressive war, war crimes, and crimes against humanity. Eleven leading Nazis were sentenced to death, though Goering managed to commit suicide before he could be hanged.

Some people still say the winning side putting the losers on trial like that was wrong, especially when the Russians were just as guilty of atrocities as the Germans. Still, the Nuremberg Trials set the precedent for other courts to try people under international law for crimes against humanity, which has to be a good thing.

Marshall Aid was meant to help the whole continent to recover from the war; in the end, the money helped western Europe to rebuild much more quickly than anyone could have expected, and to surge ahead of eastern Europe. Europe was quickly dividing right down the middle – the middle of Germany.

Disconnecting People

Once the war was over, the western allies handed over thousands of anti-soviet Russians and Cossacks they'd captured, and Stalin had them shot. Russian troops who'd been captured by the Germans were welcomed home – and sent straight to the gulags (slave labour camps; see Chapter 22). Stalin didn't trust them one inch.

The Russians cleared thousands of Germans from their homes and to make room for Russians or Poles the city of Königsberg became a Russian city, Kaliningrad. This was exactly what Hitler had planned to do to the Russians, though that doesn't make it right.

The Russians had sat by and watched as the Germans crushed a big rising by the Polish resistance in Warsaw, in 1944. Now Stalin had the rest of the Polish wartime resistance fighters rounded up and shot, while he held blatantly rigged elections and imposed his own Polish communist government.

Britain and France had gone to war to help Poland in 1939; they couldn't help her then and they couldn't help her now, either.

Slices of salami

Stalin had promised his western allies that he would hold free elections in eastern Europe. In fact, they were carefully rigged in favour of communist candidates. Communists would get control of the police or the army, and start to have their opponents arrested. Gradually, little by little, the whole country had been taken over, like slicing salami; the process was called *salami tactics*.

Romania, Bulgaria, and Hungary all suffered the salami treatment. So did Czechoslovakia. In 1948 the charismatic Czech leader, Jan Masaryck was found dead under an open window. He, er, fell.

Greece: The Truman Show

Salami tactics only really failed in Greece, where a civil war raged between the communists and their opponents. The British were fighting to keep the country out of communist hands. When trying to defend Greece got too much for them, the British asked the Americans to take over.

Truman took the opportunity to make an important announcement. The president said that the United States would help any country in the world trying to resist communism – this policy was called the Truman Doctrine.

A Cold War

The conflict between the communist East and the capitalist West that followed the end of the Second World War was called the Cold War, which describes the atmosphere of icy suspicion and distrust on each side. Luckily, both sides managed to keep their cool and avoided actually opening fire – just as well, because both sides were armed with the latest nuclear weapons.

Although the Cold War was a global confrontation, the conflict was always centred on Europe, divided down the middle by the Soviet Union and the western allies. 'From Stettin in the Baltic,' declared Churchill, 'to Trieste in the Adriatic, an *iron curtain* has descended on the continent.' Churchill's analogy was widely used in the West to describe the Soviet Union and its 'satellite' states – as he probably intended. For nearly half a century, Europeans across the continent lived in a state of constant fear that they and their continent would be destroyed.

Deutschland, Deutschland unter Alles: Germany Divided

The four zones of Germany created at the end of the Second World War were meant to join together again, but things didn't work out that way. The Russians brought in a German communist who had sat out the war in

Moscow, Walter Ulbricht, and put him in charge of their eastern zone. The western allies joined their three zones together into a single trading zone, which, thanks to American money and aid, was soon doing very well.

Ulbricht and the Russians turned the eastern zone into a separate state: the *German Democratic Republic (GDR)* usually known as East Germany.

High noon in Berlin

The GDR's capital was Berlin, or rather it was the eastern sector of Berlin; the western sector was still in the hands of the western allies. Stalin was worried that the people of East Germany would be tempted to get out and go to West Berlin, where there were goods in the shops and the money was worth something; he also thought that the West would use Berlin as a base for spying on him – he was right on both counts.

In 1948 Stalin cut off all access to West Berlin by road or rail. The city's supplies would quickly dry up and the West would have to pull out – or so he thought.

Instead, the western allies organised an airlift, sending hundreds of planes every day into Tempelhof airport to keep West Berlin supplied with essentials. Eventually, Stalin realised that the allies weren't going to give in, and he called off the blockade. The Russians and East Germans would have to find another way of dealing with West Berlin.

This is Hungary calling the world: Come in, please . . .

In 1953 Stalin died, and three years later the Soviet leader Nikita Khrushchev made a speech at the Twentieth Soviet Party Congress saying publicly that Stalin had committed appalling crimes – which wasn't news to anyone in Russia, though saying it openly was.

The world sat up; did this admission of Stalin's crimes mean that they were about to see a new caring, sharing Soviet Union? In Hungary, the new prime minister, Imre Nagy (pronounced 'Nodge'), promised to introduce free elections and a free press, and he also said that he was going to pull Hungary out of the new Soviet military alliance, the *Warsaw Pact*.

The sharing caring Russians sent in tanks to crush Nagy and his government. The Hungarians fought back as best they could with rifles and petrol bombs, and they appealed desperately to the rest of the world for help. The Russians crushed the rising by force. The West protested but didn't dare intervene.

Spies, lies, and WMD

In 1949 the Soviet Union successfully tested an atom bomb, and when the Americans developed the hydrogen bomb, the Russians quickly got one of those too. The Russians had been able to catch up with the Americans thanks to a number of spies in western countries, including the British physicists Alan Nunn May and Klaus Fuchs (originally an anti-Nazi German who had fled to Britain) who sympathised with communism and didn't think that America should have a monopoly on weapons of mass destruction. Others, including the British diplomat Kim Philby, worked in secret for years as double agents for the Soviet Union.

This wall has ears – and machine guns, too

By 1961 so many East Berliners were slipping over to West Berlin that the East Berliners were beginning to write reminders to the last person to switch off the lights. On 13 August 1961 East German soldiers suddenly appeared all along the border with West Berlin accompanied by bricklayers. The bricklayers built a wall, all around the western sectors; no one was allowed out of East Berlin, and if you tried to cross the wall, you were shot.

The Berlin Wall stayed in place for 27 years.

Chapter 24

Eurovision

. . . .

In This Chapter

▶ Following Suez, decolonisation and the Algerian War

▶ Introducing the European Community and Union

▶ Looking at 1989 and the end of the Cold War

▶ Contemplating Europe at the start of the new Millennium

. . . .

*E*urope had dominated the world for two centuries or more, but in the new age of the superpowers, the United States, the Soviet Union, and China, the Europeans seemed very small fry indeed.

Communist eastern Europe was cut off from western Europe, where the growing strength of the European Union offered a tempting vision of unity and prosperity. After 1989, when the communist regimes of eastern Europe suddenly collapsed a New Europe appeared. Unfortunately, as the people of Yugoslavia found out, the new Europe could be just as cruel and destructive as the old one.

Watch Where You're Pointing That Missile: NATO and the Warsaw Pact

Post-war Europe was divided in two by the Cold War (see Chapter 23). The Americans and Canadians had formed a special alliance with western Europe, the *North Atlantic Treaty Organisation (NATO)*, to guard against attack from the Soviet Union. The Russians formed their own alliance with the communist states of eastern and central Europe, the 1955 *Warsaw Pact*. Each side started arming with the latest weapons, *Inter-Continental Ballistic Missiles (ICBMs)* – missiles that could fire from Russia to America or vice versa. The Europeans were in the middle. Each alliance had trouble with one of its members. The Russians threw Marshal Tito of Yugoslavia out of the Warsaw Pact for showing worrying signs of independence from Moscow, and General de Gaulle pulled France out of NATO. De Gaulle never liked taking orders, especially from anyone who spoke English.

Who Do You Think You Are Kidding, Colonel Nasser?

In 1956, the Egyptian premier, Colonel Nasser, wanting money for a huge new hydro-electric dam on the Nile, announced that he was nationalising the Suez Canal Company on behalf of the Egyptian people.

The British and French governments, which controlled the Suez Canal Company, declared that Colonel Nasser was the reincarnation of Hitler, and, in conjunction with Israel, invaded Egypt to get the canal back – er, I mean safeguard world peace and protect the Egyptian people from their mad leader.

The United States told the two governments to get their troops out of Egypt fast, and put pressure on sterling to make sure that they did so. Britain and France found themselves completely isolated; they had to pull out. Nasser started flirting with the Soviet Union, and frankly, are you surprised?

The Suez crisis was important because it showed that the European powers could no longer throw their weight about as they had always done in the past. The Suez crisis also meant that everyone was too busy shouting at each other to do anything when the Russians sent in tanks to crush the Hungarian revolution (Chapter 23 explains why that was such a tragedy).

Should I Stay or Should I Go?

The peoples of Europe's overseas colonies decided that the time had come for the sun to finally set on the British empire – and the French, Dutch, Belgian, and Portuguese empires, too.

Considering how long the European empires had existed (you can trace the story of Europe's overseas colonies in Chapters 11, 15, and 19) they collapsed surprisingly quickly:

- ✔ **India:** The British divided the country in two, Hindu India and Muslim Pakistan, and got out fast in 1947. People on the 'wrong' side of the partition line had to up sticks and move to the other state. This provoked fierce anger and violence – about *1 million* people were killed in the riots surrounding Indian partition.

- ✔ **Palestine:** Britain governed it under mandate from the old League of Nations (see Chapter 22). Jewish terrorist groups trying to pressurise Britain into allowing more Jewish settlers into Palestine made the region too hot to handle, so Britain pulled out and the United Nations set up the State of Israel in 1948.

- ✔ **Malaya:** Communist guerrillas tried to take it over in 1948, but the British defeated them in a long drawn-out war that lasted until 1960. The new state of Malaysia could now become a repressive capitalist state instead of a repressive communist one.

- ✔ **Indonesia:** The Dutch had a go at reimposing colonial rule after the war but the Indonesians resisted. Very sensibly, the Dutch got out and granted Indonesia its independence in 1949.

- ✔ **Indo-China:** The Vichy government (check out Chapter 22 for what this was) let the Japanese take the region over during the Second World War and then expected to be welcomed back afterwards. The communist *Viet Minh*, defeated the French in 1954 at the Battle of Dien Bien Phu. The French set up three new states – Vietnam, Cambodia, and Laos – and scarpered. The Viet Minh still controlled the north, and the South Vietnamese wondered if the Americans might perhaps be interested in having a look round. . . . As you've probably guessed, this was the origin of the Vietnam War; for more details see *The Vietnam War For Dummies* by Ronald B. Frankum and Stephen F. Maxner (Wiley).

- ✔ **Cyprus and Malta:** Cyprus was a British possession. Greek Cypriots wanted to join up with Greece, but the Turkish Cypriots didn't. In 1960 the British set Cyprus up as an independent republic under Greek Cypriot leader Archbishop Makarios. Hardline Greeks thought that Makarios was a traitor for keeping Cyprus separate from Greece, so in 1974 they launched a *coup* to get rid of him. Turkey was so alarmed that it invaded the island and took over the northern part, where the Turks remain to this day. In Malta, the people actually voted to become part of the United Kingdom; Britain granted them independence but kept their room free in case they ever wanted to come home.

Rock the Casbah: The French Won't Go Quietly

Algeria wasn't just a French colony; the French had made it part of France. A large population of French settlers lived in Algeria, known as *pieds noirs* (literally 'black feet', because of the colour of the original French soldiers' boots, not to any lack of personal hygiene), for whom Algeria was as French as runny cheese or crusty bread and they intended to keep it that way.

The Algerian *FLN* (*Front de la Libération Nationale* – National Liberation Front) started shooting and bombing French settlers by way of a hint that maybe the time had arrived for them all to go home (the ones who hadn't been bombed or shot, that is). The French, however, had had enough surrenders for one century; they sent in their crack parachute brigade who introduced martial law and torture. Torture works (which is why people use it) and the French kept control of the cities, but the FLN started operating from bases in the countryside and over the border. And soon the French settlers had another threat to worry about – from Paris.

The politicians in Paris were thinking that pulling out of Algeria might be the best option, if only to save lives, but the *pieds noirs* and the French army said they'd resist if Paris tried to sell them down the river.

The crisis brought down the French Fourth Republic. General de Gaulle drew up rules for a Fifth Republic, with himself as President. De Gaulle went to Algeria, met the settlers and the soldiers, and made a big public speech in Algiers where he lifted his arms in a great V shape for victory and Vive la France and called out '*Je vous ai compris!*' – 'I have understood you!' The crowd went wild with excitement.

In fact de Gaulle had seen the *pieds noirs* as bigoted, narrow-minded, and racist, and he was going to wash his hands of them. Paris started secret talks with the FLN at Evian, just over the Swiss border, and on 3 July 1962 Algeria became an independent nation.

Four French army generals based in Algeria threatened to stage a military strike on Paris, but they lost their nerve. One of them, General Salan, set up a terrorist group, the OAS (*Organisation de l'Armée Secrète* – Secret Army Organisation), which killed some 12,000 Algerian Muslims and machine-gunned de Gaulle's car at Petit-Clamart, outside Paris. De Gaulle didn't bat an eyelid; they missed. The OAS leaders were rounded up and the movement collapsed.

Let's Be Friends: France and Germany

The French and the Germans had been fighting and scoring points off each other for years. Result of this rivalry: two world wars and one shattered continent.

The French foreign minister, Robert Schuman, decided to tackle this mutual animosity head-on. Since both countries were busy trying to rebuild their towns and railways, Schuman suggested that they get together on the two most important ingredients: coal and steel.

The European Coal and Steel Community

The result of France and Germany's co-operation was the *European Coal and Steel Community,* which was actually a more interesting name than it looks: it was 'European', not just Franco-German, and it was a 'community', not just a trading agreement. Schuman put one of his civil servants, Jean Monnet, in charge of the Community, and sat back to watch developments.

Schuman wasn't the only one thinking in terms of some sort of union of European states. In 1949, the Europeans launched the *Council of Europe*. This Council was meant to be like a United Nations for Europe, solving disputes by common agreement, but because the governments who founded it made sure not to give it any power to enforce its decisions, the Council wasn't able to do very much. But the Council of Europe did design a rather natty European flag of gold stars on a blue background.

Six of one, more than half a dozen of the other: The Common Market

Thanks to the coal and steel arrangement, France and Germany recovered much more quickly than anyone would have predicted. Soon the neighbours got interested: How about establishing a full-scale trading club?

In 1957, six countries – France, Germany, Italy, Belgium, Luxembourg, and the Netherlands (though everyone called the last three Benelux) – signed the Treaty of Rome setting up just that: a European trading club. This organisation was called the *European Economic Community (EEC)*, which is a bit of a boring name, so most people called it the *Common Market*. The six founder members of the EEC had invited the British to join, but Britain was a bit wary of talk of communities and unions. Britain set up a separate *European Free Trade Area (EFTA)* instead, which was a sort of Betamax to the EEC's VHS. (EFTA was comprised of seven countries so you could make jokes about Europe being at sixes and sevens if you really felt the urge to.)

All these organisations called themselves 'European', but they only operated in the western half of Europe. Eastern and central Europe had their own economic community called *Comecon*. Slipping into the habit of saying 'Europe' when you mean '*western* Europe' is easy, but try to resist doing so all the same.

Climb every butter mountain

One of the EEC's most important jobs was sorting out the chaotic state of Europe's farms. The organisation came up with a *Common Agricultural Policy (CAP)*, which basically meant paying farmers large sums of money to produce as much as possible, whether there was a market for the produce or not.

Europe's farmers set their milking machines to 'Superfast', and pretty soon Europe was faced with the unusual phenomenon of huge stocks of food and drink that no one wanted to buy – and more on the way. Over the years the CAP has been changed, but, according to some countries, nothing like enough.

The EEC proved a big success story. The Council stimulated trade and got industry and agriculture going again, and in 1962, after much agonising, Britain applied to join. The other member countries were only too pleased, but General de Gaulle vetoed Britain's application; he said that Britain would just be a stalking horse for America (the French were already getting very sniffy about the Americans). Britain was only granted membership in 1973.

Generals Come, and Generals Go

Military figures played an important part in ruling a number of western European states in the 1960s and 1970s, including France, Greece, Spain, and Portugal:

- **France 1968:** Serious student riots broke out in the Left Bank area of Paris against the government of General de Gaulle, and against the Vietnam War, the capitalist system, bourgeois conformism, having to get up for nine o'clock lectures, and the general unfairness of life. De Gaulle was badly shaken by 'the Events of '68'; he even contemplated calling in the army and establishing military rule.

- **Greece:** In 1964 a group of right-wing army colonels overthrew King Constantine II and set up a military dictatorship; they pulled Greece out of the Council of Europe and even denounced the European Convention on Human Rights, which was not so unusual, because they didn't allow any. In 1974 the Greeks forced them out of office; Greece became a democratic republic. By 1987 the country had put its dictatorship years far enough behind it to be accepted into the European Community.

- **Spain:** General Francisco Franco, known as the Generalissimo or *Caudillo* (leader), (see Chapter 22) ruled Spain until his death in 1975. Franco handed over to the next in line to the throne, Prince Juan Carlos. The new king proved a very good, democratic ruler; he even managed to put down an attempted military *coup* in 1981 by sheer force of personality. In 1985, Spain joined the European Community (see the Section 'Six of one, more than half a dozen of the other: the Common Market' above), which was fast becoming an acid test of how democratic you were.

- **Portugal:** Portugal was ruled by its dictator, Dr Salazar, from 1928 until 1968, when he fell off his deckchair and lost his marbles. In 1974 a group of left-wing army officers seized power and arranged for Portugal's first free elections since the 1920s. Portugal became a fully-fledged democracy and in 1985, along with Spain, it too, joined the European Community.

Ding dong! The Boss is dead!

Stalin, the ruthless dictator of the Soviet Union since the 1920s who led Russia through the Second World War (check out Chapters 21–23 for loads more about Stalin) died in 1953. Stalin had a stroke, but everyone in the Kremlin was scared that he was tricking them to see what they said about him behind his back, so they didn't actually call a doctor till it was too late – they also kept his death secret for days through force of habit.

After 'the Boss' (as the Politburo called him) was safely embalmed and placed next to Lenin's body in the mausoleum in Red Square, the members of the Politburo had the KGB chief, Lavrentii Beria, shot (he was a thoroughly nasty piece of work with a lot of blood on his hands, and no one would miss him – except the firing squad of course). Then the council sat down to work out what to do next.

Who's the new boss?

No one quite trusted anyone else, so at first the politburo all ruled together: Georgi Malenkov was prime minister, Nikolai Bulganin was his deputy, and Nikita Khrushchev was in Stalin's old job as party secretary. Of course, these three men were all furiously scheming against each other: Malenkov was the first to fall from power, then Bulganin, and in 1958 Khrushchev took over, but not before he had made a rather remarkable speech.

Usually when you make a speech you tell people something they don't know, but Khrushchev's speech to the Twentieth Party Congress told the audience something they all knew but no one dared say: that Stalin had been a murderous tyrant and that they were well rid of the man.

Rocket man

Right at the end of the Second World War the Germans launched over a thousand V-2 rockets against targets in London and the south of England. The allies were so impressed that the Americans and Russians raced to capture the man who had designed them, Wernher von Braun. The Americans got him and whisked him off to the States so he could design rockets for them.

While the Americans dithered about whether making use of a former Nazi was morally right (von Braun's V-2 rocket programme had made extensive use of concentration camp slave labour, and more people died building the things than were killed by them in action), in 1957 the Russians launched the world's first space satellite, *sputnik*. They followed that achievement up in 1961 by sending the first man into space, a young air force pilot called Yuri Gagarin.

The audience were scared stiff; they expected to see Khrushchev taken away by the secret police, but when he wasn't, they all applauded like mad. The speech was meant to be a secret – the press weren't present – but within a few days Khrushchev's speech was headline news all over the world

The Russians took Stalin's body out of the Lenin mausoleum and took down all the Stalin statues and pictures – they even renamed Stalingrad to Volgograd.

Goodbye, Khrushchev

In 1964 the Politburo got rid of Khrushchev. Khrushchev was a rather coarse character who rather overdid the old 'My dad was a miner so I can be as rude as I like' routine. On one occasion, Khrushchev outraged world opinion when he interrupted a session at the United Nations by banging on the desk with his shoe and shouting out 'No! No! No!' (though the interpreters probably enjoyed it).

More importantly, Khrushchev was taking too many risks. In 1962 he put nuclear missiles on Cuba and came within a day of nuclear war with the United States. But Khrushchev didn't get away with placing missiles on Cuba, and in the end he had to back down and take them away again. Khrushchev got into a row with Mao Zedong of China, which looked as if the two countries might degenerate into war at any moment.

The time had definitely come for Khrushchev to go. However, in a sign of how Russia had changed since Stalin's day, Khrushchev wasn't shot or sent to the gulag; he was allowed to resign and retire to write his memoirs. The new soviet leader, Leonid Brezhnev, had bushy eyebrows and did so little for Russia that his time in charge is still known as the Years of Stagnation. Nothing was stagnant about his activities abroad, however.

Reality Czech

In 1968 the Czechs installed a more liberal communist regime headed by Alexander Dubcek. The Czechs didn't see why you couldn't be a good communist and still speak your mind without having to worry about being arrested by the secret police.

The Russians listened carefully while Dubcek explained the Czech plans for the umpteenth time, and then they sent the tanks in. Huge protests took place all over the world at the destruction of the 'Prague Spring'. One very brave young student, called Jan Palách, died after setting himself on fire in protest at the Russian invasion. The Soviets dubbed their move the Brezhnev Doctrine; it meant that the Russians could come along and take over whenever they wanted to.

The Cold War Gets Frostier

In the 1970s, with the Russians and the Americans spending money hand-over-fist on bigger and better nuclear missiles, the two sides decided that maybe they ought to talk.

The talks were called SALT – Strategic Arms Limitation Talks – but don't get the idea that anyone was actually stopping building nuclear missiles. They reduced the rate of increased production.

Still, a general relaxing of tension occurred, which the Americans and Russians called *détente*; even James Bond worked together with the Russians to foil the villain in the 1977 film *The Spy Who Loved Me* (Anglo–Russian relations get even more intimate at the end).

Then in 1979, the Russians invaded Afghanistan to impose a socialist government, and the West got two new hard-line anti-soviet leaders, the British Prime Minister Margaret Thatcher in 1979 and Ronald Reagan, who became US president in 1981. No more Mr Nice Guy. The Americans poured more money into their defence budget and started deploying medium-range nuclear missiles in western Europe; the Russians did the same and put their missiles in eastern Europe. The Cold War was on again, with a vengeance.

Anyone who says there's no freedom of speech will be arrested

The Russians dealt very harshly with people who spoke out in favour of democracy or free speech.

The Russian writer Alexander Solzhenitsyn, who described life in the gulags from first hand in *One Day in the Life of Ivan Denisovitch*, won the Nobel Prize for Literature, but he was still arrested and thrown out of the country. The eminent physicist Andrei Sakharov called for more freedom of speech, and was sent into internal exile; he had to live in the town of Gorky, in the middle of absolutely nowhere, and wasn't allowed out.

Another tactic was to lock political prisoners up in mental asylums; if they weren't mad when they went in (officially, criticising the soviet system was proof that you must be unhinged),

then they certainly were by the time they came out – if, indeed, they ever did.

All contact with the outside world was strictly controlled. Post was opened, phones were tapped, and in East Berlin you could even be arrested for having your television aerial pointing towards the West.

Dissidents circulated their ideas or western literature in little clandestine typewritten versions called *samizdat,* run off secretly on old printers and passed to people in the know or left lying around for people to pick up. The penalties for reading samizdat literature, let alone producing it, were severe.

Poles apart

The first victims of this new freeze in the Cold War were the Poles. Workers in the docks in Gdansk (formerly the German city of Danzig, but the Germans were all forced out after the Second World War) formed a trade union called *Solidarity* led by Lech Walesa, which called not only for better working conditions but for more freedom of speech and expression.

The Cardinal Archbishop of Cracow, Karol Wojtyla, was elected Pope John Paul II in 1978, and one of his first acts was to visit Poland and encourage the Poles to stand up for their rights. But in 1980 the Polish leader General Jaruselski banned the union, put Walesa and the other union leaders in prison, and imposed martial law.

Gorbymania

In 1985 the Soviet Union got a new leader, Mikhail Gorbachev. At 54, Gorbachev was a spring chicken compared with the aged fossils he was replacing. He made a very good impression in the west; the British Prime Minister Margaret Thatcher declared that he was a man she could do business with, and Gorbachev met US President Reagan for a series of summit meetings which managed to halt the arms race by the simple tactic of just stopping building the things. The soviet system was riddled with corruption, and a flourishing black market existed. The rouble was worthless; massive spending programmes on missiles and spaceships had left the country virtually bankrupt.

The first thing Gorbachev did was to encourage Russians to get used to speaking out openly. Gorbachev called this policy *glasnost* (openness). The Soviet Union started to talk openly about some of the appalling crimes that had taken place in Stalin's time and afterwards.

Next, Gorbachev needed to restructure the entire soviet system, clearing out all the corrupt officials, ending state subsidies to non-productive industries, and opening Russia to normal market forces. This policy was called *perestroika* (restructuring). The Russians weren't going to like it and they didn't.

And the wall came tumblin' down

In 1989, Gorbachev announced a change in foreign policy; the Soviet Union would no longer interfere if any of its neighbours wanted to change their system of government. Some called this policy the Sinatra Doctrine – 'You do it your way.' The eastern Europeans decided to take Gorbachev at his word:

✔ **Poland:** Solidarity (see the Section 'Poles apart' earlier in this chapter) came out of hiding and won Poland's first free elections since the 1930s. Poland became a multi-party democracy.

✔ **Hungary:** The country dismantled the border fence with the west (and sold it off in little packets – 'Buy your very own piece of the iron curtain': they cottoned on to capitalism very quickly) and held free elections. Virtually the entire population of East Germany suddenly decided to go on holiday to Hungary . . .

✔ **East Germany:** Protest meetings in Leipzig called for free elections. Gorbachev came to visit, kissed GDR leader Erich Honecker on both cheeks and told him 'You're on your own, matey.' Honecker resigned, and the new leaders decided to open up the borders. Telephone from a checkpoint on 9 November 1989: 'Does that include the Wall?' Someone in the government offices said, 'I suppose so', and the people of East Berlin surged through into the west, then took sledgehammers to the hated Wall. And they started selling the pieces – genuine Berlin Wall rubble, 100 per cent guaranteed . . .

The next year, Chancellor Helmut Kohl of West Germany met his East German opposite numbers and negotiated a deal to reunite the whole country for the first time since the First World War (Chapter 22 explains why it had been divided after the First World War).

✔ **Czechoslovakia:** Czechoslovakia became a democracy under Vaclav Havel, a playwright who'd been imprisoned under the communist regime. The change of government went so smoothly that this event was called the 'Velvet Revolution'. The Slovaks decided they'd had enough of being married to the Czechs and wanted their own state. Again, the change went smoothly, becoming known as the 'Velvet Divorce'. (Havel's dissidents were not called the Velvet Underground, but perhaps they should have been.)

✔ **Romania:** The country was ruled by Nicolae Ceaucescu and his wife Elena, supported by the feared secret police, the Securitate. By 1989 he'd become a paranoid little dictator,building a vast palace for himself while his people were reduced to developing world-style poverty. The Securitate murdered protesters at the town of Timisoara, but in December 1989, the people of Bucharest took over the television studios and controlled the news bulletins. After fierce fighting, the protestors and their allies in the army overcame the Securitate and captured Ceaucescu and his wife. The couple were given a hasty trial and shot, on Christmas Day 1989.

✔ **Bulgaria and Albania:** These two countries forced out their hard-line communist leaders, but the communists managed to stay in coalition governments in the elections that followed.

The non-Russian peoples of the Soviet Union started demanding independence, too. Gorbachev was caught off-guard, and at first he reacted in the time-honoured soviet fashion; he sent tanks in to crush the demonstrators in Lithuania and Estonia.

In 1991, a group of hard-line Russian communists tried to stage a *coup;* they arrested Gorbachev at his holiday home in the Crimea, cut off his telephone, and then, er, weren't too sure what to do next, and the *coup* collapsed. But so did the Soviet Union. The Baltic States declared themselves independent, Georgia fell into civil war, Armenia and Azerbaijan nearly went to war over territory, and states such as Ukraine, Moldova, and Belarus prepared to operate as independent states for the first time in centuries. On 31 December 1991 the USSR ceased to exist.

Bloodbath in the Balkans

Yugoslavia was a federation, with power alternating between Serbs and Croats and Slovenes, but when all the other peoples of the old communist bloc started declaring independence, the Croats and Slovenes decided to do the same.

The Serbs made a half-hearted attempt to stop the Slovenes, and a much more determined effort against their old enemies, the Croats. They shelled the beautiful Renaissance port of Dubrovnik and besieged the Croat capital Zagreb.

In 1992, Bosnia-Herzegovina, which was a mixed area of Serbs, Croats, and Muslims declared independence. The Serbs retaliated with what they called *ethnic cleansing*, which means mass murder. The Serbs decided to clear the land of Croats and especially Muslims by rounding them up and shooting them.

The United Nations intervened and set up safe havens, but the Serbs attacked and took them back; one of the most notorious massacres of Bosnian Muslims took place in the supposedly safe haven of Srebreniça.

The United States took a hand and knocked heads together, sitting the different representatives down at Dayton, a dull US air force base in Ohio where there was absolutely nothing to do except get on with the talks. The Serbs accepted Bosnia-Herzegovina as a separate state. Meanwhile, the UN was putting up wanted posters for leading Serb commanders on war crimes charges.

When the Serbs started bombing the region of Kosovo to stop it pulling away as well, NATO finally took a hand, bombing Serbia heavily until it gave in.

Appalling cases of murder and torture were evident on all sides in the Yugoslav civil wars, and no one really emerges with much credit, least of all the European Union; it recognised Croatia's independence without considering the consequences, and then proved utterly incapable of getting any of the parties to pay it any attention whatsoever. Not a good omen for a body that was trying to get itself taken seriously on the world stage.

A new united states?

By 2000 the EEC had become the European Union (EU), one of the most important trading areas in the world, with its own parliament, and its own international government, the *European Commission*. In 2002, the EU launched the single currency, the *euro*. The euro has had mixed fortunes, and three countries, Britain, Sweden, and Denmark, decided to have nothing to do with it. In 2004 ten new states joined the EU, bringing its total to 25.

The EU was also planning to introduce a constitution, making the government more like a proper federal state, but the idea was decisively rejected by the French and Dutch people in their referendums in 2005. No one seemed to know if a body that had been designed for six member states could carry on now it had grown so large. Meanwhile, EU citizens travel all over Europe in search of opportunities for work and wealth; the helpful Polish plumber became a symbol of this new breed of mobile, flexible Euroworker.

What Comes Next?

In September 2001, Arab terrorists of al-Qaeda attacked New York and Washington, and President George W. Bush declared a global war on terror. Europe broadly supported the US-led attack on Afghanistan that followed, but was deeply divided over the 2003 attack on Iraq. The British Prime Minister Tony Blair supported the US, as did Spain and Poland; in revenge Muslim terrorists carried out devastating bomb attacks on Madrid's and London's transport systems. President Jacques Chirac of France and Chancellor Gerhardt Schroeder of Germany led international opposition to the war. US Defence Secretary Donald Rumsfeld dismissed France and Germany as 'old Europe', behind the times, though some of the democracies of 'new' Europe, such as Ukraine and Belarus, looked decidedly shaky. Like Stalin and Khrushchev before him, Russian President Vladimir Putin sent tanks in to crush a bid for independence, this time in Chechnya. In retaliation, Chechen terrorists carried out a series of appalling attacks on Russian civilian targets, resulting in bloodbaths at a Moscow theatre and a school in Beslan in southern Russia.

Throughout its history, Europe has changed through a mixture of conflict and migration. The 21st century looks no different from any other.

Part VII
The Part of Tens

LITTLE KNOWN LANDMARKS of EUROPE

The Not-So-Great Wall of Liechtenstein

The Magnificent Fence of Switzerland

The Noble Banister of Marseilles

The Ominous Bulkheads of Prague

In this part . . .

This is the fun part. I've chosen my top tens from
European history – Europeans who dominated the
continent (and not just the obvious ones), places to visit,
important ideas, and things that Europe has given the
world that the world could have done very well without.

Now comes the fun. You don't have to agree with me.
You don't have to agree with *any* of this. You can come up
with your own list or you can sit back and enjoy tearing
my list to pieces. For maximum enjoyment, try this with a
group of friends sitting up into the night after a good meal.
In the end, these choices are all a matter of opinion, and
who's to say mine is better than yours?

Chapter 25

Ten Europeans Who Dominated the Continent

In This Chapter

▶ Meeting some of Europe's conquerors

▶ Discovering the lighter side of European domination

Here's my list of people who have set out to dominate the continent. Some are military rulers; some dominated Europe in rather different and unexpected ways.

Gaius Julius Caesar circa 100 B.C. – 44 B.C.

If Julius Caesar had been around in more recent history, we'd have recognised him as a political thug, but we usually see him all wrapped up in ancient Roman togas and busts, which somehow make him look respectable.

Caesar didn't actually set out to conquer Europe – doing so just happened to fit in with his political plans. Caesar deliberately let himself get drawn into Gallic politics, and ended up conquering the whole of Gaul.

Looking back and saying, 'Hey, but look at the *benefits* of Roman rule' is easy, but Caesar didn't march across Gaul, invade Britain, and leave every other tribe in Europe wondering if they were going to be next so that they could all appreciate baths and roads; he did it for the advancement of the career of G. Julius Caesar Esq. End of story. So Caesar's dying in the very place – the Roman Senate House – that he really did want to dominate is nicely ironic.

Take a look at Chapter 4 for more about Julius Caesar.

Philip II of Spain, 1526–1598

Philip lived very modestly for the monarch of the first European superpower, in a sort of bedsit behind the altar in the chapel of the royal palace of El Escorial. From this bedsit, Philip ruled Spain, Portugal, the Netherlands, Italy, the Mediterranean, parts of North Africa, not to mention America (North and South), the Caribbean, and the Pacific. Mind you, Philip was such a control freak – keeping everyone waiting while he read *every* letter pertaining to his kingdom before it was despatched – that the very idea he ruled anything at all seems amazing.

Philip thought that his duty was to use his enormous power to keep Europe safe for God – the Catholic version of God, that is – and if that meant setting loose the Inquisition or overthrowing other monarchs for following the wrong religion, so be it. Philip didn't ask to control Europe, but if that was what God wanted him to do, he would do it and do it properly.

For more on Philip II, head to Chapter 11.

Louis XIV of France, 1638–1715

Louis XIV is probably the first monarch who actually thought to himself, 'Yes, I am going to control Europe' and set about doing just that. The result: a whole generation of Europeans who knew nothing but war.

Louis was determined to decide who should rule Spain, England, Germany, Italy – you name it. The subtler nuances of 'Keep your nose out' were, unfortunately, lost on him. When Louis put his grandson on the throne of Spain, he declared loftily, 'The Pyrenees no longer exist,' as if even the mountains bent to his will.

My own favourite Louisism is '*J'ai failli attendre*' – 'I *nearly* had to wait' – the ultimate in lordly condescension. Luckily, thanks to his opponents, Louis also had to say 'I *nearly* conquered Europe.' Nearly, Louis, but not quite.

Check out Chapters 13 and 14 for more on Louis XIV.

Napoleon Bonaparte, 1769–1821

Napoleon was an outstanding general, and a very good administrator, but he was also a warmonger of the first order. Quite simply, Napoleon did not *need* to fight all the wars that he did, but he made so many enemies that he was never able to really relax.

Napoleon always said he stood for law and liberty and the rights of man, but he wasn't above bending the law when the opportunity suited him. Napoleon had the poor Duke d'Enghien kidnapped in Germany and brought back to France in a straightforward case of judicial murder; he manipulated popular votes shamelessly; he overturned the constitution to seize power for himself – twice; he abandoned his troops to their fate in Egypt and then again in Russia; and he stole art treasures from all over Europe and shipped them off to France.

Napoleon always defended his wars by saying that he was fighting against the crowned heads of the *ancien régime* (the old regimes of 18th-century Europe), but the peoples of Europe were the ones who finally rose up against his men and brought him down – and quite right, too.

For more on Napoleon, read Chapter 16.

Adolf Hitler, 1889–1945

Unlike some of his predecessors, Hitler wasn't trying to control Europe just for the sake of doing so – he wanted to destroy communism and, of course, Europe's Jewish population. Hitler spoke of a thousand-year *Reich*, and had many plans for how this empire would look. Actually, Hitler's plans were mainly for building oversized domes in his favourite cities and making every railway line terminate in Berlin – a bit of a nuisance if you're trying to get to Plymouth.

Hitler's vision of German settlers heading east into Russia's virgin lands like settlers in the American west never really caught on, and no wonder: Germany didn't actually *need* the *Lebensraum* or 'Living Space' created by seizing other European countries, though you would have to have been very brave to tell him so.

Hitler didn't actually dominate Europe for very long, though it didn't seem that way to people at the time, and in his case every day was a day too long.

Read Chapters 22 and 23 for more on Hitler.

The Volkswagen 'beetle', 1938–2003

The VW beetle was one of Hitler's better ideas. Adolf wanted an affordable family car to run up and down his new motorways, and he commissioned Ferdinand Porsche to design one. The capacity to transform into an all-weather armoured car was an advantage.

Porsche came up with a classic design, though after the war Volkswagen had to pay damages to the Czech firm Tatra for pinching most of the design off them. Originally, the vehicle was to be called the *Kraft durch Frieden Wagen*, or 'Strength Through Joy' car, but who wants to drive something called that?

The military version did very well in the North African campaign, and after the war the British military ordered 20,000 of them, and sales took off. The car was small, cheap, and a wonderfully silly shape – and also had its engine at the rear, just to be different. Europeans were very fond of the car, especially 1960s' hippies, who coined the name 'beetle' for it in 1968 (not only did they like the shape, but the added fun was that Hitler would have *hated* them driving his favourite car).

In 1972, the VW beetle out-produced the Model T Ford to become the most produced car in history. The car even starred in the Disney 'Love Bug' films (bug = beetle, geddit?).

The VW beetle eventually fell victim to competition, especially from the Japanese, and what was expected to be the last beetle ran off the production line in Mexico in 2003, but in a cheering example of demand-led economics, public affection for the car has led to a revival in its fortunes. Sales are booming on both sides of the Atlantic.

Thomas Cook, 1808–1892

Next time you pop into Thomas Cook to change some currency or book a holiday, try to keep your mind on higher things – he wanted you to do just that.

Thomas Cook was born into a poor god-fearing labouring family in Derbyshire in 1808. He became a full-time Baptist preacher, travelling round villages preaching the gospel and denouncing drink. Cook thought that travel, which, as you know, broadens the mind, was just the thing to take that mind off drink and the temptations of the flesh. Obviously, whatever else Cook envisaged, he didn't anticipate Club 18-30.

The first Cook's tours, as they became known, were temperance picnics to North Wales and Scotland. When the Scots refused to take any more of his railway tours, Cook turned his attention to Europe and started leading tours to France, Switzerland, and Italy.

'The Napoleon of Excursions' was how one commentator described Thomas Cook. The man virtually invented modern tourism as we know it; his son John (as in Thomas Cook & Son) took up the business side of the venture and developed its banking role. Sadly, the two of them had an almighty quarrel later, and never really made up.

Thomas Cook certainly deserves his place in this list; many people have dominated Europe through war; not many have dominated Europe through a vision of bringing people together in a spirit of peace and mutual understanding. And soft drinks.

Pasta

Giuseppe Garibaldi once said that if anything managed to unite the Italians, it would be macaroni. Garibaldi had a point there, because from being a regional Sicilian dish, pasta has spread into a world-wide industry.

Pasta's origins are disputed. Marco Polo may have brought some sort of noodle back from China, but even if he did, the Italians seem to have discovered pasta some time earlier, possibly from the Arabs (like the French croissant, some of Christian Europe's most distinctive dishes are Arab in origin).

Eighteenth-century dandies were nicknamed *macaroni*; like the pasta dish, they looked sophisticated but were actually very simple. The name macaroni may be related to the Sicilian word *maccarruni*, meaning 'making dough by force', which seems a strange thing to have a special word for, but fits the case – until the 18th century, Italians kneaded pasta by foot. Maybe that's where the cheese flavour came from.

Italians ate pasta dry, until the Spanish brought tomatoes back from America, and someone had the bright idea of making a sauce from them. The rest, as they say, is history.

Real Madrid, 1956–1960

Many football teams have dominated the European scene for a while, but none has yet matched Real Madrid's winning streak when they won the European Cup five years running, from 1956 to 1960.

Opportunities for manipulating football for political purposes are nothing new. Franco used the game to promote the virtues of his rule in Spain and was particularly pleased about Real Madrid's success. Stalin, meanwhile, was infuriated that Soviet teams didn't do better on the international scene. In more recent times, Italian football has provided the forum for tensions between the north and south of the country. Some sides, such as Inter Milan and Roma, have been associated with the left in Italian politics, while others, such as AC Milan and Lazio, have been associated with the right and with Italy's emergent neo-fascists.

No individual club has dominated Europe for very long – even Real Madrid's run of victories came to an end – but the game itself has dominated European weekends for years, and shows no sign of loosening its grip.

ABBA, 1972–1982

By the time they split up in 1982, Björn, Benny, Agnetha, and Anni-Frid had changed the face of European music. Until ABBA came on the scene, serious pop music was either British or American; European acts only got a look-in outside their homelands if they were dishy (Sacha Distel) or dirty (Serge Gainsbourg and Jane Birkin getting all steamed up in '*Je t'aime . . . Moi non plus*').

The Eurovision Song Contest held in Brighton in 1974 was ABBA's third go at the title, though their first under their new name (before that they just strung their first names together – half their act was over by the time they'd been introduced). 'Waterloo' was the perfect Euro-song: about a battle in Belgium that everyone had heard of, fought between the French, British, Germans, and Dutch, sung in nearly-but-not-quite-perfect English (crucial to their future success) by Swedes. That song and those *clothes*: the ABBA style of floppy shirts and glitzy dresses was inimitable, thank heaven.

Even when punk arrived and the group were deeply uncool, a whole secret Abba-loving scene existed, where people hurried home, locked their bedroom doors, plugged in their earphones, and hummed along to 'Dancing Queen'. More recently, ABBA fans have come out of the closet and tribute bands and spoofs abound. Even hardened critics speak with respect of how Abba faced up to the pain of their real-life marital break-ups in 'One of Us is Lying', and 'The Winner Takes It All'.

Benny and Björn have gone on to write hit musicals, and won an Ivor Novello Award for their contribution to popular music. ABBA never quite swept the States they way they did Australia, but they certainly conquered Europe. *A-ha!*

Chapter 26

Ten Days That Shook Europe – and the World

In This Chapter

▶ Europe finds religion

▶ Europe reaches out to the world

▶ Europe proclaims freedom – and denies it

Ten Days That Shook the World was the title of American journalist John Reed's eye-witness account of the Bolshevik revolution in Russia in 1917. Reed was describing events that he knew were of worldwide importance (Reed's life is very well portrayed in the film *Reds* if you can face a long film with Warren Beatty in it).

But what about individual days that made history? Here's my list of ten days when Europeans did something or achieved something that (eventually) made the world sit up and take notice.

22 May 337: Constantine the Great is Converted

This date is significant because it was Constantine who turned Christianity from a minority sect into a major force in Europe (refer to Chapter 5 for more details about Constantine and Christianity). Up until this point, Christianity was just one religion amongst an awful lot of others.

But after Constantine converted, even though it happened right at the end of his life, this new religion was on a whole new plane. From then on, Christian missionaries always went straight to the top – after they'd converted the king, the people were sure to follow.

29 May 1453: Constantinople Falls to the Turks

Europeans had got used to the idea of a great Christian city in the East, rather as you take the fact for granted that lifejackets are under your plane seat. Now this great Christian metropolis became an equally great centre of Islamic culture, and the new capital of the Ottoman Empire – until the 20th century.

Forty years later, in 1492, the Spanish monarchs Ferdinand and Isabella got revenge for Constantinople by taking the last Muslim stronghold in the West, Granada. (You can find out more about them in Chapter 9). That year the Spanish rulers also gave their approval to a young man who had an ambitious plan to outflank the Muslims by sailing all the way round the world directly to the Indies. His name was Christopher Columbus.

22 November 1497: Vasco da Gama Rounds the Cape of Good Hope

The Portuguese voyager, Bartholomew Dias, had reached the southern tip of Africa, the 'Cape of Storms' as he called it, but the voyage was very hard going and he'd had to turn back. Da Gama learned from Dias's mistakes; he sailed far out into the Atlantic, where the sailing was much easier, before turning east and heading for the African shore. Da Gama rounded the Cape (rechristened 'Cape of Good Hope': much better for PR) and sailed into the Indian Ocean, the first European ever to do so. Da Gama reached India and established a direct contact between Europe and the East that was to develop right up to today.

Da Gama's landing in India initiated an epic story first of trade, then of colonialism, and finally of immigration. He was sailing for the greater glory of the king of Portugal (okay, the greater wealth of Vasco da Gama came into the equation, too), but you could say that his voyage led eventually to Bollywood and the high street curry house. A day that shook the world – and the bowels.

21 September 1520: Martin Luther Is Excommunicated

Kings had quailed at the prospect of excommunication, but Martin Luther simply took the papal bull of excommunication and threw it in the fire. Luther wasn't the first person to call the Pope's bluff and challenge his authority, but he was the first who got away with it, and dealt the Catholic Church a blow from which it never really recovered.

The great divide between Protestant and Catholic had huge implications. What started as a rather obscure debate about theology led to devastating warfare across the continent. Catholicism became associated with autocratic government; Protestant states saw themselves as champions of freedom and representative government, though they weren't necessarily right.

26 August 1789: Declaration of the Rights of Man and of the Citizen

For centuries, European society was based on the idea that people are born with different rights and privileges, and that differentiation was how society ought to be organised. The French weren't actually the first to challenge that idea – England's Magna Carta (1215) and the American Declaration of Independence (1776) both predate the French Declaration of the Rights of Man.

But the French were the first to set about a radical restructuring of society along the lines of equality, to abolish class – not just wish it away – and to try to spread their ideas beyond their own frontiers. The Declaration of the Rights of Man was the basis for later UN and European Conventions of Human Rights, so in that sense the French Revolutionaries, produced a document that made the world sit up and listen very carefully indeed. Head to Chapter 16 for more on the French Revolution and its impact on the world.

13 December 1901: Marconi Sends the First Transatlantic Radio Signal

Guglielmo Marconi came from a rich Italian family, but his mother was Irish and he went to school in England. In fact, Marconi was always more at ease speaking in English than in Italian, though he was proud of his Italian nationality and lived all his life as a dual citizen of both countries.

Marconi was always fascinated by electronics, and was excited by German scientist Heinrich Hertz's discovery of electromagnetic waves whose frequency could be measured precisely. Marconi wanted to know if you could make use of these waves to transmit messages.

In 1899, Marconi managed to send the world's first international radio signal – nothing special, just a few letters of Morse – and in 1901 he attempted the big one: sending a signal across the Atlantic. However, his aerials on both sides of the Atlantic kept being blown down by gales. Eventually, Marconi got a kite up into the air above Poldhu on the Cornish coast with an aerial that sent a simple Morse signal: dot-dot-dot – 'S' – to St John's, Newfoundland. This signal was the start of the age of instant telecommunications.

In 1910 radio transmission helped catch the London murderer Dr Crippen, who was fleeing to Canada on board an ocean liner. Ironically, Crippen had looked in at the radio room during the crossing and remarked on how wonderful this new invention was! Two years later radio was crucial in getting help to the sinking *Titanic*.

If any invention marked the 20th century out as different from every age that had gone before, it has to be radio and telecommunications – and Marconi led the way.

29 May 1906: Finnish Women Get the Vote

Finland was the first European country to give women the vote, 12 years before Britain and 38 years before France. How had a little country like Finland stolen a march on its bigger European neighbours?

At the start of the 20th century Finland was an autonomous province of Russia. Some 75 per cent of the Finnish population, male and female, had no vote and as Finland's population grew, this proportion was actually getting smaller. Ironically, the Finnish women's movement wasn't very strong; the Finns were interested in gaining rights for everyone, male and female. The Finns chance came in 1905 when revolution broke out in Russia (you can find out about this in Chapter 21) and the tsar had to grant the Russians a parliament. The Finns demanded a parliament as well, with universal and *equal suffrage* – that means giving the vote on equal terms to every adult. The tsar, who was thinking along the line 'in for a penny, in for a pound', agreed. On 29 May 1906, the tsar's decree was ratified by the Finnish diet. The only people who opposed the ruling were Finland's Swedish-speaking nobles, who were afraid they would lose power. The nobles were right – they did.

Norway and Iceland granted women the vote in 1913 and Denmark in 1915. The suffragettes in Britain had to wait until the end of the First World War to get the vote; women in France had to wait until the end of the Second World War; and women in Switzerland, incredibly, had to wait until the end of the century. It took time, but eventually the Finns made all of Europe sit up and take notice.

25 May 1940: Penicillin Is Successfully Trialled

In the course of your life, you'll have hundreds of little infections: in scratches, cuts, bites – and just one visit to the Ikea sale can give you those. Until the 1940s, if a wound got infected, you either had the infected part amputated or, nine times out of ten, you died. The situation was as simple as that.

The Scottish scientist Alexander Fleming noticed in 1928 that mould in a petri dish destroyed staphylococcus bacteria; he named this mould penicillin. Unfortunately, no one took much notice of this discovery, and even Fleming didn't pursue the matter.

In 1940 a team of scientists working in Oxford, led by Howard Florey, an Australian, and Ernst Chaim, who had fled to England from Nazi Germany, came across Fleming's paper and began growing the penicillin mould. On 25 May 1940 these scientists tried penicillin on mice and found that it worked.

Before long the scientists had their first human trial. An Oxford policeman had scratched himself pruning his roses and was dying fast from streptococcal infection. The scientists rushed around growing as much penicillin as possible in pots and pans, and the policeman made a remarkable recovery. Sadly, however, the penicillin ran out, the infection took hold again, and the policeman died. But this trial showed what could be done if only a way of producing the penicillin in sufficient quantities could be devised.

Once the Americans had paid for research on mass production of penicillin, it was available for the world to use. No other medical discovery has made such a difference to basic life expectancy throughout the world.

1 December 1934: Sergei Mironovich Kirov Is Murdered

Sergei Kirov was the good-looking, popular leader of the Leningrad branch of the Soviet Communist Party. On 1 December 1934, when going up to his office in the Smolny Institute in Leningrad, Kirov was shot twice in the back of the head by a man called Nikolaev. That Stalin ordered the assassination (which was certainly very convenient for him) has long been suspected, though no direct evidence has been found.

Kirov's murder signalled the unleashing of the full horror of Stalin's purges. The secret police, the NKVD, began arresting people in their thousands, accusing them of fantastical crimes against the state and beating them into signing confessions.

Some of the leading Bolsheviks, men who had stood alongside Lenin through thick and thin, were hauled up in front of the state prosecutor, a singularly nasty little man called Andrei Vyshinsky, in what were known as the Moscow Show Trials. About a million people are estimated to have been arrested in the immediate aftermath of Kirov's murder – how many people does it take to assassinate one man? – and most of them were executed.

Those people who weren't executed were sent off to the Gulags, the labour camps, many of them within the Arctic circle. By 1937 possibly *ten million* people had died in these camps.

We think of mass killing in terms of the Holocaust, or Rwanda in 1994; Stalin's killings dwarfed these, and they began with one of the few murders that he may not have authorised. 1 December 1934 – definitely a day that shook the world.

6 August 1991: Tim Berners-Lee Launches the World Wide Web

Tim Berners-Lee was an Oxford graduate working at the CERN European Particle Physics Laboratory in Geneva when he got the idea for a global hypertext network that he christened *the World Wide Web*. The first files were launched on the Internet, in a rather modest, low-key form, on 6 August 1991.

No discovery since the invention of radio, not even television, has had such an impact on the way the world communicates. The Web has put everyone with access to a computer, in however remote a corner of the world, in instant touch with information on absolutely anything. That little mantra 'www' ('dubbly-dubbly-dubbly-dot') has entered every language in the world.

Yet Berners-Lee himself has maintained a very low profile – he made his invention available to all for free, and declined any sort of patent or royalty. So next time someone tries to claim that Bill Gates invented the Web, you can put them right; the credit belongs to an Englishman in Geneva.

Chapter 27

Ten Places (apart from Naples) to See Before You Die

*Y*ou don't need me to tell you to go to see Venice or the Louvre; you already know about those. But if you're enjoying this book and want to see where some of the events took place, you may need to alter that package tour itinerary. So here's my list of ten places – among many, *many* more – that you may not have thought of, but which deserve a visit. These sites all have a tale to tell about Europe and its history.

The Standing Stones of Carnac

Most tourists do Stonehenge and leave the Neolithic period at that; well, that's their loss. Hop on a ferry to Brittany and head down to Carnac. This site is one of the wonders of Stone Age Europe.

In Carnac, you see some 3,000 neolithic standing stones arranged in 12 parallel rows. The stones go on for miles, and originally there were probably Stonehenge-style stone circles at either end. You see single standing stones, called *menhirs*, and table-like chambers called *dolmens*, though quite what they're for we just don't know (you could see that coming, couldn't you?).

The stones were excavated, and in many cases put back up again, by a Scotsman called James Miln and his assistant, a local lad called Zacharie le Rouzic, after both of whom the local archaeological museum is named. In the 1970s an Englishman called Alexander Thom did a survey and noticed that the lines aren't quite parallel – they converge. Is this fact significant, or does it just mean Neolithic people needed a better ruler?

The latest thinking is that initially one or two lines existed and the others were added later. Each stone is possibly in memory of an individual, which raises many questions about Neolithic people and what they believed. We'll probably never know the stones' meaning for certain, but you can't take a guess if you don't go to Carnac and see them for yourself.

Knossos: Palace of the Minotaur

So many people visit Athens and the Parthenon that the place is in danger of crumbling away, but if you want to really see the birthplace of European civilisation you need to head out to Crete and visit Knossos.

Knossos was where the Minotaur skulked in the famous labyrinth under King Minos's royal palace. If you don't believe me, visit the palace and its great city complex, all excavated by the great archaeologist, Sir Arthur Evans. Minos's throne room is still there, and so is his throne. Archaeologists have reconstructed little sections, to give you an idea of how big the palace must have been in its heyday, and everywhere you can see that strange bull's horns motif the Minoans were so attached to.

Crete was also the scene of an epic battle in the Second World War, when the Germans attacked from the air and forced the British defenders to surrender; the British didn't realise that the Germans had suffered such heavy casualties they were on the point of pulling out themselves. So Crete is an island rich in history. But okay, you can take time off and head for the beach as well.

Ostia: A Roman Town in the Roman Suburbs

Everyone does Pompeii. Now don't get me wrong, if you haven't been to Pompeii, you should go. Be aware, though, that an awful lot of other people will have the same idea as you, and on a hot summer afternoon, when Pompeii is full of tour groups, recapturing the magic of the place can be pretty difficult.

But why not take a half-hour suburban train ride from Rome to visit Ostia? Ostia was the port of ancient Rome, and its ruins are perfectly preserved, including an amazing theatre, an imposing forum, and the inevitable baths – everything you'd expect from a Roman town. Best of all, I think, is the Forum of Corporations, a market area where each stall is decorated by a wonderful floor mosaic illustrating the business that went on there.

Ostia is a gem, and judging by the times I've been there, relatively under-visited. Oh, and Ostia also has a seaside lido – you can thank Mussolini for that.

Hagia Sophia – Church and Mosque Where West Meets East

For centuries, Byzantium was *the* power in Europe, Constantinople was '*the* City' (its present name, Istanbul, means just that), and Hagia Sophia, the Church of Holy Wisdom, was '*the* Great Church'. Justinian, the emperor who revived Byzantium's fortunes and recaptured Imperial Rome, had Hagia Sophia built as the cathedral of his Christian empire, and it was built to stun.

The Greeks and Romans usually built gabled roofs. In contrast, Hagia Sophia had a great dome arising out of a square central block – an amazing architectural accomplishment. Just to add to the effect, immediately under the dome is an arcade of windows, so the roof seems to float of its own accord.

'Solomon, I have surpassed thee!' said Justinian, when Hagia Sophia was finished in 537, which was tempting fate because 20 years later an earthquake made the dome fall in. The Romans rebuilt the dome, but historians don't think that they did it in quite the same way. Even so, when Sultan Mehmet II 'the Conqueror' captured Constantinople, he was so taken aback at Hagia Sophia's beauty that he took the building as his main mosque – a backhanded compliment, if you think about it.

In 1935 Kemal Attaturk turned Hagia Sophia into a museum. The Turks, true to Islamic teaching, had plastered over the mosaics of human beings, but recently they've stripped the plaster away, so you can see Hagia Sophia in its original glory. People travelled from all over Europe to wonder at Hagia Sophia in its heyday; now you can do the same.

Aachen – Palace of Charlemagne

Aachen, also known as Aix la Chapelle, is just where a European centre should be; on the borders of Germany, Belgium, and the Netherlands. Hot springs bubble here so the Romans built their inevitable baths, and in 1748 Europe's statesmen came here to sign the peace treaty that ended the War of the Austrian Succession (refer to Chapter 15 for more on this).

But Aachen's real claim to fame is that Charlemagne chose the city as his capital. Charlemagne's still there, buried beneath Aachen's magnificent cathedral, the oldest in northern Europe. Medieval emperors were in such awe of Charlemagne that they kept digging him up to put him in ever more ornate tombs. When they couldn't get to Rome, Aachen was where the Holy Roman Emperors had themselves crowned.

The city of Aachen awards a special prize, named after Charlemagne, to the person who has done most to promote peace and unity in Europe. I think Charlemagne himself would have approved.

The Islamic Beauty of the Alhambra

Europe's Christian heritage is so widespread and beautiful that, especially today, appreciating that Europe also has an Islamic heritage is very important.

The Alhambra is a palace-cum-fortress built by the Moors as the capital of the Caliphate of Cordoba. From a distance, the Alhambra looks like any other Spanish castle, but when you get close, the building is breathtakingly beautiful; every inch of every pillar and arch is covered in the most intricate decoration. Islam forbade painting the human figure, so Islamic artists made up for it by lavishing beautiful decoration in swirling geometric patterns on every available surface.

The name Alhambra means 'The Crimson Castle', because it glows red in the sunlight; by starlight the building appears silver. The Emperor Charles V demolished some of the Alhambra to make way for his own palace, but the real vandals, as always, were Napoleon's men, who used it as a barracks and blew some of the palace up. More than enough of this wonderful building is still left to warrant a visit, though; don't miss the opportunity to go.

The Vasa: The Ship That Rose from the Sea

On 10 August 1628, King Gustavus Adolphus of Sweden gathered his court and all the foreign ambassadors, plus anyone else who had nothing better to do that day, to watch the launch of his latest warship, the *Vasa*, named after the king's royal dynasty and, with 64 guns, the match of any ship on the seas.

Or rather, *under* the seas. The captain may have been at fault for leaving the gunports open, or it may have been badly designed, but the *Vasa* fired a salute, keeled over, and sank. Incredibly, of the 150-odd people on board, all but 30 or so were saved.

However, the ship was a write-off until 1956, when a marine archaeologist called Anders Franzén found the *Vasa* and determined to bring her to the surface. Franzén managed this feat in 1961, by which time the project had gripped the imagination of the whole country and was shown live on Swedish TV. The ship went on display and is now housed in a handsome museum specially built for it. The *Vasa* is beautifully preserved all in one piece, and with everything there, from the masts and bulwarks to the intricate Dutch and German figures carved on the stern.

I once had a morning to kill in Stockholm and asked people what I should see; every one of them said 'The ship'. They were right.

Sarajevo – Moving On from the Bullets

For most of the 20th century, Sarajevo was best known as the site of the most famous assassination in European history – that of Archduke Franz Ferdinand, which precipitated the First World War.

The people of Sarajevo were delighted when the city hosted the very successful 1984 Winter Olympics. Little did they know that within ten years, Sarajevo would be in the headlines again, for all the wrong reasons.

In 1992 the Muslim people of Bosnia-Herzegovina declared independence from Yugoslavia. From 1992 to 1996, the people of Sarajevo had to endure a terrible siege by the forces of Slobodan Milosevic's Serbia, which the UN peacekeepers, hurriedly flown in, seemed powerless to halt. One of the most symbolic moments came with a surprise visit to Sarajevo to demonstrate solidarity with its besieged inhabitants by the French president, François Mitterand, on 28 June 1992, the anniversary of the 1914 assassination, as he doubtless realised.

Sarajevo is a beautiful city, which has undergone a remarkable transformation since the siege. It's a fascinating example of the ethnic and religious diversity that makes up the Balkan region, with a Catholic cathedral, an Orthodox cathedral, and a large mosque. This city *deserves* a visit.

Berlin: The City That Came Back from the Dead

If you want to get a sense of the dramatic movements of Europe's history Berlin is a very good place to start. Amazingly, considering how completely the city was destroyed in the war, you can still see parts of the elegant Berlin of the 18th century in the beautiful tree-lined Unter den Linden and the majestic Brandenburg Gate. A little way outside Berlin you can visit Frederick's the Great's beautiful palace at Potsdam. And don't miss the imposing Reichstag building, gutted by fire in 1933 and now sporting a dramatic glass dome designed by the British architect Sir Norman Foster.

Berlin was a front-line city during the Cold War. A small section of the Berlin Wall has been retained, and you can visit a good museum at the site of the famous Checkpoint Charlie, but otherwise all traces of the Wall have been erased. You need to use a map and a lot of imagination to picture how it once divided the city.

After the Wall came down developers moved in to reconstruct the city. Potsdamer Platz, an empty no-man's land during the Cold War, now rebuilt, boasts exciting new buildings including a film museum. You can see the collections of ancient and Middle Eastern art in the Pergamon Museum, and Berlin's excellent Jewish Museum. And don't miss Berlin's famous zoo.

Berlin retains its taste for cabaret and for a more relaxed and irreverent approach to life, especially in the Kreuzberg district and around Alexanderplatz in the heart of the old East Berlin. Hitler never really liked Berlin. You will.

The Tragedy of Oradour sur Glane

Oradour shouldn't be on this list. The place was a small French town near Limoges, in central France, with a church and a boulangerie and everything else you'd expect. Nothing special.

But then on 10 June 1944, four days after D-Day, an SS Panzer division arrived. They cut the village off, shut all the men in barns and garages and gathered all the women and children in the church. Then they shot the men, and poured grenades and gunfire into the church, killing all the women and children. Finally, the SS set fire to the town. Only five men and one woman survived.

We still don't really know why the SS committed this atrocity. Maybe they were seeking revenge for heavy resistance activity in the area, or possibly trying to recover stolen gold, as one theory says. Whatever the reason, Oradour, and its neighbouring village, Tulle, where the SS hanged their victims from lampposts, joined the melancholy list of other towns and villages, most of them in Poland and Russia, deliberately destroyed by the Nazis during the Second World War.

The French preserved Oradour just as the town was when the Germans left, and you can still see it today. Various other places of horror from the world wars also merit a visit – Verdun, Ypres, the Somme, Bergen-Belsen, Auschwitz-Birkenau; sadly, Oradour is up there with the worst of them.

Chapter 28

Ten Things Europe (and the World) Could Have Done Without

In This Chapter

▶ Torture and tragedies

▶ Lesser irritants of life

*W*ars, deaths, massacres – European history can seem a gloomy tale. Some of the appalling things Europeans have done to each other were so dreadful that they can take your breath away. Yet Europeans have also found smaller ways of making life just that little bit harder than it really needs to be. So here's my list of things I think Europe would have been happier without, from the really tragic and ghastly to the irritating and everyday.

Antisemitism

If you think that the story of European antisemitism begins and ends with the Nazi Holocaust, think again. Antisemitism is a recurring theme all the way throughout European history.

The Jews were blamed for the Black Death (why? what could the Jews hope to gain from it?), and for many years a popular story circulated that Jews kidnapped babies for sacrifice. Jews were expelled from medieval England and Spain, and in Germany Martin Luther preached violent hatred against them.

Hitler learned his antisemitism in turn-of-the-century Vienna, whose mayor, Karl Lueger, was almost rabidly antisemitic, but he would've encountered much the same attitude in France or in Russia, where regular *pogroms* (organised attacks) took place against Jewish communities. Even after the Second World War, some Polish Jews struggled home from the concentration camps, only to be murdered by their neighbours.

Many explanations have been given for antisemitism. Christians blamed the Jews for demanding that Jesus be put to death (though they never seem to have stopped and thought: 'Wait a minute – wasn't Jesus Jewish?'). Jewish communities kept to themselves and didn't allow intermarriage, which made them seem rather snooty and stand-offish. The Catholic Church had laws against lending money at interest, so Jews made a living out of small-scale money-lending – and a very useful local service it was, too, but I suppose no one particularly *likes* people they're indebted to. But these are explanations – not excuses.

The Inquisition

According to the popular version of events, if you were arrested by the Inquisition, you fell down trembling to your knees and cried out, 'No! No! Not the Inquisition!' Then some burly rugby players in monks' habits carried you to a spacious dungeon, where you were stretched on the rack, tied to a wheel, or incarcerated in an iron maiden (not the heavy metal group, but a woman-shaped coffin with spikes on the inside). A stern-looking monk with rotating eyeballs shouted in your face 'Confess! Confess!' – if you were inside the iron maiden presumably he used a megaphone. Finally, you'd be dragged out for a public burning at the stake known in Spanish as an *auto da fe* or Act of Faith. Once you'd been reduced to a pile of ashes, the Inquisitors went home to tea, and the whole business started again the following morning.

The Inquisition, or Holy Office, was set up to inquire into the Cathar Heresy in 13th-century France, and its famous Spanish branch dates from 1478. The Inquisition's main task was to check up on Jews and Muslims who claimed to have converted to Christianity and it made relatively little use of torture. Our image of the Inquisition comes from a couple of 16th-century Spanish Protestants with a grudge writing under the pseudonym Montanus, a few 19th-century writers with overactive imaginations and what looks like a penchant for S&M, and a Monty Python sketch.

Nevertheless, the Inquisition fixed the idea that public trial and humiliation could be used to silence dissent. In that sense, the Inquisition was the ancestor of Stalin's show trials, of the McCarthy 'un-American activities' hearings, and of the worst aspects of Mao's Cultural Revolution in China. We may have got the Inquisition out of perspective, but Europe, and eventually the world, would have been a much happier place without its example.

The Black Death

Unless you believe that populations need culling from time to time, the Black Death should certainly feature in this list. Being precise about figures is impossible, but we're probably looking at a death rate across Europe as whole of about a third, and sometimes a lot higher than that. Some places, like Milan, escaped, for reasons we still don't really know, but not many; the Black Death even reached Greenland.

The Black Death had a profound effect upon Europeans' outlook on life and death and prompted a cult in European art of skulls, skeletons, and reapers. Only the wars of the 20th century caused as much misery, despair, and general sense of helplessness as the Black Death.

Sugar

Sugar cane was a pricey luxury in medieval Europe, imported at considerable expense from the East. Columbus took sugar from Europe to see whether it would grow well in the Caribbean. Would it grow well? Is the Pope a Catholic?

However, sugar cane is a very labour-intensive cash crop, and the locals were already being worked to death in the Spaniards' silver mines, or dying from flu or the common cold. The Portuguese then hit on the idea of moving Africans – strong lads, used to working in the sun – over the Atlantic to harvest the sugar. Economically, this idea was a shrewd move: 18th-century Europe developed a very sweet tooth, and the sugar trade became phenomenally lucrative. But all those pastries and dainty lumps were subsidised by the slave trade and the appalling misery the whole affair produced on the high seas and on the sugar plantations. Later, Europeans discovered how to grow their own sugar beet, so the demand for cane sugar shrank, but by then the damage to Africa had been done.

King Leopold II of Belgium

Leopold II was king of the Belgians between 1865–1909. At first sight, Leopold looks much like any other 19th-century European monarch: lots of gold braid, ribbons and medals, a big beard, married to a Habsburg princess, four children, one of them a son named after his father. So far, so dull.

Now add a touch of spice: An assassination attempt and two illegitimate children by a rather dominating prostitute called Blanche Delacroix, with whom Leopold went through a sort of marriage ceremony a few days before he died.

The reason for Leopold's appearance on this list, however, is because of his actions in the Congo. Leopold was obsessed with getting hold of an African colony for his people, whether they wanted one or not (on the whole, they didn't). Leopold hired Henry Morton Stanley to go out and claim a vast area of the Congo basin for him (for Leopold, that is, not for Belgium) and then used every diplomatic trick he knew to get the rest of the world to recognise his new colony. Once Leopold had gained control of the Congo, he authorised the ruthless exploitation of slave labour to produce rubber for his personal profit.

Those who looked into the situation in the Congo were shocked by the evidence they found of wholesale murder, rape, and mutilation taking place in the king's name on the king's personal estate. The death rate was upwards of *three million people*. Eventually the international outcry was so loud that the Belgian government had to take the colony off the king's hands. Leopold did his best to destroy the most incriminating evidence, and Belgium's museums and public statues make no mention of the appalling misery he inflicted upon a vast area of Africa.

The Berlin Wall

Many cities have walls built round them, but a peculiar sort of mentality is needed to build one down the middle. When this barrier was first erected in 1961 – to keep East Berliners in and stop them being tempted by the affluence and freedom of expression in the West – the wall ran across streets and even through houses. Street signs still directed you towards places in the east, without adding that a very large wall was in the way.

A whole generation now exists who never saw the Berlin Wall, and if you visit Berlin you'll find very little trace of it, so visualising what the effect was like is difficult. From the eastern side, the Wall was more or less what you'd expect to see: sentry posts, trip wires, guard dogs, and lots of machine guns. From the western side, however, the Wall was surreal; halfway down an ordinary street you'd suddenly find it in front of you.

Nothing was surreal about the people who were shot trying to cross the Berlin Wall, though, or the desperate lengths they went to – tunnelling or hiding in ever more ingenious places in cars. The Wall symbolised everything that is wrong with an oppressive government that doesn't trust its own people.

Russian Passport and Border Control

You step off the plane in Moscow or St Petersburg, dreaming of romantic troika rides down starlit avenues piled high with snow . . . and then you meet Russian passport control – a small booth in which you are confronted with an unsmiling security guard who appears to be 13. The guard looks you directly in the eye, unblinking, while you try smiling, staring back, squirming, laughing, and looking around casually as if waiting at a bus stop. Eventually, the security man looks down at your passport, leafing through every page slowly, as if reading all that tiny writing printed on the page to make it harder to forge. You're now feeling intensely guilty and prepared to own up to anything he suggests, when eventually a buzzer goes off, the exit door opens slightly, and you're allowed through. But you're not free yet.

As you go through customs, a large woman officer of a certain age hails you and with a bored expression, evading eye contact, tells you to open your bags. Then, the woman goes through your belongings, holding them in finger and thumb as if every item is unwashed. Then, just as you can see your coach through the window, revving its engine, the customs inspector contemptuously pushes your underwear back across the desk and tells you to go. You scramble to cram everything back in your case and run across the concourse, scattering socks or knickers as you go. You arrive gasping on your coach to be greeted by the unsmiling, unsympathetic faces of your fellow travellers, who clearly think that you've been keeping them waiting on purpose, and a telling-off from your guide (who's called Olga; they're all called Olga) for being late. Welcome to Russia.

French Plumbing

For most of the 20th century, going to the toilet in any public building in France meant negotiating what the French liked to call, rather disingenuously, a Turkish toilet. This toilet arrangement consisted – and in some places still consists – of a porcelain-covered pit set into the floor with a couple of ribbed platforms for your feet on either side of small round hole in the ground, rather like a slightly larger-than-normal hole on a golf course.

The French also came up with the *pissoir*, a metal street latrine for men, which you can still see in some French towns and smell from even further. Gabriel Chevalier's comic novel *Clochemerle* is entirely based on the upheaval caused when a *pissoir* is installed in a small French town.

Nowadays, French towns are finally getting rid of these contraptions and replacing them with automatic toilets, where you insert a coin to open a sliding door, which then encloses you in a tiny space and forces you onto a white shaped plastic seat. If you're not claustrophobic when you go in, you are by the time you come out, but I advise you to get on with the business in hand because when your allotted time is up the door opens whether you're finished or not.

France is a modern, hi tech country, with something of a national love affair with the futuristic in design and engineering; all they need to do is apply some of the ingenuity that went into designing the superfast TGV train to the simple, everyday process of emptying the bladder. Someone let me know when it happens.

Lederhosen

Why? *Why?* Lederhosen, which is German for leather trousers, originated in the 18th century as eminently practical shorts, with braces to keep them up, for children in the Bavarian countryside, and they should have stayed that way. However, in a terrible tragedy for European culture and taste, the tradition evolved for grown men to wear lederhosen, too.

Whether this style development began with men copying their children or the leather was so tight the children could never get them off and wore them till they died, I don't know. What I do know is that no grown man looks good in lederhosen. That combination of knobbly knees and the cross strap of the braces makes a man look as if he's just landed by parachute and left his trousers in the plane. A photo was taken of Hitler relaxing in a pair of lederhosen, and frankly, anyone who can vote for someone looking that daft deserves everything they get. Quite enough misery exists in the world without our adding to it with the sight of overweight men in leather shorts yodelling and slapping each others' bottoms.

Kraftwerk

Now I'm prepared to concede that this item is a matter of taste. Some people revel in the sound of robots moving to the sound of what appears to be the beeps from a cashpoint machine. German electrogroup, Kraftwerk, have been credited with influencing a whole range of musicians, including Madonna and Elton John, though some may say that that alone justifies their inclusion on this list. Kraftwerk's first big success was the album *Autobahn* (motorway) in 1974, boasting a title track of 22 minutes, which is almost long enough to drive down one.

Two of the original line-up left in a huff after *Autobahn,* and the two original founders, Ralf Hütter and Florian Schneider Esleben, have since developed something of a reputation for their obsessively eccentric behaviour. If your musical tastes encompass strange things like a tune, and a human being or two singing it, then steer clear of Kraftwerk; if you enjoy listening to electronic beepers, this is the stuff for you. Though perhaps you should still get out more.

Index

• *G* •

• O •

• R •

• S •

FOR DUMMIES®

Do Anything. Just Add Dummies

HOME

UK editions

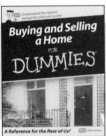
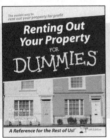

0-7645-7027-7   **0-7645-7016-1**   **0-7645-7054-4**

PERSONAL FINANCE

0-7645-7023-4   **0-470-02860-2**   **0-7645-7039-0**

BUSINESS

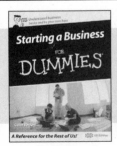

0-7645-7018-8   **0-7645-7025-0**   **0-7645-7026-9**

Other UK editions now available:

Answering Tough Interview Questions For Dummies
(0-470-01903-4)

Arthritis For Dummies
(0-470-02582-4)

Being The Best Man For Dummies
(0-470-02657-X)

British History For Dummies
(0-7645-7021-8)

Building Confidence For Dummies
(0-470-01669-8)

Buying a Home On A Budget For Dummies
(0-7645-7035-8)

Cognitive Behavioural Therapy For Dummies
(0-470-01838-0)

Cleaning and Stain Removal For Dummies
(0-7645-7029-3)

CVs For Dummies
(0-7645-7017-X)

Detox For Dummies
(0-470-01908-5)

Diabetes For Dummies
(0-7645-7019-6)

Divorce For Dummies
(0-7645-7030-7)

eBay.co.uk For Dummies
(0-7645-7059-5)

Formula One Racing For Dummies
(0-7645-7015-3)

Gardening For Dummies
(0-470-01843-7)

Genealogy Online For Dummies
(0-7645-7061-7)

Golf For Dummies
(0-470-01811-9)

Irish History For Dummies
(0-7645-7040-4)

Kakuro For Dummies
(0-470-02822-X)

Marketing For Dummies
(0-7645-7056-0)

Neuro-Linguistic Programming For Dummies
(0-7645-7028-5)

Nutrition For Dummies
(0-7645-7058-7)

Pregnancy For Dummies
(0-7645-7042-0)

Retiring Wealthy For Dummies
(0-470-02632-4)

Rugby Union For Dummies
(0-7645-7020-X)

Small Business Employment Law For Dummies
(0-7645-7052-8)

Starting a Business on eBay.co.uk For Dummies
(0-470-02666-9)

Su Doku For Dummies
(0-470-01892-5)

Sudoku 2 For Dummies
(0-470-02651-0)

Sudoku 3 For Dummies
(0-470-02667-7)

The GL Diet For Dummies
(0-470-02753-3)

Wills, Probate and Inheritance Tax For Dummies
(0-7645-7055-2)

8264_p1

FOR DUMMIES®

A world of resources to help you grow

HOBBIES

Poker FOR DUMMIES
A Reference for the Rest of Us!
0-7645-5232-5

Sewing FOR DUMMIES
A Reference for the Rest of Us!
0-7645-6847-7

Drawing FOR DUMMIES
A Reference for the Rest of Us!
0-7645-5476-X

Also available:

Art For Dummies
(0-7645-5104-3)
Aromatherapy For Dummies
(0-7645-5171-X)
Bridge For Dummies
(0-7645-5015-2)
Card Games For Dummies
(0-7645-9910-0)
Chess For Dummies
(0-7645-8404-9)
Crocheting For Dummies
(0-7645-4151-X)

Improving Your Memory
For Dummies
(0-7645-5435-2)
Massage For Dummies
(0-7645-5172-8)
Meditation For Dummies
(0-471-77774-9)
Photography For Dummies
(0-7645-4116-1)
Quilting For Dummies
(0-7645-9799-X)
Woodworking For Dummies
(0-7645-3977-9)

EDUCATION

Cooking Basics FOR DUMMIES
A Reference for the Rest of Us!
0-7645-7206-7

The Koran FOR DUMMIES
A Reference for the Rest of Us!
0-7645-5581-2

Anatomy & Physiology FOR DUMMIES
A Reference for the Rest of Us!
0-7645-5422-0

Also available:

Algebra For Dummies
(0-7645-5325-9)
Astronomy For Dummies
(0-7645-8465-0)
Buddhism For Dummies
(0-7645-5359-3)
Calculus For Dummies
(0-7645-2498-4)
Christianity For Dummies
(0-7645-4482-9)
Forensics For Dummies
(0-7645-5580-4)

Islam For Dummies
(0-7645-5503-0)
Philosophy For Dummies
(0-7645-5153-1)
Religion For Dummies
(0-7645-5264-3)
Trigonometry For Dummies
(0-7645-6903-1)

PETS

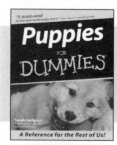

Puppies FOR DUMMIES
A Reference for the Rest of Us!
0-7645-5255-4

Dog Training FOR DUMMIES
A Reference for the Rest of Us!
0-7645-8418-9

Cats FOR DUMMIES
A Reference for the Rest of Us!
0-7645-5275-9

Also available:

Labrador Retrievers
For Dummies
(0-7645-5281-3)
Aquariums For Dummies
(0-7645-5156-6)
Birds For Dummies
(0-7645-5139-6)
Dogs For Dummies
(0-7645-5274-0)
Ferrets For Dummies
(0-7645-5259-7)

German Shepherds
For Dummies
(0-7645-5280-5)
Golden Retrievers
For Dummies
(0-7645-5267-8)
Horses For Dummies
(0-7645-9797-3)
Jack Russell Terriers
For Dummies
(0-7645-5268-6)
Puppies Raising & Training
Diary For Dummies
(0-7645-0876-8)

FOR DUMMIES®

The easy way to get more done and have more fun

LANGUAGES

Spanish FOR DUMMIES®
0-7645-5194-9

French FOR DUMMIES®
0-7645-5193-0

Italian FOR DUMMIES®
0-7645-5196-5

Also available:

Chinese For Dummies
(0-471-78897-X)

Chinese Phrases
For Dummies
(0-7645-8477-4)

French Phrases For Dummies
(0-7645-7202-4)

German For Dummies
(0-7645-5195-7)

Italian Phrases For Dummies
(0-7645-7203-2)

Japanese For Dummies
(0-7645-5429-8)

Latin For Dummies
(0-7645-5431-X)

Spanish Phrases For
Dummies
(0-7645-7204-0)

Spanish Verbs For Dummies
(0-471-76872-3)

Hebrew For Dummies
(0-7645-5489-1)

MUSIC AND FILM

Guitar FOR DUMMIES®
0-7645-9904-6

Filmmaking FOR DUMMIES®
0-7645-2476-3

Piano FOR DUMMIES®
0-7645-5105-1

Also available:

Bass Guitar For Dummies
(0-7645-2487-9)

Blues For Dummies
(0-7645-5080-2)

Classical Music For Dummies
(0-7645-5009-8)

Drums For Dummies
(0-7645-5357-7)

Jazz For Dummies
(0-7645-5081-0)

Opera For Dummies
(0-7645-5010-1)

Rock Guitar For Dummies
(0-7645-5356-9)

Screenwriting For Dummies
(0-7645-5486-7)

Songwriting For Dummies
(0-7645-5404-2)

Singing For Dummies
(0-7645-2475-5)

HEALTH, SPORTS & FITNESS

 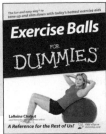 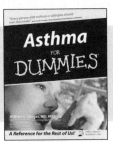

Fitness FOR DUMMIES®
0-7645-7851-0

Exercise Balls FOR DUMMIES®
0-7645-5623-4

Asthma FOR DUMMIES®
0-7645-4233-8

Also available:

Controlling Cholesterol For
Dummies
(0-7645-5440-9)

Dieting For Dummies
(0-7645-4149-8)

High Blood Pressure For
Dummies
(0-7645-5424-7)

Martial Arts For Dummies
(0-7645-5358-5)

Menopause For Dummies
(0-7645-5458-1)

Power Yoga For Dummies
(0-7645-5342-9)

Thyroid For Dummies
(0-7645-5385-2)

Weight Training For Dummies
(0-471-76845-6)

Yoga For Dummies
(0-7645-5117-5)

FOR DUMMIES®

Helping you expand your horizons and achieve your potential

INTERNET

0-7645-8996-2

0-7645-8334-4

0-7645-7327-6

Also available:

The Internet All-in-One Desk
Reference For Dummies
(0-7645-1659-0)

Internet Explorer 6
For Dummies
(0-7645-1344-3)

Internet Privacy For Dummies
(0-7645-0846-6)

Researching Online
For Dummies
(0-7645-0546-7)

eBay Bargain Shopping
For Dummies
(0-7645-4080-7)

Google For Dummies
(0-7645-4420-9)

2005 Online Shopping
Directory For Dummies
(0-7645-7495-7)

DIGITAL MEDIA

0-7645-1664-7

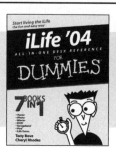

0-7645-7347-0

0-471-78278-5

Also available:

CD and DVD Recording
For Dummies
(0-7645-5956-7)

Digital Photography
All-in-One Desk Reference
For Dummies
(0-7645-7328-4)

Home Recording For
Musicians For Dummies
(0-7645-8884-2)

MP3 For Dummies
(0-7645-0858-X)

Paint Shop Pro 9
For Dummies
(0-7645-7935-5)

Photo Retouching &
Restoration For Dummies
(0-7645-1662-0)

Scanners For Dummies
(0-7645-6790-X)

Photoshop Elements 4
For Dummies
(0-471-77483-9)

Digital Photos, Movies &
Music Gigabook For
Dummies
(0-7645-7414-0)

COMPUTER BASICS

0-7645-8958-X

0-7645-0819-9

0-7645-7326-8

Also available:

PCs All-in-One Desk
Reference For Dummies
(0-7645-3941-8)

Pocket PC For Dummies
(0-7645-1640-X)

Troubleshooting Your PC
For Dummies
(0-7645-7742-0)

Upgrading & Fixing PCs
For Dummies
(0-7645-1665-5)

Buying a Computer
For Dummies
(0-7645-7653-4)

Windows XP All-in-One Desk
Reference For Dummies
(0-7645-7463-9)

Macs For Dummies
(0-7645-5656-8)
